T0346339

THE BLACK LEGEND

George Bascom, Cochise, and the Start of the Apache Wars

DOUG HOCKING

TWODOT®

GUILFORD, CONNECTICUT
HELENA, MONTANA

A · TWODOT® · BOOK

An imprint of The Rowman & Littlefield Publishing Group, Inc.
An imprint and registered trademark of The Rowman & Littlefield Publishing Group, Inc.

Distributed by NATIONAL BOOK NETWORK

British Library Cataloguing in Publication Information available

Library of Congress Cataloging-in-Publication Data

Names: Hocking, Doug, author.
Title: The Black Legend : George Bascom, Cochise, and the start of the Apache Wars / Doug Hocking.
Description: Guilford, Connecticut ; Helena, Montana : Two Dot, [2018] | Includes bibliographical references and index. |
Identifiers: LCCN 2018016995 (print) | LCCN 2018026787 (ebook) | ISBN 9781493034468 | ISBN 9781493034451 (hardcover)
Subjects: LCSH: Bascom, George Nicholas, 1837-1862. | Cochise, Apache chief, 1805?-1874. | Apache Indians—Wars—Arizona. | Chiricahua Indians—Wars—Arizona.
Classification: LCC E99.A6 (ebook) | LCC E99.A6 H59 2018 (print) | DDC 973.8—dc23
LC record available at https://lccn.loc.gov/2018016995

Printed in the United States of America

To my children, Eric and Jennifer, and to my wife, Debbie.
And to George N. Bascom who always deserved better.
A Pox on Lying Self-Promoters

CONTENTS

ACKNOWLEDGMENTS

ENOUGH CANNOT BE SAID TO THANK RICK COLLINS, FORMER BOARD president of the Tucson Presidio Trust, volunteer coordinator for the Anza Trail in southern Arizona who personifies Juan Bautista de Anza at the Tubac Presidio Park and Tumacacori National Historic Site. Rick is a park ranger and an interpretation specialist at Tubac Presidio and a recognized authority on the Spanish Colonial Army. He also served with the council that brought Chiricahua Apaches back to Arizona for the Geronimo Centennial in 1986. In other words, he's one heck of a guy and if you happen to see Juan Bautisa de Anza at Tubac or Tumacacori, be sure to say hello. He provided me with notes that he had compiled over more than thirty years concerning what has become known as the Black Legend: a long-circulated myth that an altercation in 1861 between an Army lieutenant and an Apache chief at Apache Pass in Arizona sparked a war that lasted over a decade. These notes included information from the regimental returns and other sources I'd previously found difficult to access. Their value cannot be overstated. During our discussions about the affair, he presented many ideas and interpretations that had differed slightly from my own. His was the idea that Lieutenant Bascom never attempted to take Apache Chief Cochise as hostage against the return of a kidnapped boy, Felix Ward. This would have been counter-productive, as Bascom in his report says he agreed to allow Cochise ten days to go find and then return with the boy. Sergeant Robinson, who wasn't in the tent with Bascom and Cochise during their negotiations, tells a slightly different tale, saying Bascom told Cochise he would be a hostage, but Robinson may have misunderstood. Johnny Ward, Felix's father, was, unfortunately, the interpreter between the lieutenant and chief, and his tone and objection to not getting the boy immediately may have alarmed Cochise. We both agree that Bascom should be exonerated. He did not start the Cochise War. He did nothing wrong and was neither a drunk nor a pig-headed fool, as some accounts would have us believe.

Ben Sacks, Constance Altshuler, and Robert Utley should be mentioned for the wonderful work they did in the 1960s that began the process of unearthing the truth of Bascom's tale. Utley worked out the timeline that had become confused by the injection of material from people who were not at Apache Pass during the parley between Bascom and Cochise. Dr. Sacks and Ms. Altshuler were the first to explore the newspapers of 1861 and the military reports and post returns. They began the process of exonerating Bascom and showing how far from truth the accounts of others were.

Dr. John Fahey knows more about Surgeon Bernard John Dowling Irwin, who came to rescue Bascom and his troops at Apache Pass, and Fort Buchanan (where Irwin was stationed) than any living human being. We have walked the site of what little remains of the fort together, and he has loaned me valuable papers from the packet Irwin submitted concerning his application for the Medal of Honor for heroic efforts at the pass.

I shouldn't forget to thank Debra Chatham, librarian at the Sierra Vista Public Library, who has pursued difficult-to-locate articles and books for me time and again. I gratefully acknowledge her assistance. Gene Baker has been my constant companion walking the ground and helping me to locate many of the sites from the Apache Wars.

Susie Goll Szynalski, a relative of George N. Bascom, provided information about the Bascom family and George's early life. Larry Ludwig, park ranger at Fort Bowie National Historic Park, provided information on the archaeology of the site of the Bascom Affair and his article, co-written with Douglas McChristian, was invaluable in setting the record straight and making the world aware of the writings of Daniel Robinson.

Chapter One

AN OVERVIEW OF THE BLACK LEGEND OF COCHISE AND LIEUTENANT BASCOM

HIS BLUE UNIFORM NOW ALMOST GRAY WITH DUST, THE YOUNG OFFICER rode a mule over the rim of the valley down along the Overland Mail trail into Apache Pass. His men, many of them mounted, carried their long .58 caliber rifle muskets on their left shoulders. Many rode mules but there weren't enough to go around, so others marched. All were tired and now showed many days' growth of beard. They had moved at the speed of the men afoot, about eighteen miles per day, for five long days and slept on the cold February ground each night. Behind them came four blue wagons with white canvas tops now dingy from travel carrying their bedding, tents, ammunition, and food for twenty days. The lieutenant looked around at the men he was proud to lead, his long beard grazing the shoulder boards that showed he was a lieutenant. They were hot under their heavy woolen coats. The sun of southern Arizona beats down hard even on winter days.

At the lieutenant's side rode grizzled Johnny Ward, a man twice the lieutenant's age, perched on a sturdy horse. He spoke to the officer in an Irish brogue, "I want my boy back from these thieving savages and my cattle, too. It's only been a week but he's in danger. They might kill him at any time."

"We'll get him, sir. And the cattle, too." The lieutenant pondered the wisdom of his colonel ordering him to take this man, so deeply involved and enraged, along as interpreter. Johnny spoke excellent Spanish, and it was known that Cochise could speak that tongue as well. But still, the man might be trouble if the Indian refused to produce the boy and cattle.

As the column passed, the station keepers emerged from the Apache Pass Overland Mail Station and the lieutenant waved, then called to one of his men. "First Sergeant Huber, I'm going to stop at the station and ask these men if they know where I can find Cochise. We'll go into camp at the base of the hill half a mile beyond the station."

"Aye, sir. I'll see to it."

The lieutenant turned off and Johnny Ward followed as the infantrymen continued their march. The young man reviewed what needed to be done and what he'd say to the station keepers. Colonel Morrison had sent him to confront the Chiricahua Apache chief, Cochise, to force the return of the boy and cattle. He would show his strength and ask politely, over a meal perhaps. He might even offer some gifts. Everyone knew that Cochise was guilty. He'd raided along Sonoita Creek before and the trail the lieutenant took pointed to the chief's home at Apache Pass. The colonel had entrusted him with the mission of confronting Cochise.

The lieutenant knew himself to be honorable and hoped he was brave as well. His men trusted him and so did his colonel. Little did he suspect that one day he would be villainized and reviled as the man who started the Apache Wars.

The Black Legend is a myth that has persisted for over a century and a half, and places the blame for eleven years of Apache depredations in Arizona squarely on the shoulders of one man: Lieutenant George Nicholas Bascom. According to this legend, or variations of it, in October 1860, Apache raiders abducted Felix Ward, the son of Johnny Ward, a drunken, abusive father, and carried him into captivity; or, possibly, Felix had run away to the Apache to escape the abuse. Sometime later, Johnny's oxen wandered off. Unable to find them, the drunken man complained to Lieutenant Colonel Morrison, the commander at Fort Buchanan, that Apaches had stolen his cattle and son. Months later, Lieutenant Bascom, leading a patrol of twelve cavalrymen including Sergeant Reuben Bernard, happened upon a random band of Chiricahua Apache that included Cochise.[1] Inviting them to parley in their tent under a flag of truce, the soldiers made hostages of seven, and the drunken lieutenant demanded that Cochise return Felix Ward. Cochise assured the lieutenant that he did not have the boy. The soldiers bound Cochise and imprisoned him in a tent for the night. Since they had failed to relieve him of his knife, he cut his way free. Cochise then captured James Wallace, an Overland Mail[2] employee, and offered to exchange him for the lieutenant's hostages. The lieutenant stubbornly refused to make the trade without the boy. Sergeant Rueben Bernard implored him to save Wallace's life, becoming so adamant that the lieutenant had Bernard court martialed.

Angered by Bascom's refusal to trade hostages, Cochise dragged Wallace to death behind his horse. Bascom played a card game called 7Up with Surgeon Bernard John Dowling Irwin to determine the fate of the woman and two boys among his hostages. Losing to Surgeon Irwin, the lieutenant hanged the adult males, despite Irwin's objections, but allowed the woman and boys to live. Cochise, who prior to this incident had not only been friendly to Americans and even protected the Butterfield Overland Mail, was enraged at the violation of the white flag, at the lieutenant calling him a liar, and at the hanging of his relatives. He began an eleven-year war of vengeance against Americans, starting by attacking a stagecoach. The stagecoach careened down the trail at high speed, leaping a chasm where Cochise and his men had destroyed a bridge.

This memorable story has stayed in the popular imagination, fed by rumors that a stupid lieutenant started the Cochise War. The presumption is that lieutenants in general are young and stubborn and refuse to listen to their wise sergeants. The only problem with this story is that, apart from the names, none of it is true. This version of the story began with a soldier, Captain Reuben Bernard,[3] who returned to Arizona in the final months of 1868 to find that he was the only one left out of all of the soldiers who had been there in 1861, when the incident at Apache Pass occurred. According to his version of events, Bernard had been not only an eyewitness, but the hero of the story. In the 1880s, two others added their presumed eyewitness accounts. To further confuse the account, Bernard seems to have told his tale different ways, but always claiming that the boy had gone missing in October 1860. These three accounts do not agree with each other, much less with verifiable sources. And then the accretions began. The story grew like a snowball rolling downhill picking up new elements. If the version the reader is familiar with doesn't quite match the one above, it's because the parent versions don't agree on particulars and many of the accretions don't fit at all.

Early historians of Arizona[4] reported that a confrontation between the U.S. Army and Cochise started the war with the Chiricahua Apache. They referred to this event as the Bascom Affair. They lacked the resources that we have today. They did not have easy access to back issues of newspapers long out of print, nor to out-of-state papers. They lacked access to military reports. They were heavily reliant on the accounts of old-timers who presumably had been there and to recent newspapers bearing the recollections of old-timers. Sidney DeLong, Arizona State Historian Thomas Farish, Frank Lockwood, and Don Russell, who was Reuben Bernard's biographer, all repeated versions of the Black Legend. Often realizing that something wasn't quite right, they attempted to reconcile the irreconcilable by adding elements of imagination to the already confused accounts.

Only in the 1960s did a version of the story closer to the primary accounts, those of people actually present, begin to emerge with the work of Robert Utley, Dr. Ben Sacks, and Constance Altshular. The real story is that the affair began in January 1861 along Sonoita Creek, about three miles south of modern Patagonia, when Apache raiders took a pre-teen boy, Felix Ward,[5] along with his stepfather's herd of cattle. Soldiers at Fort Buchanan located a hot trail that pointed toward Cochise's home at Apache Pass between the Chiricahua and Dos Cabezas Mountains. The commander of the 7th Infantry, Lieutenant Colonel Pitcairn Morrison, sent Lieutenant George Bascom and fifty-four men of Company C to confront Cochise and demand return of the boy and the cattle. Morrison allowed the boy's stepfather, Johnny Ward, to accompany Bascom as interpreter. Bascom met Cochise and allowed the chief ten days to bring in the boy. But something went wrong. Enraged, the chief called to his people and ran. Six of his people ended up by mischance as Bascom's hostages against the eventual return of the boy. Cochise took his own hostages and subsequently killed four of them and a stagecoach driver, along with eight Mexican teamsters.[6] Before the affair was over sixty dragoons[7] had joined the sixty-six[8] men of Bascom's Company C, 7th Infantry Regiment[9] at Apache Pass. There were four officers senior to Bascom present when the hostages were hanged; one of them, Lieutenant Isaiah Moore, had assumed command. Disgusted at the mutilated condition of the bodies of Cochise's former captives, Surgeon John Irwin, who had captured three Apache, suggested hanging the Indians the Army held hostage. Bascom objected, but Lieutenant Moore allowed the hanging of six Apache to proceed.

From this recounting of the story, it would seem there is little reason to blame George Bascom. Even though Bascom followed a hot trail to Cochise's doorstep, he was mistaken. Cochise didn't have the boy. In fact, according to the best account, Aravaipa[10] Apaches who made their way home by way of the Sulphur Springs Valley at the western side of Apache Pass had taken Felix Ward and later traded him to the Coyoteros (White Mountain Apaches).[11] Although the lieutenant seemed genuinely surprised at Cochise's reaction to his agreement to allow the chief ten days to bring in the boy, he may, indeed, have attempted to take Cochise hostage. That was common practice before the Civil War. To further muddy the facts, Johnny Ward was the interpreter. We don't know what he said to Cochise. Perhaps he didn't want to allow the chief to depart. Whatever he said, it drew out an unfortunate, extreme overreaction from Cochise. This alone would not be enough evidence to lay the blame for eleven years of warfare at Bascom's feet. Historians have realized this and try to make more of these facts than is here. They adopt Apache culture as a crutch to a crumbling theory, asserting that the lieutenant should have known not to take an Apache chief hostage, unaware that it was common practice.

Other historians have expressed the wish that an older and wiser commander like Captain Richard S. Ewell[12] had been there, asserting that he'd have known what to do. He had confronted Cochise twice before, demanding the return of livestock. Approaching Cochise with but few men, he granted the chief a few weeks to come up with the livestock, and then returned with a larger army. Previously, he had exchanged hostages with Pinal Apaches for an abducted girl. However, for Bascom, returning to Fort Buchanan for more men wasn't an option. Besides, Bascom already had more men with him than Ewell had.[13] In addition, Bascom was aware of Ewell's experiences and had four of the captain's former subordinates advising him.

Historian Edwin Sweeney wrote, "to blame this Bascom incident for the following decade of war, as Cochise and others have maintained, is a gross oversimplification."[14] Sweeney's evidence that Cochise held Bascom to account is based on an unfortunate misquote of General Oliver Otis Howard's recollection of what Cochise said. Sweeney wrote, "The worst place of all is Apache Pass. There five [six] Indians, one my brother, were murdered. Their bodies hung up, and kept there till they were skeletons. . . . I have retaliated with all my might." The problem is in what the historian left out with his use of an ellipsis. Missing is the sentence, "Now Americans and Mexicans kill an Apache on sight."[15] This changes the emphasis. Cochise was responding to the indiscriminate slaying of Apaches, not the hanging of his brother. Sweeney continues, "As one prominent historian wrote, even if the Bascom incident had not occurred, 'there doubtless would still have been an Apache war.'"[16]

George Nicholas Bascom deserves very little of the blame. However, the Black Legend, which held sway until the 1960s, told a different story. Unfortunately, despite the emergence of new scholarship and previously unavailable primary sources that chip away at the legend, it continues to come up and is still prevalent in popular writings. The legend began with former Sergeant (later Captain) Reuben Bernard, a man of infinite ambition and self-promotion, who returning to Arizona in 1868, realized that he was one of very few who had been there before the Civil War.[17] He saw the opportunity to impress Colonel Thomas Devin, his commander, with a story that explained the start of the Cochise War[18] and made him a hero. Devin passed the story along to Governor A. P. K. Safford, who repeated it in a letter to the *Arizona Citizen*, a Tucson newspaper.[19] For many years, Captain Bernard, stationed at Fort Bowie, associated with Sidney DeLong, the sutler[20] who in 1903 produced one of the first histories of Arizona, spreading Bernard's account.[21] Mining company owner Charles Poston, who had been in Arizona in 1861, but who was not at

Apache Pass during Bascom's confrontation with Cochise, produced several accounts of Arizona history and a book relaying and modifying the Bernard tale.[22] In 1886, former regimental musician Hubert Oberly joined the anti-Bascom bandwagon with his account:

> *If it were not for the insensate folly and drunken stupidity of a young West Point cadet there would never have been an Apache war. I was at the first outbreak, and I assert the truth has never yet been told, or if it has been I have never seen it. . . . In 1860 the Apache were as well behaved and friendly a tribe of Indians as any in the States. They were then guarding the Butterfield mail route against the attacks of roving bands, and acted in good faith.*[23]

Here, Oberly added new "facts" to the story, implying that Bascom was a drunk and a cadet, although the lieutenant was neither,[24] and that the Apache were peaceful and guarded the Overland Mail (aka Butterfield Mail). In fact, Cochise's band had raided along Sonoita Creek and had stolen livestock from the Overland Mail Company.[25] Oberly also stated that Bascom wanted to hang the prisoners, while Surgeon Irwin objected, implying that this hanging was because Bascom was enraged over Cochise's escape. Oberly's article so upset Irwin that he wrote a rebuttal saying that he, Irwin, had wanted to hang the hostages after viewing the mutilated bodies of Cochise's hostages more than a week after Cochise's escape.[26] Oberly adds one more cut, saying that cards were borrowed from a soldier, and a game of 7Up determined the Indians' fate. Like so much of Oberly's reported interview, this card game does not appear in any other account. In fact, Oberly wasn't at Apache Pass during this particular time period. He was at Fort Buchanan nursing a sick child.[27]

We don't know why Hubert Oberly so viciously attacked George Bascom. Perhaps there was some personal animosity, though he didn't seem to know the lieutenant very well, calling him a cadet fresh from the Point. Perhaps he was inflating his own importance and ego by enhancing the stories then circulating. In some ways, Oberly's is the most difficult of anti-Bascom accounts to refute. He claimed to be a primary source, someone who was actually there at Apache Pass, although unit records indicate he was at Fort Buchanan. He was accurate in some of what he said—noting, for instance, the presence of Sergeant Daniel Robinson and Surgeon Irwin—and grossly mistaken on other points.

This raises the question of how we determine what should and should not be recorded as history. Primary sources, accounts from people who were actually on the scene, who participated, are the gold standard. Historians rightly consider primary sources better than secondary and more reliable. Secondary sources include written accounts such as newspaper stories taken down by others who heard or were told about the event. The issue is anything but simple. Charles Poston is a secondary source to the events at Apache Pass; he wasn't an eyewitness. However, because he claimed that he knew Johnny Ward personally, he poses himself as a primary source where Ward is concerned. Ward stayed at Poston's house one night when he first came to Arizona in 1858. From this meeting, Poston made some conclusions about Ward's character and habits, saying that he was on the run from the law and was a drunkard. But this does not square with other accounts. Ward built an apparently prosperous ranch with a large house.[28] Nor does Poston's caricature square with Johnny Ward taking in partners, as evidenced by a newspaper ad that ran for many months to tout new blacksmith and wheelwright services available to the public on Ward's ranch. At least one of those partners was still with him in 1861, and even witnessed the Apache raid on Ward's ranch from his sickbed.

Sometimes a secondary source tells something about a primary source we might not have known otherwise. Both Charles Poston and Captain Bernard claimed that Apache took Felix Ward in October 1860. A letter published in a February 11, 1861, newspaper had something else to say:

On the 21st [actually January 27, 1861][29] they stole cattle from the ranch of Mr. John Ward, eleven miles from the post,[30] and seized a lad of twelve years within three hundred yards of the house, whom they carried into captivity. An infantry officer with a small command was sent to rescue the captive as soon as the news reached the post.[31]

We already know Poston to be a secondary source, so confusing the date may be understandable. However, this one error tells us that we should closely examine everything else he says about events and verify it with other sources before we accept it. Historian Allan Radbourne, the acknowledged expert on Felix Ward, said: "In fact, Poston's account of the circumstances leading up to the Bascom-Cochise confrontation is wildly, and demonstrably inaccurate."[32] Captain, former Sergeant, Bernard may also have had a lapse of memory writing many years after the event. However, the length of the gap between the kidnapping and the pursuit becomes an important element in the story, which relates that Bascom picked on random Indians months after they took the boy, when the lieutenant was actually on a hot trail. Here the secondary source, the newspaper article, helps to show that there are problems in Bernard's account.

Historians have a greater knowledge of the times, events, and personalities involved than the average layperson, and thus are supposed to interpret those events and, to the best of their ability, tell the reader what happened. When we encounter two diametrically opposed primary accounts, it is up to the historian to determine where truth lays. "Someone is lying so the truth must lie in the middle" is unacceptable. If only one side is lying, this approach is unfair to the side doing its best to tell the truth. Considering Poston and Bernard's accounts, we see where a secondary account points to their error.

Memory degrades with time and errors creep into the story, so accounts written soon after events are to be preferred. Different people see different things depending where they are standing and what their experience causes them to deem important. We can speculate about different perspectives and which is most correct, but since we can't see into a person's mind, speculation is usually fruitless. However, when comparing multiple accounts and established facts, we may be able to determine bias and fabrication. Sergeant Daniel Robinson's accounts written thirty years later are so detailed and agree with other accounts so completely— accounts that he did not have access to when he wrote his own—that I believe he must have kept a journal and used it later to produce his three accounts. His writing becomes a basis for forming the center of the story.

We need to watch for contamination. All of the Apache accounts are secondary and most were recorded long after historians had brought the Poston/Bernard/Oberly accounts into currency. All bear the earmarks of being war stories, that is to say, exaggerated. Many have Bascom killing his hostages before Cochise killed his. The primary accounts agree on when and why the hangings of Bascom's hostages took place. In December 1872, Governor Safford interviewed Cochise. Safford didn't speak Apache, so the interview took place either in Spanish or through an interpreter. Safford already knew the Bernard account and implies that Cochise said that eleven years of warfare were the result of Lieutenant Bascom mistreating him. Since Bernard's account is dubious in the extreme, one gets the feeling that Safford told (rather than asked) the chief why he, the Apache, had fought and Cochise nodded. Of course, he did. Safford was telling him that an American lieutenant had wronged him and his people, and thus neither Cochise nor his people nor Americans more generally needed to take responsibility for the war. It was the lieutenant's fault. How neat for both leaders. The governor's rendition of the tale exonerated Americans generally and their leader, the governor, as well as the Chokonen,[33] Cochise's band of the Chiricahua, and their leader. Of course Cochise agreed. Cochise was nobody's fool.

Safford's account, while it is a primary account of an interview with Cochise, is a secondary account where the Bascom Affair is concerned. It is also one in which the interviewer appears to be leading the witness.

Make no mistake—Cochise was a great chief who kept his word. That does not mean he never told a lie. War is rife with deception. When Captain Ewell approached Cochise, he denied having the livestock he had stolen and kept them hidden. Cochise was a man of wisdom and war-fighting ability. Apaches followed him in numbers greater than they followed any other leader. In their society, following a leader was voluntary and done out of respect and confidence in his leadership. Heredity did not make him a leader. Unlike Geronimo, he was not a loud-mouth who was made out to be a leader by the Army and the press, with no real standing among the Apaches.[34] Cochise was real, although legends grew around him. He did not protect the Overland Mail; in fact, he stole livestock and threatened to destroy their stations. He was not always peaceful. He was always Apache and that meant that when times were hard, he raided Mexicans, Americans, and other Indians for food and supplies. The story of the always peaceful Chiricahua chief who guarded the Overland Mail struck a chord with the eastern press, novelists, and later historians enamored of the "Noble Savage."

The legend of the Bascom Affair persists because it chimes with something in the American imagination. It captures an element of how we see ourselves and thus it makes a good story that we uncritically accept, remember, and repeat.

In 2017, at a writers' conference, a well-known historian talked about the Bascom Affair. He said that the story of the stagecoach careening down the trail at top speed and leaping a chasm was too good to pass up even though the physicists say it was impossible.[35] That's an interesting standard. This prominent historian has done a great deal of truly brilliant work showing how legend and history have impacted our culture. Legends have shaped our perceptions of ourselves as a nation. They're not history, though they have a history and are important. However, it's also important to know as nearly as we can what really happened. Understanding history, as well as the legend, allows us to predict, as well as we might, the probable outcomes of policy and law. The legend makes great reading, but it breaks down under scrutiny. On the trail from Apache Pass to the Overland Mail Station, there is no chasm to leap. Nor is there a bridge that Cochise and his warriors burned. Rather, the Overland Mail Company built up the bottom of one wash to form a platform several feet high, much like a modern dip where water flows over the road.[36] A version of the story from the 1930s says that Cochise and his warriors removed stones from the sides, making this platform too narrow for the stage, which slid across on its axles. Even this is problematic. This story doesn't appear in the primary accounts of the people who were actually on the stage, nor does it appear in early secondary accounts until much later. Maybe it happened. It is a good story, too good to pass up, but it isn't a leap over a chasm. It conveys the frantic rush from ambush where the Apache wounded the driver and slew a lead mule. The excitement of deadly peril was real enough. Except that isn't what occurred, either. One early account noted, "The road was barricaded with rocks for over two miles, but Mr. Culver will return in the next stage and put on a force of forty men to remove the obstructions."[37]

A few days after this account, Mr. William Buckley, the superintendent of the line who was on the stage, commented on the slow trip from Apache Pass to the Overland Mail station. This was the stagecoach that was supposed to have leapt the chasm in its flight from the attacking Apache. Instead, it took more than an hour to go two miles when the Overland Mail normally traveled at better than nine miles per hour.

> *As soon as we could put the wounded driver inside the wagon, we started for the station. As the road was very heavy, it seemed impossible to reach the same, as the Indians had filled the road in several places with heavy rocks.*
>
> *With the assistance of the passengers we were able to remove the rocks and push the wagon up the hills. Soon after leaving, we were fired at again. We arrived at the station about two o'clock, A.M.*[38]

There was no chasm to leap and no fast ride down to the station. It was a slow trek over a rock-strewn trail that the passengers cleared as they went. The story of the chasm came along many years later and started with a statement from a secondary source that the Apache had dug a ditch across the road.[39] That source had much else confused on other counts as well. By the 1930s, embellished in Don Russell's *One Hundred and Three Fights and Scrimmages*, the trench became a built-up wash bottom, an improved dip where Cochise had removed the rocks from the sides, making it too narrow for the stage, which slid across on its axles. Imagination turned the ditch into a chasm. Since the stage couldn't leap a chasm, the chasm became a bridge with the planks burned away and only the stringers remaining.

I recently told this story to a person who sputtered, "but I read, but I read." Apparently, this exciting tale, "too good to pass up," was one of their favorite stories of the Old West. The individual stubbornly refused to give it up. Somehow the statements of the people who were really there counted less than the thrill of the flying stagecoach. In her book *Give Me Eighty Men*, Shannon Smith wrote:

Their influence has continued for generations as later historians used the sources written by the Carrington wives almost without question. Like Custer's Last Stand, the Fetterman Massacre became mythologized in popular culture. Books, novels, and articles have launched the story of Fetterman and this military debacle into the forefront of America's western heritage.[40]

She speculated that because Victorian women supported mythologized versions of the stories of the military disasters of George Custer and Fettermen, men found it impossible to challenge and demythologize these nineteenth-century stories until after the wives of those involved had passed away in the twentieth century. This writer suspects that whatever causes myth to linger in the face of all evidence must go further than the influence of Victorian women. Stories that are "too good to pass up" linger as well as do those that resonate with something in our psyche.

Many know in some form the story of the stubborn lieutenant and the wise sergeant. We expect it to be true. It resonates with our egalitarian culture. Officers come from the upper classes. They are college boys with no experience out to prove themselves to experienced men. The Army draws common soldiers and sergeants from the working classes. Sergeants come up through the ranks learning hard lessons along the way. Many think it the sergeant's role to teach the young officer his business.[41] The young officer, eager to prove himself and take charge, often feels he must resist and show his men that he is in command. When a former sergeant told the tale with himself as the hero and Lieutenant George Bascom as the man who started a war with the always friendly Cochise, the story took hold and has stayed with us for over 150 years.

Today we have available records that scholars in earlier periods did not have access to: newspapers, military records, letters, and magazine articles. Our preference must be for primary sources, records laid down by people who were there, and for near-primary secondary sources such as contemporary newspaper accounts. When scholars set down the first histories of Arizona, these early historians had access to old-timers who had lived through the events. Unfortunately, memories fade and sometimes folks had reason to twist the tales. Few old-timers who had been in Arizona, then part of New Mexico, in 1861 remained there after the Civil War. When the military withdrew, the unprotected civilian population fled, and few returned. Southern Arizona was off the transcontinental mail route. Mining activity had shifted to the north around the new territorial capitol, Prescott. A few of those who were in Arizona, but who were not part of the action, contributed accounts as if they had been present and, unfortunately, these have been considered primary sources.

James H. Tevis led an exciting life as an Overland Mail station keeper, Arizona Ranger, Confederate officer (with the rank of captain), friend of Moses Carson (Kit's elder brother), rancher, miner, and entrepreneur. Tevis wrote *Arizona in the '50s* to amuse and delight an audience. In 1886, he reconstructed his lost memoirs working with his daughter with the intent of having the book published. His book is a first-person account and a primary source, but like many others of the time is full of exaggeration and fantasy. We can only employ it with extreme care and not blind acceptance. If some of the events he described had occurred, they would have left signs elsewhere, like ripples in a pond moving outward from a tossed stone. Other people would have reported the event; the story would have been in the press. Cochise didn't kill 150 men at Doubtful Canyon in April 1861, as Tevis reported. The chief and his warriors killed five. There are many accounts of the event in other sources. J. J. Giddings and four companions were making their way west in a stagecoach assessing the work needed to reopen the mail line across Arizona for the San Antonio and San Diego Mail, aka the Jackass Mail.[42] Two of the men ended up tied upside down to trees over small fires where a rescue party found their bodies. In Tevis' account, the two men were his friends captured by Cochise near Pinos Altos, and he alone escaped. Tevis made himself the hero of an event in which he did not participate. On March 17, 1860, Apache raiders, probably Aravaipa, abducted Larcena Pennington Page and Mercedes Quiroz. Most of the male population of Arizona, led by Captain Richard Ewell, joined in the pursuit and rescue. Tevis placed himself at Ewell's side, giving advice and thereby saving the life of one captive. He made Cochise the villain when, in fact, the captives had been taken by Pinals or Aravaipa Apaches. Larcena prevented Tevis from publishing his account during her lifetime. He passed on before she did, and the account went unpublished until the 1950s. Some think this is because she did not want the story of her captivity told, but she had already given her account to the press in 1860. There must be another reason, and Tevis' gross inaccuracies may well be it.

For the confrontation between Bascom and Cochise, we have available the two reports made by Bascom himself, a report by Lieutenant Isaiah Moore, an account by Surgeon John Irwin, one by Superintendent William Buckley of the Overland Mail, and by William Oury, station keeper in Tucson, as well as contemporary newspaper accounts. We also have two accounts by Sergeant, later Captain, Daniel Robinson, and these are lucid, detailed, and complete. These accounts are in substantial agreement, differing only in minor details concerning information to which a particular individual did not have direct access but learned from others. There is no need to quibble about minor differences. Memory fades and people misunderstand things. The accounts are straightforward, and there is no indication of cover-up.

If one account tells us that Cochise came to Bascom with his wife and two boys and another says only one boy was there, we may look for confirmation of the presence of the second boy but shouldn't suspect fabrication. Perhaps there is a defect of memory and we will honor the earliest written account. Perhaps the writer perceived the elder boy as an adult. What is important is that Cochise arrived with his family not expecting trouble. If a source says an event took place at 6 a.m. and another at 7 a.m., unless someone was actually minding the clock, we have agreement. This writer has seen accounts of a fight where participants had it lasting five minutes, an hour, and several hours. So it must have seemed to them, though the latter account was probably a deliberate exaggeration. If, on the other hand, one source says the event took place "at sunrise and the sun was in our eyes so that we couldn't see the enemy" and another says it happened "at noon and the blazing sun beat down and we had no water," we may have a problem to unwind. We must ask ourselves how the writer came by the details and if and why they were important to him and the story.

Historians have relied heavily on the accounts of men who weren't at Apache Pass in February 1861 during the confrontation between

Lieutenant Bascom and Chief Cochise. It is significant that these latter accounts do not agree with each other, let alone with the accounts of people who were actually there. Oberly claimed to have been at Apache Pass with Lieutenant Bascom. However, unit records do not include Oberly's name among the men of Company C, 7th Infantry that accompanied Bascom to Apache Pass (see Appendix A), and the number of men in the company who were available for duty squares with the number reported as following Bascom to the pass.[43] Unit records also indicate that Oberly was left behind at Fort Buchanan and unable to transfer with his unit because he was nursing a sick child. He was a musician, not an infantryman. Surgeon Irwin went out later with hand-picked men whose names also were included in unit records; Oberly was not among them, either (see Appendix C). Moreover, he's wrong on many verifiable facts important to the story. Surgeon Irwin wrote a refutation of Oberly's account:

> *Some months ago there appeared in a prominent New York newspaper under the caption "Why the Apaches Made War" a statement in the form of an interview with a person represented as having served in Arizona in the 7th U.S. Infantry, which, if allowed to remain unexplained and uncontroverted, distorts a conspicuous incident in the early history of that territory, and, at the same time, does gross injustice to the reputation and memory of a brave and efficient officer of the Army, Captain George N. Bascom. . . .*
>
> *In some particulars the published account of the occurrences that led to the summary execution of six Chiricahua Apache warriors at Apache Pass, Arizona, in February, 1861, was correct, but, owing to the possible effects of time on the mental faculties of the narrator (Sergeant Oberly)—twenty-six years having elapsed since the tragic affair, or to his having been incorrectly reported—the interview contained palpable errors and misstatements of a nature so coarse that justice to truth and the vindication of the character of one whose life was given in defense of his country's cause require that the imputations cast upon his courage and judgment should be repelled by a comrade who knew him as one officer whose reputation for all soldierly qualities was above suspicion.*[44]

First Sergeant (later Captain) Reuben Bernard in 1863. His lies made him a hero and Bascom a villain.
U.S. CAVALRY ASSOCIATION

The most influential of these tales came from Reuben Bernard who had the ear of Colonel Thomas Devin, commander of the Sub-District of Southern Arizona, of Governor A. P. K. Safford, and of Sidney Delong, who wrote a 1903 history of Arizona.

There are many versions of the Bascom Affair, all filled with misstatements and inaccuracies. Captain Reuben F. Bernard was the first to provide a version that made Lieutenant Bascom out to be a stubborn, inexperienced young lieutenant who would not listen to his wise sergeant. In 1861, Bernard had been a sergeant of the First Regiment of Dragoons assigned to Fort Breckenridge ninety miles northeast of Fort Buchanan where Lieutenant George Bascom, commander of Company C, 7th Infantry, was assigned. In 1868, when Bernard returned to Arizona, everyone wanted to know how the war with Cochise had begun. Bernard, realizing that there were no old-timers from 1861 still around, told a story with himself as the hero first to his commander, Colonel

Devin, then to Governor Safford, and finally to Sidney DeLong, the sutler at Fort Bowie where Bernard was assigned. DeLong wrote one of the first histories of Arizona and repeated Bernard's fantastic story. This is the version of the story used by the makers of the 1952 movie *Battle at Apache Pass* and the basis of what many people think they know about Bascom and Cochise. Here is DeLong's story:

> *The commanding officer of the fort sent out a new lieutenant named Bascom, accompanied by twelve men under Reuben F. Bernard . . . with orders to proceed to Apache Pass . . . where he would likely find Indians who could give some information regarding the lost boy. . . . The lieutenant . . . upon arriving at the station with his party found there Chief Cochise and another Indian. Cochise professed entire ignorance of the depredation, . . . but said he would find out and see that the boy was returned. This explanation and promise did not satisfy Lieutenant Bascom and he at once made prisoners of the . . . Indians. . . . Bascom pitched camp giving his . . . captives a Sibley tent to themselves, stationing a guard in front and rear of the tent but with unloaded*[45] *muskets.*
>
> *Cochise . . . had been left his sheath knife [and] he slashed a long cut in the tent and darted through. . . . The next day the stationkeeper named Wallace,*[46] *who spoke the Apache language fluently and had always been on friendly terms with those Indians, thought by his influence he could arrange matters and make peace and in his confidence ventured too near or too far among the hills surrounding the station and the Indians made him a prisoner. . . . About 4 p.m., of the same day, Cochise, in full war paint and mounted, appeared upon the hill within gunshot of the station and with an imperial haughtiness demanded that the Indian prisoners be set at liberty, and stated that those he held would be liberated and sent in as he had captured three Americans, besides Wallace. This was done through Wallace, who acted as interpreter, and who begged that it be accepted as he stated they would be all killed were it rejected. Lieutenant Bascom would not accede to the proposition and the Indians disappeared from the vicinity of the station. . . . The next morning no Indian signals; no Indians*

were to be seen. The command of Lieutenant Bascom, with the seven prisoners, started to return to Fort Buchanan. Upon reaching the mouth of the Apache Pass, some three miles west from the station . . . on the side of the road were the bodies of four Americans, and that of Wallace was one of them. . . . Lieutenant Bascom halted his command; about one hundred yards north of the road, an oak tree, which is yet standing, was selected, trimmed up to suit the purpose, and without ceremony the seven Indian prisoners were hanged and the command proceeded on to Fort Buchanan. It is but justice here to state that Sergeant Reuben F. Bernard refused to have anything to do in the proceedings and was placed in arrest by the lieutenant.[47]

DeLong, with long residence in Arizona beginning when he arrived with the California volunteers in 1863, cleaned up the story and included factual elements that came to hand. For instance, he corrected the dates from one of Bernard's versions. "Bernard had arrived three months before. In a letter Bernard gives the date of October 1860 for the raid on Ward's ranch."[48] If there was a delay in the pursuit from October until February, Lieutenant Bascom would appear to be guilty of randomly accusing Cochise, as he would have lacked evidence that Cochise was responsible. The date of the pursuit is well reported in post returns (a monthly report by the military unit that detailed strength and told of patrols and fights), Bascom's two reports, and in the newspapers (see Appendix G). We have to wonder how Bernard got the date so wrong. We also have to wonder what the commander of an infantry company was doing leading a patrol of twelve dragoons from a post ninety miles away. Post returns[49] would have reported any cross-attachment of men and a summary of any combat patrol. It would have been extremely odd for an infantry lieutenant to lead dragoons. The arrest and court martial would have been recorded in several places, including in Bascom's reports. It wasn't. We might also wonder why unit records, newspaper accounts, and the recollections of others who were there show Bascom at Apache Pass with sixty-six infantrymen of Company C, 7th Infantry, and no dragoons at all. The story relies on Bernard being the only sergeant there to advise the lieutenant, but we have the names of five infantry non-commissioned officers from Bascom's company who were there.

There are interesting omissions in the story. Lieutenant John R. Cooke,[50] 8th Infantry, son of Philip St. George Cooke, arrived on the eastbound stage[51] early on the third day of Bascom's long confrontation with Cochise, and although senior to Bascom, placed himself under Bascom's command. Bascom acknowledged gratitude to Cooke in his report to Colonel Morrison "for his kind advice and gallant assistance."[52] Bernard's story omits this crucial piece of information. Nor did he recall that Surgeon Irwin had arrived on the tenth day and shortly after that Lieutenants Isaiah Moore and Richard Lord of the 1st Dragoons arrived from Fort Breckenridge (see Appendix C). This omission is especially surprising since Lord was Bernard's commander.[53] All of these officers were senior to Bascom. Lieutenant Moore assumed command and thus he—and not Bascom, as Bernard insisted—was responsible for hanging six hostages. It seems very likely that Bernard was not in Arizona in February 1861.[54]

Reuben Bernard claimed that Lieutenant Bascom ordered him court martialed for insubordination in the field. There is no record of any such court martial. In his report, Bascom had this to say about his men and the non-commissioned officers who served under him: "The men behaved excellently well, always ready for the discharge of any duty; the non-commissioned officers zealous and untiring in the discharge of their duties."[55]

Some might call me a revisionist historian. It seems that a revisionist is someone with a political agenda who wants to remake history to support a cause. That's not what I'm doing. The historian must review and analyze primary sources. If the sources don't confirm the current version of history, then the historian should write about what did happen. If those who don't remember history accurately are doomed to repeat it, then it is up to the historian to do his or her best to learn and to say what really happened. In George Nicholas Bascom we find a humble young officer well-liked by his peers and superiors, willing to accept advice, who was maligned by a few individuals for their own reasons. He became the villainous, stubborn drunkard who started a war. Even as the evidence against Bascom crumbles to dust, we find that the legend persists and the lieutenant is still held up as a scoundrel.

In *The Man Who Shot Liberty Valance*, the newspaper editor says, "When the legend becomes history, print the legend." I can't really accept that as the role of the historian. The historian should seek truth. It's often elusive. Noted southwest historian John Kessell said:

> *First off let us ignore the postmodernists' claim that none of us can possibly know objectively what actually happened, only objectively what is said to have happened. As historians, that is our business—to say what happened, to pursue historical truth as objectively as possible. Historians Jacques Barzun and Henry F. Graff suggest in* The Modern Researcher *(1992) that practitioners of the craft apply six rules: accuracy, orderliness, logic, honesty, self-awareness, and imagination (I might add calmness). Evidence gathered in this way one bit reinforcing or challenging another, provides us with the probability upon which to base our "truth," that is, the probability that something actually happened pretty much the way we say it did.*[56]

A cultural historian of my acquaintance once said that if the legend is too good not to be true, we need to make the legend history. After all, the story in a case we were discussing at the time was said to have come from an historical figure, Tom Jeffords, who was self-effacing, and thus, wouldn't have lied. Tom Jeffords became a friend of Cochise in 1871. Their friendship and mutual trust became the basis for the peace achieved in 1872.[57] In a sense, Jeffords' story is the ending to the story of Cochise that begins with Bascom. In fact, the story he referred to did not come from Jeffords. It was a secondary account of what another person claimed Tom Jeffords had said. Jeffords is said to have told many stories about himself, and the accounts conflict acutely. Did he lie? Was he misunderstood? Were the stories filtered through others' experiences? Knowing a little about Jeffords, I think he was accomplished at letting greenhorns believe what they wanted to believe, thus avoiding arguments. How can we tell? It is the historian's duty to sort the possible from the impossible, the probable from the highly unlikely. I do that by searching out the ripples in the pond and looking for the shadows that should be them. I have some sympathy with preserving the legend. After all, legends tell us who we think we are and what our aspirations should be. Still, history should be a bit more than legend.

The past has not blessed historians with perfect intelligence of what occurred nor left complete records. We have to improvise by drawing logical suppositions. When presented with a conundrum, I try to figure out other things that must be true if the story is true. We toss a stone into a pond and it disappears, but the ripples remain. I look for the ripples. Turning back to Tom Jeffords again—whose story I am familiar with, having written his biography—I find examples of how accounts can be shown to be improbable by the lack of ripples in the pond. Historians and others who knew Tom attributed to him a statement that, during his time as superintendent of the mail from Socorro to Tucson, Cochise had slain variously twenty, twenty-one, or twenty-two mail riders. Every time a rider was attacked, there were panicked stories in the newspapers and a great deal of excitement. I could find accounts of only two attacks. The mail service was so successful with two riders per week that they soon added a weekly stagecoach. If they had lost the mail twenty-two times, the contract would have been cancelled. It wasn't. Moreover, on such a dangerous line, new hires would have been difficult to procure. Was there a shortage of mail riders? High pay goes only so far and soon the contract becomes unprofitable. The mail carrier was highly successful. The cavalry would have responded after each incident and the forays would appear in the post returns, which in fact include no such mentions. If I can confirm some of these, then the story has a high likelihood of being true. And if none of them pan out? Then the story is probably false. As good as the story is, it remains legend, not history. In exploring the accounts of the Bascom Affair, I have discounted accounts like Oberly's, which claims that Cochise attacked a Texas wagon train at Apache Pass and killed two hundred men, women, and children. There were no ripples in the pond to bolster his account.

Although the legend may not reflect the facts of an incident, it may expose a truth about how we later felt about the incident and ourselves. The legend often resonates with elements of our national or cultural heritage, providing insight into who we think we are. That makes the legend interesting. This definitely has a place and is important to the cultural historian, but it does not make the legend the history of the original event.

As we write history, we rely on memory and notes. Memory plays tricks. Things we've heard and only imagined as we picture the past creep in and become new "facts." We create accidental misquotes. "Four men killed near Dragoon Springs" becomes "four men buried at Dragoon Springs." It seems an unimportant distinction until we find ourselves with seven candidates to lay under four burial cairns. The historian has to check their notes and check the footnotes of sources to ensure that the evidence supports what is written and what we are writing.

In the nineteenth century, tales of the Wild West were popular. Those writing their own accounts, which might be considered primary sources, frequently juiced up their stories with heroic acts and deeds of infamy that never occurred. The same standard we use for any legend must apply. Can the story be supported by other evidence, by other reports? What other things must have occurred if the story is true? Has the story been influenced by earlier reporting?

Primary sources are the reports of people who were actually there and participated in events. There are numerous sources of contamination. A source that was written down immediately after events occurred is to be preferred over one written many years later. Recollection of detail is often an indicator that a source is referring to notes or a diary written at the time rather than relying on failing memory. Comparing sources to each other can be helpful, but an untruthful source cannot be reconciled to a valid one by averaging their content. How do we know when a source has fabricated data?

This is a difficult question. We can ask, was the source really present? Is there evidence that places the source somewhere else? Is the source's account consistent with the accounts of others? Is the evidence presented consistent with the tools, techniques, and social organization of the time? Here the historian's thorough knowledge of the era is important. What was the source's motive in writing? John Bourke, aide de camp to General Crook, wrote brilliant, detailed, accurate diaries that followed on careful observation. The Army sent the general to Arizona in 1872 to subdue the Apaches. He returned in the 1880s to pursue Geronimo. However, Bourke wrote *On the Border with Crook* for a popular audience; he juiced up the facts to make the account more exciting and included details of events in which he did not participate, as though he had. The result is a wonderful tale that is not to be completely trusted without confirmation from other sources.

Secondary sources—newspapers and the contemporaneous accounts of non-participants—can be useful in verifying facts given in primary sources. If someone claiming to be a primary source says an event occurred in October of 1860 in the Whetstone Mountains, while another primary source says it occurred in January of 1861 in the Chiricahua Mountains seventy-five miles distant, we might look to the newspapers, which we learn reported the event in January and in the Chiricahua Mountains. The first source begins to look doubtful and should be rejected; it cannot be reconciled. It is just wrong.

Like ripples from a stone tossed in a pond, events have effects. Many of us drift through life without appearing in official reports or in the newspapers. Even so, some events in our lives get reported: marriages, property transfers, yard sales. Important events should find their way into reports and the papers. When we read an account and want to affirm its veracity, we can look to the ripples for confirmation. If the ripples aren't present, there's a good chance the story isn't true. Raphael Pumpelly, writing in old age of his time in Arizona, recalls Apache raids on Fort Buchanan after the Cochise-Bascom confrontation. If the raids do not appear in the post returns, some might conclude that the military was conducting a "cover up," but the loss of livestock could not go unreported. That too creates ripples and the commander would know that he couldn't hide the loss of equipment, men, or livestock. Ten Apache might become one hundred in his report to explain how he was overwhelmed and livestock stolen, but the report would appear. Both Dr. Irwin and Sergeant Robinson report a raid in June 1861, followed by a pursuit in which they participated, with Lieutenant Bascom in the lead. Both report four men killed. Robinson implies that they were soldiers. The post returns show only one man slain: "Pvt. Driskell of Company C, 7th Inf. killed in action by hostile Indians on the 22d June 1861 while guarding government property."[58] The others may have been civilian herders.

Much has been made of the wrath of Cochise after his confrontation with Lieutenant Bascom. Other writers have shown the extent of this wrath using accounts such as those of Oberly and this report from Tevis:

Some few days after this, Major McNeece withdrew the coaches from the Overland Mail Route, taking coaches, stock and employees. When his party, consisting of 122 men, was about two miles southeast of Stein's Peak Station the Indians attacked them and all were killed. Among them was my old partner, Anthony Elder. After this massacre, three prospector friends from Pinos Altos, Burke, Donahue and Malcolm, were taken prisoners by the Indians at Stein's Peak.[59]

The names and other details show that Tevis is referring to the deaths of J. J. Giddings and four companions, a well-reported event.[60] In April 1861, J. J. Giddings and his companions, Elder and McNeese among them, set out from El Paso to inspect the Overland Mail stations to the west toward Tucson in order to determine what would need to be done to reopen the line as the San Antonio and San Diego Mail. Cochise ambushed them near the Stein's Peak Station at Doubtful Canyon. Giddings, who survived the firefight with one companion, surrendered to the chief. People who knew them discovered their bodies suspended upside down from a tree where they had been tortured to death. Donohue was one of four teamsters reported in the papers as having disappeared near Doubtful Canyon in March 1861. Tevis increased the death toll from five to 122 and then added three "prospectors." There are no ripples in the pond to support Tevis' version of events, while the nine deaths are well reported. Similarly, Oberly includes in his account of Bascom's confrontation with Cochise a reference to a party of two hundred Texas emigrants being slain at Apache Pass in the spring or early summer of 1861. Irwin handily dispatches this fantasy, which is also absent from any other report of the time.[61] Oberly says he saw the burned remains of the wagons and may have seen the remains of the Montoya wagon train destroyed by Cochise during his confrontation with Lieutenant

Bascom. Eleven men lost their lives in that incident and its aftermath, as we'll detail in a subsequent chapter. The ripples are there for the eleven who show up in reports, accounts, and newspaper stories, but not for the two hundred. Such exaggerations make it appear that Cochise slew five hundred or so men, women, and children in the spring of 1861, when the actual number was below thirty.

Sidney DeLong, one of Arizona's first historians and a pioneer himself, noted that a gentleman had:

> published a book on Arizona, which came out in 1874, called "The Marvelous Country." From its careful perusal one can hardly avoid the conclusion that the author was never in what now is Arizona, but only in that portion along the Rio Grande at Mesilla, and Donna Ana, which finally fell to New Mexico; so his "book" is largely made up of fancied adventures and descriptions of scenery that are fictitious or taken at second-hand from descriptions of others.[62]

The historian must say what happened. It's a daring course because subsequent documentation may show that some of his conclusions were wrong. The best he can do is present his reasoning and let the reader decide if he is correct. The historian must have a greater knowledge of the era, the personalities involved, the lines of communication (roads, trails, and rivers), the technology available, and the customs of the people than the average reader. For instance, we are shocked that Bascom invited Cochise in for parley and then took his people hostage against return of the boy and the livestock. In our own time, the police have made false announcements of prizes won to lure criminals into their custody. To an extent, the Army saw Indians as criminals, so hanging on to them until restitution or compliance was gained seemed reasonable. The taking of hostages was common practice before the Civil War. Bascom was not acting outrageously in so doing. Hostages were usually well treated, though as we'll see this had not been Cochise's experience in dealing with the Mexicans, who also took hostages. It only made sense. The Indian[63] was apt to depart into the hills and never be seen again if the Army didn't maintain control while they had him.

Culture as an explanation of Indian behavior is a dangerous course. Too many use it as a *deus ex machina*, god from the machine, an expression that harks back to ancient theater. When the playwright wrote himself into a corner, he arranged to have god lowered by crane to the stage to miraculously cure the problem. To use culture as an explanation in history, the historian should first show that the particular cultural element existed and was agreed upon by a substantial element of the group whose culture is being described. Ideally the writer claiming the existence of this cultural artifact should demonstrate its application in group behavior and not just in informant reporting. During a ceremony, I questioned some Apache friends about something I'd read and expected to see coming up next in the ceremony. The response was, "Well, maybe in some families." Next, the writer should show that the individual being written about was prone to respond to this cultural element in this way. Needless to say, this is almost never done and we should be very suspicious of such explanations.

It is hoped that the reader will come to see Lieutenant George Nicholas Bascom as a young man of temperate humor on the eve of being promoted to captain (October 24, 1861) already in command of a company, and doing his best in difficult circumstances. Other historians have compared Bascom unfavorably to Captain Richard S. Ewell, whom they claim would have handled the affair differently. To my knowledge, neither officer was prescient. Ewell had promised bloodshed if he ever had to deal with Cochise again, and it seems likely he would have followed through on his threat. The evidence against Cochise, although circumstantial, seemed quite sufficient.

Bascom was gallant and hard charging, but far from being stubborn and headstrong, he welcomed advice. Bascom acknowledged gratitude to Cooke for his assistance at Apache Pass.[64] Even in the most intense circumstances, Bascom was willing to listen to the advice of his sergeant and surgeon Irwin. In June 1861, Cochise killed four herdsman, including one soldier, and drove away part of the Fort Buchanan herd. Bascom, Robinson, Irwin, and a local man, Paddy Graydon, along with a number of soldiers went in pursuit, chasing Cochise and his warriors as far as the Whetstone Mountains, twenty miles from the fort. According to then

Sergeant (later Captain) Daniel Robinson of Company C, 7th Infantry.

DANIEL ROBINSON, 1881. NATIONAL PARK SERVICE/FORT LARAMIE NATIONAL HISTORIC SITE MUSEUM, FOLA 16854

Sergeant Daniel Robinson, "The officer in command [Bascom] seemed to have recovery of the stolen stock in view, regardless of consequences to himself or others. The trail ran through intricate gorges, and as we were about to enter one, the surgeon counseled caution before going further. A halt was ordered and no sooner made than we were assailed with a shower of arrows."[65]

Surgeon Irwin had this to say:

From the foregoing [commendation of Bascom from the Department Commander] it will be perceived that the imputation circulated against Lieutenant Bascom's experience and conduct are utterly unworthy of credence, and it was a painful surprise to those who knew that gallant young officer to learn that anyone professing to have served in the same regiment with Bascom could be brought through hearsay or misrepresentation to speak unjustly of him and especially of his conduct on that trying occasion. Subsequently it was my fortune to share with him the dangers of conflict with the Chiricahuas on occasions where lack of coolness and courage on his part would have involved destruction of himself and his companions.[66]

Chapter Two

GEORGE NICHOLAS BASCOM

[The] classic image of Bascom is that of a green lieutenant, fresh from West Point, who was both arrogant and imprudent.[1]

There is an Apache story in it [June 1896 *Sports Afield*] *that does great injustice to a brave and gallant officer. . . . The lieutenant is charged with hoisting a white flag over his tent and inveighling (sic) Cochise and other chiefs into our camp. This is absurd and the most painful part of the story.*[2]

Some months ago there appeared [an article in a New York newspaper, which] *distorts a conspicuous incident in the early history of that* [Arizona] *territory, and, at the same time, does gross injustice to the reputation and memory of a brave and efficient officer of the Army, Captain George N. Bascom.*[3]

HE STOPPED, PANTING, AT THE SCHOOLHOUSE STEPS. HE'D WON THE race against his peers. He smiled, but the sadness still showed in his eyes. He missed his parents and his siblings. The death of his father three years earlier had ended the comfortable life he'd known in a wealthy east Kentucky family. Now they were all separated, and he missed them, his father most of all. As the other boys gathered around him, he could see that they were not as well dressed as himself. Many wore homespun and a few wore buckskin. The frontier was never far away and never far from mind.

The boy liked the forest and enjoyed hunting. He could be alone and for a while he didn't have to feel beholden. His relatives treated him well and tried to love him as their own, but it was different from being with his parents and brothers and sisters. He knew they were showing him kindness, but he also knew he was an outsider and so he pushed himself. If he hunted, he could bring home game for the table and contribute something. He pushed himself to do well in school so that they would be proud.

"You've won again, Geordie," exclaimed one of the boys.

Geordie was their leader. It had always been this way. He was the oldest of seven children. When his father died, he stepped into the role. He suffered through his mother's long last pregnancy before relatives realized she was incapable of tending to the children. They'd sent her away to a home where, as they said, "she can rest."

Another boy piped up, "We only let you win because it's your birthday."

Geordie didn't really know when his birthday was. It was in the spring, he was sure. April, maybe May. He knew he was born in 1836. His mother was no help in this regard. She'd forgotten and his relatives, the Guerrants, had never known for sure.

A red-haired boy called out, "You promised to tell us about the war! You said you'd read it from the newspaper."

"So I did," said Geordie pulling the paper from his back pocket. "It says here that the Cotton Balers—that's the 7th Infantry—really took a pounding at their fort on the Rio Grandie. Their commander, a major, got killed and they're renaming the fort after him, Fort Brown. There's more. There was a man's wife, a big woman, over six feet tall, with red hair, whose husband was killed. She jumped right in and started serving his cannon. They call her the Great Western, after that big steamship."

Geordie wanted to be a hero like Major Brown and to travel to Mexico and Santa Fe and exciting places like that. He wanted to serve with a unit like the Cotton Balers and meet beautiful, brave women like the Great Western. Geordie wanted to be a soldier.

In February 1861, when he met with Cochise, Lieutenant George N. Bascom was neither "green" nor "fresh from West Point" as the author of that quotation goes on to show. At twenty-five years old, he was a man who welcomed advice from both officers and his sergeants. Sergeant Daniel Robinson and Assistant Surgeon Bernard John Dowling Irwin liked and admired him and in the 1890s, when Bascom was accused in print of cowardice and misbehavior, they came to his defense. George Bascom was brave and a gentleman liked by his peers. Lieutenant Colonel Pitcairn Morrison, commander of the 7th Infantry Regiment, the Cotton Balers, entrusted his first major campaign into Chokonen Apache territory to Lieutenant Bascom. Bascom lived a hard life, but he managed to graduate from West Point.

In 1795, Thomas Dye Owings made his way from Maryland to what would become in 1811 Bath County, named for natural springs thought to have medicinal qualities. His father dispatched him to operate one of the first iron furnaces in this region of northeastern Kentucky, which Virginia had only recently agreed to cede. On June 1, 1792, the Union admitted Kentucky as the fifteenth state. Within fifteen years, Owings had amassed a good deal of wealth and land. He and Richard H. Menefee founded the community that took Owings' name, Owingsville. Owings and Menefee each owned significant parcels of land in the immediate area. To select whose name the community would take, the two men wagered that the man who built the finer home the quickest would be the namesake of the town. Building a home for the munificent sum of sixty thousand dollars, Owings won the contest. They founded Owingsville in 1811.

Owingsville would become the birthplace of two notable soldiers: Civil War Confederate General John Bell Hood and Captain George Nicholas Bascom, a scion of the Owings family, who died in the service of the Union at Valverde on the Rio Grande.

Sylvanus Clarke Bascom (born 1801, died January 21, 1844), the father of George Nicholas Bascom, was the first of his clan to settle in Kentucky. He married Mary Nicholas Owings (1812–1865) of the prominent Owings family. George was born to this couple related by blood and marriage to some of the most powerful families in Kentucky in either April or May of 1836, at Owingsville, Kentucky. He was the eldest of seven siblings. His mother gave birth to the seventh, Colgate Bascom, on August 13, 1844, when George was eight years old.

The Bascoms were a prominent family and probably well-off, with servants to assist Mary in caring for her many children. Her eldest children were still too young when Colgate was born to be of much assistance. George's father, Sylvanus, passed on eight months before the youngest child was born. The strain on the young mother was too much to bear. The family farmed her children out and relatives raised them. They sent Mary, unable to cope with life, to an institution, where she died in 1865. These catastrophic events separated George from his siblings. Peter and Margaret Guerrant of Bath County, Kentucky, took over raising George and brother Alpheus Washington Bascom. They were related to the Owings family by marriage.[4]

Kentucky was Southern and Western in outlook and no longer wilderness, but still not as "civilized" as the states on the coast. The frontier past was too recent in memory and wilderness still abounded. The frontier drew boys to physical pursuits rather than academic. At the U.S. Military Academy (USMA), West Point, there was a division between Northern cadets, who had a better grounding in mathematics and academics, and their Southern counterparts, who often lacked depth in such schooling. Young George spent much of his time outdoors in athletic pursuits, riding, and hunting. At West Point he did not perform well academically. The attrition rate was around 50 percent and reduced the ranks of Southern and Western gentlemen. "It is not thought a disgrace to be dismissed from here," wrote George Derby, a cadet, "for the studies and discipline are very hard, and a man who succeeds should be thought uncommonly talented, and one found deficient should not be blamed, for I verily believe that not one half of those appointed can possibly graduate."[5]

The record shows that George grew up disciplined, well-mannered, respectful of authority, and grateful for assistance and advice. This may be a product of having been raised at the sufferance of relatives, but it would appear his parents already had him on the right track before they passed from his life. As the eldest, he must have had responsibility thrust upon him after his father's demise, during his mother's final pregnancy.

Among George's relations, which included Doctor Henry Guerrant, Thomas Owings, and Judge Eliha Owings, was one who obtained for him an appointment to USMA. It might even have been his uncle, Southern Episcopalian Methodist orator, Bishop Henry Biddleman Bascom. The Methodist pastor was a friend of Henry Clay and won an appointment as chaplain to the House of Representatives. The only way into the door of the military academy was through political appointment and by passing an academic examination. USMA admitted George in July of 1853 when he was seventeen.

West Point was the premier college of engineering in the United States, the curriculum heavily weighted toward mathematics, chemistry, geology, mineralogy, and engineering, both civil and military. Cadets also studied French, so that they could read French tactical treatises, and drawing, so that they might produce maps and terrain sketches, as well as physics and astronomy. On the military side they studied ordnance, that is, weapons and munitions, and gunnery. They also got a dose of English grammar, geography, ethics, and rhetoric, as well as law, both military and civilian. All cadets studied the same subjects.

In the hot, humid summer, dressed in thick woolen uniforms topped with a heavy cadet shako, George marched to and fro with his peers learning the school of the soldier from upperclassmen in turn learning to be leaders and trainers of the men they would someday command. Summer encampment was the first taste of the military life where upperclassmen taught, hazed, and drilled the first-year cadets in the practical side of soldiering. "Drills began at 5:30 a.m. and continued until 5:00 p.m. During the day cadets took instruction in riding, dismounted drill, infantry tactics, musketry, artillery drill and firing, and fencing."[6] The cadets also walked guard, served on fatigue (work) details, and paraded. The tactics of the day prepared the young soldiers for a European-style battlefield where armies massed against each other and fought in ranks. The weapons of the day, muskets, had a maximum effective range[7] of about one hundred yards and could be fired about three times in a minute[8] by a well-trained soldier provided that there wasn't too much wind or rain. The evolutions of the infantry, their tactics, were fairly simple. They formed in line when enemy infantry approached, to present the maximum number of firing weapons to the front. Skirmishers were sent out a few hundred yards to snipe at officers and the enemy colors, causing confusion in the enemy ranks. When cavalry approached, the infantry formed square, with bayonets to the fore to discourage horses. When artillery fired on them, the infantry lay down or took open order to keep from presenting a masked formation for the artillery to shoot at. It was critical that the evolution from line of march to line to square and so on be done rapidly without confusion, even under fire. This is what the infantry practiced until it was second nature. The artillery often operated in front of the infantry firing grape (like a huge shotgun shell) and canister, which exploded over the enemy, raining down fragments of metal. The artillery also fired solid round shot. The range was five hundred yards to a mile for some weapons (very short by today's standards), and the gunners could see their targets.

The U.S. cavalry of the day was dragoon cavalry, who fought both as cavalry and as infantry. The dragoons trained in the saber. If they encountered infantry in open order or line, the dragoons could cut the infantrymen to shreds. They also battled other cavalry with sabers. The dragoons served as scouts to find and fix (hold in place) the enemy, and as flank and rear guards to prevent surprise. They trained with musketoons (shortened muskets) and horse pistols to fight dismounted as infantry, as their weapons were much more accurate when the men were steady on the ground. One man in four held the horses. At Apache Pass, Bascom would lead his men as mounted infantry. They rode mules to the fight, but dismounted to engage the enemy, performing traditional infantry roles.

The U.S. Army did not train to fight Indians. The massed tactics and steady rate of fire was devastating against Indians if one could just get them to cooperate and attack en masse. It happened occasionally with usually devastating effects on the Indians, who soon learned to avoid soldiers. Disciplined fire will hold a much larger enemy force at bay. There wasn't much need for artillery in the West, though on occasion it was used to great effect. Usually artillerymen found themselves used as infantry and the Army frequently tried to issue mules to the infantry, so that they might serve as mounted infantry.

The role of the Army in the West was difficult. From 1835 to about 1855, the First Regiment of Dragoons kept the peace on the plains without a fight, using only disciplined show of force.[9] There was little reason to change tactics. In New Mexico after 1847, there were new challenges. Apaches, Navajos, and Comanches raided for food, livestock, and captives. By the time word reached the Army, the enemy already had a significant lead and the cavalry would have to ride its horses nearly to death trying to catch up. Many writers have assumed that the cavalry had inferior stock unable to subsist on native grasses as Indian ponies could. The need to make up distance alone accounts for much of the supposed weakness. When cavalry did manage to approach the enemy, they scattered like quail, leaving the military little to pursue. The Indians operated more like bandits than a military force. The military was not a police force. The most logical change of tactics for fighting Indians would have been to become police.

Sherlock Holmes[10] had not yet made forensic science or detective work such popular pursuits. Police worked from eyewitness accounts or circumstantial evidence. When Indians conducted a raid, their tactics, location, and style of dress and arms usually showed which tribe had committed the act. There was little chance of identifying the actual individuals involved. For the military, it was enough to know the tribe or the band. The Army held the band collectively responsible for the acts of the few. They'd follow the enemy to his village, if they could, or attack the first persons of that tribe they encountered. It was brutal and frustrating. When soldiers captured an Indian, they held him or her and their children hostage against the good behavior of the tribe. If released, the Indian would surely disappear into the wilderness, hidden by his tribe and rough country, never to be seen again. One in hand seemed a better bargain than many in the bush. From the military perspective, the entire band benefited from the plunder brought back by raiders; the entire band hid the culprits. The United States treated Indians as nations at war, collectively responsible for the actions of their warriors. To an extent, this worked to the Indians' benefit, with a few horrific exceptions. As a rule, the government did not hang captured Indians or send them to prison or to the firing squad. The government did not usually treat Indians as criminals. However, the Army routinely destroyed villages and the supplies and equipment they contained, forcing already starving tribes to sue for peace and seek annuities from the Indian agencies.

Throughout the Indian wars, military tactics did not change much. This lack of change was not the result of stubbornness or because military minds were slow. The tactics learned from the French and British were what the Army needed to protect the country from border threats raised by Britain, France, and perhaps Spain, both real and perceived. The tactics had worked well in the Mexican War of 1846 to 1848. The United States still looked to Europe for science and technology. The changes that came were not great. The Army did not adapt well to fighting bandits or guerillas, which in every respect except political motivation is much the same thing. The tactic that works is to deny the guerilla the use of terrain by stationing small forces at key points and having available a large mobile force to crush the guerilla when pinned down. This requires communications, the means to mobility, and knowledge of the terrain. In the 1880s, this is how the Apache were subdued. In Vietnam, the Army accomplished this end with aircraft, air mobility, and tanks. The lesson has been learned and lost many times. In guerilla warfare, whether fighting American Indians or Viet Cong, junior officers lead the fighting operating on their own, using techniques that don't hold up in battles between nations. If the enemy can threaten the small outliers with a large mobile force, denying terrain in this manner does not work.

In the 1850s, the Army did not yet know the land. There were no good maps available. Scouts, both Indian and white, were hired who knew the countryside, the springs, mountains, and rivers. Historians tell us that General George Crook perfected the pack train, freeing the Army from slow, cumbersome wagon trains. They credit him with the use of Indian scouts, though these had long been in use. He recruited them in large numbers. They moved swiftly through well-known terrain to hidden campsites and springs, thus denying terrain to hostiles. By the 1880s, the Army scattered troops in small parties at springs and choke points, narrow defiles, and places where trails came together, thus denying terrain. The military used the heliograph, a device of mirrors reflecting sunlight, to communicate over long distances so that blocking forces were sent in a timely fashion to capture raiders. Eventually, the Army moved troops swiftly by rail. Basic tactics changed very little until after World War I, and then only in response to automatic weapons, improved artillery, and armored forces.

West Point did not produce martinets, although it did produce disciplined soldiers. That was not the American way. Officers from the American West, like Bascom, were especially independent minded. In the American service, thinking for yourself has been the accepted way. The U.S. military seldom found itself in set piece battles conducive to junior officers acting as mere puppets for the generals. American officers had to think on their feet, often operating hundreds of miles from their next higher commander and out of communication. During the Mexican-American War in 1847, at Cerro Gordo, Santa Anna, who styled himself the Napoleon of the West, planned the perfect set piece battle. It would have destroyed any European army of the day. As great a military thinker as the Duke of Wellington, who defeated Napoleon at Waterloo, proclaimed that the Americans stood no chance. The Americans "unfairly" followed a junior officer around Santa Anna's flank and completely routed his army, capturing his carriage and best wooden leg. West Point also produced fine engineers and scientists—men who could think. They mapped the West and developed new techniques for doing so. Western flora and fauna include in their scientific names the names of many soldiers who identified them as new species. Many officers were in sympathy with the plight of the Indians who starved when settlement denied them hunting lands. "We have to feed them or exterminate them" is not a call for genocide but rather a recognition of reality. The country was forcing starvation on the Indian, and they would either die slowly or fight. Either road led to extermination. If the Indian fought, the Army would defend the citizens of their country. If they didn't fight, they would starve.[11] Congress, more than corrupt Indian agents, frequently forced starvation on the Indian. Little enough was promised by treaty and frequently even that was not provided or was delayed as Congress wrangled over budgets. Settlers, miners, and hunters invaded lands reserved for the Indian and when the Indian objected, the Army was called on to defend the invaders even though the officers often sympathized with the Indian.

The military knew the futility of pursuing Indians with regular army forces. A change in tactics would have helped but little and made the military less able to defend the country from conventional threats. According to Calamus, a pseudonym for an officer assigned at Fort Lyon, New Mexico Territory, writing to the *Missouri Republican*:

> *There are no settlements here or near Fort Defiance, and the location at either place was not well adapted for a military garrison. The mountains, and glens, and hiding places in this Territory are so numerous, vast, and extensive, that it would require an army of 100,000 soldiers to penetrate the Indians' paths and defiles, and follow the savages to their places of retreat. Like Rob Roy McGregor and Roderick Dhu, amid the highlands and glens of bonnie Scotland, the Indians here can elude all pursuit from a small army; and it would be a perfect waste of time for infantry, especially, to attempt to pursue them.*[12]

In 1869 and 1870, Lieutenant Howard Cushing shone as an example of an active officer who pursued the Apache aggressively. It wasn't tactics that made Cushing special. He was used to attacking villages and creating havoc. On May 5, 1871, he attacked aggressively into an ambush and lost his life, ending four years as one of the most experienced Indian fighters in the American Southwest. What had made him great was that in December 1869, he had captured a herd of Apache ponies. While most officers found themselves able to pursue Indians for a few weeks before they had to return to their home post to recruit, that is, fatten, their horses for a month or more and then found themselves belabored by escort and post duties so that it was months before they could take the field again, Cushing had two herds of horses—one was always resting and fattening. The district commander had also relieved him of all extraneous duties and given orders that Cushing's troop should remain continuously in the field. The realities of being a great Indian fighter are somewhat mundane.

George Bascom is often compared unfavorably to Captain Richard Stoddard Ewell, who had preceded him at Fort Buchanan, departing just before Bascom arrived there in October of 1860. Historians and his contemporaries thought of Captain Ewell as a real Indian fighter, and he did well in New Mexico and Arizona. We'll revisit some of his accomplishments in a later chapter. Ewell graduated from USMA in 1840 and joined the First Regiment of Dragoons at Fort Leavenworth, Kansas. There he learned Indian fighting from Colonel Stephen Watts Kearny and Captain Philip St. George Cooke along the Santa Fe Trail. Kearny used his dragoons to make an overwhelming show of force. Ewell followed the clear trails of Indians driving slow-moving herds of stolen livestock to their camps and used a small force to make contact without spooking the Apaches into flight. When they refused to return the livestock, he departed and returned with overwhelming force. When Apaches abducted an eleven-year-old girl from a logging camp in the spring of 1860,[13] Ewell followed the trail to the country of Pinal Apaches.[14] Approached, they claimed not to have the girl, but said they would intercede with the Tontos who had her, if Ewell returned the Pinal hostages he was holding. He made the trade and rescued the girl. Paying ransom encourages more kidnapping and it wasn't at all clear that it wasn't the Pinals themselves who had had the girl all along. Richard Ewell dealt with Cochise on several occasions over stolen livestock and wrote that if he had to deal with the Chiricahua chief again there would be bloodshed.

USMA admitted George Bascom in 1853 to a class of more than fifty-five cadets. In 1855, at the beginning of Bascom's third semester, West Point dismissed him for conduct deficiencies, he having accumulated more demerits than were allowed in a semester. Secretary of War Jefferson Davis, himself a graduate of USMA, restored Bascom and six others, including Marcus Reno. Readmitted in 1856, into a class reduced to thirty cadets, he ranked fifteenth academically. Bascom's class had diminished remarkably. He would graduate twenty-sixth in a class of twenty-seven in June 1858. He had survived attrition and had graduated honorably. Those at the top of his class selected their branch assignments. Top academic performers generally chose the engineers and those just behind them the topographical engineers, then cavalry and artillery, while those near the bottom went to the infantry.[15] George's class at graduation was much smaller than many classes that decade. We are left to puzzle why the attrition rate was so high. The West Point "goat,"

Lieutenant
George N. Bascom.
ARIZONA HISTORICAL SOCIETY

that is the cadet graduating at the bottom of his class, is legendary, and by all accounts a difficult position to achieve. One must manage to be at the bottom academically and still manage to graduate. Many "goats" have gone on to great things.[16] George wasn't the goat but came close and managed to survive. Those who earned demerits showed an independence of mind and adventurous spirit. They often turned out to be exceptional field officers.

Consider Cadet George N. Bascom's accomplishment: He had come from Kentucky where education was not up to the standards of the Northeast. Nonetheless, he passed the entrance exam, an academic achievement not yet widely accepted in the universities of the East Coast, where wealth alone was the entrance requirement. USMA eliminated many Southerners and Westerners on academic grounds, but George survived. It was not unusual for a first-year class to lose more than half its members before graduation. USMA was an engineering school, the best of its type in the United States. Graduating twenty-sixth in a class of twenty-seven was much the same as saying Bascom ranked twenty-sixth among the most highly educated men in the United States. This level of education showed in the works of the graduates in the field. They wrote books on ethnography, biology, geology, and mineralogy. Scientists named many of our plant and animal species for the USMA graduates who first identified them. In a sense, George was not at the bottom of his class; he ranked among the most brilliant college graduates of 1858. The education provided by West Point was not then as narrow as many consider it today.

Bascom would wait almost a year, until April 1859, before the Army commissioned him a Second Lieutenant. In the meantime, he served as a Brevet Second Lieutenant in the 9th Infantry at Fort Columbus, New York. The brevet position did not count against authorized unit strength. There he drilled recruits.[17] He was in close contact with soldiers and men new to the Army, giving them their first instruction in how to be soldiers. It was further practice for him in the lessons he had learned at summer encampment. On April 23, 1859, Bascom was commissioned a second lieutenant in the regular army and assigned to the 7th Infantry Regiment.

The 7th Regiment of Infantry was a proud unit organized in July 1798. The first battle ascribed to the unit colors occurred at Fort Harrison, Ohio, on September 4 and 5, 1812. A large band of Indians attacked the day prior and set fire to one of the block houses of the fort and followed with a resolute attack. Captain Zachary Taylor, "Old Rough and Ready," Mexican War hero and twelfth president of the United States, was in command. Colonel Russell and the rest of the 7th Infantry relieved the beleaguered post in a timely fashion. At Viller's Plantation on December 23, 1814, the regiment was cited for conspicuous bravery under fire. The 7th next fought under General Andrew Jackson against the British at the Battle of New Orleans where it earned its nickname, the Cotton Balers.[18] In the words of the song: "We stood beside our cotton bales and didn't say a thing." In the Mexican War, fighting under General Taylor, the regiment erected a large fort with extensive works called Fort Taylor. When the balance of the American force moved away, the Mexican army bombarded the fort for many days, killing the 7th's commander, Major

Brown, for whom the post was renamed.[19] An army wife who lost her husband in the shelling became the heroine of Fort Brown. Six foot, two inches tall with flame-red hair, the lady who ministered to soldiers under fire is known to history as Sarah Bowman, the Great Western.[20] She would later reside along Sonoita Creek, running an establishment near Fort Buchanan while Bascom was assigned there. For a soldier, his regiment's history and honors is something to which he aspires, something he wants to live up to.

There was a great deal of military traffic across the plains and mountains to Utah supporting the Mormon War in which the 7th Infantry participated along with about one-third of the U.S. Army. The Army routinely put new lieutenants in charge of recruits and replacements being sent to join their units. This would have been command and field experience for the new officer.

The first casualty of war is the truth.
                                    –SENATOR HIRAM JOHNSON

In Utah, truth was a casualty long before war came. Between 1846 and 1848, while the United States was distracted by taking the greater Southwest from Mexico, Brigham Young moved his people to the promised land, the Kingdom of Deseret. Deseret included all of what we today know as Utah and Nevada, western Colorado, southern California, parts of Arizona, New Mexico, Wyoming, and Idaho. His people, the Latter-day Saints, came with a nurtured sense of victimhood. Their leaders taught that their strange doctrine was the reason their neighbors had driven them from Ohio, Missouri, and Illinois. There is a degree of truth in this since their doctrine led to the formation of militias, the intimidation of neighbors, block voting to exclude those not of their faith from office, and theft of land and property.

In Deseret, the people were isolated enough that the prophet Brigham had almost total control of the flow of information. The church claimed ownership of the land, and people had the use of it as long as the church allowed. The church separated people from their land, land they'd developed, in order to send them to pioneer the frontier. The church also took property when people fell into disfavor. One way to fall into disfavor was to become an apostate. Anyone seeking to leave Utah left behind all his wealth and property and the very means of making the move. Once they arrived in Utah, they were trapped. The existence of Avenging Angels and Blood Atonement is hotly debated. People believed it was so. Some sins were so severe that only the spilling of the sinner's blood could atone. One such crime was leaving the church. After the slaughter by Mormons of 120 travelers at Mountain Meadows on September 11, 1857, there was little reason to doubt the church's potential for violence. The U.S. Army, the Mormon leaders taught, was coming to kill all of the Saints because of their religion.

Brigham Young declared himself governor and refused to step aside for the territorial governor appointed by the president and sent out from Washington. Mormon leadership roused their people against government officials with claims that they were debauched, vile, and sinful. As bad as many appointees were in the nineteenth century, it's unlikely that all of them were as corrupt as the Mormons claimed. Prophet Young controlled the press and the information flow in and out of Deseret. He wanted the legally appointed officials gone as they represented a challenge to his political power. The power of religion, the state, and the fourth estate were all in his hands, and the isolation of Deseret allowed him to maintain his complete hold over the people. The government of Utah was totalitarian in every imaginable sense. Officials of the government land office and judges sent to Utah were run out of the territory with claims about their lack of morality. Mormon juries voted as their church leaders told them to vote. Brigham Young ran Deseret and when challenged, he threatened the trails to Oregon and California and sought to create an Indian uprising to harass travelers.[21]

Finally, in 1857, President Buchanan had had enough. He sent the Army on the Utah Expedition to subdue the rebellious Mormons. The Army started west in September. Colonel Albert Sidney Johnston of the 2nd Dragoons was in command. However, he and the dragoons were diverted to Bleeding Kansas to settle the violence there and did not join the expedition until later. The infantry led the way without cavalry support. The lines of communication and supply were lengthy, and the means of supporting the Army were stretched thin using civilian drovers and teamsters. The Army ended up camped in the vicinity of South Pass on Utah's doorstep and there passed an uncomfortable winter. The people of Utah trembled as their prophet told them the Army had come to annihilate them once and for all. He moved them south, burning towns and stores as he went, leaving scorched earth behind. People formerly ordered to far frontiers in southern California were ordered back to Utah to assist in the resistance. Attempts were made to stir up the Indians, the Lost Tribes of Israel, against the Americans with some minor success. The Oregon-California Trail became unsafe for travel. Mormons massacred emigrants at Mountain Meadows, the worst wagon-train disaster in American history, and blamed the affair on Paiutes and on the behavior of the emigrants. Brigham Young prepared safe-haven fortresses for himself at places such as Pipe Springs in what is now the remote Arizona Strip. At last, the prophet came to his senses faced with this threat and agreed to allow the expedition to enter Utah unopposed.

The army ended up at Camp Floyd away from the principle Mormon settlements, forty miles south of Great Salt Lake City. They were encamped amid a hostile population, many of whose less savory members preyed upon the soldiers while the more upstanding Mormons remained unwilling to convict a nominal Mormon of an offense against a gentile, as they called non-Mormons, presuming themselves to be the literal descendants of the children of Israel.

The Army had brought a large number of teamsters with it to the valley of the Great Salt Lake and in an economy measure discharged them without the means to return across the plains. They became the core of another unsavory element that preyed on soldiers. The Mormons under license distilled Valley Tan. The name was supposedly drawn from tanning fluid. It was green whiskey, aged all of a week or less. A town grew up outside the camp, Fairfield, which came to be known as Frogtown, the haunt of whores and gamblers.

Commissioned in the 7th Infantry on April 23, 1859, Lieutenant Bascom joined his regiment soon after. Over the ensuing year Bascom learned about the tedium of garrison life, mounting guard, leading escort parties, and serving as provost in Frogtown. He came to know his men, who he could rely on and who he could trust, and they in turn came to know their officer. In the late spring of 1860, the unit received new orders. The 7th assembled at Fort Bridger on the Green River in what is today southwestern Wyoming and on June 7, began the march, two companies at a time, to New Mexico where the regiment would disperse to different camps, with Bascom's Company C going all the way to Fort Buchanan near Tucson. The march was arduous, with the unit averaging eighteen miles per day. Bascom learned to place sentries to watch at night for hostile Indians and thieves. They marched east on the Cherokee Trail, passing to the eastern flank of the Rocky Mountains before turning south toward Santa Fe. Lieutenant Colonel Morrison, an old man in poor health, commanded the regiment. During this long march, Bascom learned about commanding troops and operating in the field.[22] On October 3, 1860, Lieutenant George Nicholas Bascom arrived at Fort Buchanan with two companies, C and H, of the 7th Infantry and the regimental headquarters.[23] Lieutenant Colonel Pitcairn Morrison was the senior officer in what was coming to be called Arizona. Captain Samuel Hayman commanded Company C and his first lieutenant was Gurdin Chapin, who was selected to serve as regimental adjutant, a duty that took him away from the company. On December 15, 1860, Captain Hayman departed on leave and Bascom became company commander. At Fort Buchanan, Bascom also met and earned the respect of Assistant Surgeon Bernard John Dowling Irwin, the "Fighting Doctor," who had served at the fort since 1857. The doctor later wrote that a newspaper article written about Bascom did "gross injustice to the reputation and memory of a brave and efficient officer of the Army, Captain George N. Bascom, who was killed in battle in one of the earliest conflicts of the War of the Rebellion."[24] Bascom held the Fighting Doctor's esteem, as well.

In October 1860, two companies of dragoons of the 1st Regiment rode ninety miles to the north to take up station at Fort Breckenridge along with Company B, 8th Infantry. Brevet Lieutenant Colonel Isaac Van Duzer Reeve, serving in his regular rank of captain, commanded Company B, although he had previously commanded Fort Buchanan and all of the troops in western Arizona. Company B built Fort Breckenridge. The new fort was located on the San Pedro River at the mouth of Aravaipa Creek, near where the San Pedro joins the Gila. This put the dragoons well into Pinal and Aravaipa Apache territory and on the raiding trails of Tontos and Coyoteros, but it moved them away from the centers of population on Sonoita Creek, at Tubac, and Tucson, all of which now felt unprotected.

Chapter Three

RICHARD S. EWELL, THE OCCUPATION OF ARIZONA, AND THE FOUNDING OF FORT BUCHANAN

ACCORDING TO ARIZONA SETTLER EDWARD DUNBAR, CAPTAIN EWELL was "[A] most efficient officer . . . and had Fort Buchanan and the Department of New Mexico been under the management of such officers as Capt. Ewell . . . little or no complaint would have been heard from the people."[1]

He stood up in the stirrups and looked all around. Even standing like this it was clear he wasn't a tall man. He took off his tall hat, now somewhat crumpled and stained from wear, and beat the dust out of his blue uniform, and then pulling out a handkerchief, he mopped his bald pate. He looked up the steep sides of the canyon at pine trees and rock. The Apache could be hiding anywhere. He had to be alert. They'd fired at his men the night before as they sat around their campfires. Nothing hurt but their pride. Cochise's people were hostile. That was certain. They lived one hundred miles away from the settlers on Sonoita Creek and only raided occasionally.

"Too far away," he said under his breath, "and too many dragoons for their taste, I expect." His commander had told him to head out with all his dragoons and bring those Apaches to heel. It wasn't working. He'd learned from the best, Colonel Kearny and Captain Philip St. George Cooke, how to intimidate and awe Indians. It had worked well for twenty years on the Plains. But how was he supposed to awe anyone with this

48

ragtag lot? His horse moved, and his saber rattled under his leg. The country killed horses so he could hardly keep the men mounted. His men's uniforms were in rags and they wore whatever replacement civilian attire suited them. They didn't look like an army.

He turned to his men and called out in a high pitched, squeaky voice, "You sons of whores, get in line there! Try to ride like soldiers even if you are hell spawn scalawags."

Sergeant Paddy Gradon turned to the man riding beside him. "Aye laddie, be sure the captain's not feeling hisself today. He's made cursing a right art form but he's off it today."

"Aye, mate," his partner replied, "'e's the Shakespeare of harsh language."

They both laughed.

From somewhere behind the long column a rider approached at high speed.

"'e'll kill that horse in this heat."

Reining in beside the captain the rider saluted and said, "Change of orders, Captain Ewell, with all due respect, sir. Yer to leave off chasing Cochise and continue northeast to join Colonel Bonneville on the Helay River where there's big doin's. The whole New Mexico army is gonna attack the Patches."

"Damn! They fired on us last night and I need to strike a blow. Damn that hostile, arrogant, son of a dog, Cochise. Damn these new orders!"

Graydon smiled. "Now he's in the mood."

Some historians have suggested that matters at Apache Pass might have gone differently if only Captain Richard S. Ewell had been there instead of Lieutenant George Bascom. Ewell had the experience and temperament for fighting Indians. He would miraculously have known that Cochise was telling the truth when he said he didn't have Felix Ward. From 1858 through 1860, Ewell was the most influential officer in Arizona[2] and one of the most dominant personalities. His record as an Indian fighter was based on a limited number of encounters. His contacts came when no one else was able to achieve contact. He had encountered Cochise and attempted unsuccessfully to force the chief to return stolen livestock. In 1860, Captain Ewell wrote that the next time he visited the

Chokonen leader he would "strike a blow."[3] In other words, there would be a fight. Despite this, in many respects, Lieutenant Bascom seemed to be emulating Ewell, the great Indian fighter and negotiator. His behavior was especially similar to the captain's in his March 1860 encounter with Pinal Apaches. Captain Ewell was a remarkable soldier and an excellent role model. Although they never met that we know of, Bascom would have been familiar with the captain's record and had fellow officers at hand who had served with Ewell.

On February 8, 1817, Richard Stoddert Ewell was born at Halcyon House, his mother's family home in the District of Columbia's premier neighborhood, Georgetown. Both his father's and mother's families had distinguished places in the history of the colonies and the Revolutionary War. His father died when he was nine,[4] and Richard grew up poor and close to his mother. His family owned two slaves, although one, Fanny Brown, had technically been manumitted and stayed on with the family. Ewell spent his boyhood at Belleville Farm in Virginia, which the family called Stony Lonesome for the condition of its soil. Through much of his life Richard Ewell dreamed of returning to farming.

In 1836, Richard Ewell managed an appointment to the U.S. Military Academy. Being poor, he and the family had wished this as a way for him to attend college. West Point was a four-year government scholarship with pay. A Southerner with poor academic background, Ewell worked hard to succeed.

At West Point he grew particularly close to William Tecumseh Sherman, whom he later described as being "in every sense a gentleman[,] generous & high toned."[5] Ewell did not graduate at the top of his class. Upon graduation cadets selected their branch assignments in class order, those with the highest standing generally selecting the Engineers or Topographical Engineers. Farther down the ranks Ewell selected the dragoons and, in 1840, was assigned to the 1st Regiment of Dragoons.

In 1840, there were two regiments of dragoons in the U.S. Army, numbering 750 men apiece. The United States created its first two cavalry regiments in 1855. In the summer of 1861, the dragoons were reorganized as cavalry. Dragoons were cavalrymen taught to fight from horseback, as well as on the ground as infantry. They wore sky-blue trousers and navy-blue jackets trimmed in orange. They were heavily armed for their dual role with large caliber percussion cap pistols, single short carbines or musketoons,[6] and heavy sabers known to the soldiers as "wristbreakers." According to biographer Donald Pfanz, this was only an ideal and the Army seldom came up to standard. For instance in the late 1850s, when regulations called for Sharp's carbines and Colt revolvers, Ewell's command still carried a heterogeneous collection of firearms that one soldier described as no better than "old rattletraps."[7]

In the late summer of 1842, while assigned to Company A, Lieutenant Richard Ewell accompanied renowned cavalryman Captain Philip St. George Cooke, escorting a caravan of traders across the Great Plains to Santa Fe. Ewell commanded Company A's complement of troops. While waiting for Cooke to assemble the expedition at Council Grove, Richard Ewell and many of his men contracted malaria.[8] It would haunt him the rest of his life. Writers have called it his "Fort Buchanan ailment," but he had it long before he arrived at that post and it returned in the damp, warm summers to debilitate him.

Neither Cooke nor Ewell arrived at Santa Fe during this late summer trip. Heavy rains and deep mud slowed the caravan to a crawl. Nearing the Cimarron River, Captain Cooke had to decide whether to continue and have no chance of returning to Kansas before winter. He would need to winter at Bent's Fort and return to Council Grove in the spring. Returning to Council Grove would leave the caravan exposed to attack by Indians and freebooting Texians. Cooke decided to go on, a decision that met with approval from all hands, especially the troops who wanted to visit the fabled city of the Southwest. They were soon met with a force of Mexican troops who assumed escort duties and Cooke turned back to Council Grove after all. Ewell would wait until 1850 before visiting Santa Fe.[9]

In 1845, Lieutenant Ewell accompanied Colonel Stephen Watts Kearny on a march along the Overland Trail to South Pass in modern Wyoming. This was the trail to Oregon and California that crossed the Rocky Mountains at a low point with a gentle grade. The other great route across the mountains lay far to the south in the thirty-second degree corridor that ran through Apache Pass. Ewell's biographer said: "The dragoons set out on 18 May 1845. Each company rode horses of a distinctive color: black for Companies A and K, bay for C, chestnut for F, and gray for Company G. The dragoons rode two abreast with a 100-yard interval between companies in order to avoid each other's dust."[10] They returned to Fort Leavenworth by way of Bent's Fort, a trading post on the Arkansas River, then the border with Mexico.

By this time, Ewell's appearance bordered on the grotesque. According to the *Encyclopedia of Frontier Biography*, "He was slight of build with a great beak of a nose and bright eyes that seemed to be on the verge of popping from a prematurely bald bomb-shaped head. Such features, combined with a shrill, squeaky voice and a bird-like habit of cocking his head to one side when he spoke, reminded many of a little woodpecker. He was sharp-tongued, witty, and quaint in speech, pronouncing his words with a bad lisp. (In profanity) he had few peers."[11] Nonetheless, he had few peers as a soldier.

Assigned to Company F, 1st Dragoons, Lieutenant Ewell did not accompany Colonel Kearny and the Army of the West to New Mexico and California. Instead, the company was sent south and served in General Zachary Taylor's army in Mexico, arriving too late to take part in the great battles fought by that army. Assigned to General William Worth's division, Company F joined General Winfield Scott's expedition to Mexico City acting as Scott's mounted escort. Richard Ewell first came under fire at Pedregal outside Mexico City, turning the enemy's flank. He assaulted the gates of Mexico City only to find himself, his commander, and a handful of dragoons alone, the rest of the assault force having been called back. He was breveted to captain.

His regular promotion to captain came on August 4, 1849, and he took command of Company G, 1st Dragoons, in New Mexico Territory in 1850. En route to his new assignment Ewell commanded 160 recruits on the trip from Fort Leavenworth to the frontier. With them rode Captain Abraham Buford, 1st Dragoons, Lieutenant Alfred Pleasonton, 2nd Dragoons, and Lieutenant Henry Heth, 6th Infantry. Two days out of Taos, New Mexico, the party encountered Kit Carson rushing east with a party of ten dragoons to rescue Santa Fe trader Elias Brevoort and his partner who were returning to Missouri with the profits from their sales in Santa Fe and Taos. Carson had information that the traders had hired the wrong men as escort. Fox, the man leading their escort, and several accomplices intended to rob them. Ewell and twenty-five of his recruits went with Carson and caught up with Brevoort near the Cimarron River, placing Fox under arrest and taking him back to Taos where he subsequently escaped and was never heard from again, perhaps having been slain by those who aided his jailbreak. The frontiersman and the soldier became friends. In 1856, Elias Brevoort traveled with Ewell to Tucson and became the sutler (post trader) at Fort Buchanan. In 1858, Brevoort was one of Ewell's partners in the Patagonia Mine.

Captain Ewell took command of Company G at Rayado, then Kit Carson's home. It was a two-company post on a tributary of the South Fork of the Canadian about ten miles south of Cimarron and twenty miles north of Fort Union, eighty miles from Santa Fe and forty from Taos. The commander of the 9th Military Department (later Department of New Mexico) assigned the companies to Rayado to intercept raiding Jicarilla Apache who dwelt on the plains to the east and across the mountains south of Taos. By the time word arrived of a raid, pursuit had been delayed and was unlikely to catch up to the raiders. Nonetheless, the presence of the dragoons discouraged the Jicarilla. Eventually, a new department commander dispersed the dragoons away from the towns and Company G took up residence at Los Lunas, some forty miles south of Albuquerque on the Rio Grande.

Although a strict disciplinarian, Captain Ewell recognized and attended to his men's needs. At Los Lunas the unit established a large company fund to purchase luxuries for the men. They built a bowling alley and collected books for a library. Ewell directed the planting of gardens, which provided much needed variety in the soldiers' diet and saved them money as local prices ran high. Danger was not the only negative aspect of a soldier's life. Hardship was constant and comforts few. They built and maintained their own quarters. Discipline was often harsh and food bad, prepared by soldiers in rotation rather than regular cooks. Pay was low and irregular. Ewell complained in June 1851:

It has been nearly 3 months since we have been paid at this Garrison &
for the men it is unfortunate. Tobacco is a necessary & the temptation

to sell clothing or public property in their charge is very much increased when the Pay Master's appearance is a rare or uncertain event. The Uncertain movements of troops make it more difficult to obtain credit, except at exorbitant prices.[12]

He went on to urge the department to pay soldiers their back pay in small increments over a long period of time rather than in a lump sum, to prevent giving them the means and incentive to desert.

In December 1854, Captain Ewell and Company G pursued Mescalero Apaches to their stronghold in the Sacramento Mountains. Captain Henry Stanton, with fifty infantry and twenty-nine additional dragoons out of Fort Fillmore, joined them on the march. On January 18, 1855, the Indians attacked the soldiers' camp. Ewell pursued them upstream into the mountains. Stanton went ahead to investigate an apparently abandoned enemy camp and was slain in what proved to be a trap. Ewell's men killed about fifteen Apaches including their war chief Santa Anna, but a rear guard action by the Indians allowed them and their families to escape. Shortly after Ewell returned to Los Lunas, a party of fifteen Mescaleros attacked the guards on his horse herd, wounding four soldiers, one of whom died. This was the enemy's last gasp. They sued for peace and Ewell's stature as an Indian fighter grew.

He pursued Indians at every opportunity, leading patrols in person. On May 14, 1856, Captain Ewell received a report that Indians were plundering settlers along the Rio Puerco. He led a patrol of twelve dragoons, all that were available, in pursuit but was too late to make contact and was only able to determine that the marauders were Mimbres Apaches. With only a handful of dragoons at his back, he dared not follow them into their own country.

That summer, orders arrived dividing the 1st Dragoons between New Mexico and the Pacific Coast. The Army ordered four companies to Tucson to take possession of the Gadsden Purchase. By the 1848 Treaty of Guadalupe Hidalgo, which ended the war with Mexico, the United States for seventeen million dollars purchased former Mexican lands south and west of the Arkansas River including the modern states of New Mexico, Arizona, and California. The all-important thirty-second degree corridor was part of the purchase. This was a series of low passes through the Rocky Mountains extending westward from El Paso on the Rio Grande to the Colorado River. Topographical Engineer William Emory, traveling with General Kearny's Army of the West, had recognized and reported the need to acquire this corridor as it was one of the few feasible routes for a railroad and wagon road to the West Coast. Through the incompetence of Border Commissioner John Bartlett, the United States accidentally gave this land back to Mexico. Negotiator James Gadsden proceeded to Mexico where, in late 1853, he succeeded in buying the land for an additional ten million dollars by a treaty ratified in the spring of 1854. Mexican troops continued to occupy Tucson until March 1856.

Major Enoch Steen assembled his four companies at Fort Thorn on the Rio Grande and on October 19, 1856, began the arduous 340-mile trek across the desert to Tucson, arriving there in November. There the major could not find decent accommodations for his troops, only "miserable huts." Grain and forage in the area was insufficient for his horses. The whiskey sellers, gamblers, and prostitutes of Tucson had a debilitating effect on his soldiers. Since 1849, Tucson had become a collecting point for men on the run, especially from committees of vigilance in California. It was a land beyond the reach of the law and remained that way until at least 1863 when Arizona finally became a territory, although some attempt at providing local government was made when Arizona became a separate county of New Mexico in January 1860 with Tubac, forty-five miles south of Tucson, as the county seat. Up until then, the Gadsden Purchase had been part of Santa Ana County, New Mexico Territory, which stretched from Texas to the Colorado River, with the county seat three hundred miles from Tucson at Mesilla. Raphael Pumpelly, historian and early resident, described Arizona as follows:

There was hardly a pretense at a civil organization. Law was unknown, and the nearest court was several hundred miles distant in New Mexico. Indeed, every man took the law into his own hands, and the life of a neighbor was valued in the inverse ratio of the impunity with which it could be taken. . . . Murder was the order of the day.[13]

Steen moved his force south of Tubac to Calabasas on the Santa Cruz River near where it is joined by Sonoita Creek. There was immediate outcry from the citizens of Tucson, especially from the grog sellers, gamblers, and pimps thus deprived of victims and income. Although the grazing was better and the post closer to sources of fresh supply of meat and vegetables, the claim was put forward that Tucson and the Overland Mail had been left exposed to Indian attack. Department headquarters ordered a change of location. The major dispatched Captain Ewell, who had made a number of scouts through the area, to find a better location. He located a post near *Ojo Caliente*, Hot Spring,[14] at the headwaters of Sonoita Creek, east of the Santa Rita Mountains. The site had water and grass and room for four companies. There was wood nearby for construction, heating, and cooking. Moreover, it sat astride the routes that Apache raiders used to return from the populated regions along the Santa Cruz River and in Sonora, Mexico, and it was twenty miles closer to Tucson although separated from the Old Pueblo by a mountain range. The new site was excellently located, but naturally there were objections from Tucson to which Ewell replied, "the only sufferers by our absence [in Tucson] would be the whiskey sellers & those who hope to profit from the dissipation of the Soldiers."[15]

Far from being "always at peace with the Americans," the Chiricahuas routinely conducted raids in Sonora and Chihuahua, Mexico, and famine was prompting them to attack American settlements as well.[16] In April 1857, Colonel Benjamin Bonneville,[17] acting commander of the Department of New Mexico, ordered Major Steen to take the field with a major expedition against the Chiricahua. Steen, an old man and sickly, was unable to lead the command of 110 men that rode out from Calabasas on May 3. Instead Captain Ewell was in the lead and directed his course northeast toward the Chiricahua Mountains. On May 12, he established a camp near the mountains. The next day with sixty-five men he rode around the southern end of the range.

At one point a band of Chiricahuas appeared with a white flag. They sent a captive Mexican boy to talk to the dragoons, making, as Ewell described it, the "usual professions of friendship, when they are in trouble." Unimpressed with these declarations of peace, Ewell ordered an immediate attack.[18] Captain Ewell experienced little success with the Chiricahua. Both sides fired on each other several times with no casualties on either side. Orders soon carried Ewell and his command north and east to join Colonel Bonneville's Gila Expedition against the Mogollon Apaches.

Bonneville's orders divided his command of six hundred dragoons and infantry into two columns advancing westward from the headwaters of the Gila River on either side of that stream. Progress was slow. Ewell referred to this mass of soldiers as a "solumn" (a solid column) and had little hope of its achieving anything beneficial.

I am very tired of chasing a parcel of Indians about at the orders of men who don't know what to do or how to do it if they knew what they wanted. I would prefer the less romantic but hardly less inhuman business of raising potatoes and cabbages—I say hardly less inhuman because as we now are about starting in a "solumn" (solid column) of 600 men, we will NOT be apt to see Indians, and mules and horses will be the only sufferers.[19]

Finally, Pueblo Indian scouts detected an Apache village and Captain Ewell pushed forward with eighty infantrymen, thirty mounted riflemen, and sixty dragoons to find that only a handful of women remained in the village. Ewell sent his Pueblo Indian scouts ahead again and they made contact, a fight ensuing. He sent Lieutenant Chapman forward with twenty men to support them, but the Apache withdrew.[20] After this aggressive action by his subordinate, Bonneville grew fearful of ambush and was ready to withdraw entirely from the mountains. Ewell convinced him to push on.

Within sight of the Gila River, the Pueblo scouts discovered an Apache village, which remained somehow unaware of the advancing soldiers. Ewell ordered an immediate attack on forty warriors and their families found in the camp. The shock of the attack scattered the Indians. The battle of the Gila was a success. Two officers and eight men lay wounded, but they had killed no fewer than twenty Apache warriors and had taken forty-five women and children prisoner. The only downside to this was that the people attacked were Coyotero Apaches, and not Mogollons.

The band sued for peace. Soon after, Indian agent Dr. Michael Steck uncovered evidence that Coyoteros had taken part in attacks on travelers and had been harboring Mogollon Apaches, including the man who had murdered Navajo agent Henry L. Dodge.[21] Out of this huge campaign, only Ewell had made contact with the enemy, and he had killed many, taken prisoners, and caused the Indians to sue for peace. His star was on the rise and his commanders recognized him as the premier Indian fighter in the department.

Meanwhile, on June 3, 1857, Major Steen had led the remaining soldiers at Calabasas to Ojo Caliente. There the tired, hot soldiers with little direction from Steen began to construct Fort Buchanan in the *cienega*, marshy area, and along the steep hillside, below the mesa Ewell had selected. This would prove unfortunate, making the new fort one of the unhealthiest in the West as malaria raged each summer among the troops. In a hot, dry June, it wasn't obvious that the site, surrounded by water on three sides, would become a marsh with the arrival of the rains in July and August. When Ewell returned in late August, it was too late to undo the mistake.

In May 1858, Captain Ewell bought an old Spanish mine shown to him by a Mexican herder. Joining him as partners were James W. Douglass, Richard M. Doss, and Lieutenants Isaiah N. Moore, Richard Lord, and Horace Randal.[22] The Patagonia mine produced silver and lead, and was in production off and on into the twentieth century. It was about fifteen miles southeast of the fort, and Ewell hired workmen and worked on it himself whenever time allowed. In the winter of 1858–1859, Elias Brevoort, the trader Ewell had saved with Kit Carson in 1850, and erstwhile sutler at Fort Buchanan, bought out two of the captain's co-owners thus acquiring a controlling interest. He was a good businessman, but in Ewell's estimation a poor judge of men. Under Brevoort's direction production decreased and along with it the value of the mine. Ewell sold out at a profit but a profit much less than it would have been before Brevoort took over. Brevoort soon sold out to former filibuster Henry Titus, who in turn sold the mine to Sylvester Mowry for twenty-five thousand dollars. Under the supervision of Mowry's brother, the mine eventually showed a profit of thirteen hundred dollars per day.[23]

On April 11, 1858, departmental headquarters approved Major Enoch Steen's request for sick leave and he turned over command of Fort Buchanan to Major Fitzgerald. Requirements of the Mormon War led the Army to transfer the four companies of dragoons at Fort Buchanan to California, but before the orders arrived, sense briefly prevailed, and Army headquarters in Washington decided to leave two companies at the fort. Lieutenant John Davidson left that spring at the head of two companies bound for California. In July, Surgeon Bernard John Dowling Irwin declared Major Fitzgerald unfit for duty due to pulmonary hemorrhaging. He returned east to die of tuberculosis. Captain Ewell assumed command of the post and of all the dragoons still in Arizona. Ewell remained in command from July 1858 until the end of March 1859 when Captain (brevet Lieutenant Colonel) Isaac Reeve arrived. He stayed until January 1860 when he requested sick leave, placing Captain Ewell again in command until September of that year.[24]

During his first period of command, July 1858 through March 1859, Ewell's principal problem besides Mexican bandits and unruly Americans was Pinal Apaches who lived in the mountains near where the San Pedro River flows into the Gila, about one hundred miles north of Fort Buchanan. It cannot be overstressed that Captain Ewell was the only governmental authority in Arizona. There was no sheriff or marshal, no courts or judges, no mayor. Apart from Captain Ewell's authority every settler was a law unto himself, and Mexicans and Indians as well as other Americans took advantage of this. Ewell reported:

> *The Indians are constantly committing depredations in the valleys of the Santa Cruz and Sonoita. They come in small stealing parties of from 5 to 8 on foot at night [and] drive off the stock. On being closely pursued by citizens or soldiers, they leave that portion of the stock that cannot travel with celerity and make a run for the mountains, when it is impossible to trail them.[25]*

Ewell kept small patrols constantly in the field but they were of little use. On January 27, 1859, Pinal warriors attacked three of Ewell's soldiers who were on leave, killing two. Captain Ewell proposed a punitive expedition but lacked the horses and supplies to make it possible. In the early months of that year, he had 170 men at the fort with fifty recruits on the way. He had only 108 horses and 12 of them were unfit for service. He also lacked horseshoes, cavalry boots, uniform drawers and socks, ammunition, and rations. "I am [as] helpless without these supplies as if I were without horses."[26]

During this period the Chokonen, Cochise's band of the Chiricahua, were relatively quiet in relation to the settlers of Sonoita Creek, Tubac, and Tucson. Cochise had nothing to gain by picking a fight with Americans whose army was close at hand. Dr. Steck, the Indian agent, was making biannual gifts of a wagonload of goods and food in exchange for the good behavior of Cochise's people. He was getting additional trade goods from the Overland Mail. Relations were tense, but peaceful, as his people continued to raid into Chihuahua and Sonora. When Chokonen from outside Cochise's immediate band conducted a raid on Americans, he was quick to proclaim his innocence to Captain Ewell, knowing he would be blamed. On another occasion his own people took more than eighty mules from the Sonora Exploring and Mining Company, presumably without his knowledge as he was quick to apologize and ordered the stock returned.[27]

During 1859, Captain Reeve repeatedly reported the need for a campaign against the Pinal who had been raiding southern Arizona frequently. He lacked the forces necessary for such a project. Nonetheless, Colonel Bonneville, at department headquarters in Santa Fe, ordered him to take the field. On October 26, he sent Lieutenant Cooke, Company B, 8th Infantry, to establish an advance supply base on the San Pedro River. On November 8, the campaign commenced. Captain Ewell was away in Mexico on a diplomatic errand. The campaign did not go well. In December, when Ewell returned, Reeve made a second attempt. This time Ewell located a Pinal village and attacked, killing eight warriors and wounding a ninth. The captain captured twenty-three Apaches, mostly women and children. He was the only U.S. casualty, suffering a slight wound to the hand. Nonetheless, he pressed his troops onward for twenty more days, returning to Fort Buchanan on January 3, 1860. Department headquarters approved Reeve's request for an extended leave of absence due to illness and he left Arizona. Captain Richard S. Ewell was again the senior officer in command of the fort.

On April 3, 1860, a letter signed Hesperian, the Westerner, datelined Tubac, March 18, 1860, appeared in the St. Louis *Missouri Republican*:

> *Intelligence was sent in this afternoon by an express rider that an American woman [Mrs. Page] and a little girl had been stolen by the Indians from the pinery thirty miles distant, and carried into captivity. The woman is a daughter of one of the oldest settlers, and was married not more than two months since to a lumberman in the pinery. This is the first instance I have had to record of captives being taken by the Indians. It is doubtless designed as a retaliatory measure because of the detention at Fort Buchanan of the captives taken during the campaign of last fall. Truly, we are in the midst of trying times. A courier has been dispatched to Fort Buchanan with information of the abduction and every effort will be made to recover them. The town is alive with excitement. "What family will be next?" is asked; and some of our sturdy farmers have made arrangements for bringing their women and children into town for the present.*[28]

Larcena Pennington had recently married former filibuster John Page. The newlyweds took in eleven-year-old Mercedes Sais Quiroz to educate her and teach her English. Mercedes was the ward of rancher William Kirkland and his wife, Missouri Anne. At first they lived at the Canoa ranch and then moved to her husband's pinery, a logging operation at Madera Canyon in the Santa Rita Mountains. There the women cooked and maintained the camp. While the men were away logging and preparing lumber for market, Apache raiders struck the camp. As the women watched horrified, the raiders looted everything they could carry with them on foot and despoiled the rest, dumping flour out on the ground. Larcena believed that the Apaches had already slain her new husband and the other workers, but the Apache had bypassed the men. They led the two women away at lance point. Larcena, and later Mercedes as well, tore her clothing and broke branches on bushes as they went north along the spine of the mountains to leave a clear trail for the help she hoped would come.

Wherever possible the women stepped to the side of the trail to leave clear tracks showing that they were still alive and with this band of Indians.

That March there was still snow on the ground in the high country. The Apache kept up a grueling pace, which Larcena found difficult to maintain. They prodded her repeatedly with their lances, breaking her skin, leaving her with many wounds. At sunset, fifteen miles from the lumber camp, the Apache saw pursuers in the distance. Briefly the Apache carried her but there was no way to maintain their pace bearing the woman. The Apache stripped her of her heavy clothing, leaving her only a thin chemise. They took her shoes and one of the Apache put them on. Still too slow, she was pierced in the back with a lance thrust. Recovering from illness, she was unable to keep up. The Apache lanced her repeatedly to encourage her to move more swiftly. Finally, they pushed her off the edge of the ridge and threw rocks down on her. In a hurry to escape pursuit, they didn't take the time to make sure she was dead. Battered, she lay senseless. The Indians left, assuming she was lifeless or would soon die. The little party continued to leave tracks resembling Larcena's.

In Tubac, the following dispatch was received from Lieutenant Randal, at Fort Buchanan:

> *I have received an express from Capt. Ewell to the effect that Mrs. Page and the girl have not been taken from the mountains. That the Indians have been left afoot, and are trying to steal animals that they may get their captives off. It is, therefore, desired that a strict guard should be kept over all animals for the present, and that all persons who can join in the rescue will be thankfully received and liberally rewarded. Send me fifty or one hundred "Papago" men if possible. Tell them that I will pay them well and give them all the beef, &c., they can eat. Send them up to-night, as quick as possible. Capt. Ewell wishes to surround the mountain, and I will distribute them. Capt. Ewell desires no hostile movement toward these Indians, and will be glad to have every information of interest sent to the post.*[29]

Captain Ewell was in hot pursuit as the trail split in two. One party presumably took Mercedes Quiroz and the other, using the purloined shoes, apparently had "Mrs. Page." Ewell feared that if confronted or pressed too hard, the Apache would slay their captives.

Larcena Pennington Page woke to the sound of her husband's voice above her following the trail of the Apache. Too weak to cry out, she lay there, and the pursuing loggers passed her by. John Page had already alerted Canoa ranch, Tucson, and Fort Buchanan. Mrs. Page later told her own story.

I had been married but little over two months and was living with my husband Mr. J.H. Page, in a rude cabin at the mouth of the grand cañon leading to the pinery of the Santa Rita Mountains. Our family consisted of myself and husband, a little Mexican girl eleven years of age Miriam Kirkland [Mercedes Sais Quiroz] and Mr. Wm. Randall, who was engaged with my husband in the lumber business.

On the morning of the 16th of March, after an early breakfast, my husband left us at camp for the purpose of putting some Mexicans to work and, Mr. Randall going out to kill a deer, Miriam and myself were left quite alone. As it was washing-day, I had started to procure some water when the little girl screamed and said the Apaches were on us. They came up in a run. Having a six-shooter (Colt's Revolver) in my hand, I turned to fire at them but they were already so close that before I could pull the trigger they had rushed upon me and secured the weapon. They then proceeded to plunder, seizing on everything they could carry off—flour, blankets, clothing &c.; and not satisfied with this, they destroyed the balance. We hallooed and screamed for assistance but the Indians struck me with their lances, and told us to keep quiet or they would kill us. They packed up what they could take and marched us off, hand-in-hand, in a hurried and barbarous manner. After proceeding thus for a quarter of a mile they separated us, in order to prevent our talking together, the little girl being a little in advance of me.

We traveled thus all day over a very rocky and mountainous trail, penetrating deeper and deeper into the mountain and finally almost reaching the summit. Having suffered much from recent attacks of fever and ague I was in a very enfeebled condition, totally inadequate for the fatigues of such a journey; and my inability to travel at the speed which they desired was the cause of my receiving the most brutal treatment at their hands. They several times pointed a six-shooter at my head, as much as to say that my fate was already decided upon and that I was to be made a victim of savage barbarity. The little girl, who was ahead, would occasionally fall back crying, and tell me that the Indians were going to kill me. They spoke but little Spanish yet enough was understood to awaken my fears and fill me with apprehension. I knew that my strength, which was rapidly failing, would admit of my proceeding but little further and that unless my husband and other parties were following to rescue me, I must fall a victim as soon as my strength entirely failed.

We had proceeded then about sixteen miles as nearly as my limited ideas of distance will enable me to judge, and I now lagged behind so much that my savage captors grew impatient and resolved to kill me. They stripped me of my clothing including my shoes, and left me but a single garment. They then thrust their lances at me, inflicting eleven wounds in my body, threw me over a ledge of rocks or precipice some sixteen or eighteen feet high, and hurled large stones after me to make sure of their victim, and then left me, supposing that I must die and too barbarous to end my misery by entirely extinguishing the spark of life. This occurred near sunset. I had nine lance wounds in my back and two in my arms, and my head was cut in several places by the rocks which were thrown after me, but most of the latter glanced without striking me.

I had alighted on a bank of snow, almost in a state of nudity and in a senseless condition. In counting up my camping places before reaching home, I think I must have laid there in a state of unconsciousness for near three days. When I came to I took some snow and put on my wounds. I recollected the direction traveled and the position of the sun from camp at sunset, and with these guides started for home. My feet gave out the first day and I was compelled to crawl the most of the distance. Did not dare to go down to the foot of the mountain for I could find no water, and was therefore compelled to keep on the steep and rocky mountain. Sometimes after crawling up a steep ledge, laboring hard for half a day, I would lose my footing and slide down lower than the place from which I started. As I had no fire and no clothing, I suffered very much from the cold. I was at a point said to be six thousand feet above the sea, and only wonder that I did not freeze. I scratched holes in the sand at night in which to sleep, and before I could travel was obliged every day to wait for the sun to warm me up. I traveled what I could every day and in the meantime had to subsist on grass alone. On the fourteenth day I reached a camp of some workmen in the pinery which was untenanted. There I found a little food and some flour which had been spilled on the ground. The fire was not quite out and I kindled it up. Scraped up some of the flour and made me a little cake, the first food I had tasted since I left home. I was now near the workmen in the pinery and within two miles of my home, but was too weak to go on. I could hear the men at work and sometimes saw them, but could not attract their attention. At length I crawled along to the road over which they must pass and was found there and carried home, after being out sixteen days.[30]

Captain Richard Ewell took immediate action upon being informed of the abduction. He followed the Apache trail north of the Overland Mail road to the Santa Catalina Mountains.

[A] dispatch sent in by Capt. Ewell announced that the Indians had escaped from the mountain, having previously divided into two parties each having a prisoner. The course of the party having the little girl in custody was traced to a point where it crossed the route of the great Overland Mail, and a point some thirty miles east of Tucson. The child had left articles of clothing at intervals along the trail as guides to those in pursuit, and when in soft ground where footprints could be readily detected, had taken a long sidewise step in the dark, where there would be little likelihood of her savage companions obliterating it. The trail of the party which had Mrs. Page in charge was also followed, but after proceeding some distance there seemed no evidence that she was still with them, and Capt. Ewell thought it most probable that she had been killed after giving out and no longer able to travel. He stated that he would send one of the Indian

prisoners with him to his home in the Indian country, mounted on a dragoon horse, and well armed, to ascertain if the prisoner were there, giving him eight days to meet him at the Canon del Oro. The Envoy Extraordinary is empowered to offer a transfer of prisoners. Should both be brought in alive he will give all the Indian prisoners at the post in exchange for them. Should the messenger fail to return, he was assured that the vengeance of the American people would be visited upon his nation with no [sic] unsparing hand. Thus invested with instructions the messenger had set out, and yesterday morning Captain Ewell started for the Canon del Oro to await the expiration of the eight days. He will hoist a flag of truce in his camp and endeavor to prevail upon the savages to come in.[31]

Captain Ewell reported to his superiors in Santa Fe that "I have sent two Apache men, prisoners at this post, with a party under Lieutenant John H. Cooke, 8th Infantry. These Apache [will] be turned loose on the trail for the purpose of negotiating an exchange of prisoners if possible. . . . It is evident that if the Indians are hard pushed they will murder these women."[32] He justifiably suspected that if pressed too closely, the Apache would murder the women, just as they killed slower-moving livestock to escape pursuit.

Hesperian, a term that translates roughly as the Westerner, was Thompson Turner, who corresponded from Arizona with the Missouri and California newspapers from 1859 through 1861. Turner believed this abduction "[i]t is doubtless designed as a retaliatory measure because of the detention at Fort Buchanan of the captives taken during the campaign of last fall," as noted above. Captain Ewell thought so as well and thus had offered to make a prisoner exchange.

Ewell's prisoners were Pinal Apaches. The Pinal[33] said they did not have the girl and that the woman was dead. They blamed everything on Tonto Apaches who had passed through their country on the way north. The Pinals then proposed that if Ewell returned with the Pinal captives he was holding, they would force the Tontos to give her up. It seems unlikely that they would risk war with the Tontos to assist Ewell and therefore very likely that they were the culprits in the abduction. Some

66

later versions of the story say that the Pinals asked for and received a wagonload of supplies for their assistance in making the exchange.[34] Captain Ewell believed that Pinals had taken the girl and he exchanged Pinal captives for Mercedes Quiroz. He rode into Tucson with her on the day of a convention proposing Arizona as a separate territory from New Mexico. The delegates showered honors on him, including naming one of four proposed counties Ewell in his honor, which he reported with some disconcert in a letter to his niece.[35]

Fort Buchanan, N.M.
May 2, 1860
Miss Elizabeth Ewell
Dear Betty:
The last mail brought your note, enclosed with one of Benjamin's, in which you take me to task for not writing oftener. Since November I have written several times to you, probably fully as often as I have received letters. During this time I have been on several detached duties, three of which required an absence of over twenty days each, besides constant minor duties of ten to fifteen days at a time. Adding to these the time required for preparation and the many things to be attended to at once on my return you will easily see without much calculation has kept me pretty much occupied during that time. In March I was absent for three weeks, the Indians having taken off two captives. An American woman and a girl of nine or ten. The woman was left for dead and managed to crawl back to her people—the child was taken to their country and finally exchanged again for some Indian prisoners that were here. The people made a great fuss about the child and not knowing how to thank Providence for the sage recovery vented their gratitude in making a fuss over me. I was marched into the convention, had county called after me and a public hall, all of which, under a different description, would appear very ridiculous. The fact is, they had not time to think over the matter, being taken, as it were, by surprise.[36]

Today we would question the wisdom of trading prisoners for the kidnapped girl as this encourages further kidnapping. Ewell had to know that once detected, the Apache were likely to kill the girl rather than be caught in possession by an armed force. In 1849, he was in New Mexico when Kit Carson and elements of the 1st Dragoons caught up with Jicarilla Apache holding Anne White and her infant daughter. The Jicarilla killed Mrs. White just as Carson entered their camp. So Ewell may have felt compelled to make the trade. All of the contemporary sources state that the exchange was for Pinal hostages held at Fort Buchanan and neither Ewell nor Hesperian mention a wagonload of goods thrown in to pay the Pinal for their services as intermediaries. Ewell would have had to account for goods from Army stores. It was not uncommon to provide food and trade items to Indians for their good behavior. Maybe there was no such wagonload. If so, the Pinal got only the return of their captives and the Tonto Apaches didn't even get a share of the wagonload of goods, making a peaceful interaction between Pinal and Tonto even more unlikely. Perhaps Captain Ewell had been correct from the start and the culprits were Pinals. In the final analysis, it seems to have been a straight up prisoner exchange with the Pinals simply attempting to deflect blame from themselves.

This story was still fresh when Lieutenant George Bascom arrived in Arizona a few months later in October 1860. He would have heard it and learned from it. Meanwhile, the fall and early winter of 1860 brought seriously deteriorating relations with the Apache.

The Pinal and other Western Apaches continued to raid. Meanwhile, Cochise and the Chokonen, his band of the Chiricahuas, in constant contact with travelers on the Southern Emigrant Trail and Overland Mail employees who lived within their territory, experienced numerous negative incidents. The Overland Mail station keeper at Apache Pass helped a long-held Mexican captive, Merejildo Grijalva, to escape. The Chokonen made off with livestock from Ewell's Station and Dragoon Springs Station.[37]

Tubac, January 14th, 1860
The driver of the Overland Mail stage brought the news on his last trip that friendly Indians at Apache Pass had given intimations of extensive preparations for a total extermination of the Overland

Mail line through their country, to be followed by a decent [sic] *upon the settlements. Everything seems to portend lively times here for a season.*[38]

In early June, Cochise's band, the Chokonen, raided the Santa Rita Mining Company, and made off with the company's substantial herd of livestock. On June 6, Captain Ewell set out from Fort Buchanan with forty dragoons. In the Chiricahua Mountains, he met with Cochise who pled innocence. Ewell refused to accept these pleas and warned the chief that he would return in a few weeks and at that time he would expect Cochise and his people to return the livestock.[39] In the meantime, Lieutenant Lord and Company D, 1st Dragoons, returned to Fort Buchanan from the Rio Grande. The St. Louis *Missouri Republican* reported:

Tubac, June 28, 1860
Capt. R.S. Ewell started on the 25th, with seventy five men and several volunteers, for the purpose of meeting the Chiricahua Indians at Apache Pass.[40]

Tubac, July 18th, 1860
Capt. Ewell has returned to Fort Buchanan with his command without having achieved success in the object of his expedition. . . . The Indians met at the place of rendezvous with their women and children, the entire collection numbering about one hundred and fifty. They brought in a few worthless animals which the Captain declined receiving, and after waiting in vain for a better assortment, he gave them notice that he would proceed to force them to terms.

Capt. Ewell's command consisted of seventy-five dragoons and several volunteers, but although he continued over a fortnight in the field, nothing was affected. Not a single engagement took place, no prisoners were taken, and the campaign was a complete failure.[41]

Before departing from Arizona for the last time in September 1860, Captain Richard S. Ewell wrote to his superiors in Santa Fe explaining that the next time he went to Apache Pass to confront Cochise and his

Chokonen, he would not ask for restitution but would instead engage the Chokonen in battle.[42]

Ewell had had enough. Cochise was not friendly. At best he was prudent. With starvation facing his people, irritated in his encounters with Americans, and dissatisfied with Dr. Steck's "gifts," he had begun raiding Americans in 1860. Accomplished Indian fighter Captain Ewell had been unable to bring him to terms. Ewell's tactics consisted of finding and attacking Indian villages, taking hostages, and being willing to exchange them for hostages held by the Apache. He recognized that, pressed too hard, Apaches would slay both livestock and hostages. Like many frontier officers, Ewell recognized that the Indians faced starvation and were raiding to feed themselves. Many officers, frontiersmen, and Indian agents repeated the phrase "we'll have to feed them or exterminate them." It expressed a reality recognized and not a preference for genocide. The American advance was not going to stop and it would result in the starvation of the Indians unless the government did something. The public would demand retribution when attacked.

Lieutenant George N. Bascom knew of Ewell's exploits. He had the advice and assistance of four officers, all senior to him, who had been Ewell's acolytes. Lieutenants Richard Lord and Isaiah Moore had served alongside the captain in his Indian campaigns. Surgeon Irwin had served with him since coming to Fort Buchanan, and Lieutenant Cooke had been with Ewell in the Indian campaigns of 1859 and the recovery of Mercedes Quiroz in 1860. Bascom welcomed their advice and assistance. The Black Legend depends on Bascom being alone at Apache Pass with only Sergeant Reuben Bernard to advise him. That wasn't the case. Bernard wasn't there and officers long associated with "the master Indian fighter," Richard Ewell, were.

Chapter Four

THE SETTLEMENTS OF ARIZONA

We went down the valley of the Sonoita creek . . . The valley closes, sometimes into canons, rocky and precipitous not thirty yards wide, at others forming openings so as to give farms of a hundred acres . . . The Sonoita creek may be looked upon as a branch of the Santa Cruz river, although it sinks before reaching it.[1]
—COLONEL B. L. E. BONNEVILLE TO ADJUTANT GENERAL,
JULY 15, 1859

HE EMERGED FROM HIS ONE-ROOM ADOBE HOUSE SLOWLY SQUINTING AT the early morning sun just appearing over the hills to the east. He sniffed the air. Javelina stank almost as bad as a skunk and stumbling in among those nearly blind wild pigs could be deadly. He remembered Ole Mose, Kit Carson's elder brother, said he could smell Indians. Maybe, but more likely that was just Mose's blather. Mose said a lot of things. He scanned the ground looking for sticks that hadn't been there the night before. It wouldn't do to get too near the ones that rattled and hissed. He looked across the flat valley floor two hundred yards to the hillside looking for anything that moved, flashed, or hadn't been there when he bedded down. Some days he got lucky and a deer or an antelope come to drink at the creek would be close enough to shoot with the caplock rifle he kept loaded inside the door. Chickens wandered near the house. They kept down the insect population, especially the scorpions. Everything seemed to be in order. He checked the loads on the two pistols tucked into his belt. They were heavy and pulled at his suspenders, but it was better to have them than not. Mexican or Apache raiders might show up at any time.

The door creaked as his Mexican "wife" stepped out into the yard. There was no church of any kind in Arizona, so he couldn't marry her proper. Her kitchen was outside the house where she had a flat sheet of iron for cooking tortillas and an *horno*, a beehive-like adobe oven for baking. He shook his head. *This climate*, he thought, *too warm to cook inside*. He'd built a hearth, but it was seldom cold enough to light a fire. He stretched, a little stiff from sleeping on the floor. That was what she had grown up with and it was her house. He looked at the door. It was stout but the wood was drying and cracking. He'd have to repair it soon. Guadalupe was just getting used to having a door. Her family's home had only a blanket across the entrance. The door would remain open all day. He checked the firing ports he'd made in the walls. They let in drafts and a little light while they made the house a fortress.

Next he walked around and checked the stock corrals, pigs on the south side and horses and cows to the north. High adobe walls closed them in. They drew flies and smelled bad, but having them close made it more difficult for the Apache to steal them, and the dog and chickens gave warning. His woman checked about in all the places the chickens hid eggs, then cut a few slices from the slab of bacon hanging from the extended *vigas*. A ristra of chilis hung nearby. They'd end up in his breakfast, too. And there would be tortillas. He wished she'd learn to bake real bread, or biscuits. Biscuits would be good, with preserves and butter.

Today he'd saddle the horse and head out to his new field by Sonoita Creek. It was only a quarter mile away, but he wanted the horse to graze and to be near if anything happened. He'd take the rifle, too. He'd divert water from the creek into the new irrigation ditch he was working on and let the water soften the face where he wanted to extend the ditch. The water would show him how to keep the ditch to level. He was doing all right, selling a little produce to the soldier boys at Fort Buchanan five miles to the north. He had a little money.

He thought that in the late afternoon he might take Guadalupe up to the sutler's store and let her buy some of the things she needed. Then on the way back, they'd stop at the Casa Blanca and get a real, American meal, drink some rot gut whiskey, and play a little Monte. Life was good if a man was careful.

The short, beautiful valley of the Sonoita was home to Felix Ward, the boy kidnapped by Apaches, and to the soldiers of Fort Buchanan. With nearby Tubac and Tucson in the Santa Cruz Valley, it was the only place in Arizona populated by Mexicans and Americans. Sonoita Creek rises on the eastern slope of the Santa Rita Mountains and flows south and southwest around those hills to join the Santa Cruz River. Its valley is pleasant, with a flat grassy plain less than a mile wide. It is bounded on the east by the Patagonia Mountains across which the Santa Cruz rises, flowing south into Mexico only to turn back to the north and flow once again into the United States. The area is distinguished by an oddity in North America. Southeast Arizona has three rivers that flow north to join the Gila. From west to east they are the Santa Cruz, which flows by Tubac and Tucson, the San Pedro, and the San Simon. Between the San Pedro and the San Simon, or more properly, between the Dragoon and Chiricahua Mountains, lies the Willcox Playa into which all local streams of the Sulphur Springs Valley flow and sink. In all these streams, water rises where rocky outcroppings dam their underground flow and force it to the surface only to sink again into the sand. For thousands of years, people have gathered where water rises to the surface. The following description of the area was published in the May 12, 1859, edition of the *Weekly Arizonian*:

> *The total length of Sonoita valley is about eleven miles, its breadth from fifty feet to half a mile; the sides precipitous, and very rough. The road winds along the bed of the stream most of the way, between tall cliffs, occasionally, where the passage is very narrow. The Sonoita, a clear, rippling brook, runs through the valley, like all streams in this country, intermittent, and before it reaches the Santa Cruz, toward which it runs so briskly, dives into the sand and disappears. Now and then the valley widens a little, leaving a small interval which can be irrigated, and here are the farms, hemmed in by the adjacent hills, which roll away into formidable mountain ranges. . . . It is a romantic ride along*

the banks and channel of the little stream, which is a treasure beyond price to the farmers of the neighborhood. "Sonoita," in Spanish, signifies clover, and there was never a more correct appellation, for the narrow valley is matted with a luxuriant growth of clover, which when short and green is much relished by cattle.[2]

The mountains, which bound the valleys of southeast Arizona, were home to the Apaches. The Santa Ritas dominate the western horizon and to their east are the Patagonias, and then a string of three ranges, the Huachucas, Mustangs, and Whetstones, north of which are the Rincons and Santa Catalinas that dominate the Tucson skyline. East of these ranges are the Mules and Dragoons and beyond them the Sulphur Springs Valley and Willcox Playa. Still further east are the Chiricahuas and Dos Cabezas, between which lies Apache Pass. Finally, the long thin chain called Peloncillo bounds the eastern edge of this world. The name is a mystery, a confusion of two Spanish words. It either means little baldies or sugar cones. The cartographer spelled it one way and gave the definition for the other. Emigrants and the Overland Mail, often called the Butterfield, crossed these Peloncillo Mountains at Doubtful Canyon. There Stein's Peak station serviced the mail coaches. The name is a misspelling. It honors Major Enoch Steen of the 1st Regiment of Dragoons.

This isn't the ghost town, Stein's, by which travelers on Interstate 10 pass. That's a later railroad town. Stein's Peak and Doubtful Canyon lie nine miles to the north, with Stein's Peak at the eastern entrance to the canyon. What today we call the I-10 Corridor is the reason for the Gadsden Purchase and for General Kearny's Mexican War march to California. The string of low passes that stretch from El Paso, Texas, to Tucson are one of the few places that wagon trains and, more important, railroads can cross the Rocky Mountains. The next such passes to the north are at South Pass in Wyoming and that route is snowed in part of the year. The same forces that built the mountains and passes gave southeast Arizona great mineral wealth and the availability of roads made it accessible to exploitation. Without a means of transportation, miners would be left to stare dumbly at their pile while shooting gold and silver bullets at marauding Apaches.

Arizona drew an odd lot of the wildest sort of frontiersmen and women. They had to be tough and brave to survive. The nearest court was in Santa Fe nearly six hundred miles away as the government organized Arizona as part of New Mexico's Santa Ana County, with the county seat at Mesilla on the Rio Grande three hundred miles from Tucson, Tubac, and Fort Buchanan. It was impossible to take a case to court and so Arizonans pleaded to be organized as their own territory. Edward Cross, editor of the *Arizonian*, Tubac and Arizona's first newspaper, said:

There is no presence of law, no sheriffs, judges, juries, and courts. Everyone goes armed, and acts as his own court, jury, and execution-ers, using his weapons whenever he sees fit—preserving his own life and taking the life of any person if deemed necessary.[3]

Very soon after the United States completed the Gadsden Purchase, people began to refer to it as Arizona. It included Mesilla and Pinos Altos, which today are in New Mexico.

With no official law and order, Arizona became a haven for those on the run, particularly from committees of vigilance in California. Charles Poston thought Johnny Ward was one of these, though other records show a gentleman named Ward arriving too late to join the Crabbe filibustering expedition[4] to Sonora. This would have been fortunate for Johnny as the Crabbe expedition was surrounded in a church in Sonora and surrendered with the understanding that they'd be allowed to return peacefully to the United States. Instead the Sonoran governor executed them, possibly to cover up his own complicity in the plot. These would-be filibusters added to the problems of southeast Arizona as Jeff Ake, a young teenager at the time, had to say:

This second bunch come down a little too late to join 'em. In this bunch was Bill Ake, my cousin, and John Page;[5] Cyril Scott, John Delaney, John Ainswirth, old Cap'n Sharp, Alt Scott, Bob Phillips (who after-wards owned the hotel in Tucson), a feller named Davis, Three-Finger Jack, McAllister, Poker Jack, a feller named Ward,[6] another called Dyvelbits, who could eat more bacon than any man I ever saw.[7]

The central government in Mexico City was weak and in debt. It held little sway in the outlying provinces. This invited bold Americans to form armed parties intent on cutting out a part of Mexico for their own. They weren't alone in this. The government in Mexico City owed money to both the French and the English, and they looked covetously at Mexico. France tried its hand at a takeover in 1841 and twice during the Civil War. Cinco de Mayo celebrates the Mexican defeat of the French in the unsuccessful 1862 French attempt. A second attempt installed the Emperor Maximilian. Filibusters formed a lawless and rowdy element in the tiny Arizona community, as illustrated by a news article in the *San Francisco Evening Bulletin*:

> *Tucson, November 3, 1860*
> *On the afternoon of the 30th October, William Beattie was shot in the principal thoroughfare of Tucson by Miller Bartlett. He received five balls from a six-shooter in his breast, and expired immediately. Much excitement prevailed at first in consequence of Beattie having been shot down without weapons of defense about his person; but public opinion underwent a rapid change on learning about his conduct just prior to receiving the shots. It seems that the deceased was compelled to exile himself from California on account of some difficulty which occurred at Murphy's Bar, Calaveras county. He arrived hereabout [sic] two months since, and during this brief sojourn won the unenviable reputation of being the most unprincipled desperado in the country. He evidently delighted in fomenting quarrels, and scarcely a day passed without his being either a principal or accessory in some disturbance. . . . He had declared on his way in that he was returning to Tucson for the purpose of killing Bartlett.*[8]

Six ounces of prevention were worth a pound of cure in frontier Arizona.

There were also boosters like Charles Poston in company with mining engineers like Ehrenberg and Brunckow. The boosters, renowned for their casual acquaintance with the truth, convinced easterners to invest in Arizona's mines. The engineers worked and developed them. Most of these latter were Germans as the only school for mining engineers at the time was in their homeland. Poston started the Sonora Exploring and Mining Company, which operated out of Tubac and had mines at the Hacienda Santa Rita on the western flank of the mountains of that name. There was another set of mines near Cerro Colorado west of the Santa Cruz River. In the Patagonia Mountains, south and east of Fort Buchanan and the Santa Ritas, Captain Ewell developed his Patagonia mine, which he eventually sold out to Elias Brevoort.

The Spanish mined on the *sistema del rato*, the rational system, which German engineers nicknamed the "rat hole" system from the appearance of the mines which very closely followed veins of ore twisting and turning, seldom cut bigger than the vein itself. They often look like little more than natural caves or animal dens. They worked the ore with *arrastras*, which consisted of a stone floor, a central pivot, large stones suspended from the pivot arm, and stone walls. Quartz ore was placed inside and the large stones broke it to powder as the pivot arm turned. Mercury was added, which formed an amalgam with gold and silver. Placed in a retort the mercury was boiled off and recovered for reuse leaving behind "sponge gold."

Elias Brevoort had come west as a Santa Fe trader. In 1856, he was the sutler at Fort Buchanan. The sutler was the precursor to the Post Exchange. He supplied soldiers' needs for needle and thread, buttons, replacement clothing, candles, writing implements, tinned food, and whiskey. The sutler also served as the first general store on Sonoita Creek. In 1870, Brevoort partnered with Indian agent Tom Jeffords as Indian traders at the Canada Alamosa Reservation in New Mexico near modern Truth or Consequences.

Beer was not usually available in those days. It was bulky and expensive to transport. Beer became available when someone set about brewing it locally. There was from the 1850s a beer garden in Tucson. The wealth of broken wine bottles around officers' quarters on Fort Buchanan and at other posts attests to the expensive transportation of wines. One has to wonder what condition they arrived in after coming west by wagon. Part of the aging process of wine is allowing yeast to settle to the bottom of the bottle. Shaking the bottle reverses this and spoils the wine. Whiskey was sent out nearly pure, that is two hundred proof. This was the most economical way to transport heavy liquid. Once it arrived, the bartender or sutler would mix it by half with water and add brown sugar for color and flavor, tobacco for color and bite, and, some said, snake heads. This was snakehead, red-eye, or rot gut whiskey. With such stuff the only thing that was certain was the hangover.

Apart from alcohol the isolated communities of the Southwest offered few opportunities for recreation. It's not too surprising that many became alcoholics or that, with everyone carrying guns, so many drunken affrays turned into shooting affairs, though the unreliability of muzzle-loading weapons often gave all but the most inebriated pause to reflect. Indeed, sometimes reason "interfered" and lives were spared, as reported in an April 1859 issue of the *Weekly Arizonian*: "The difficulty between Messrs. Graydon and Burr, which caused an exchange of shots between the parties a few days since, has been satisfactorily adjusted by the interference of friends."[9]

Another account of a potential disaster averted appeared in the July 14, 1859, *Arizonian*:

A difficulty having occurred between the Hon. Sylvester Mowry and Mr. Edward E. Cross, editor of the Arizonian, *in reference to certain publications made by both parties. Mr. Geo. D. Mercer, acted as the friend of Mr. Mowry, and Captain John Donaldson as the friend of Mr. Cross. Mr. Mowry being the challenging party, no compromise being effected, the parties met on the 8th inst, near Tubac, weapons Burnside rifles, distance forty paces; four shots were exchanged without effect; at the last fire Mr. Mowry's rifle did not discharge. It was decided that he was entitled to his shot, and Mr. Cross stood without arms to receive it, Mr. Mowry refusing to fire at an unarmed man, discharged his rifle in the air, and declared himself satisfied. The settlement appended, signed by the principals, is approved by the undersigned.*

George D. Mercer,
John Donaldson
Tubac, Arizona, July 8, 1859

The following is a copy of a document sent to the Washington States for publication, by the two principals:

Mr. Edward E. Cross withdraws the offensive language used by him, and disclaims any intention to reflect upon Mr. Mowry's veracity or upon his reputation as a gentleman, in any publication he has made in reference to Arizona.

Mr. Mowry being satisfied from personal explanations that he has done injustice to Mr. Cross' character and motives, in his letter to the press of July 2nd, takes pleasure in withdrawing the imputations against Mr. Cross as a man of honor and veracity contained in the letter. Any difference of opinion which might exist between them in reference to Arizona is an honest one, to be determined by the weight of authority.

Sylvester Mowry,
Edward E. Cross[10]

Born in Rhode Island, Sylvester Mowry was an 1852 graduate of West Point who came west as an artillery officer. Until 1854, he explored with the survey of a railroad route to the Pacific. He is said to have become entangled with the daughter-in-law of Brigham Young while Young's son was away on mission and that the Army transported him secretly out of Utah. Something occurring in this period set up a hostile relationship with Captain James H. Carleton, who later, as General Carleton, commander of the California Column and New Mexico, had Mowry arrested and his mine confiscated for supporting the Southern cause. He sold or gave, perhaps unwillingly, lead and powder to the Confederate forces occupying Tucson in 1862. The Army assigned Mowry to Fort Yuma from 1854 to 1858, perhaps as punishment, where he met Sarah Bowman, the Great Western. In 1858, resigning his commission, he became active in Arizona mining and politics, and he was nominated to be delegate from the provisional territory of Arizona. Separation of Arizona, the Gadsden Purchase, from New Mexico was a cause supported by many with Southern sympathies. While in Tubac, he became one of Arizona's greatest boosters and the owner of its most successful pre-war mine. Mowry stayed in Arizona when others departed, resisting increasing Indian attacks.

Sylvester Mowry, James "Paddy" Graydon, William Buckley, and Surgeon Bernard John Dowling Irwin found themselves embroiled in almost every significant event in southeast Arizona between 1856 and 1861. The population was small, but these men always stood out as volunteers. The community was beset from the inside with its own troublemakers and duelists and from without by both Apaches and Mexicans.

Thomas Farrell marched into New Mexico with the 7th Infantry in 1860 and took his discharge there, finding employment as a station keeper with the Overland Mail. He provides something of the tenor of the times in his story of an attack on an eastbound mail coach. His description is probably of Cochise's ambush of the mail on February 6, 1861. "They got through all right, and to this day it is not known whether the hold-ups were Mexicans or Indians, as many of the crimes committed in those days were traced to Mexican employes [sic] of the company."[11] Mowry missed out on the confrontation at Apache Pass, but was present for the rescue of Silas St. John at Dragoon Springs Station in October 1858.

According to legend, soldiers of the 1st Regiment of Dragoons discovered Dragoon Springs in 1856. In 1857–1858, the first transcontinental mail, the San Antonio and San Diego Mail (the so-called Jackass Mail)[12] used the site as a watering place, even though water was never plentiful. After John Butterfield won the contract from Congress in 1857 for an Overland Mail to run from St. Louis and Memphis to San Francisco, he ordered ten stations to be constructed of rock, instead of adobe, in Apache country. The Butterfield station at Dragoon Springs was the farthest west of these fortress mail stops. (The actual springs are located in the canyon about one mile south of the station.) Butterfield armed his station keepers with revolvers and with fast, breech-loading Sharp's rifles, and he arranged for gifts to be given to the Chiricahua.

William Buckley, the superintendent of the line from Mesilla to Tucson, put Silas St. John in charge of a six-man team to complete the station at Dragoon Springs. St. John's assistants were fifty-year-old James Burr, a blacksmith from Watertown, New York; thirty-year-old

Preston Cunningham, from Wisconsin and Iowa by way of California; and twenty-five-year-old James Laing, born in Kentucky.[13] Working with them were three Mexican laborers, Guadalupe and Pablo "Chino" Ramirez and Bonifacio Mirando. The station was a "corral of stone, 45x55 feet. . . . It was constructed especially strong, as this was a passing point for the Apaches going to and coming from Sonora."[14] By early September 1858, the walls and gates were up but the living quarters and storeroom, in the northeast and southeast corners respectively, still required roofing.

At midnight on September 8, 1858, Silas St. John changed the watch, replacing Laing with Guadalupe. Laing retired to the room in the center of the east wall, while Cunningham slept in the storeroom. The two remaining Mexicans and Burr (who didn't like sleeping near the stock) slept outside the gate. It was a clear, starlit, moonless night. About 1 a.m., a disturbance in the stock corral awakened St. John. The mules were excited, and St. John heard blows and feeble cries. As he rose from his pallet, the three Mexicans confronted him in the doorway. Guadalupe was armed with a broad axe, Bonifacio with a chopping axe, and Chino with a stone sledge. St. John kicked Chino away. He saw the glint of stars off Bonifacio's axe, which allowed him to parry, but the blow intended for his head cut deep into his hip. A strike to Bonifacio's face felled the Mexican. "As St. John reached for his . . . rifle, which was standing against the wall at the head of his bed, Guadalupe got in a successful stroke which severed St. John's arm midway between elbow and shoulder."[15] Silas knocked the axe from the Mexican's hands with his rifle. All three Mexicans fled out of the gate. With his arm useless, Silas dropped the rifle and reached for his pistol. The three assassins re-entered the station, but hearing the pistol's hammer being cocked, turned and ran. St. John got off one shot.[16]

Wounded in hip and arm, Silas was unable to pursue the attackers. He bound up his wounds as well as he could and climbed to the top of some sacks of barley. From this vantage he could see over the walls. There he waited for daylight, listening to the moans of Cunningham and Laing. Burr was silent, his head completely smashed in. Laing, his skull split in twain by the axe, rose briefly and staggered blindly about. When daylight came, St. John dragged himself to his friends. Cunningham had taken three axe blows to his head but still breathed. Partly conscious, Laing now lay still with his brains exposed.[17] Movement caused St. John's wounds to open and bleed freely. He made a tourniquet for his arm with a handkerchief, stone, and stick. All day on September 9, he listened to his friends' groans but was unable to assist them. The day was hot, and there was no water in the corral. The three survivors suffered much from thirst. That night, coyotes came in, attracted by the smell of blood. The coyotes howled and the hungry and thirsty mules brayed, creating pandemonium. Around midnight, Cunningham passed away, joining Burr in death.

At dawn on September 10, buzzards, crows, and magpies came to sit atop the walls waiting for a chance at the bodies in the unroofed compound below. St. John waved his arm to keep them away. He was unable to intervene as they mutilated the face of Burr who lay outside the compound. The night became hideous with the sounds of his thirsty, starving animals and with an increase in the number of coyotes and wolves. A few shots from St. John's revolver kept them at bay. On the morning of September 11, the coyotes departed, but the birds returned. The day was torture as St. John lay in the sun with no roof to cover him. That night the coyotes attacked Burr's body, quarreling and fighting over it as they tore the flesh from the bones.

Sunday morning, September 12, the correspondent for the Memphis *Appeal*, a Mr. Archibald,[18] arrived from Tucson on his way to the Rio Grande. He was alarmed that there was no flag flying over the mail station, and he could hear the hideous sounds of thirsty mules from within. He halted half a mile away and then approached cautiously with gun cocked. His hellos went unanswered. He found St. John within the station, with swollen tongue and throat so parched that he could not make a sound. Archibald started for the spring a mile distant to get water. As he did so, the Jackass Mail was westbound with Colonel James B. Leach, the government road-builder, Major N. H. Hutton, and Sylvester Mowry aboard. "In the party . . . veterans, who quickly dressed St. John's wounds, which were full of maggots. They [Leach's men] buried the bodies of [Burr] and Cunningham in one grave. Laing still hung to life tenaciously."[19] The next day, September 13, 1858, after he died, the men buried him in a separate grave.

Hence, the first two graves at Dragoon Springs contain three bodies: those of Burr and Cunningham, who rest together, and that of Laing. In 1860, H. C. Grosvenor, manager of the Santa Rita mines, made a sketch of the station showing the two graves. It appeared in *Our Whole Country* in 1863.[20,21]

Rescued and given water, Silas St. John's ordeal was not yet over. Colonel Leach sent an express for the doctor at Fort Buchanan but as Colonel Leach considered the direct road to the fort to be unsafe, the two lone men went a long way around, arriving three days later. Assistant Surgeon Bernard John Dowling Irwin started at once with an escort. He did not arrive until September 17, the ninth day after the Mexicans had wounded St. John.[22] Doctor Irwin described St. John as "the only survivor of his party, alone in a rude hovel in the wilderness, without food or water, unable to move; his wounds undressed, stiffened, and full of loathsome maggots; his companions had died one by one a horrible death, and lastly, to add to the horrors of his suffering, the hungry wolves and ravens came and banqueted upon the putrefying corpse of one of his dead companions which lay but a few feet from his desolate bed."[23] Despite his mental and physical sufferings, St. John bore his hardships with the "fortitude of a martyr."

St. John was weak from the loss of blood and sleep. The doctor found that the wound in his thigh was eight inches long and three inches deep. His arm, the bone severed, was now hanging by a bit of skin. Irwin determined to remove it. The escort made up a bed of some bags of corn and placed St. John upon it. The doctor then informed these men of how to compress the artery in the limb. He inserted a catling—catgut in the form of a garrote—through the wound and used it to cut through the remaining skin. He then disarticulated the shoulder joint and closed the wound. Chloroform was not at hand, so the doctor gave St. John a "few drachms of essence of ginger" for the pain. "The celerity with which the operation was performed, and the fortitude and excellent disposition of the patient, saved him from everything like protracted suffering." In the evening, Irwin gave St. John tincture of opium. On the 21st, the doctor and his patient started out on the two-day trip to Fort Buchanan, sixty miles away by wagon. Half a grain of sulphate of morphia helped to relieve the pain. At the fort, St. John occasionally suffered from frightful dreams and imaginary pain in the lost arm. Twenty-four days after the amputation, Silas St. John was up and walking about. In less than six weeks, he was ready to return to work.[24,25]

This was not an isolated incident. In July 1860, Jeff Ake and his brother, preteen sons of Felix Grundy Ake, drove a wagon thirty miles across Apache country along the Babocomari Creek to the San Pedro River, twenty miles south of Dragoon Springs, to deliver produce to the miners there. Arriving after dark, they made a gruesome discovery. Two dead men lay on the floor of Brunkow's adobe. "On the morning of Monday, 23d inst. the peons, 11 in number, working at the San Pedro mine, headquarters of the St. Louis Mining Company, arose and surprised the whites, murdering them and decamping with all the movable property. The murdered men were Frederick Brunckow, Mining Engineer; John C. Moss, Chemist and Assayer; James Williams, Machinist."[26] The Mexicans had stabbed Brunckow with a mining drill and tossed his body down the mine shaft.

Filibusters and other rough elements occasionally rode up and down the Sonoita Valley exacting revenge on any Mexican who came to hand. The local ranchers, farmers, and mine owners quickly subdued these rough elements, as they didn't care to have their inexpensive Mexican labor run back to Sonora. Settler Grundy Ake dealt with some of them after one outrage. "Little Bill knowed [sic] Dad meant it, so the filibusters went away to the fort, and made Paddy Graydon's saloon their headquarters like. It was a pretty tough joint, but a good saloon at that. Out in the wild country, saloons was always a kind of headquarters for most of the men."[27]

The *Arizonian* gave this account of one incident:

In another column will be found an account of the murder of Mr. Byrd, by some Mexican peons, who have escaped from the country. It was a cold-blooded murder, and if the perpetrators could be found, they would receive no mercy from the people of this neighborhood.

This murder, together with the fact that Americans have lately been ordered out of Hermosillo, in Sonora, was the cause of a cruel and unjustifiable attack upon some Mexicans, made on Sunday, the 9th instant, by a gang of self-constituted regulators, who proceeded up the Sonoita valley, and with force and arms compelled every Mexican employed upon the different ranches to leave, under penalty of extermination for disobedience.[28]

Elsewhere in the same edition the editor described the regulators:

Three of the gang engaged in the murderous affair at the mescal distillery, are in irons at Fort Buchanan, namely, Page, Bolt, and Scott. Wm. Ake,[29] *J. Pennington, Sam Anderson, and a man named Brown, are yet at large. Pennington is a very young man, evidently led into the affair by his older associates, and as he did not take an active part in the affray, he will probably only be required to give his evidence. Ake and Anderson, two notorious rascals, are yet at large, and we believe Brown has not been arrested. Ake is a young man, but has committed several murders. He was one of the ringleaders of the party. Anderson is a cowardly, sneaking fellow, a great liar, a carpenter by trade, and has a bad scar across his face—Messrs. Marshal, Graydon and Hall, with a party of soldiers, are yet in pursuit of the fugitives, who it is believed have not left the country.*[30]

Paddy Graydon joined the posse looking for excitement as he often did. Those that were captured remained in irons, chained to a tree, for some while until finally the post commander concluded that there was no reasonable possibility that the regulators and the witnesses against them could be transported three hundred miles to Mesilla for trial, nor was it likely that the judge would visit Mesilla from Santa Fe to hear the case. The officer released them. Page, William Ake, and J. Pennington were relatives of Sonoita Valley settlers.

There were few settlements in the Gadsden Purchase, which the settlers called Arizona. These were the farms along Sonoita Creek, a settlement at Calabasas near where Sonoita Creek enters the Santa Cruz, at

Tubac on that river, and at Tucson. After May 1860, a small community grew on the San Pedro River near Fort Breckenridge. There were no other towns in Arizona. Colorado City near the confluence of the Gila and Colorado Rivers sprang to life in 1860 and was all but abandoned that same year when its founders moved on to Pinos Altos and a new gold strike. Fort Yuma was across the river in California, although Sarah Bowman operated a restaurant and bawdy house on the Arizona side. There were no towns to the east before Pino Altos, six miles north of modern Silver City, and 250 miles east of Tucson. The county seat was at Mesilla on the Rio Grande.

James "Paddy" Graydon, an Irishman, rode into the area as a soldier with the 1st Dragoons and took his discharge at Fort Buchanan. He soon established himself three miles from the post, just outside the boundaries of the military reservation, at Casa Blanca Canyon. There he built the United States Boundary Hotel catering to the needs of soldiers, ruffians, and settlers. He provided relaxation of all kinds: women, whiskey, cigars, food, and gambling. A local newspaper advertisement read:

UNITED STATES BOUNDARY HOTEL
LOCATED ON THE SONOITA-VALLEY ROAD
three miles from Fort Buchanan.
The above hotel has been opened by the subscriber, and he is now pre-
pared to accommodate travelers in the best style the country affords.
He will also keep on hand a fine assortment of wines, liquors, cigars,
sardines, etc., etc. He will also insure all horses committed to his care.
Persons visiting the Fort will find good accommodations for the night
at my establishment.

JAMES GRAYDON[31]

Jeff Ake, son of Grundy, recalled:

Right soon after the filibusters come in, they raised a lot of trouble. I
remember the feller named Davis got killed at Paddy Graydon's. He
beat up another filibuster, Wilson—this Davis was an overbearing
cuss—and another feller, Jim, shot him with a shotgun. I remember

Davis lying out there asking for a drink, and Jim took him one in his hat. Davis died, and Wilson and Ward pulled out. Then the soldiers told 'em to keep away from the fort.[32]

According to James Tevis, "Paddy Graden [sic] had a gin mill just off the fort reservation and made more money from it than all the ranchmen put together."[33]

The United States Boundary Hotel's adobe walls were plastered in white clay and it came to be called locally the *Casa Blanca*, White House. The Casa Blanca must have been an interesting place. Jeff Ake recalled what his father Felix Grundy Ake told him:

But Dad had time to gamble once in a while. He was fond of cards, poker 'specially. He would go up to Paddy Graydon's and play with the soldiers and others. One night he let me and Will go up with him to watch the play. Dad still wore his long black beard. When the drinks come round, Dad would pretend to drink, but pour the liquor in his beard.[34]

Faro was the game of choice in the Old West. It is a simple game requiring no skill and the odds vis-à-vis the house were almost even. In the twentieth century, casinos gave it up because their margin wasn't large enough. It is similar to Spanish or Mexican Monte, which is played with a forty-card Spanish deck whose suits are clubs, coins, cups, and swords. It is not to be confused with three-card monte, an entirely different game. The Faro layout is a cloth with a representation of each card one to ten and face cards. Suits do not matter. Players place a chip on the card of their choice. The dealer draws two cards. The first is the dealer's card and he wins any money placed on that card on the cloth. The second is the player's card and any player who has bet on that card wins double his bet. Chips placed upon cards that did not come up may be allowed to ride or may be recovered and new bets placed. Chips may also be placed between cards thus betting on two or four. Bets may be "coppered" by placing a copper marker on the chip thus reversing the bet. The dealer plays through the entire deck and a counter keeps track of which cards have been played, thus card-counting is not only legal but also part of the game. The rules change and the stakes go higher on the last three cards in the deck. This bet is called "Bucking the Tiger."

The game is so fast that it is hard to keep up and by sleight of hand and calling the cards out of order, picking up and paying bets incorrectly, the dealer can cheat. Imagine a few drunken players trying to keep up with many chips on the board, each player running several bets, and the dealer turning cards, calling them, paying, and recovering bets in a steady rhythm. It's fun. The bets are usually small, the pace exciting, and now and then, adding to the fun and excitement, a player shoots a cheating dealer.

Graydon, perhaps tiring of running a saloon and hotel, took on an odd partner, or he may have leased or sold the property to her sometime after 1859. It is hard to imagine two such strong-willed individuals existing as partners in one establishment. Nonetheless, both are reported as running Casa Blanca.[35] Sarah Bowman, the Great Western, went by many names as husbands died or were traded in. Albert Bowman was her husband in the 1850s and 1860s. She was over six feet tall, perhaps as much as six feet two inches, with flame-red hair and a temper to match. She first came to public notice in 1846 during the Mexican War as the heroine of Fort Brown, later Brownsville, Texas, where her husband was killed in the shelling. She continued to carry food and water under fire to the men despite the danger. The *Great Western* was the largest steamship of the time and the name clung to her.

She had been a laundress. The Army allowed that there would be one laundress for every seventeen men or no more than four per company.[36] Soldiers paid laundresses for their work and the women also received army rations and quarters, commonly referred to as "suds row." With money, rations, and quarters the laundresses were great catches as brides for soldiers and sergeants. Some supplemented their income as casual brides. Pioneers in Arizona and Sylvester Mowry at Fort Yuma called Sarah a madam and so she may have been among those seeking supplemental income.

In the Mexican War she organized the laundresses and the open mess[37] and claimed that she emerged from that war with over ten thousand dollars. She went west with the 2nd Dragoons and settled in across the river from Fort Yuma in what came to be known as Colorado City. There Raphael Pumpelly saw her in the summer of 1861. "I looked with interest on this woman as, with quiet native dignity, she served our simple meal. She was a lesson in the complexity of human nature."[38]

Jeff Ake recalled her at Casa Blanca:

They called her old Great Western. She packed two six-shooters, and they all said she shore could use 'em, that she had killed a couple of men in her time. She was a hell of a good woman. I used to take eggs and stuff up for her to buy, and she would feed me. When the Civil War come . . . she moved away where she could be near an army post. She had been one of the first residents of Ft. Yuma and she used to tell us that there was just one thin sheet of sandpaper between Yuma and hell.[39]

Ake recorded that in August 1861, "the Great Western, 'the greatest whore in the West' my Dad called her, and our family, all pulled out. Great Western sent her girls back to Mexico, where they come from."[40] She added interest to an already interesting community.

Paddy Graydon's ranch must have been separate from the Casa Blanca, though nearby. Sergeant Daniel Robinson described it.

Graydon was quite a character—a good type of the frontier man of that day—fearless, quick-tempered and quick to shoot when an occasion demanded it. He could speak Spanish like a Mexican, and was a man of expedients and ingenuity. In building his ranch he had an eye to defensive operations. It was loop-holed on all sides with a turret on top, on which was mounted an old-fashioned blunderbuss, primed and loaded to the muzzle and fixed on a revolving pivot so that it could be aimed in any direction. Besides, he had other arms ready for use at a moment's warning. The turret was reached by a portable ladder from the inside, so that he could draw it up at will. On top was a pole on which he hoisted his flag on special occasions, but recently[41] it had been kept up from sunrise to sunset. Besides all this he made an underground passage from the cellar to a gulch nearby, and in the cellar a well of water. On one side of the ranch the corral was situated

which was also loop-holed. The whole structure was built of adobes on
open level ground beyond the reach of arrows of the wily Apaches who
frequently appeared in the surrounding ravines.[42]

Land ownership was informal, there being no land office to record a claim, no surveyors, nor fixed points from which to start a survey, and no nearby county records office to keep track. Settlers did stick to a pattern. They laid claim to 160 acres, a square half a mile on a side, as what they thought the government would allow. Jeff Ake said that William Wadsworth had seven farms along Sonoita Creek. Jeff may have been referring to separate plowed fields rather than homestead claims. Or it may mean Wadsworth had his ranch hands stake claims, which he helped them develop and bought from them. General William Wadsworth, about thirty years old when he came to Arizona from Texas by way of California in 1856, was a man of some prominence. The provisional territorial governor appointed him commanding general of the territorial militia, a title that didn't amount to much because the militia was never raised and the territorial government never became anything more than provisional, a dream. Wadsworth and his wife had a dark secret, which the Akes, with whom they had come to Arizona, kept for them. Back home both had abandoned spouses and children, and they weren't legally married.

The Felix Grundy Ake family was large, with two married daughters and their husbands. Preteen son Jeff Ake recalled some of their activities: "We raised green stuff, and had a big bunch of hawgs, and of co'se, beef out in the grama. The hawgs lived in the *cienegas*,[43] fattening on *cienega* roots. Bears and lions killed quite a few of 'em, so Dad built a rock house, one room, at the hawg ranch and set a guard there."[44]

Besides the Akes, and their two sons-in-law, Thomas Thompson and Bob Phillips, there were the Cottons, the Davis', the Keith's and the Elias Pennington family. Elias, a son-in-law, Page, and four sons would die in Apache attacks. In 1859, the *Arizonian* described the farms as belonging to Findlay, Elias Pennington, B. C. Marshall, William Wodsworth (Wordsworth or Woodworth), Johnny Ward, and Felix Grundy Ake.[45] The southernmost of the settlers was Johnny Ward with his common-law wife,[46] Jesusa Martinez, and his stepson, Felix, aged twelve, and step-daughter, Theodora, aged ten.[47] In the August 1860 census, the pairing was noted as having a five-month-old daughter, Mary Ward. Their youngest son, Santiago Ward, was born after the 1860 census. Jesusa had previously married a man named Tellez, who may have been Irish, like Johnny Ward, and was the father of Felix and Theodora. After 1858, she was the wife, common-law or otherwise, of Johnny Ward, who in his fifties was many years her senior.[48] They ranched where the valley narrowed and rocky canyon walls rose high above. It is a well-watered spot of great natural beauty and there are signs—pottery and an irrigation ditch—that Sopaiburi Indians had farmed there hundreds of years before Ward arrived.

The ruins of their house remain about three miles south of modern Patagonia, cut through by the new paved road. The house has been repurposed many times over the intervening years. Windows were added and the house much enlarged.[49] John Cady used the house as a store in 1881–1882.[50] It is hard to imagine Johnny Ward taking the time to build more than a one- or two-room adobe. Glass windows would have been an incredible extravagance as the glass would have had to come by wagon from St. Louis or San Francisco, and it would have been a danger during Indian attacks. Surviving buildings from the era resemble the home of Paddy Graydon, with firing ports instead of windows. Ward kept a herd of cattle and sold hay and beef to the Army at Fort Buchanan, though he apparently did not contract directly with the post.

The Ward family was not alone at the ranch. There must have been significant outbuildings housing a wheelwright shop and smithy, as evidenced by an ad in a local newspaper for the services of "Andrew J. Nicherson & Cole, Blacksmiths and Wheelwrights."

These two tradesmen must still have been living and working on Ward's ranch in January 1861, as a "Mr. Cole" is mentioned in the February 16, 1861, edition of the *Los Angeles Star* as a witness to the abduction by nine Indians of Ward's twelve-year-old stepson.

There was plenty of evidence elsewhere that life was not peaceful on Sonoita Creek. As the *Arizonian* noted on March 3, 1859:

In order that our readers in the "the States" may have an idea of the manner in which the people of Arizona are plundered by Indians we give a few cases that have come to our knowledge within the past few weeks. There are a number of other instances which are omitted for want of names and dates. Most of these depredations were committed by the Pinal and Coyotero bands of Apaches.

Jan. 4 Took two cows and a mule from Patagonia Mining Company; traced to the Chiricahui [sic] mountains.[51]

Dec. 11. Apache killed a New Mexican trader, near Calabasas Ranche, took the mule train, destroyed the goods and escaped.

On the 12th, took eight mules from Señor Ochoa,[52] who resides eight miles from Fort Buchanan. No pursuit.

On the 13th, took twenty head of cattle out of the corral at Fort Buchanan—followed, and fifteen head recovered.[53] Also on the same day, took eleven mules from Mr. Yancy, at Tubac, and being pursued lanced three mules.

On the 19th, three horses taken from Fort Buchanan. No recovery.

On the 20th, twelve cattle taken from the fort.

On the 16th, four oxen taken from Captain Rowlet, near Tucson. No recovery.

On the 22d, twenty-two oxen taken from Señor Chavis, near Tucson. No recovery.

25th, Attack on Sergeant Berry's party, at Whetstone Springs, twenty-two miles from Fort Buchanan; sergeants Berry and Kelly killed; also, three mules killed and one carried off. Kelly was a native of Ireland and had been 20 years in the service. Berry was an American, from Weston, Mo., and had served fifteen years. Both had just received an "honorable discharge" and were on their way to "the States."

On the 28th took two cattle from Mr. Goodrich. No recovery.

On the 28th, took eleven head of horses from Findlay's Ranche. None recovered.[54]

Feb. 12, killed a mule belonging to James Grayden, at Casa Blanca, three miles from the fort.

On the 15th, drove off all the cattle belonging to Mr. Ake. Immediate pursuit by Messrs. Ake and Davis, the property recovered.

On the 16th, killed a donkey and a cow and calf at Arivaca Ranche; also stole two horses.

On the 20th, all the animals belonging to Tomocacari Mission, three miles from Tubac, taken in broad day. Immediate pursuit by Mr. McCoy and Captain Sharp, and the animals retaken.

On the 18th, a band of Papagoes took three horses from Hoyt's Ranche. Pursued by Lieut. Lord, to the Mexican town of Santa Cruz; three men and five horses taken.

On the 21st, a cow, belonging to Mr. Wodsworth, killed, within a short distance of the dwelling house. The same night, Indians were shot at and driven away from Mr. Ake's house.

On the 28th, two oxen belonging to a Mexican taken on the road between Tubac and Tucson.[55]

Overland Mail Stations were built at fifteen- to twenty-five-mile intervals from Doubtful Canyon to Tucson. Each station was occupied by two to four men who tended the mules and prepared them for harness at the sound of the hunting horn on the approaching stage. There was a station keeper, a hostler (the mule tender), and often a relief driver. At larger, more important stations, there might also be a wheelwright and blacksmith. Wheels made "back east" where the humidity was high shrank and fell apart in the arid Southwest. Their metal tires had to be shortened, heated, and refit. It was a lonely life. The stage came by four times per week, twice from each direction. Employees spent their time bringing in fodder and firewood, preparing meals for passengers, and watering the stock. At Ewell's Station they transported water by tanker from five miles away at Ewell's Spring, and at Dragoon Springs stock was taken a mile to water in the canyon. They were isolated, the nearest military assistance often one hundred miles away, as at Apache Pass. The May 25, 1860, edition of the *Missouri Republican* reported how unnerving that isolation could be:

Tubac, May 6th, 1860
The Pinals have been very quiet while the Tontos have appeared in large numbers at various settlements on the Gila. Two stations of the

Overland Mail Company in that section have been deserted through
alarm at their unusual boldness, and the road agent[56] has gone down
to re-open them with increased numbers of men.[57]

Overland Mail stations were well defended with their high stone walls. Butterfield kept his men well-armed with revolvers and Sharp's breech-loading carbines—arguably the most effective firepower available in the West—and the company offered for trade or gift things the Apache wanted. Although the Apache occasionally threatened to wipe them out, up until February 6, 1861, the Chiricahua Apache did not attack the coaches and apart from a few incidents of stock theft, and they left the stations alone as well.[58]

Overland Mail employees took great pride in their company and their work. Butterfield recruited many of his men in upstate New York where he had previously run stage coach lines. He carefully selected them. John Butterfield laid down strict rules and policies. Isolated as they were, his men needed to be capable of operating independently and disciplined enough to follow the rules when supervisors weren't handy. This feeling of independence and pride led to problems at Apache Pass when Overland Mail employees failed to heed a wise warning from Lieutenant Bascom.

The beginning of the end of a period of relative peace for the Overland Mail came when the Military Department of New Mexico ordered two companies of infantry to Fort Buchanan. In May 1860, Company B, 8th Infantry left Fort Buchanan and moved to the mouth of Arivaipa Creek at the San Pedro near its confluence with the Gila River. This was ninety miles north of Buchanan and many miles north of the Overland Mail and emigrant trails. It was at the edge of Pinal and Aravaipa Apache territory and interdicted the raiding routes of Western Apache and Coyoteros depredating along Sonoita Creek, the Santa Cruz River, and in Sonora, Mexico. There Company B constructed Fort Breckenridge. In October 1860, the 7th Infantry arrived at Sonoita Creek and Companies D and G of the 1st Dragoons moved to the new fort.

The dragoon cavalry was no longer available to protect the miners, ranchers, and farmers in the south. The cavalry was no longer close enough to defend Tubac and the Overland Mail route. The presence of cavalry in the north changed Apache raiding patterns. They no longer went north along Sonoita Creek, to Ciénega Creek, Redington Pass, and finally the San Pedro. Instead they turned east along Babocomari Creek and headed through South Pass in the Dragoon Mountains to Soldier's Holes on Whitewater Draw, the Sulphur Springs Valley, Turkey Creek, and Apache Pass. Southern Arizona noticed the increase in violence immediately, although many were slow to understand its cause.

When the dragoons moved north, the settlers felt abandoned by their government. In April 1860, they formed a local provisional government, which included Wadsworth as general of the militia, an organization aimed at a defense from Indians that the government was not providing.[59] Indian attacks were increasing. The newspaper declared, "We have almost daily reports of Indian depredations, and from the activity of the savages it would seem that they are determined to give the settlers as much trouble as possible."[60] The infantry was not effective as far as the settlers were concerned. According to one newspaper report in February of 1860, "The Indians, notwithstanding the presence of several infantry companies in Arizona, are not awed into quietness; indeed, they seem to fully appreciate the uselessness of infantry troops and, having less fear of pursuit than formerly, are bolder and more daring."[61]

A growing sense of frustration with an army that was not protecting them led to the formation of the first company of Arizona Rangers, of which Jack Swilling and James Tevis were members. These feelings fueled anger when Apaches kidnapped Felix Ward and led to an overwhelming response by Lieutenant Colonel Pitcairn Morrison. He dispatched an entire company of infantry to deal with the problem, sending all the men he had available and one of the largest forces yet ordered to take the field on this sort of mission. He also allowed the boy's stepfather to accompany this force as translator. He needed to send a translator, but it seems both Paddy Graydon and Antonio, who worked at Fort Buchanan, might have been available. Sending Johnny Ward was unwise, but Morrison needed to demonstrate his resolve and could hardly refuse the stepfather who wanted to accompany the troops.

On February 12, 1861, while Bascom's fate at Apache Pass was still unknown, settlers held a meeting at Tucson. As a result, Tucson formed

Fort Buchanan, ca. 1900. ARIZONA HISTORICAL SOCIETY

a Ranger company of twenty men, which took the field within a week. Citizens reached the following agreement:

> *WHEREAS, The citizens of this Territory have of late suffered from the depredations of Apache Indians to an extent heretofore unknown, compelling many to abandon their homes and seek protection in the more thickly settled sections, thereby checking our progress in agriculture and mining; and*
>
> *WHEREAS, We are now threatened with an interruption of our mail facilities for communication with the States; therefore,*
>
> *Resolved, That we deem it the duty of every good citizen to aid, to the extent of his ability, in the suppression of those depredations, and the restoration of peace and quiet to our homes.*
>
> *Resolved, That it is expedient to organize a body of efficient men to act as Rangers, and to continue in the field as long as their services are required.*

Resolved, That a committee of five be appointed by the meeting to act as a Committee of Ways and Means, to provide for equipping and rationing such Ranger Company; and that such Committee be instructed to forward to the commanding officers at Forts Buchanan and Breckenridge a copy of these Resolutions, with a request for them to co-operate with our citizens.[62]

According to these citizens, the depredations had increased before Bascom took his company to Apache Pass, not as a result of it. The people were angry enough to pay for a well-equipped Ranger company to defend them. Pioneers did not easily or willingly part with a dollar, but on this occasion they volunteered to raise funds.

Apache problems increased after October 1860 when the dragoons departed for Fort Breckenridge. Citizens noted the increase in depredations along Sonoita Creek, and they put considerable pressure on Colonel Morrison to do something. The December 4, 1860, issue of the *San Francisco Evening Bulletin* reported: "[T]he policy of Government in sending infantry soldiers to defend the frontier, instead of mounted troops, has contributed to cast still further doubts on the stability of Arizona investments."[63]

Chapter Five

LIFE AT FORT BUCHANAN

Tucson, November 19, 1860

The citizens of Sonoita Valley have long kept up a rivalry with Tucson in the line of "amusements" and "innocent recreations." Last week they indulged their taste by having two shooting affrays, and one attempt at shooting, but the latter happening on the reservation at Fort Buchanan, was interrupted by the commanding officer, who is so antiquated in his views that these sports of the people are not relished by him.[1]

—St. Louis *Missouri Republican*, December 7, 1860

Dressed in an immaculately tailored uniform the colonel stooped to pass through the low doorway of post headquarters, which doubled as the post commander's residence followed by Lieutenant Colonel Isaac Reeve, commander of the post and of Company B, 8th Infantry.

Reeve spoke, "There it is, Colonel Johnston, Fort Buchanan."

The inspector general looked at two small adobe structures of earthen ugliness, the officer's quarters, and then behind him at the post headquarters. He shook his head. These were the finest buildings on the fort. Below them down the hill, spread out wherever a little flat space allowed, were the jacals that formed the rest of the housing.

"They're scattered all over like a Mexican village. I can't even see your commissary and quartermaster buildings," said the tall officer shaking his head. He glanced up and down the little valley with the flat parade field along its bottom and buildings, if you could call them that, scattered in no particular order along the eastern hillside.

Below them, naked Mexican children ran playing and yelling between the buildings.

The two colonels were joined by Assistant Surgeon Bernard Irwin and Captain Richard Ewell, commander of Company G, 1st Dragoons.

Irwin spoke up, "The jacals are unhealthy. They're falling down. Adobe chinking and loose bark hide scorpions, spiders, and rodents. They fall onto the men whenever there is a rain. The roofs leak and drip mud. They're hot in the spring and summer and drafty in the winter. The rodents attract rattlesnakes."

Colonel Johnston nodded.

Irwin continued, "See the streambeds? In the summer they flood the whole parade field and the evil vapors make the men sick."

Ewell spoke up, "Not to mention the mosquitos, but all that water does make some lovely grass grow to feed the horses."

Johnston looked closely at Ewell. He must have been about forty years old and bald. He was probably older than any of his men. No wonder soldiers called their commander "the old man." Johnston had heard whispers that Ewell's men had named a mountain after him, Mount Baldy. He'd also heard that Ewell was the best Indian fighter in the Department of New Mexico.

The colonel shook his head again. "It must be over half a mile from here to your commissary. This post is ten times as big as it should be and on a sidehill. That can't be much fun for anyone. How do you guard this place?"

Reeve frowned. "With the greatest of difficulty, sir. Now, if we could discuss the lack of supplies. Our weapons are old and nearly useless, we're in need of uniforms, food, horses, ammunition, everything."

Today, not much remains of Fort Buchanan. In 1882, the New Mexico and Arizona Railroad excavated a deep cut through the post cemetery and sutler's store and then built a grade across the parade ground. In 1926, the State of Arizona built a road through the heart of the post. The quarters of the commander and post headquarters, one of the few adobe buildings, repurposed a few years later as either the Camp Crittenden sutler's store or a storage building, remain today as low walls in front of a private residence. Diligent searching can locate a few foundations and quantities of period trash. In the 1960s, the area was gone over with metal detectors and the Museum of the Horse Soldier in Tucson displays many of the items recovered. There was also a salvage archaeology project undertaken when the state department of transportation moved Highway 82 to its current location.[2] Most of the buildings were of *jacal*. Upright, unpeeled logs were set in the ground and chinked with adobe plaster. Such buildings don't last long. They leak and rot, and insects and their predators live under the loose bark. They can't have been much fun to live in. In dry weather, dust settled on everything. When it rained, the ceiling and walls dripped mud and scorpions. When the weather was cold and the wind blew, it found its way in between the upright timber. The boundaries of the old post are difficult to fix. Today the land is heavily wooded with mesquite, oak, and cottonwood.

Fort Buchanan today. DOUG HOCKING

In March 1856, the Mexican military departed from the Tucson Presidio and the Gadsden Purchase. In November of that year, Major Enoch Steen arrived with four companies of the 1st Regiment of Dragoons and raised the U.S. flag over the Presidio[3] in Tucson. It had been a hard journey across the desert from Mesilla on the Rio Grande, three hundred miles behind them. Along the way they left their names on the terrain at Stein's Peak, named for the major, the Dragoon Mountains, and Dragoon Springs. Legend says that even Soldier's Farewell is a recollection of this trip. One soldier, thinking he'd reached the end of the world or perhaps distraught over a Dear John letter, ran about camp shaking hands and bidding farewell to all his comrades. When finished he put his dragoon Colt to his head and stayed behind forever at Soldier's Farewell. The story is probably apocryphal, but we lack a better explanation for the name.

As hard as the journey had been on men and horses, Major Steen found Tucson even harder. In Steen's words, Tucson was "built for no other reason than that there was protection [the presidio], and now requiring protection because it has been built."[4] Perhaps it was the heat, which even in March can be quite brutal in the Old Pueblo, as Tucson is known. The dry late spring is the hottest time of the year. Or perhaps he found the grazing exceptionally poor. Then again, he may have found the population objectionable. Even then, it was a gathering place for scoundrels run out of or on the run from California. Liquor flowed, and the cards and women were as hot as the climate. Steen moved his force south to Calabasas near where Sonoita Creek joins the Santa Cruz and there established Camp Moore. This drew instant complaint from the people of Tucson, who said that the Army wasn't close enough to protect them.

There may have been some truth in this, although the officers of the 1st Dragoons seemed to think the issue was that the Army was no longer close enough to exploit. The Apaches are mountain Indians and their homes were in ranges north and east of Tucson. Although Tucson was large enough that the Apaches only attacked it once, they did raid very close to town. Major Steen may have had some concern for protecting the border from raiding Mexicans and perhaps even the possibility that Mexico would try to retake her lost frontier. The Department of New Mexico, headquartered in Santa Fe, ordered the garrison to move to a site closer to Tucson. Steen sent Captain Richard Stoddard Ewell to select a site.

On March 4, 1857, he recommended a small mesa near the headwaters of Sonoita Creek at a spot known as Ojo Caliente. It was a wise choice. Ewell knew the Apache raiding trails. Raiders hitting Sonora, the Santa Cruz, and later Sonoita Creek settlements, returned north along Sonoita Creek. A few miles north of the headwaters, the Apache crossed into the north-flowing Ciénega Creek, which ran on to join the Rillito, which flowed westward, north around Tucson. From the junction of Ciénega Creek and the Rillito, the Apache would proceed eastward over the Redington Pass between the Santa Catalina and Rincon Mountains to the San Pedro River and then north to its junction with the Gila and thus to their mountain homelands. The site for the fort sat astride their route and interdicted their raiding trails. The new site was twenty miles closer to Tucson than the camp at Calabazas, although with the Santa Rita Mountains between the fort and Tucson, it may have seemed just as far away as Camp Moore. It was ideally located to defend the settlements and had a good supply of grass for grazing, water, and firewood. And it kept the soldiers away from the hells of Tucson, much to the relief of Captain Ewell.

Three months after Captain Ewell had scouted the site for the new post, Major Steen, then ill, sent soldiers ahead to build the new fort. Ewell was away on campaign and not there to supervise.[5] On June 3, 1857, the dragoons arrived at Ojo Caliente. The exhausted men dropped their gear on a "flat, narrow, meadow-like plain at the foot of a high plateau."[6] It wasn't obvious after the long, hot, dry spring, but the parade ground was a *cienega*, a marsh, surrounded on three sides by water. The new fort stretched along the low ground and the soldiers constructed buildings up the steep hillside rather than half a mile above on the plateau Ewell had selected. Construction was haphazard with no particular order, the post coming to look more like a Mexican village than an army camp. Colonel Joseph E. Johnston, touring the post on inspection, found that the officers' quarters and post hospital had been built of adobe, but other buildings were no more than logs or wooden slabs, set on end in the ground and the intervals closed with mud, most of which had fallen out, leaving them drafty. When Captain Ewell and the Gila Expedition returned in late August, construction was already underway and it was too late to move the camp.

Captain (brevet Lieutenant Colonel) Isaac Van Duzen Reeve commanded Company B, 8th Infantry. On March 29, 1859, he arrived with his company at Fort Buchanan and assumed command. He remained until early 1860. Of the fort, he said that it occupied "ten times the ground it ought to, being on & around a side hill of considerable abruptness—and does not admit of any considerable improvement in a military point of view—the buildings being located with great irregularity & irrespective of defence (sic)."[7]

Southeast Arizona is a malarial climate and in this and succeeding summers the disease incapacitated many of the troops, including Captain Ewell, with fever and chills. The diagnosis was not available at the time, but today qualified doctors believe the symptoms were those of malaria. Fort Buchanan had one of the highest rates of illness in the Army. The only people to have escaped were some employees of the sutler, and Nancy, Captain Ewell's old nurse.[8] In 1858, several soldiers died of malaria.[9] According to one source every man was suffering from some touch of the disease. Ewell was sick every summer and was still sick in January 1861 when the department commander finally granted his request to return home on a convalescent absence. On October 4, 1859, Army Inspector Colonel Joseph E. Johnston wrote: "The garrison present is Bvt. Lt. Col. Reeve's Co. B, 8th Infantry, & Capt. Ewell's G, 1st Dragoons. The first, a Capt. (sick) & 56 enlisted men, including 6 on extra & daily duty & 22 sick. The second, a Capt. & 74 enlisted men including 22 on extra & daily duty, 17 sick & 4 confined, with 57 horses, 4 of which are reported 'unserviceable.'"[10]

In 1858, in conjunction with the Mormon War in Utah, the Army transferred the four companies of dragoons in Arizona from the Department of New Mexico to the Department of the Pacific. The cavalry was badly needed to defend mines, settlers, and the Overland Mail. Army General Orders No. 2, dated January 16, 1858, reported: "The General commanding the Department of New Mexico will either abandon Fort Buchanan . . . or relieve the dragoons now stationed there."[11]

This meant that there would be no soldiers left in the Gadsden Purchase. Fortunately, even before department headquarters in Santa Fe received these orders, rare daylight dawned in Washington, DC, and the Army amended the orders: "Two companies of the dragoons will remain to garrison Fort Buchanan . . . [and] will hereafter be under the same obligation with respect to the department commander as the other posts within his command."[12]

On April 11, 1858, the Army approved Major Steen's request for sick leave and he departed Arizona, turning command over to Major Fitzgerald. In July, Dr. Bernard John Dowling Irwin declared Fitzgerald unfit for duty and command devolved on Captain Ewell, who held it until the next March, when Captain (brevet Lieutenant Colonel) Reeve arrived with Company B, 8th Infantry, replacing Company D of the 1st Dragoons, which was reassigned to Fort Fillmore near Mesilla, leaving Fort Buchanan with one company of dragoons and one of infantry. When Reeve departed in early 1860, Captain Ewell again assumed command until September 1861, when he departed to sit on a court martial board at Fort Bliss, Texas, never to return.

By May 1858, Ewell had formed a partnership with lieutenants Isaiah Moore, Richard Lord, and Horace Randal to open the abandoned Patagonia Mine. Ewell reputedly bought information about the mine's location in the Patagonia Mountains from a Mexican sheepherder in exchange for a pony and few other small articles.[13] For a while Ewell's quarters looked more like an alchemist's laboratory than a soldier's home, set up as he was with the tools of a mine assayer. He had learned chemistry at the U.S. Military Academy as part of the curriculum that all cadets studied, but he took particular interest in it and in March 1858, he converted his quarters.

My room is completely filled with chemical machinery & my table boasts of several crucibles & books; blow pipe, scales, charcoal, supports & at least 6 different kinds of minerals. Maj. Steen left a piece of mineral with me which he thought was rich but appeared ordinary to me. He begged me for a long time to try it & at last thinking of 'Tool for luck' did so & found it very rich then reduced some & found it worth at the rate of two dollars the pound of ore—ten cents is considered good from the same amount of ore.[14]

Small in stature, Captain Ewell was nevertheless rated by the people of Arizona as a great Indian fighter. His men idealized him and behind his back called him "Old Baldy," an endearing term they dared not use to his face. They renamed a mountain visible from the post, Mount Wrightson, in his honor, designating it Mount Baldy. Tevis said of him, "[W]hen vexed he was not very particular about his language and would 'cuss' the soldiers very lustily; but no other man dared do it in the Captain's presence for he loved his soldiers and, although he talked roughly to them, he always took care that they were made as comfortable as possible, and his soldiers all liked him."[15]

Ewell did indeed take good care of his men. The company kept a garden and he believed himself to be the first man ever to successfully raise potatoes in southern Arizona. They were much in demand. The garden ensured the health of his men, at least as far as freedom from scurvy was concerned. The company fund was well maintained and quite wealthy, providing food and amusements for the men. All too often on the frontier the only amusements available to soldiers were bad whiskey, bad gamblers, and bad women. The commander used the company fund to buy books, musical instruments, and supplemental food for the men. Informal organizations of soldiers kept libraries, formed bands, and put on musical and theatrical performances. They also engaged in sports and sports competitions, including foot and horse races. Musical evenings accompanied by drinking could become rowdy, and the bands might end up in a brawl over whether to play Irish or German tunes.

At Los Lunas in New Mexico, before coming to Arizona in 1856, Company G, 1st Regiment of Dragoons, was noted as having made many improvements to the post, including the construction of a nine-pin bowling alley and the cultivation of a flourishing garden. Captain Ewell was an exceptional gardener. When the company departed from Los Lunas headed for Fort Buchanan, it took with it a large and valuable library and a company fund of no less than twenty-five thousand dollars that, in the opinion of one historian, made it "the wealthiest and probably the most comfortably provided company in the department."[16] The amount of the company fund seems entirely fantastical, amounting to $333 per man in the company, the equivalent of about two years' pay for each of them.

Ewell found himself bored with garrison life. He read Shakespeare, studied French, wrote some very amusing letters to his female relatives, and played cards. Nothing seemed to help, and boredom grew more oppressive each day. "This place is dull beyond anything I ever imagined."[17] He spoke of the fort's quarreling ladies. By that he meant the officers' wives. He, Surgeon Irwin, and some of the subalterns were bachelors, so there can't have been very many of them. Lieutenant Lord of Company D, 1st Dragoons, was married and had his wife with him. In the summer of 1860, the census recorded forty civilians on the post. These included the officer's wives, the enlisted wives, children, interpreters, carpenters, adobe brick makers, and herdsmen. There was a gulf between Victorian ladies, the officers' wives, and the laundresses married to enlisted men.

Something of that gulf appears in a letter Ewell wrote in 1859. It also tells us about the Victorian ladies that accompanied their husbands to frontier posts untrained and unable to cook and clean, needing servants and finding them hard to come by.

After a journey of twelve months, my second lieutenant and his wife arrived a fortnight since, without a servant, and she perfectly helpless, having almost lost her sight. It is very fortunate for them that I have a good servant woman and a comfortable house. The lady is, of course very miserable and wishes herself back in Connecticut. I think it must require a great deal of affection to make a man willing to degrade a lady almost to a cook or washerwoman. As for any love standing such trials, it is absurd to think of it. The woman can justly complain of the selfishness and neglect of the man, while the natural fretting and complaining, under the circumstance, will disgust him, not withstanding her sufferings may have been great.[18]

Ewell complained that people treated his home as a wayside inn and that he thus had more uninvited guests than he cared for. The company garden occupied some of his time, and he searched the area for edible wild food. The woods provided wild berries and sour currants to keep away the scurvy.[19] Living arrangements were difficult in an age where processed and frozen foods were not available. Ewell was lucky to have his loyal servant to cook for him. A soldier lacked the time and often the skill to cook for himself when the task might consume much of the day. Officers made arrangements to maintain an open mess, when there were enough bachelor officers present to support such an establishment, and hire servants, often enlisted men or the wives of enlisted men seeking supplemental pay. On a small post, an officer might arrange to take his meals with a family. Ewell tells us that at one point, "I am now keeping or about to keep bachelor's hall. One of my subalterns, Lt. Moore, is about going on recruiting service and the other is married, so that I will have to live by myself."[20] A few months later he had companions. "There are two bachelors here now—one an Irishman, doctor U.S.A., red head and hot tempered, the other a lieutenant from Ohio, who, on a march we made together sometimes since, where he catered, provided, to my dismay nothing but a big hog which we were to eat fresh."[21]

The Irishman was Doctor Bernard John Dowling Irwin, a man as remarkable as you'll find anywhere, who would participate in the great events of early Arizona and Fort Buchanan. In fact, Irwin received the very first Medal of Honor for his heroic efforts at Apache Pass in February 1861. He led twelve soldiers to the relief of Lieutenant George N. Bascom's force intending to break the cordon of five hundred Apaches.

Irwin occupied his time developing improved techniques for treating wounds and was always the first to volunteer for any chance of action. Some call him "The Fighting Doctor" and decry his participation in battle[22] but times were different, medical ethics and the treaty status of combat doctors evolving. The assistant surgeon did as he thought best and those around him appreciated his participation.

Irwin's medical school instructors included William Phipps Blake, who would one day become director of the Arizona School of Mines as well as serve as the Territorial Geologist. On one of his first assignments, Surgeon Irwin worked at Fort Defiance, New Mexico Territory, with Major Henry L. Kendrick, who had been professor of Chemistry and

Mineralogy at West Point. Helped by Kendrick, Irwin became a field agent for Spencer F. Baird, director of the Smithsonian Institution, and as such collected specimens of birds, plants, animals, and minerals, first at Fort Defiance and later at Fort Buchanan. Baird wrote to Irwin, "I do earnestly hope that you will set to work at the systematic collection of all the animals of your vicinity."[23] The surgeon developed a lifelong relationship with the Smithsonian and also was responsible for forwarding the Tucson Ring Meteorite to the museum. The massive iron ring had been in use as a blacksmith's anvil.[24]

Captain Ewell's boredom stemmed from enforced idleness. Some of the commanders over him were sickly old men who didn't care to stir themselves to fight Apache or know how. Moreover, they lacked the men and horses for sustained pursuit. The Apache were will-o'-the-wisps who saw no reason to stand and fight a superior force. Soldiers had to catch them off guard and that required skill and lengthy pursuit. Fort Buchanan stood as close to the end of the world as a military post could be. Its supply lines were lengthy and the fort was at the very end of them. The post bought some supplies locally, such as hay, beef, pork, and vegetables, but prices were high. The soldier companies, as already noted, kept gardens. Everything else came from Fort Leavenworth on the Missouri River in Kansas, along the Santa Fe Trail to Fort Union, New Mexico, and then five hundred miles to Fort Buchanan. Alternative routes included by sea to San Francisco to the Gulf of California, then up the Colorado by steamboat to Fort Yuma and across the desert. In January 1859, Fort Buchanan had 170 men with fifty recruits en route. However, there were only 108 horses and 12 of those were unfit for service. There were also shortages of horseshoes, cavalry boots, socks, and ammunition.[25] Sylvester Mowry, local mine owner, politician, and former officer wrote, "the small cavalry force in the Territory, although mostly ably handled by Capt. R. S. Ewell . . . was entirely unable to make a campaign with decisive results against the Indians.[26] Ewell trained his men well and Colonel Johnston reported: "The Dragoon Company is better instructed than any other of the mounted troops I have seen in New Mexico. The men ride more like soldiers & the horses are better broken. It is evident that a regular course of instruction has been followed, instead of that of beginning with the school of the platoon, which I judge to have been the practice in this department."[27]

Although well trained, the state of their armaments was deplorable:

The men are well clothed & their personal accoutrements & horse equipments [sic] *are good. There is, however, a great variety of fire arms, Sharp's, Hall's & the pistol carbine, the rifle (cal. .54) & musketoon—Colt's revolver of both sizes, & the old Dragoon pistols. Capt. Ewell advocates Sharp's Carbine, in comparison with the musketoon, for he has had no opportunity to compare it with others of the same kind. The Capt. has made two requisitions for carbines annually for several years. His sabres (sic) are of the old pattern.*[28]

It is hard to imagine entering combat with such a collection of arms. Officers place their men with a thought to the respective range of their weapons. A proper line of defense cannot be formed when one soldier's weapon has a range of fifty yards while that of the man next to him is two hundred yards. Moreover, there is a great difference between the rate of fire of a musketoon and Sharp's Carbine. The unit needs to carry ammunition for each of the different weapons, complicating supply.

Many of the officers who came to Lieutenant Bascom's aid at Apache Pass in February 1861 had long served in Arizona, many under or with vaunted Indian fighter Ewell. A soldier could easily stay a lieutenant for ten or more years. Promotion was based on seniority, although political promotion during reorganization was not unknown.[29] Through much of the nineteenth century, regiments consisted of ten companies commanded by a colonel, assisted by a lieutenant colonel, and a major. A captain assisted by a first and second lieutenant commanded each company. Each company was usually authorized one hundred men. That was all Congress would pay for. There was no paid retirement until the 1890s. The Army pulled officers from their regiments and companies to serve as staff officers (quartermaster and adjutant), recruiting officers, to serve on special assignment, to serve on courts martial, and to serve on special commissions. Additionally, officers were away on leave and sick leave. Sick leave was an especial problem with senior officers like Steen and

Morrison, who returned home on sick leave and never returned to their units, although they were still on the books against unit strength. The next senior man moved up to take the position of an officer on the sick list, so a major or captain often commanded a regiment. Men in training, on detached service, and en route were carried against unit strength so a company of one hundred could seldom field more than fifty men and often had no more than one officer present for duty. A lieutenant with three or four years' service with a regiment might well have served as an adjutant, quartermaster, company commander, and even post commander of a two-company post. Before he was promoted to captain, a lieutenant would likely have experienced more time in service than a major in today's army would have. It's not surprising that the company commander came to be called "the Old Man." A lieutenant was often in his forties before he was promoted to captain and thus was one of the oldest men in the unit. The December 7, 1860, edition of the St. Louis *Missouri Republican* reflected the reality of understrength units and the inability of infantry to cope with Apaches, reporting:

> *Tucson, November 19, 1860*
> *Lieut. Plympton, of the 7th Infantry, arrived last week with forty-two recruits for the two companies of infantry at Fort Buchanan, which will increase them to seventy-five men each, a number quite sufficient to do guard duty, as infantry can do little more in this country.*[30]

Up until the Civil War, there were no medals given for military service. In 1862, Congress created the Medal of Honor, which was initially for enlisted men and not for officers. Up until the late 1860s, officers got brevet rank instead. The Army awarded brevet promotions for heroism in combat. An officer wore his brevet rank and was entitled to be addressed by it.[31] If no officer was present who held higher regular rank, the brevet officer's rank prevailed. Congress still paid the officer at his regular rank as authorized by his position in the regimental rolls. If an officer with regular rank of captain was brevetted to colonel, he outranked all captains who were only captains and brevet majors and brevet lieutenant colonels. But if a regular major was present, that officer outranked the brevet colonel. Increased regular rank and pay waited on seniority within the regimental roll.

Life for soldiers at Fort Buchanan was a mixture of boredom, terror as the Apache walked between their buildings in the night, and frustration at lacking the tools and manpower to do their jobs properly. The soldiers faced pressures from settlers and superiors to make an impact on marauding Indians and Mexican bandits. Society was divided by a gulf between suds row and officers' wives who bickered with one another. Single officers hired servants to prepare their meals or arranged to dine with a family. Victorian ladies, helpless to conduct their own housework, sought out competent servants. Everyone suffered from malaria during the warm, wet summer.

Officers assigned to Fort Buchanan and Breckenridge in late 1860 and early 1861 included Lieutenants Isaiah Moore, Richard Lord, Horace Randal, John Cooke, Andrew Evans, Charles Ingraham, Gurdin Chapin, and George N. Bascom, as well as Captain (brevet Lieutenant Colonel) Isaac Van Duzer Reeve, Lieutenant Colonel Pitcairn Morrison, and, finally, Assistant Surgeon Bernard John Dowling Irwin.

Born in Pennsylvania about 1826, Isaiah N. Moore was a sober and efficient officer[32] and one of Ewell's partners in the Patagonia Mine with Richard Lord and Horace Randal. On July 1, 1851, after he graduated from West Point, the Army commissioned him in the 1st Dragoons. Serving with Company G in New Mexico under Captain Ewell, he fought Navajos, Mescalero, and Mimbres Apaches. Ewell welcomed Isaiah, as his previous lieutenants had been less than efficient; one was a confirmed alcoholic. Finally, the captain had someone he could rely on. The lieutenant frequently assumed command of Company G, 1st Dragoons, when Ewell was away. Moore operated successfully in the field in 1855, when Company G attacked the Mescalero Apache in the Sacramento Mountains. In 1856, Moore rode into Arizona with Major Steen to take possession of the Gadsden Purchase. By 1861, he had been in Arizona almost five years and had as much experience fighting Apaches as any officer in New Mexico Territory. With almost ten years in service, knowing Ewell's methods as no other officer did, and many months in command, he brought Company G, which he commanded, to the assistance of Lieutenant Bascom at Apache Pass.[33]

Lieutenant Richard S. C. Lord was born in Ohio and graduated the U.S. Military Academy on July 1, 1856. He gained a spot in the 1st Dragoons in June 1857. Posted to Arizona, he brought along his wife to the frontier, where she suffered hardships both in attempting to find a reliable servant and in operating her household without one. When Company B, 8th Infantry, was assigned to Fort Buchanan in March 1859, Lieutenant Lord went with Company D, 1st Dragoons, to Fort Fillmore near Mesilla and didn't return until June of 1860. Shortly thereafter, his unit was assigned to Fort Breckenridge. In February 1861, he was commander of Company D, and came with Lieutenant Moore to Bascom's aid at Apache Pass.[34]

Lieutenant Horace Randal was born in Tennessee about 1834 and graduated from the U.S. Military Academy in 1854. As a lieutenant with the 1st Dragoons, he fought Apaches in New Mexico in 1855 and 1856 before coming to Fort Buchanan in command of the escort for a wagon train from Albuquerque. Escort duty, guard duty, escort for the mail, and construction duties on post ate into the number of soldiers available for campaigns against marauding Indians. In December 1860, he departed for the East on leave and on February 27, 1861, resigned his commission to accept service in the Confederate Army, rising to be a brigadier general. He was slain at Jenkins Ferry on April 30, 1864.[35]

Among Captain Ewell's final actions in Arizona was the selection of a site for a new fort, one that would be better placed than Fort Buchanan to protect the Overland Mail road and Leach's Wagon Road.[36] Ewell knew his enemy. He selected the site at the mouth of Aravaipa Creek where it entered the San Pedro in the heart of Aravaipa Apache country, near the Pinal Apache and on the raiding trails of the Tontos. It would prove a fateful decision. Hesperian wrote about the site in a letter to the *Missouri Republican*:

Tubac, May 15, 1860
Capt. R.S. Ewell is now at Aravaipa Canon, engaged in laying off the Military Reservation of ten miles square for the new six-company

*post. A company of infantry under the command of Lieut. Cooke is
already on duty there, and it is probable that Lieut. Lord's company of
dragoons now en route for Fort Buchanan, will also be ordered there
for the present.*[37]

Lieutenant John Rogers Cooke was the son of Lieutenant Colonel
(later General) Philip St. George Cooke of the 1st Dragoons, and was
born at Jefferson Barracks, Missouri, in 1833. He was commissioned a
lieutenant in the 8th Infantry in 1855 and stationed at Fort Buchanan by
March 31, 1859. He fought in several skirmishes against Pinal Apaches.
In May of 1860, he was in command of Company B, 8th Infantry, in the
absence of Captain Isaac Reeve. Under his direction Company B built
Fort Breckenridge at the mouth of the Aravaipa Creek on the San Pedro
River a few miles south of its confluence with the Gila River.

In 1858, James B. Leach was superintendent of the building of an
emigrant wagon road to California. Congress instructed him to use no
heavy grading or bridging, to make provisions for collecting and preserving rainwater, and not to go as far south as Philip St. George Cooke
had in building his road, parts of which ran through Sonora, Mexico.
Leach gathered forty wagons, pulled by oxen, loaded with seventy-five
rifles, twenty Colt's pistols, 11,500 rifle cartridges, three thousand pistol
cartridges, and thirty-five kegs of blasting powder.[38] Much of Leach's
road followed the same course as the Overland Mail, with significant
deviations. He ran his road north to Tres Alamos on the San Pedro River
and then built his Wagon Road along that river, departing from the river
near Fort Breckenridge going overland to the Gila, which it followed
west to California. The wagon road cut many miles off the journey, but
since it avoided Tucson, the only town in the area, few travelers used it.
The new fort was in the heart of Pinal and Aravaipa Apache country and
interdicted their raiding routes to Sonoita Creek and the Santa Cruz.
However, it was very far from the mines and population centers and left
them exposed. In October 1860, Companies D, Lieutenant Richard Lord
commanding, and G, Lieutenant Isaiah Moore commanding, of the 1st
Dragoons, were reassigned from Fort Buchanan to Fort Breckenridge,
leaving Companies C and H, 7th Infantry, as guardians of the south, a

task for which they were ill-suited, as they were unable to move rapidly against Apache raiders.

In the summer of 1860, after the return of Captain Reeve, Cooke was no longer in command. In February 1861, Lieutenant Cooke took leave and departed Tucson by Overland Mail coach, heading home. There he would resign his commission and join the Confederacy. On February 6, Cochise and his warriors attacked Lieutenant Cooke's stage as it crossed into Apache Pass.

Brevet Lieutenant Colonel Isaac Van Duzer Reeve was a regular captain who graduated from West Point in 1835. He fought in the Mexican War, winning brevets, and fought Indians in Texas, New Mexico, and Arizona. He came to Fort Buchanan in March 1859 with the 8th Infantry and briefly assumed command of the post, fighting campaigns against Pinal Apaches. In February 1861, while stationed at Fort Breckenridge, he received orders to take Company B, 8th Infantry, to Fort Bliss, Texas, on the Rio Grande to defend against invading Texans. Between February 7 and 9, while Bascom and his company were surrounded by hundreds of Apache at Apache Pass and awaiting help, Company B was marching along Leach's Wagon Road passing north of the Dos Cabezas Mountains. The dust of their passing was visible from Apache Pass and Cochise and Mangas Coloradas thought this a treacherous attempt by the Army to surround them while they were confronting Lieutenant Bascom.[39]

In October 1860, Companies C and H of the 7th Infantry marched into Fort Buchanan, having come from Utah by way of South Pass, Colorado, and New Mexico. By mid-December the *Arizonian* reported, "The Indians were still troublesome and depredations had been committed in the immediate vicinity of Fort Buchanan."[40]

In January 1861, six officers were present for duty at Fort Buchanan. Lieutenant Colonel Pitcairn Morrison was the commander of the 7th Infantry Regiment and Fort Buchanan. He was sixty-five and would soon return home on sick leave. Lieutenant Gurdin W. Chapin was his adjutant. An adjutant is a sort of military secretary who composes orders and reports, and receives and sends mail. It is an important position, and the officer is taken from company strength. He would otherwise have been commander of Company C. While in Utah, Chapin had served as infantry escort with a Topographical Engineer expedition to locate a new road to Nevada, and this had gained him some experience in confronting hostile Indians.

Lieutenant Andrew W. Evans was commander of Company H, 7th Infantry. He was born in 1829 and commissioned in 1852, and then served with the unit in the Mormon War of 1857. He returned to Arizona in 1870 as a major with the 3rd Cavalry and served on General Crook's staff. Evans earned a brevet promotion at the Battle of Valverde in February 1862. Lieutenant Charles H. Ingraham was born in Ohio in 1836 and was commissioned in 1858, joining the 7th Infantry in Utah. He died in 1867.[41] Company H took to the field after Apaches in December 1860. The post returns reported: "1st Lieut. A. W. Evans, & Lieut. Chs. H Ingraham and 36 enlisted men of Company 'H' 7th Infantry return from scout to this post January 14, 1861."[42]

They were recovering from their winter ordeal and were not available to assist Lieutenant Bascom in early February. The last of the six officers were Dr. Irwin and George Bascom. Assistant Surgeon Bernard John Dowling Irwin had been assigned to Fort Buchanan since 1857. Lieutenant George N. Bascom had been in command of Company C since December 1860.

Life in the infantry garrison must have continued much as life on Fort Buchanan had been when the dragoons were there, except the officers suffered heavy criticism from the civilian populace for being unable to police the Indians. Forts Buchanan and Breckenridge were the very end of the military world, as remote as any American Army post, undersupplied, and at the end of extremely long lines of communication. The infantry, newly arrived, was under intense pressure to show that it could do something besides "guard duty," as Indian raids were occurring ever closer to the post. The officer in command, Colonel Morrison, was old, sickly, and inactive. This placed even more pressure on his subordinates to act. Lieutenant Evans' January foray after Apache raiders was ineffective in locating or chastising them. Somehow the Apache managed to all elude infantry, even when the foot soldiers were mounted on mules.

Ewell had been out to Apache Pass to confront Cochise several times, forcing the Chiricahua leader to return stolen livestock. It was a frustrating business, with the chief prevaricating and concealing stolen stock and attempting to return malnourished stock for good. Before he left Arizona, Captain Ewell wrote, if Cochise's band raided again he would not ask for restitution but would instead "strike a blow."[43] For all that, Ewell and many of the officers around him were aware of the reason for the thefts and had some sympathy for the Indians. Ewell wrote that the "Indians [are] in starving condition, stealing to eat born of necessity."[44]

Chapter Six

COCHISE AND THE OVERLAND MAIL

[O]ne of the worst Indians now on the continent is Coches. This Indian was always at peace with the whites until 1860 when he and his family were invited to dine with an officer of the Army, who had his company ready to arrest him for the purpose of keeping him as a hostage for the return of a boy stolen by the Pinals.
—CAPTAIN REUBEN BERNARD, 1869[1]

CAPTAIN, FORMERLY FIRST SERGEANT, REUBEN BERNARD HAD ONLY casual acquaintance with the truth. Throughout his military career he endeavored to enhance his standing with stories that overstated his role in events. His greatest contribution to the corruption of history was the harm he did to Lieutenant Bascom's reputation and the manner in which he built up that of Cochise. Cochise was not always at peace. Bernard is also the source of the story that Cochise guarded the road for the Overland Mail.

Brevet Brigadier General Thomas C. Devin commanded the Sub-Department of Southern Arizona and the 8th Cavalry in 1869. As such he was Bernard's immediate commander. On January 25, 1869, shortly after the latter's return to Arizona, Devin made the remarkable assertion in a report to higher headquarters that Cochise guarded the road "before the attempt to take him prisoner caused him to make war." In fact, in the fall of 1860, when Lieutenant (later General) George Crook traveled

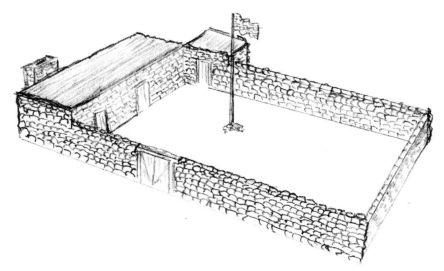

The Overland Mail Station at Apache Pass as it may have appeared in 1861.
ARTWORK BY DOUG HOCKING

east by Overland Mail stage, he noted that some stations had no horses because of a Chiricahua raid.[2]

John Warren Butterfield was a wise man who knew how to run a stagecoach line and deliver the mail on time. In Apache country, he built ten stone stations with walls eight to ten feet high. The stations were approximately sixty–by–forty feet. Inside were two or three ten- by ten-foot covered rooms. The rest of the enclosed area was a corral open to the sky. The hostler and the station keeper brought the stock inside each night so as not to tempt the Apache.

Butterfield armed his men with revolvers and Sharp's rifles, which were early percussion cap breech-loading weapons. This was still the age of the muzzleloader and the percussion cap. Powder and ball went down the barrel and then a cap was placed on the nipple. Rifles were slow to load as the ball had to be forced through the rifling, that is, grooves in the barrel. A man might get off two shots per minute. Muskets could be loaded more swiftly but were only accurate to one hundred yards. The Sharp's was breech loaded with paper cartridges. A lever lowered the breech, and a paper cartridge was inserted. When the breech was raised it cut off the end of the cartridge exposing the powder charge, which drove the bullet through the rifling. A man could fire a phenomenal six rounds per minute, and with the accuracy of a rifle. This gave Overland Mail personnel a very real advantage in firepower over both the military and the Indians.

Along with the lance, the bow and arrow was the primary weapon of the Apache at this time; they could launch five arrows in the time it took to reload a musket. In addition, arrows were more likely to wound than kill immediately, which gave the Apache another advantage: Soldiers could abandon dead men, but the need to attend to wounded comrades took both some able-bodied and the wounded men out of the fight. And, unlike bullets, arrows were capable of high-angle fire and could hit soldiers hiding behind cover. However, soldiers and Overland Mail employees had a real advantage in both the lethal threat and range of their firearms, discouraging the approach of Apaches who, unlike many Plains tribes, were not out to prove their courage. Surviving battle and returning with loot was enough. Even beyond rock walls and fast-loading, long-range weapons, a possibly greater advantage that helped to keep the scattered handfuls of Overland Mail employees safe was their usefulness as a source of supply to the Apache. Butterfield's men not only purchased hay and firewood from Indian women, giving the tribes incentive to tolerate them, but also made gifts of cornmeal and other items of food and manufacture.

Overland Mail Stations were strung out every fifteen to twenty-five miles from Doubtful Canyon to Tucson. The route crossed the San Simon Valley to Apache Pass between the Dos Cabezas and Chiricahua Mountains, and then crossed the Sulphur Springs Valley and Playa de los Pimos (Willcox Playa). From there the route was north of the Dragoon Mountains, across the San Pedro Valley and north of the Whetstone, Empire, and Santa Rita Mountains. Although this was often called the Butterfield Overland Mail after John Butterfield, the man most instrumental in putting the company together and winning the mail contract with the U.S. government, the company emblazoned its coaches with the name Overland Mail, not Butterfield.

There were stations at Stein's Peak, San Simon, Apache Pass, Ewell's, Dragoon Springs, San Pedro Crossing, Seneca, and Tucson. At each station were usually three or four men: In addition to a station keeper, a hostler to handle the stock, and a relief driver, some stations hired a local cook, and at others Butterfield hired tradesmen such as wheelwrights and blacksmiths. Some stations served meals to passengers. Most were simply change stations where the stage, which traveled at nine miles per hour, stopped to change mules or horses. Stops lasted twenty minutes. In that time passengers were allowed to eat and/or visit the privy, but they'd best make it back in time, or the stage would leave without them, leaving them three days' wait for the next scheduled stage. The Overland Mail had a schedule to keep. The U.S. government contracted the company to deliver the mail from St. Louis, Missouri, to San Francisco, California, within twenty-five days. The Overland Mail published a schedule showing departure times at key stations. At others the stage passed through early or late, not stopping for more than twenty minutes.[3]

El Paso - Saturday and Tuesday 11.00 AM
Soldier's Farewell - Sunday and Wednesday 8:30 PM 150 miles
Tucson - Tuesday and Friday 1.30 PM 184½ miles
Gila River - Wednesday and Saturday 9.00 PM 141 miles[4]

Passengers found the ride on the Overland Mail challenging. They were an afterthought. The company received six hundred thousand dollars annually for semi-weekly service running simultaneously in both directions on a six-year contract as a mail carrier.[5] For a fare of over two hundred dollars, a princely sum in that time, nine passengers were crowded into a celerity wagon, which the Overland Mail used in the West. The wagon had a canvas top and sides, and everyone sat on the same level. The driver and conductor faced forward, while three passengers behind them faced backward, their knees interlocked with those of the passengers on the middle seat facing forward. In the rear, three sat in relative comfort facing forward. Comfort was only relative as the wagon was only forty-two inches wide. The average human is about twenty inches wide and three on a seat are sixty inches wide, meaning that the two outermost passengers had to dangle one leg over their side of the coach. The seats were not padded. The wagon rolled night and day. With passenger comfort in mind, Butterfield arranged to have the middle seat fold down to form a bed. As Waterman L. Ormsby, the first westbound passenger wrote in 1858:

The first travelers will find it convenient to carry with them as much durable food as possible. As for sleeping, most of the wagons are arranged so that the backs of the seats let down and form a bed the length of the vehicle. When the stage is full, the passengers must take turns at sleeping. Perhaps the jolting will be found disagreeable at first, but a few nights without sleeping will obviate that difficulty, and soon the jolting will be as little of a disturbance as the rocking of a cradle to a suckling babe. For my part, I found no difficulty in sleeping over the roughest roads, and I have no doubt that anyone else will learn quite as quickly. A bounce of the wagon, which makes one's head strike the top, bottom, or sides, will be equally disregarded, and

Overland Mail celerity wagon used in the West. COURTESY OF GERALD AHNERT *"nature's sweet restorer" found as welcome on the hard bottom of the wagon as in downy beds of the St. Nicholas.*[6]

Raphael Pumpelly didn't find the ride quite so comfortable.

At El Paso we had hoped to find a larger stage. Being disappointed in this, I took a place outside, wedged between the driver and conductor. The impossibility of sleeping had made me half delirious, and we had gone but a few miles before I nearly unseated the driver by starting suddenly out of a dream.

I was told that the safety of all the passengers demanded that I should keep awake; and as the only means of affecting this, my neighbors beat a constant tattoo with their elbows upon my ribs. During the journey from the Rio Grande to Tucson my delirium increased and the only thing I have ever remembered of that part of the route was the sight of a large number of Indian camp-fires at Apache Pass. My first recollection after this is of being awakened by the report of a pistol, and of starting up to find myself in a room, where a number of people were gambling. I had reached Tucson, and had thrown myself on the floor of the first room I could enter. A sound sleep of twelve hours had fully restored me, in both mind and body.[7]

In 1858, the Indian Bureau sent Dr. Steck to confer with the Chiricahuas about travel through their country. Cochise agreed to allow the Overland Stage to pass through and to build stations in his country. He agreed not to molest travelers in small parties.[8] Nonetheless, Cochise's father-in-law, Mangas Coloradas, on October 1, 1858, arrived at the Stein's Peak Overland Mail Station and demanded twenty sacks of cornmeal.[9] Although Mangas Coloradas was a Chiricahua Apache, he was from a different band (Bedonkohe) and Cochise (Chokonen) had no authority over him. Nonetheless, this gives some idea of what "peaceful" relations were like. Cochise did not guard the Overland Mail. He tolerated it. He did not openly attack a stagecoach until February 6, 1861, but he did raid the line for stock and his people made some dire threats against the station at Apache Pass. An account in the *Weekly Arizonian* attests to this:

Tubac, March 10, 1859
The Apaches are collecting in large numbers along the Overland Mail Route between the Mimbres and Dragoon Springs. The celebrated chief, Mangus Colorado, who for three years past has been very quiet, is in the field again with a large party of warriors. He declares that if government does not give him more beef and flour he shall let his people take it wherever they please. They have annoyed the mail company very much by filling the road with stones in Apache Pass several times, and now threaten to close the Pass altogether, complaining that government does not pay them enough for using their land.[10]

Similarly, a report in the *Missouri Republican* from mid-May of 1860 mentioned that a "'friendly Apache' reminded the station keeper at Apache Pass that 'it was the intention of the Indians to clean out the station.'"[11]

This must have made life interesting for the tiny bands of Overland Mail personnel at isolated stations fifteen to twenty-five miles from each other and often over one hundred miles from the nearest Army support. Today, that may not sound very far, but in 1860, infantry would have been five days' march away and cavalry three days'. That's a long time to wait with the Apache at the door. With some notable exceptions, Americans and Chiricahua, on the surface at least, tolerated each other. In 1859, Tevis, who hated Cochise but got on with other Apaches, wrote this letter to the weekly *Arizonian*:

Our correspondent at Apache Pass [James Tevis] *sends us the following communication dated July 3d,* [1859]*:*
Mr. Editor: About 20 of our warriors came in from Sonora yesterday, and brought 35 head of cattle and some horses and mules. They took the cattle from Oposura, or vicinity. They are going and coming in small parties all the time.

Ca-Chees [Cochise] has started to the fort with all his band that are not stealing in Sonora, or at least he told me he was going. He is afraid that Capt. Ewell will charge him with stealing the stock from the Patagonia mine, which he knew of before I did. Ca-chees is a very deceptive Indian. At first appearance a man would think he was inclined to be peacable (sic) to Americans, but he is far from it. For eight months I have watched him, and have come to the conclusion that he is the biggest liar in the Territory; and would kill an American for any trifle, provided he thought it wouldn't be found out. He fears the soldiers, and if he was not guilty he would not have cause. The chief Es-co-nella, I believe is the only one that is actually friendly to Americans; his band has not lately been out on any plundering expeditions.

The last time the Coyotero chief, Francisco,[12] was here, he asked me if the Americans were going to buy or take Sonora? I told him I thought they would. He then wanted to know if the Americans would let the Indians steal from Sonora, and I replied that I rather thought not. He then said that as long as he lived and had a warrior to follow him he would fight Sonora, and he did not care if the Americans did try to stop it, he would fight till he was killed. I think he would make his word true.

J.H.T.[13]

Tevis had a role in Cochise's subsequent hostility with the United States and in some of the hostile statements made by Cochise's people concerning the Overland Mail. The Chiricahua took a ten-year-old Mexican, possibly Opata Indian, boy, Merejildo Grijalva, captive. They raised him, and Cochise adopted the intelligent boy, using him as an interpreter. Dr. Steck noticed the boy and had Tevis spirit him out of Apache Pass on an Overland Mail coach. Steck thereafter used the boy as an interpreter.[14]

Tevis's assessment of Cochise as a "very deceptive Indian" should not be taken at face value. Tevis did not like Cochise and claims to have participated in acts that may have undercut the chief's[15] authority. Cochise's first responsibility was to his people and to keeping them fed, a daily challenge in hard times when white encroachment was impinging on available resources and the climate was being uncooperative, reducing the natural resources available. As Ewell noted, the Indians were starving and stealing to live. In such circumstances, a leader is not going to be forthright in dealing with strangers and enemies. All war is deception. When Cochise gave his word to those he thought of as dealing squarely with him, he kept it and forced his people to keep it as well.

In July 1859, returning from raiding Fronteras, Sonora, Mexico, Cochise found that a raid had been committed for which he might be blamed. He visited Fort Buchanan to proclaim his innocence to Captain Ewell.[16] Lieutenant Colonel Reeve recorded the return of the stock:

> *This morning two Chiricahua Indians of Chees [Cochise] came in and brough (sic) (11) eleven of the stolen animals. This band was encamped on the San Pedro and Chees, having heard of the robbery sent and took these animals and sent them in. He sent word that he would try and get all that had been stolen. He says they were stolen by a band of Chiricahuas headed by a chief named "Parte" that they supposed when they took them that they were in Sonora and that the animals belong to Mexicans. . . . Chees appears to be acting in good faith, prompted somewhat, I doubt not, by my visit to the Chiricahua Mountains in search of a site for a post.[17]*

Cochise was prudent, not peaceful. He didn't want to bring on an engagement with the dragoons as long as they were nearby. He also wanted the supplies, two wagonloads every six months, that Dr. Steck had agreed to provide. So it seemed wise to him to agree not to raid in the United States. He would raid in Sonora at least until times grew hard and the authorities in Fronteras offered him a greater amount of supplies with the more frequent deliveries that he preferred.

Later that summer, after Cochise's visit to Fort Buchanan, Indians stole ninety horses and mules from the Sonora Exploring and Mining Company near Tubac. Captain Ewell pursued them but rain obliterated the trail, enough of which remained that the captain concluded that the Chiricahua were responsible. Ewell confronted Cochise, insisting on their return. Cochise also insisted to his people that the stock must be returned. According to Grijalva, Cochise was so incensed that he not only took the stock from the thieves, but also killed one of the warriors responsible. Cochise sent eleven animals to Fort Buchanan. According to Grijalva, Cochise, while continuing raids into Mexico, "had strict orders never to lay hands on anybody or anything within the boundary of the United States."[18]

The extent of Cochise's authority is a matter of speculation. There is no doubt that he was a great chief, perhaps the greatest the Apache ever produced. Within their society, men were free to follow whatever leaders they chose and to stop following when they chose. The society was matrilocal. That means not that women were in charge, but that men went to live with their wives. Women had the only non-portable property. At death they passed this property on to their daughters. Within this property were their gathering sites. The climate in the Southwest is erratic, with rain falling in one place and not in another from year to year. Women respected others' claims to specific sites for gathering food.[19]

Men did not have similar claims to "real property," so they went to live with their wives, who lived with their mothers. A local band, or rancheria, was an extended family, a senior man and his wife, their unmarried children, their married daughters and their husbands and children, and possibly the senior woman's sisters and their husbands and children. Depending on fertility and deaths, a woman might inherit from a childless aunt or from her husband's mother or aunt. There was enough fluidity in this that a man dissatisfied with the leadership of the senior man could easily leave the group with his wife and take up residence with other relatives.

These arrangements tell us that hereditary chieftainship was impossible. Apache married between bands and so a man left his home band and any hereditary claim he might have had. We can see this in the death of Cochise in 1874. Cochise told Tom Jeffords that he wanted him to stay on as the agent. Tom feared that Cochise's people would not listen to him after Cochise was gone, so Cochise called in his sub-chiefs and got them to agree that his son, Taza, would be the new chief. The old chief assured Jeffords that Taza would follow his instructions and listen to the agent.

That Cochise had to call them in and get them to agree tells us that the assumption of leadership was by selection, not heredity.

Cochise's authority extended beyond his rancheria. When he called in sub-chiefs he was calling the heads of other rancherias, other family groups. There were four bands of Chiricahua who take their name from the Chiricahua Mountains where Cochise's Chokonen band lived. These were the Chihenne, from the Warm Springs area of New Mexico; the Nednhi, who lived in Sonora and Chihuahua, Mexico; the Bedonkohe, Mangas Coloradas's people; and the Chokonen. There were three groups of Chokonen. The most pacific and least in number were headed by Chepillo and Esquinaline who lived in the Animas, Peloncillo, and southern Chiricahua Mountains. More militant were the Chokonen who lived in Mexico in the Pitaichache and Teras Mountains under the leadership of Parte, Chino, and Yaque. Cochise led the most militant band of all. It was also the largest group, having six hundred or seven hundred members, living at Apache Pass, Stein's Peak, and in the Dragoon Mountains.[20] Warm Springs, Gila, and Mogollon are all used to refer to various bands of Chiricahua. Cochise seems to have had some authority over all of the Chokonen. What's more, he could count on support from the Bedonkohe. After 1863 and the death of Mangas Coloradas, the Bedonkohe assimilated into other bands. Most of the Bedonkohe opted to follow Cochise. The Apache are defined by the mountains where they lived, that produced the resources they needed. They were not desert Indians. Ed Sweeney, who has studied Cochise and his era extensively and whose writings are well known, wrote of the nature of Chiricahua tribal relations:

The tribal relationship was expressed in many ways: the three[21] peoples were usually at peace with one another, visiting was frequent, and social dances, puberty rites, and marriages were reasons for assembling. The band served as the political unit of the tribe, and an individual remained a member of the one into which he or she was born, except when a man married outside this band. In this case, it was Chiricahua custom for the man to live with his wife's people, and his offspring were known by the affiliation of her band.[22]

Cochise was on good terms with Francisco of the Coyotero or White Mountain Apache. His people intermarried with them, as well as with all of the bands of Chiricahua and to some extent the Mescalero. Relations were considerably less cordial with the Western Apache—Pinals, Aravaipas, Pinaleños, and Tontos—who raided into the Sonoita and Santa Cruz Valleys as well as into Sonora. All of them spoke one language and could understand each other's speech. Naming the bands and calling them tribes was a convenience for the American government and military. It gave them someone with whom to make treaties. For the Indians the situation was more fluid, with relationships that developed more from custom and out of respect than for political purposes. Someone following the bands over time would observe how those relationships ebb and flow, coalesce and disappear. Each man could decide for himself who to follow and where he would live. Leaders exercised influence rather than commanded obedience. A leader had to be strong in war, able to lead his people to prosperity either by raiding or by avoiding conflict, and more than anything able to handle disputes within the group diplomatically and wisely so that all parties were satisfied. Cochise was all of this. Surgeon Irwin described his physical appearance in 1861.

> He was then in the prime of life: tall and well favored in face and figure; about thirty years old and at least six feet in height. His presence was bold and warlike; presenting the attributes of a superb specimen of robust, physical manhood. Conscious of the evil reputation of his tribe and fearing that retribution for their many wicked deeds might overtake him, he declined all overtures and offers made to induce him to visit the military posts.[23]

Ed Sweeney thinks that Cochise was born before 1815, which would have made him forty-six years old in 1861 when Irwin knew him, or perhaps fifty. In 1835, Chees, one of a variety of spellings of Cochise's name, led a party that was raiding in Mexico. The same Indian appears on ration lists at Janos, Chihuahua, Mexico, in 1842 and 1843, at which time he had a wife and child.[24]

By all accounts Cochise was a tall, well-built man, physically a more commanding presence than most of his peers. If he was only five foot, ten inches tall, he would have been five inches taller than most of his followers. Fred Hughes was Tom Jeffords' clerk on the Chiricahua Reservation between 1872 and Cochise's death in June 1874. He knew Cochise intimately and described him in this way:

In conversation, he was very pleasant, and to his family and those immediately around him, he was more affectionate than the average white man; he showed nothing of the brutish nature generally attributed to him. It was astonishing also to see what power he had over this brutal tribe, for while they idolized and almost worshipped him, no man was ever held in greater fear, his glance being enough to squelch the most obstreperous Chiricahua in the tribe.[25]

The leader's name in Apache was probably closer to Cheis than Cochise, and meant oak in that language. The origin of the first syllable is uncertain.

After 1859, his rancheria of about fifteen lodges was in Goodwin Canyon. Apache Pass is in the low point between the Dos Cabezas and Chiricahua Mountains. Two canyons lead toward the pass in parallel, Goodwin and Siphon. The Overland Mail road ran up Siphon Canyon as far as the Apache Pass Station and then departed the canyon, which veered south. The trail continued over low hills going west another two miles up to the pass. Cochise lived about two miles north of the station. Apache Spring was about half a mile east of it. Overlook Ridge formed the southern wall of Siphon Canyon and the spring was on its northern slope, which is to say, the canyon wrapped around the ridge. The approach to the pass from the east is a steep, uphill climb of three miles. The approach from the west is from the gently rising plain of the Sulphur Springs Valley.

As the wives had favored gathering sites, which included stands of manzanita, canyon grape, walnut, choke cherry, oak, yucca, and agave, all of which the Apache used for food, the men had favored campsites.

Cochise had at least one in Doubtful Canyon, another in West Strong-hold Canyon, and a true stronghold at China Meadow, the latter two in the Dragoons. He had another stronghold on Turtle Mountain in Chiricahua Pass at the southern end of the Chiricahua Mountains. There was no seasonal move like the Plains Indians following the buffalo. They moved when resources grew short, and they occupied temporary camps for hunting and harvesting seasonal plants.

Mexico City exercised little control over the outer provinces Chihuahua and Sonora, which a bankrupt Mexico left to fend for themselves. There was no unified plan for dealing with the Apache. Each pursued its own, often to the detriment of the other. Chihuahua would offer regular rations and the Chiricahua would raid in Sonora. If Sonora offered more, they would raid in Chihuahua. In March 1851, in the Carrasco affair, Chihuahuans attacked rancherias near Janos, killing twenty-one Apache and capturing sixty-two, which they sent off to slavery deep in Mexico. In 1857, at Janos the local government issued the Chiricahua poisoned rations. In July 1858, at Fronteras, Sonora, Sonorans trapped and slaughtered Apaches coming in for talks and trade.[26] These were reasons that Cochise lacked trust in whites and why he sent scant few of his people in to talk to the commander at Fort Buchanan. Larger numbers might invite capture or slaughter. Dr. Steck had participated in liberating Merejildo Grijalva, showing that he could not be entirely trusted, nor were Overland Mail employees, who used their stage to smuggle him out.

The *Missouri Republican* carried an express revealing the declining relations. Far from protecting the line, Cochise was now stealing stock.

June 3, 1860

An express just in from the Rio Mimbres, reports that a pack train of 24 mules, heavily loaded with "panocha" or Mexican sugar from Sonora, was attacked by the Apaches near the Hanover Copper Mines, worked by Messrs. Hinkle and Thibault, on the morning of the 20th—five persons killed and the whole train captured. The same Indians have also succeeded in stealing all the mules from Ewell's Station Overland Mail Company as well as from Dragoon Springs Station.[27]

Ewell's Station was the next station west of Apache Pass and Dragoon Springs, at the northern end of the Dragoon Mountains. In 1874, Samuel Woodworth Cozzens produced a book detailing his adventures in Arizona and New Mexico, *The Marvelous Country*. He made reference to an April 7, 1860, stock raid by the Chokonen on the Dragoon Springs Station. Cochise himself was suspected.[28]

The decline in friendly relations between the Overland Mail and Cochise may have begun in January 1860, when John Wilson killed one of Cochise's Mexican captives, Jose.[29] The other station employees at least considered the fight fair as both were armed with knives.[30] It was soon after this, on January 14, that a stage driver noted that the Chiricahuas were giving "intimations of extensive preparations for the total extermination of the Overland Mail . . . to be followed by a descent upon the settlements."

Actions by Cochise were not without provocation. Apache Pass was on the Emigrant Trail and the Overland Mail Road. It was becoming a busy place. With more interaction between whites and Chiricahua there were bound to be more unfortunate incidents. Cochise, already wary of whites in the form of Mexicans, became distrustful of Americans as well. Mexico strengthened her border defenses even as American defenses weakened. Mexico offered more and more regular rations. The tide was turning in Mexico's favor. The picture emerging is not one of Cochise the always friendly who protected the Overland Mail Road. Rather he was Cochise the ever tolerant and always wary. He was Cochise who saw to the interests of his people and who did not provoke the army near at hand.

In 1859, Lieutenant Colonel Reeve faced a similar problem and wrote from Fort Buchanan: "Should all the available force be sent after any one of these tribes, it would bring down a war of destruction upon this greatly exposed mail route, and it would be impossible to give it protection. I do not see, therefore, any course to be pursued for the present, but the highly objectionable one of temporizing."[31]

The dragoons might occasionally intimidate the Apache, but they were too weak a force to subdue them. The Army needed Cochise's goodwill, for he was capable of closing down the vital mail route that united

California to the Union and ensured a supply of much needed specie. Even though the Overland Mail never carried bullion shipments, the mail was crucial, and the Union needed to keep the gold flowing by sea. It was fortunate that the stations and the stages were heavily armed, since the passengers were advised to carry arms, and that the stages carried little that Cochise needed.

Chapter Seven

APACHE FIGHT FOR SURVIVAL

IT HARDLY SEEMS ENOUGH TO SAY THAT THE CHOKONEN WERE hunter-gatherers. The Sioux hunted buffalo and followed the herds. Their diet leaned heavily to meat. There were no herds of buffalo in Arizona. There was very little game at all. All North American Indians hunted to some degree. The only domestic animals they kept were the turkey, the horse, and the dog.[1] All of them were aware of farming techniques and most farmed in one way or another. Apaches were known to sow crops at arroyo mouths and in other places they knew would become wet during the summer rains. They would sow, depart, and return in the fall. At least one source says the Chiricahua were the only Apaches who did not do this. That seems unlikely, and such farming techniques would be easy to miss and might well have ceased during their extended twenty-five-year war with the United States and thus not have been remembered by the younger generation anthropologists had available to interview. Some archaeologists believe that Native Americans modified their environment in ways we should think of as husbandry and farming, so that the environment would produce more of the crops and animals that they favored.

There are many accounts of the Chiricahua lighting the grass on fire over extensive areas. This would have the effect of burning out woody growths of mesquite (outside wash bottoms), whitethorn acacia, and creosote bush, all of which inhibit the growth of grass. Grass feeds the wild horse, deer, and antelope, all valuable as food. The valleys are now choked with these woody growths where the grass was high when whites arrived.

In 1846, along the San Pedro River, the Mormon Battalion fought what was once known as the Battle of Bull Run. Their descendants have since renamed it the Battle of the Bulls. The battalion shot a few wild bulls in an area of tall Sacaton grass. The bulls retaliated, their approach hidden in the high grass, goring several soldiers and tipping over wagons. In the 1830s, a Mexican family had tried to ranch on the Mexican Babocomari Land Grant along the creek of the same name which flows from the west near Fort Buchanan into the San Pedro River. After Apaches killed one of the brothers, the remaining family gave up the effort and turned their cattle loose. During the ensuing years, the Apache hunted the cows, since they were easier to bring down, for meat. What remained in 1846 was a herd of very ill-tempered, sexually frustrated bulls.

The climate of the southwest is monsoonal. That means that during part of the year, late June through September, the wind tends to blow from one direction, southwest, bringing with it higher humidity and rain from the Pacific. Because of this, the summer is cooler than the late spring and early fall. Days dawn clear, clouds build over the mountains, and late in the day there are thundershowers. From a hilltop, one can sometimes watch several storms raining on different parts of the valley floor and on the mountains while places in between remain dry. The monsoon itself is highly variable, arriving late and leaving early, coming weak or strong, depositing anywhere from five to fifteen inches of rain in its course. Winter and spring rains are usually sparse. Depending on when the rain clouds come and how much liquid they carry, plants that grow in profusion one year and in one place might not be seen again for twenty-five years or more.

Canyon grapes, which grow in the canyons where there is moisture, are small but, although native, closely related to domestic varieties. The Apache used them to sweeten their food. Manzanita, the little apple, produces in profusion a fruit about a quarter of an inch in diameter. Although unrelated, it resembles an apple in color, texture, and flavor and produces reliably on the hillsides. The Apache used acorns, although bitter, to make a kind of flour and as a thickener in stews and soups. They used mesquite beans, another very reliable producer, to make sweetish flour. The banana yucca produces a large fruit, which they ate. The agave, or century plant, which matures after seventeen or more years, sends up a tall stalk and produces evil-smelling flowers that attract bats. The Apache watch for the growth of the stalk and harvest the plant just as it begins to grow, cutting off the great, sharp leaves like a giant artichoke. They cook this for days in rock-lined pits until all the sugar can be harvested from the sweet pulp. The plant is also known as mescal, giving name to the Mescalero Apache, and is the source of Mexican tequila.

Women built wickiup lodges, poles lashed together at the top, creating a nest eight or ten feet in diameter covered with bear grass thatch or skins. They gathered plants in patches claimed by their mothers and mothers' mothers. They gathered firewood and often hay for sale and wild grain for food. They tanned skins, made baskets to carry their few possessions, ground corn on stone metates, and cooked for their families as they cared for their children. The men gambled on various games, hunted when it suited them, and planned the next raid.

The Apache are not horse Indians. They ride well but are as likely to eat a horse, a great delicacy, as ride it. The rocky soil of the southwest is not kind to horses and the Apache were great walkers. Frustrating pursuit, they would ride a horse to death, eat it, and steal another.

With variation in climate came variation in animal productivity. A good growing season would mean more rabbits, deer, and antelope followed by seasons of predator productivity. The Apache did not eat their brother the bear. It was considered cannibalism. Nor did they eat fish, which they thought of as related to snakes. The Apache did not touch snakes. Touching them, they believed, causes arthritis.

Like Vikings of old, the Apache were great traders. They carried goods from afar. When the people they were trading with proved weak, the Apache became raiders. By the nineteenth century, the Chiricahua were wearing cloth, not leather clothing. Trade and raiding had become dominant over hunting. When plant and animal productivity were down, as they were in the late 1850s and early 1860s, the Chiricahua had to raid to live. As Captain Ewell noted, they were starving, and famine prompted them to attack settlements in New Mexico and Arizona.[2] Dr. Steck was providing only a few wagonloads of food and goods. Their main complaint against Americans was the paucity and infrequency of rations and presents. Consequently, they sought greener pastures in Mexico. At Janos they resumed negotiations with their sometime adversary and sometime friend, Jose Maria Zuloaga.[3] They could buy or trade for cornmeal and beans and take it away in packs. Livestock traveled on its own feet and was thus easy to take away in a raid. Horses, mules, and cattle were all food.

The Chiricahua did not go to war for glory. They went to war for revenge when an enemy had slain an Apache. And they raided for food and for goods to trade for food. They were careful of their own lives. They fought in small parties, attacking from ambush, preserving their Apache lives. During most periods, they were not fighting to drive their enemies out of their country. They did not fight to hold terrain. They would much rather collect a "tax" on their adversaries than drive them away. If they stole from an enemy, leaving him alive, they could return in the future to steal from him again. Only when someone killed an Apache did they retaliate in kind. It might be better to allow the Apache to steal your horses than to shoot one and have them return for vengeance. For a brief period, between August of 1861 and July of 1862, the Chiricahua changed tactics and tried to drive the Americans out. This was because they thought they'd won a war. The Army left to go fight in the east and they were aware of it. The mail stopped running and they were aware of the change. The settlers left and Cochise and Mangas Coloradas attacked the wagon train. They attacked Tubac, Pinos Altos, and finally the California Column's lead companies in the Battle of Apache Pass. Attacks on towns and on the Army were not usual. This was a change of tactics prompted by their awareness of the distant Civil War and that something grave had happened to the Americans.

The Chiricahua did not usually take scalps except as an insult, after which they threw them away, unlike the Plains tribes, who made a cult of scalp taking. The Apache were unusually conscious of what bound a person to life. Basket weavers always left a flaw in their work, a trail leading from the center to the edge, by which the weaver's spirit might escape rather than be trapped forever in the basket. Likewise, things that a person loved in life followed them into the grave. Apache funerals were hasty affairs, the idea being to get rid of the body, which might contaminate the band, as quickly as possible. They did not like touching the dead. Even so, everything that a person loved in life went into the grave with him or her. In 1874, Cochise was buried wrapped in his favorite blanket given him by Henry Hooker, with his pistols strapped on and his rifle at his side. Finally, his favorite horse was shot and followed him into the grave. This wasn't so that he would have them in the afterlife. It was so that they would not call his spirit back from the grave. Even the deceased's name was not spoken again for fear it would bring him back.

It is difficult to imagine a people so repelled by touching the dead as being involved in postmortem mutilations. They did practice torture. There are many outstanding and well-known cases of torture by fire, but these may not be as common as Hollywood and dime novels make out. The bodies of six Apache hanged at Apache Pass in February 1861 remained in place for many months. There is no reason to believe that there was a cultural taboo against being hanged. It was enough that they did not like to touch dead bodies. Much of the mutilation attributed to Apache torture may have resulted from scavenger activity after death.[4]

Most of the time, especially before the summer of 1861 and the Civil War, Apache raiding was a matter of survival. They raided for food and for needed supplies. This made them easier to perceive as bands of outlaws and thieves, than as enemy soldiers. Many Americans and soldiers did see them in this light. They weren't fighting to drive the enemy from their country. The manner of pursuit employed against them was more like the capture of criminals than fighting soldiers and involved the Army in acting as a police force, a task for which it was ill-equipped and trained.

Part of Cochise's greatness lay in refusing peace terms until peace was made on the terms he demanded and he got a reservation in his own country. He came to own the Dragoon, Chiricahua, Dos Cabezas, and Peloncillo Mountain ranges and the valleys in between, the land that had always been his. In 1872, General O. O. Howard, acting directly for President Grant, gave him everything he had demanded. However, in 1860 and 1861, it was still easier to view the Apache as parasitic outlaws.

Cochise was wary of councils with the enemy. Much of his experience came from dealing with Mexicans, who were often duplicitous, treating the Apache as vermin to be exterminated. Apache researcher Ed Sweeney, who has studied the life of Cochise, concluded that "The Mexicans invited Cochise's father and some of his noted warriors to a feast and by treachery, got him and his warriors drunk and killed them."[5] He may have lost an elder brother in a similar event. In March 1837, Governor Escalante y Arvizu declared "War to the death to the enemy," the Apache. John Johnson was an Anglo living in Sonora. The governor gave him permission to track down hostiles, granting him half of the stolen stock recovered. At Fronteras on April 12, Commander Antonio Narbona gave Johnson a small cannon. He traded with the Apache in whiskey and sundries for stolen mules. On April 22, while trading, Johnson fired his cannon loaded with metallic scrap into the Apache, killing many.

In 1839, recognizing that their troops were no match for the mobile, quick-striking Apaches, the government of Chihuahua hired scalp hunter James Kirker to kill them. In 1840, Chihuahua's new governor, Francisco Garcia Conde, withdrew the contract on humanitarian grounds. On July 4, 1842, Chihuahua concluded a peace treaty with the Chokonen and Bedonkohe by which they agreed to cease hostilities, to deliver captives and stolen horses, and to establish their rancherias near Janos. Governor Conde agreed to issue weekly rations of corn, tobacco, sugar, and meat. The Chiricahua continued to raid into Sonora. Relations broke down over the course of years. In 1846, Chihuahua again hired James Kirker and his band of mercenaries. The Apache were invited to a feast and when they came, under protection of treaty, mescal and whiskey flowed freely. Kirker and his men killed perhaps as many as 130 of the inebriated Chiricahuas. Cochise had reason to be wary of councils with both Mexicans and Americans, although the Americans who had betrayed them were operating in Mexico on behalf of the governments of Sonora and Chihuahua.

With relations at low ebb with both Mexican states, Cochise was willing to accept annuities from the United States in compensation for not raiding north of the border. Initially, Pinal Apaches were Fort Buchanan's greatest worry. On January 27, 1859, Pinals killed two soldiers on leave from the fort. At about that time, the Chiricahua also began to demonstrate their dissatisfaction with the status quo. Captain Ewell accompanied Dr. Steck, the U.S. Indian agent, to a meeting with Cochise. The Indian leader agreed to stop raiding north of the border and Steck agreed to provide food and gifts twice per year.[6] Ultimately, this arrangement proved to be too little and too irregular for Cochise's satisfaction. He preferred the more regular system of rations issue provided by Mexican governments. In December 1860, he sent Yones, his brother Coyuntura's wife, along with Chiquito Teboca, to Fronteras to seek peace and rations.[7]

In late 1859, Americans killed a Chokonen in the act of stealing a horse. According to James Tevis, station keeper, Cochise was so incensed that he ordered his warriors to kill anyone who went for water at Apache Springs. This did not, however, lead to any immediate tragedy. But to Chokonen, thinking it demanded revenge. In December 1859, Thomas Smith, who ranched in Sonora thirty miles below the border, pursued raiders and killed three while recovering his stock. In January 1860, the Chokonen took their revenge, attacking two of Charles Hayden's freight wagons at Apache Pass, and killing a couple of oxen.[8] During the winter and spring of 1860, Chokonen raided regularly.

In June 1860, they raided the Santa Rita Mining Company and ran off the entire herd. On June 5, they raided another herd only four miles from Fort Buchanan. Captain Ewell took the field and set out to confront Cochise at Apache Pass at the head of forty dragoons. Cochise pleaded innocence, which Ewell refused to accept. He warned the chief that he would return.[9] Returning, Captain Ewell searched the Chiricahua Mountains without locating the stock and then after two weeks returned to Cochise with even more dragoons at his back.[10]

Even as relations with the Chokonen deteriorated, Ewell was facing problems with Western Apaches, Pinals, and Tontos. His most successful mission took place in March 1860, when he recovered a young girl stolen by Apaches. He was hailed a hero at the Territorial Convention in Tucson meeting the day he returned with the young lady. This cemented his reputation as a great Indian fighter.

This story was still fresh when Lieutenant George Bascom arrived in Arizona a few months later in October 1860. He would have heard it and learned from it. Meanwhile, the fall and early winter of 1860 brought seriously deteriorating relations with the Apache.

St. Louis Republican, *Tubac, October 2d, 1860*
Ft. Breckenridge was visited on the morning of the 28th ult., about nine o'clock, by one hundred and fifty Indians on a marauding expedition. They drove off all the stock at the post excepting three horses and one steer. The latter was well riddled with lance wounds. This was all done under the eye of the Commandant [Lieutenant John Cooke] and his troops, who were powerless to offer resistance. The settlers generally are much rejoiced over the event, and indulge in the delusive hope that the War Department will awake to a realizing sense of our defenceless [sic] and exposed condition when it is seen that a military garrison, established expressly for their protection, can not [sic] only offer them no assistance but is unable to successfully repel an attack upon the post itself.
Lieutenant Cooke, the Commandant, immediately dispatched a courier to Fort Buchanan asking for assistance. The messenger while on his way met Lieutenant Randal, 1st Dragoons, with thirty men, who was proceeding to make a reconnaissance of the pinery in the Pinal Mountains, with the hope of finding an accessible route for a wagon road to Fort Breckenridge.[11]

The newspaper writer, presumably Thompson Turner, seems sarcastic in noting that Lieutenant Randal promptly set out to find a road to the pinery rather than pursuing the Apaches and the stolen stock. If the report of a raiding party of 150 Indians is accurate, then he might have found himself outnumbered and decided to continue following the orders he'd been given, to locate a road to the pinery, instead of pursuing the raiders. The dragoons were still at Fort Buchanan but within weeks they would move to Fort Breckenridge.

St. Louis Republican, *Tucson, October 16, 1860*
At Tubac a band of Apaches, on the 11th, shot some four cows and drove off three head of horses in sight of the town *(emphasis added),*

recent successes have rendered them very daring. They were followed but not overtaken.[12]

St. Louis Republican, *Tucson, November 11, 1860*
W.F. Ward, of Dardswill, Yell County, Arkansas, was murdered on the Reserve at Ft. Buchanan about 8 o'clock in the evening of the 3d. He was shot in the breast by some person unknown, concealed in ambush, and lived but three hours. He was not more than 500 yards from the barracks when fired upon.[13]

St. Louis Republican, *Tucson, November 19, 1860*
The Apaches still continue to manifest their hostility toward the whites and, no longer content with committing depredations, endeavor to kill all whom they encounter when not intimidated by superior numbers. It is now ascertained that the murder of a young man from Arkansas who was shot on the reservation at Fort Buchanan, an account of which I transmitted you last week, was perpetrated by Apaches in ambush. We hear accounts every few days of some one having been chased by Indian parties too large for one man to cope with. Indeed, they appear to fully comprehend that our infantry soldiers can afford us no protection, and are daily becoming more daring. I learn that my strictures on this branch of the service are not well received by the officers composing it. But if my objections to placing infantry upon an Indian frontier as a protection to settlers are ill-founded, if my argument is illogical, why is it not proved so by actual results? Col. Morrison arrived at Fort Buchanan with his command nearly two months ago and the troops are now fully rested from the fatigues of their journey. If infantry are adapted to the service for which these troops were sent here, the defense from the Indians of an exposed frontier, why is not some attempt made to prevent these frequent aggressions? . . . By these remarks I do not mean to disparage the infantry branch of the service. The officers are gentlemen of finished education and would adorn any position, while the privates are able-bodied and brave, calculated to reflect honor to the nation in civilized warfare. It is not

their fault, but their misfortune, that they are placed in a position of almost utter uselessness. *(emphasis added)*[14]

The Apaches were growing bold. They had also begun killing people instead of just stock stealing. And the infantry was so powerless that the Apache were raiding close to the fort and even killed a man in the fort.

Problems with the Indians continued without respite into the winter, culminating in the abduction of Felix Ward and theft of his stepfather's cattle. There was no lull, nor was Lieutenant Colonel Morrison successful in chastising the culprits.

The Pinals were giving trouble. So were the Chokonen, who were clearly not peaceful and not guarding the Overland Mail. They were desperate, starving, and raiding for food, but in 1860 a new element entered in. They had always taken Mexican captives, but now they were taking captives north of the border. They had always raided except for a few brief months when Cochise did his best to keep his people from raiding Americans. Now they were killing people as well. Since the departure of Captain Richard Ewell and the movement of the dragoons to Fort Breckenridge distant from the population centers at Sonoita Creek, Tubac, and Tucson, it seemed the military was powerless to do anything about the Apache who were raiding the military posts as well as the settlements.

Lieutenant Colonel Pitcairn Morrison, commander of the 7th Infantry, was an old man about to apply for medical retirement. He was probably ready to go home. The lieutenants under him had their whole careers ahead of them. They were steeped in competition both academic and in sports. Military leaders have to be strong competitors who wish to win no matter how the odds are against them. Their education trains them for this role. These insults to their pride must have been galling. They were probably also aware that Captain Ewell had made it clear that his next confrontation with Cochise would not be a friendly one. He would employ all the force at his disposal.

Chapter Eight

THE RAID ON JOHNNY WARD'S RANCH

THE BOY, SMALL FOR HIS AGE, SAT IN THE CROTCH OF A COTTONWOOD tree next to clear flowing Sonoita Creek minding his father's cattle. He was happy here and so was his mother for the first time in many years. She no longer had to worry about where the next meal was coming from. Papa Juan would provide. She had given Papa Juan a baby girl a year ago and his young brother, Santiago, had just been born. There had been a sound. He spun about, tossing his long dark red hair. His one blue eye, the other blind since infancy, looked intently into the brush beside the creek searching for movement or anything that should be there. The boy had the look of one descended from northern Spain where Celtic people related to those in Ireland lived, but born in Sonora he had no inkling of this. The cattle moved about nervously, sniffing the air. There was something there, a mountain lion or lobo.

From higher up the slope toward the boy's home, Mr. Cole lay on his sickbed in the wheelwright and blacksmith shop he ran in partnership with the boy's father. He noted the discomfiture and how the cows seemed ill at ease. He reached for his rifle, but could barely lift it. He cursed. He'd be of little help to the boy.

At the house, the boy's mother and her sister and elder daughter, almost the boy's age, worked grinding corn and making tortillas. Their stove and oven were outside the two-room windowless adobe house. The youngest two children were swaddled near at hand. There was no fireplace in the house. Juan kept promising to build one when there was time, but the climate didn't really require it and the adobe held the day's heat in winter and the night's coolness in summer. The woman smiled at her children and at her home. Juan had built a stout door to keep them safe and put small loopholes in the wall so he could fire on Indios. She was glad her sister had come to help with the newborn, Santiago.

She looked across the field to her eldest son. He was running toward the house pursued by an Indian. Two others were herding the cattle north along the stream. Screaming to her sister, they gathered the young children into the house and barred the door. She peeped through a porthole and saw the Indio had captured her Felix. She began to cry. They were sure to kill him. If he were younger, they might adopt him. But he was too old.

Cole watched as another group of Indians emerged and tried to break down the door to the house. He reached again for his rifle and again found himself too weak to employ it. Better to lie still and hope they didn't notice him, he thought. Two riders appeared at a bend in the canyon. Taking in the situation they shouted a war cry. Cole recognized neighbors McCarty and Wilson returning from Tubac. Their sudden appearance startled the Apache, who headed north up the valley with the boy and the cattle.

The boy knew he had to keep up. If he lagged, they would kill him for sure. The warriors kept looking behind for pursuit. Soon they split up. One group took the cattle and he went with the other. He remembered passing Fort Buchanan and turning east along Babocomari Creek. After that he remembered little of the journey. He was exhausted, but he kept putting one foot in front of the other. His throat was dry. He staggered through the night and they continued toward the rising sun.

Johnny Ward's ranch was at the southern end of the Sonoita Creek Valley about twelve miles from Fort Buchanan where the valley narrows into the canyon, which stretches to the Santa Cruz River. It is a beautiful spot where colorful cliffs and rocky fells rise close at hand. The valley floor is still grassy and the stream flows clear between cottonwood and sycamore trees. Indians chose this spot hundreds of years before the Irishman arrived. Johnny accidentally incorporated their broken pottery into the adobe walls of the house. An ancient irrigation ditch runs almost to the door.

Johnny Ward's ranch, ca. 1900. ARIZONA HISTORICAL SOCIETY

The house is on the hillside with rocky cliffs above looking down to the stream one hundred yards away. At some point, possibly in the 1920s, road builders made a cut in the hill and took away half of the house. It's difficult to tell exactly what Johnny Ward's home was like. Today parts of three rooms remain. In one is a wall that blocks off part of the room with no apparent purpose. There is no door to the rest of the house in that wall. The structure was repurposed a number of times after the Wards left and was in use until after 1900. It shows signs of having had a number of large windows facing the hillside. It seems unlikely that Ward would have had glass windows. In the 1864 census he listed himself as a glass blower, but that requires a different technique from producing flat panes of glass. Moreover, it's doubtful that the machinery to produce flat glass panes was available in Arizona, and freighting glass panes would have been very expensive. With the Apache constantly prowling the valley, most people had firing ports for defense. Plenty of broken glass litters the home site, but it's not clear that it comes from Johnny Ward's occupation.

In 1825, the Mexican government granted eighty-six hundred acres along Sonoita Creek, the San Jose de Sonoita Grant, to Don Leon Herreras. Apaches drove him out in 1833; he returned, only to be driven out again in 1836. It is possible that Johnny Ward moved into his abandoned hacienda, but the artifacts recovered at the site do not date from the 1830s.[1] Ward arrived in the area in 1858 and worked with Pete Kitchen at Potrero Ranch cutting hay for the dragoons. In late 1858 or 1859, he moved on to Sonoita Creek along with his common-law wife, Jesusa Martinez. Ward was in his early fifties, and she was much younger and already had two children, a boy of about ten years, Felix Tellez, a very light Mexican with blue eyes and reddish-brown hair, and a young daughter, Teodora. On July 25, 1860, the second of their children together entered the world. They named him Santiago, or James.[2] Johnny Ward seems to have liked Jesusa's eldest son a great deal. Everyone came to call him Felix Ward.

Ward seems to have done well for himself selling hay and beef to the army at Fort Buchanan, although he was not the contractor and may have sold through an intermediary. He probably also sold to the Patagonia and Santa Rita Mines. He soon had partners in the ranch:

Johnny Ward's ranch today. DOUG HOCKING

Andrew J. Nicherson & Cole
Blacksmiths and Wheelwrights;
Ward's Ranche, Sonoita Valley.
The above firm are prepared to do all work in the line of their busi-
ness, in a neat and durable style. Wagons made and repaired; all sorts
of blacksmithing done, including horse and mule shoeing, with the
utmost despatch [sic] *and at reasonable prices.*[3]

This ad appeared in the first edition of the *Weekly Arizonian* and continued thereafter through every edition. We know that Cole was still present in January of 1861. We learn from this ad that Ward's ranch was so well known that it was used to give directions. The ranch was located where the wagon road from Fort Buchanan turned westward into the pass between the San Cayetano and Santa Rita Mountains and thence to Tubac. Ward had a stable relationship with his partners, as the partnership continued up until the area was abandoned at the beginning of the Civil War. Johnny Ward was a man of substance with a new wife, children, cattle, land, and business partners. He was doing well.

There were other settlers in the valley north of Ward's ranch. The United States Boundary Hotel, also called the Casa Blanca, was located near Monkey Springs, three miles south of Fort Buchanan just off the military reservation where its owner, James "Paddy" Graydon, didn't have to obey the dictates of the post commander. Sarah Bowman, the Great Western, ran the hotel for Mr. Graydon. There were other settlers and ranches: Ash, Titus, Marshall, Finley, Pennington, Grundy Ake, and Wordsworth (or Wadsworth). On January 27, 1861, tragedy struck.

The Arizonian *further says, concerning the Apache depredations which led to the attack on the Overland Mail:*

"*Scarcely a day passes without out hearing of some new foray made by the savages who infest our border, upon the unprotected settlers. On the 27th ult. a Mexican boy, about twelve years of age, was taken captive by them on the Sonoita from Ward's rancho. Nine Indians were seen by Mr. Cole, who was lying sick near Mr. Ward's residence. They tried to capture the women and children at the house, but were prevented by the opportune arrival of Messrs. McCarty and Wilson, who happened fortunately, to be in the vicinity. They succeeded however, in capturing a boy who was several hundred yards from the house. Another party were at the same time engaged in stealing Mr. Ward's cattle. Messrs. McCarty and Wilson pursued the Indians some distance, hoping to rescue the boy, but they did not succeed in overtaking the party, and they escaped with the prisoner and 20 head of cattle. Mr. Ward was in Sonora on the day of this misfortune. A courier was dispatched to Ft. Buchanan with the intelligence and next morning Lieut. Bascom started out to examine the trail. A detachment of dragoons were providentially at the post, having accompanied Lieut. Lord as an escort. The latter gallant young officer was sitting on a Court Martial, and unable himself to leave, turned over his men to the command of Lieut. Bascom. Nothing was accomplished, however, and on the 29th Lieut. Col. Morrison sent out*

60 men to pursue the Indians and rescue the prisoner if possible. The soldiers had not returned at last advice."[4]

Mr. John Cole saw the whole raid from his sickbed. He watched the Apache try to capture the women and children in the house. Cole was not living in the same house. He had separate quarters probably at his wheelwright's shop, which so far has not been located.[5] The Indians did not manage to enter Mr. Ward's house. This suggests a solid door. The lintel is still there for a wooden door. And it suggests a lack of large glass windows, which could have easily been broken. Like his neighbor, Graydon, Ward had built his house like a fortress.

On January 28, Johnny Ward returned and took word of the abduction and cattle theft immediately to Lieutenant Colonel Pitcairn Morrison at Fort Buchanan. A herd of cattle leaves a discernable trail in cow pies if nothing else. Morrison immediately dispatched Lieutenant George Bascom to search for a trail. Bascom went out in the morning of January 28 probably accompanied by some of the same frontiersmen who brought the word of the raid to the fort, Johnny Ward among them. He could not locate a trail. He returned to the post. There he met Lieutenant Lord visiting from Fort Breckenridge with an escort of dragoons. This escort undoubtedly did not include First Sergeant Reuben Bernard, since Lord was the only officer present for duty in that company.[6]

Court martial duty was onerous. Unfortunately, it was the only recourse, even for minor infractions. There was no system of non-judicial punishment as there is today.[7] The commander had to empanel a board of officers fairly and that meant drawing them from other posts. Serious violators spent months in confinement awaiting the next court martial board, and then over the course of several days, the board tried many cases. In addition, there was no charge of absent without leave. If a man wasn't present for duty, he was a deserter, even if he always planned to return and was only away a few days. This makes it appear that desertion rates were much higher than they really were, and the need for court martial and pre-trial confinement makes it appear that discipline was much worse than it really was.

In the afternoon of January 28, Bascom went out again. This time he had dragoons with him. Some of them likely had been serving in Arizona since 1856. Some had ridden with Captain Ewell in 1860 on the occasions when he confronted Cochise at Apache Pass. They knew that Cochise's people, the Chokonen, had been raiding into the Sonoita Creek area and that they had raided the Overland Mail. Working with Bascom, they located a trail that led east along the Babocomari Creek. How far they followed the trail is uncertain. They were only gone five or six hours. At six miles per hour on horseback, they'd have gone eighteen or twenty miles, perhaps as far as the Mustang Mountains, before turning back.

Before they left Fort Buchanan in October 1860, Lieutenants Isaiah Moore and Richard Lord and other officers assigned to the dragoons—along with Surgeon Irwin who stayed on at the fort—would have told the incoming officers about their experiences with the Apaches. They'd have mentioned that the most common raiders were Pinal and Aravaipa Apaches who lived near where the San Pedro River flowed into the Gila. The next most common raiders were Tonto Apaches, who lived far to the north, and Coyotero Apaches, who lived north and east of Fort Buchanan in the White Mountains. These latter were under pressure from the Navajo, who in turn were under pressure from the U.S. Army in New Mexico. The Navajo were pushing the Coyotero further south. They'd have gone on to explain how these raiders, after hitting Sonora and the settlements along the Santa Cruz River and Sonoita Creek, returned north through the Santa Rita Mountains and along Ciénega Creek between those mountains and the Whetstones. From there they followed the Rillito to Redington Pass, which took them to the San Pedro River. When the Chiricahua raided, they avoided the San Pedro Station and Dragoon Springs and instead went east along the Babocomari to the San Pedro, around the southern reach of the Dragoon Mountains to Soldier's Holes, and then on to Turkey Creek and Apache Pass. Once they reached the Dragoon Mountains, the Chokonen were in their own country. In the past, any trail that led east along the Babocomari Creek had led to Cochise and his people. Western Apache and Coyoteros went north while Chokonen went east.

Since their arrival in October 1860, the dragoons had been patrolling the northern reaches of the San Pedro River from their base at Fort Breckenridge. They were short of officers and, as always, short of horses. They were just settling in to their new home and had not undertaken any major pursuits, although raiding had increased, especially raiding by Coyoteros and Chokonen.

We may suppose that on Monday morning, January 28, 1861, when Lieutenant Bascom went out he likely was mounted on a mule with a handful of infantry in train, and perhaps a few frontiersmen, including Johnny Ward, riding from the nearby Santa Rita Mountains east across Ciénega Creek hoping to cut a trail. He didn't find one. In the afternoon he went out again, this time with the loan of Lieutenant Lord's experienced dragoon escort. The dragoons suggested that they try to cut the trail of Chokonen raiders going east. They located the trail and followed it far enough to confirm that the trail, after avoiding the fort, did not turn north along Ciénega Creek, but instead continued east along the Babocomari. Time did not allow them to go much further than the Mustang Mountains south of the Whetstones, but that was far enough to show that the trail did not lead to Western Apache (Pinal, Aravaipa, Tonto) country.

What neither Lieutenants Bascom and Lord nor the dragoons realized at the time was that there had been a change in raiding patterns. The presence of dragoon patrols on the lower San Pedro had forced a change in trails. The Western Apache and the Coyoteros were no longer going north along Ciénega Creek. They were going east around the Dragoons all the way to the Sulphur Springs Valley between the Dragoon and Chiricahua Mountains. This was especially true of the Coyoteros, who had been driven further south recently.[8] Cochise was well aware that Coyoteros were crossing his country. That was okay with him. He was on friendly terms with their chief, Francisco. He may have been less aware of the Pinals, Tontos, and Aravaipa, with whom he was not friendly. When Surgeon Irwin came to Bascom's relief at Apache Pass, he would encounter and capture Coyotero raiders returning home across the Sulphur Springs Valley. Cochise told Bascom that if the lieutenant would wait for ten days he thought he could find and bring in the stolen boy,

Felix Ward. It would have taken him about that long to ride to Francisco's camp in the White Mountains and return.

Colonel Morrison's Post Order No. 4 ordered Bascom to proceed to Apache Pass with the balance of Company C, 7th Infantry.[9] The company marched out of Fort Buchanan the morning of Tuesday, January 29. Lieutenant Bascom later reported: "I have the honor to report that in compliance with the foregoing Orders; I left Fort Buchanan on the 29th ult. and arrived at Apache Pass on the 3rd inst.; feeling confident that they [Chokonen] had the boy."[10] Bascom led a company of fifty-four men.[11] At Apache Pass twelve more would join his force.[12]

On January 29, 1861, when Lieutenant Bascom and his men marched out of Fort Buchanan, Lieutenant Colonel Morrison knew that Bascom was bound for Apache Pass to confront Cochise. The lieutenant wasn't following a trail that he somehow lost. The trail he discovered the day before had already demonstrated, rightly or wrongly, that Cochise's Chokonen were the culprits. He didn't choose Cochise as a random target. He was sent by his commander to confront Cochise. Johnny Ward knew this. Lieutenant Lord and his dragoon escort knew and so did Surgeon Irwin. Even Lieutenant Marmaduke, who left Fort Buchanan bound for the Rio Grande at about this time, knew that the Chokonen were the target.[13]

We have a hard time shaking the notion that this was a young second lieutenant at the head of a small patrol. The Bernard story tells us that Bascom led twelve dragoons. That has been the image repeated over and over in many of the secondary sources. The historian needs to free him- or herself from this notion. It's not correct. This was a major expedition. The force that Captain Ewell led against the Chokonen was barely this large. Colonel Benjamin L. E. Bonneville had led something larger in 1857, the force Ewell called the "solumn" (solid column) of six hundred men, which advanced along the Gila River to little effect.[14] That was an effort by the entire Department of New Mexico. In late fall of 1859, Colonel Isaac Van Duzer Reeve took the field from Fort Buchanan with 176 men of Companies D and G, 1st Dragoons, and Companies A, C, and F of the Mounted Rifles. This force killed eight Apaches along the San Pedro River. He rounded up more than forty Apache women and children.[15] His effort to suppress the Pinal Apache had some effect in that in January 1860, the Pinals came to Fort Buchanan to sue for peace and Reeve released some of the hostages. In March 1860, Captain Ewell exchanged the remainder for Mercedes Quiroz. Captain Ewell seldom had more than thirty-five dragoons available for field operations. Bascom's force was one of the largest yet to proceed into Chokonen country.

Bascom would lose forty mules to Cochise at Apache Pass. Sergeant Robinson reported that the command had more than fifty. When Sergeant Daniel Robinson joined Bascom on Sunday, February 3, the sergeant had four wagons, each pulled by four mules. He may have had as many as five men riding. That's twenty-one mules. The rest came with Bascom's column. The lieutenant had pack mules carrying casks and supplies, a few men mounted, and three wagons carrying tentage and supplies. He was carrying rations for twenty days, nine tents for his men, bedding, ammunition, field cooking equipment, and other supplies. In short, Bascom marched at the head of one of the largest expeditions as yet sent against the Chokonen.

The first day out Bascom may have gotten a late start. The 7th Infantry had averaged about eighteen miles per day during their march from Utah. They often arose as early as 3 a.m. to begin the long day's march. The lieutenant would stop where water was available. This pace would have brought Bascom to Cottonwood Springs near Mescal Pass on January 30. Known as Iron Springs in the 1880s, it was the place where Wyatt Earp shot Curly Bill Brocius. The next day was a long march through the short canyon emerging into the San Pedro Valley heading toward the mouth of Dragoon Wash. The San Pedro River provided water and the wash was the old stage road to Dragoon Springs. This would have been Company C's campsite on January 31. It is unlikely that Bascom would have gone the additional six miles north to San Pedro Crossing where there was an Overland Mail Station. There was no need. Bascom would have been visible to Chokonen scouts in the Dragoon Mountains as soon as he emerged from Mescal Pass. Cochise would have been aware of a very large force headed toward Apache Pass. The Army was coming their way and they didn't know why, but it couldn't be good. Some say the Apache had preternaturally keen vision. This may be so, but they also knew how to interpret what they were seeing. Sergeant Robinson wrote: "In peace, or in war, all Indian tribes have sentinels on the lookout; posted at prominent points so that none can pass without being seen by them. The Apaches had theirs on the highest peaks, from where they could see long distances in that clear atmosphere."[16] Seeing a dust cloud thirty miles away, they could estimate the size of the party, whether it was pulling wagons, and how many were mounted.

From the mouth of Dragoon Wash the next day's march took them to Dragoon Springs on February 1, where they spent the night. The station was about one mile north of the mouth of Jordan Canyon in the Dragoon Mountains where there were springs. It was near the crest of the pass in Texas Canyon. The next day's march would have been dusty even in winter. The Overland Mail road took them across the Willcox Playa. *Playa* in Spanish is "beach" and refers to a dry lake. The lake bed was covered in fine-grained white dust, which would have stirred in great clouds under marching feet. The night of Saturday, February 2, Bascom had his men camp at Ewell's Station in the Sulphur Springs Valley. From Ewell's it was a short march to Apache Pass and the spot in Siphon Canyon near Apache Spring where Bascom camped on Sunday, February 3. During this march, the Overland Mail stage passed his column going both east and west.

As Bascom's men marched they carried on their left shoulders the Springfield Model 1855 U.S. rifled musket. At nine pounds, two ounces, it was 59⅞ inches long in .58 caliber. It carried a 22½-inch long saber bayonet. It had an effective range of five hundred yards and thus could kill at ranges well beyond anything the Apache could field. Infantrymen folded the wide brim of their six-inch-tall black Hardee hats up on the left side against the crown. This was so the bayonet wouldn't cut the brim. Cavalrymen folded their hats on the right so as not to cut the brim off with their sabers. The front of the hat bore a large brass hunting horn, then the symbol of infantry. Their muskets loaded through the muzzle with a Minié ball, all lead, conical, and hollow at the base. When the soldier fired his weapon, the conical base expanded to engage the rifled grooves in the barrel, which caused the bullet to fly with greater accuracy. The soldiers carried paper cartridges. To load their weapons, they pulled a cartridge from the cartridge case at their waist, bit off the back end exposing the powder charge, dumped the charge down the barrel, and followed it with paper and ball, and then drove it home with the ramrod. The weapon could be primed in either of two ways. The hammer could be cocked and the soldier then pulled a percussion cap from a second pouch. This looked like a tiny top hat with a crown about a quarter inch in diameter. Inside was a fulminate of mercury charge, which exploded when struck by the hammer. The soldier placed the cap on a nipple under the hammer. The Springfield also used the Maynard primer system, which used a cap imbedded in a paper tape much like a child's cap gun. This made loading go a little faster.[17] A well-trained infantryman could get off three shots in a minute and perhaps four with the Maynard system when it worked properly.

Weapons were not loaded until needed. There simply is no way to unload a muzzle loading weapon except to fire it, and this wastes ammunition.[18] Left around loaded, the weapons are dangerous and might discharge if dropped or bumped. If the propellant in the barrel becomes damp, it hardens into a solid lump and will not explode. Before the Civil War at frontier posts, soldiers coming off guard duty would often ask permission to go hunting. The other option was to fire the weapon into the ground. Depending on circumstances, a soldier might stand sentinel with bayonet only. On the far frontier, ammunition was in short supply and precious.

The soldiers probably had blue overcoats, possible caped overcoats. They wore long blue woolen coats over cotton shirts and blue woolen trousers suspended by braces. They walked in laced leather half-boots. Around each soldier's waist was a belt with brass buckle carrying his bayonet case, cartridge case, and cap box. At his back was a canvas haversack containing his tin plate, cup, knife, and fork, as well as a slab of bacon and some hard tack, his field rations. A woolen blanket was rolled and tied to the haversack. He also carried a stamped metal canteen on a strap over his shoulder.

Bascom's camp contained eight or nine conical Sibley tents adopted by the Army in 1856, as well as his wagons and stock corral. The tents looked like canvas tepees. One tent was Bascom's, another was occupied

Standard uniform that would have been worn by a soldier of 7th Infantry, ca. 1861.
DOUG HOCKING

by his non-commissioned officers. Twelve infantrymen occupied each of the remaining tents.[19]

Fort Buchanan was the regimental headquarters of the 7th Infantry. In that capacity, headquarters sent out supplies, especially flour, from Buchanan to Fort Floyd. The Army designated Fort Floyd as Fort McLane in January 1861. The regiment assigned soldiers in rotation from the infantry companies to serve as wagon drivers and escort. The detail customarily made two trips, out and back, before a new detail took over. Company C assigned Sergeant Daniel Robinson to this duty in mid-December. On January 16, 1861, he and his escort departed Fort Buchanan. On February 3, he was returning to Fort Buchanan, with a detail of twelve men drawn from companies B, C, and G, when he encountered his commander, Lieutenant Bascom, at Apache Pass.[20] He and Lieutenant Bascom had served together for several years. He respected Bascom and later defended the lieutenant's reputation. His superiors considered him an excellent man in any difficult situation.

On their way out to Fort McLane, Robinson and his party had stopped at the Apache Pass Overland Mail Station and talked with the station keeper, James Wallace. Cochise and some of his people visited Robinson's camp. Two of the women Robinson mentioned in his account would become important to events later on. He engaged in a game of cards with one of Cochise's warriors.

One of them brought a pack of cards and intimated by gestures that he wished to play a game. The Apaches were expert gamblers and would stake everything in their possession on a bet.

Besides him [Wallace] and the driver, there were two squaws at the station, one older and haggard, the other young and rather good looking for an Indian mother and daughter I thought. After they had left, I spoke to Wallace about them. He said "They belong to Cochise's camp about a mile away; the oldest was part Mexican, and the other a Mexican that had been stolen by the Apaches when a child; having grown up among them, she was considered as much of an Apache as any of them, and was known by the name of Juanita." He also said, "They come to the station quite often and make themselves generally useful."[21]

When Sergeant Robinson returned with four wagons that had carried supplies to Fort McLane, he encountered Lieutenant John Marmaduke at Steen's Peak.[22] Marmaduke was returning from Fort Buchanan, where he had served on the same court martial board as Lieutenant Richard Lord, en route to his post, Fort McLane. He rode in an ambulance.[23] Marmaduke warned Sergeant Robinson that there had been Indian trouble. Apaches had taken Johnny Ward's boy Felix and his herd. He cautioned Sergeant Robinson to keep a good lookout. This caution is an indicator that Colonel Morrison suspected Cochise and the Chokonen of the crime.[24]

Robinson and his party camped the next night at San Simon Station where there was water. He got his men up early and broke camp at 3 a.m., wanting to arrive at the summit of Apache Pass by noon. As they neared the Chiricahua Mountains, a rider approached them at high speed and stopped one hundred yards off, indicating by signs that he wanted to "swap." The sergeant allowed him to approach, gave him some tobacco, and the two shared a smoke of *cigaretos*, cigarettes rolled in corn husks.

Near the narrow entrance to Siphon Canyon that leads to Apache Pass, Robinson stopped to wait for the wagons to come up and saw Apaches behaving oddly, walking bent over, apparently hiding, four hundred or five hundred yards off. He advised his men to be cautious and had them load their weapons. The sergeant set off with two men as advance guard and soon left them to scale one of the higher nearby points so as to observe the trail ahead and behind. "In this manner we reached the summit about noon, a beautiful little plateau, in the center of which was built the stage station and about 1500 yards beyond up a rocky ravine the spring is situated in an easterly direction from the station."[25] They approached the Overland Mail station around noon and camped between Apache Spring and the station. He had the mules led to water and tied them securely to the wagons.[26]

From the east the Overland Mail trail leads south into Siphon Canyon, which twists through a narrow gorge for about two miles and then opens out near the Apache Pass Station. The trail then leaves the canyon, proceeding west and uphill for another two miles to the Apache Pass. A narrow defile leads east away from the trail for about half a mile to Apache Spring. An arroyo, a dry streambed, runs west to east about one hundred yards south of the station entering the broad, sandy bottom of the Siphon Canyon stream. Oaks, walnuts, and other broadleaf trees crowd the canyon bottoms. Farther out there are mesquites. The hillsides are dotted with manzanita, bear grass, ocotillo, and yucca. Here and there are stands of agave. The station stood west of the Siphon Canyon streambed and the spring well to the east. Sergeant Robinson's camp was to the east at the entrance to the narrow defile leading to the spring, with Overlook ridge to his north and the high canyon side to his south, within sight of the trail to the pass and the station. From the western end of Overlook Ridge, the valley stretches out in a half circle for perhaps a mile on an incline rising to the west, Sergeant Robinson's plateau.[27] Robinson wrote a recollection of his conversation with the station keeper at Apache Pass:

"Halloo, boys!" Exclaimed [station keeper, James] *Wallace, "I am glad to see you back again." After responding I* [Sergeant Robinson] *then asked him, "What is up among the Apaches?" And told him that they acted rather suspiciously that morning.*

"Well, he said, "they are troubled about something that I have not found out yet, none of them have been around today." Pointing to a high peak above us, he continued, "The look-outs up yonder saw the white covers of your wagons in the San Simone (sic) *valley yesterday afternoon. They also saw a larger number and soldiers with them at Ewell's Springs, which no doubt will be here today. The Apaches don't like to see so many soldiers around, and possibly this is what troubles them."*[28]

On Sunday, February 3, 1861, while eating their noonday meal, Robinson and his men observed a column approaching and soon recognized the men of Company C, 7th Infantry. Lieutenant Bascom made camp east of the station at the foot of Overlook Ridge and ordered Robinson to join him.[29] The sergeant was put in charge of transportation, the livestock and wagons, which were corralled on a little bench above the camp.[30] Lieutenant Bascom questioned Robinson closely about Indians. "I never knew the precise nature of Lieut. Bascom's instructions," Robinson wrote, "but it was generally understood that he was ordered to the Pass to find Cochise, and through him to find the boy, and in the event of failure to hold Cochise as a hostage and bring him to Fort Buchanan."[31]

The Chokonen were already nervous when Bascom arrived. They had seen his column coming. The lieutenant had orders to find Cochise and get the boy returned. These orders probably also included directions to bring Cochise back to Fort Buchanan as a hostage if the boy wasn't returned, as Robinson had surmised. The taking of Indian hostages was common practice. Colonel Reeve had taken hostages among the Pinals a year before and used them to negotiate a peace of sorts. Captain Ewell used some of the same hostages to win the freedom of Mercedes Quiroz. Even so, Bascom may not have initially intended to take hostages. He wrote later that he thought negotiations were going well and he had agreed to allow Cochise ten days to bring in the boy, Felix Ward.[32] He may have been surprised when Cochise drew his knife to cut his way out of the tent where they had been conducting their negotiations and escape.

Chapter Nine

NEGOTIATING WITH COCHISE

ON SUNDAY, FEBRUARY 3, HAVING ORGANIZED HIS CAMP AND INTERviewed Sergeant Robinson, Lieutenant Bascom set off for the Overland Mail station with the interpreter, Johnny Ward, stepfather of the kidnapped boy.[1] There they spoke with station keeper James Wallace. The two Mexican women held by the Apache, young Juanita and the older woman, were at the station. Bascom and Ward asked them to go to Cochise's camp and request that he come speak with the lieutenant.[2] Cochise's camp was two miles to the north in Godwin Canyon. The women left, but Cochise did not appear. In the late afternoon, Bascom imposed on a reluctant James Wallace, who avowed friendship with the Apache leader, to go to his camp. He brought back word that Cochise would come the next day at noon.[3]

Monday, February 4, was a windy day and the tent flaps on the conical Sibley tents snapped in the breeze. According to Robinson there was no white flag of truce flown in the camp[4]; it was, after all, a punitive expedition and Bascom had orders to take hostages if necessary. Lieutenant Bascom waited through the morning while Sergeant Robinson tended to the livestock, leading the mules a few at a time to Apache Spring to water. Units normally divided men in the field into separate messes, those who shared a tent and cooking responsibilities. There were no specialist cooks in those days. Men took cooking duties in rotation. This was one of the reasons that army chow was bad, the other being the raw materials they had to work with. Descriptions of the event suggest that they planned to cook outside and take their dinner, the noon meal, in the tents, out of the wind. Bascom posted a few sentries armed with fixed bayonets, but not with loaded weapons. He now had sixty-six men following his commands, an ample force, he thought, to intimidate the Apache into cooperation.

Cochise arrived at noon with his wife, and two boys—one his son, Naiche, and the other his nephew, Chie—along with three adult males, one of whom was his brother Coyuntura.[5] They were likely all relatives by blood or marriage. Cochise was tall and well made, perhaps a bit haughty. He had delayed meeting Lieutenant Bascom for a full day, demonstrating to the soldier a sense of who was really in charge at Apache Pass. February was starving time when game is scarce, vegetable food unavailable, and winter stocks run low. Any conference with Indians must begin with shared food and often with gifts as well. The record does not show Bascom giving any gifts, though small amounts of shared tobacco and coffee would have gone unmentioned. The lieutenant was there to recover stolen livestock and a boy, so gifts may not have been appropriate. Acting through his interpreter, Johnny Ward, the soldier invited Cochise and his brother into the lieutenant's tent for dinner while the other Apaches were invited into one of the enlisted tents for the same purpose. Bascom gave orders to the Sergeant of the Guard to post sentinels in the rear of the tents and not allow any of the Indians to leave without permission.[6]

There were only four men in the lieutenant's tent: Cochise, Coyuntura, Bascom, and Johnny Ward. Only those four know exactly what words passed. Robinson was too far away with the wagons to overhear. Three of the men spoke in Spanish and the fourth, Bascom, may not have known what the others said. They ate dinner probably prepared by Bascom's soldier servant whose name is lost to us. Afterwards, over coffee, Bascom explained why he had come. He wanted the boy and the livestock returned. Cochise replied that he did not have them. This undoubtedly angered Ward, who had seen the trail that pointed toward Apache Pass. Bascom pressed the issue. Cochise admitted that he might know who had them and if Bascom gave him ten days, he would do all that he could to intercede and get them returned. Bascom wrote in his report:

I left Fort Buchanan on the 29th ult. and arrived at Apache Pass on the 3rd inst; feeling confident that they had the boy I captured six Indians and told the Chief Ca-Ches that I would hold them as hostages until he brought in the boy; he denied having taken the boy, or having been engaged in the depredations in the vicinity of the Fort, but said it was done by the Coyoteros and that they then had the boy at the Black Mountain and if I would wait ten days at the Station he would bring him in; to this I consented.[7]

Bascom implies that he took the hostages before discussing matters with Cochise, though events seem to have unfolded in a slightly different manner. He condenses his report. They talked, he took hostages, and the next day they talked again when Bascom told Cochise that he would release the Chokonen hostages when the Indian leader returned the boy.

Of prime importance is that Bascom agreed to let Cochise go to the Coyoteros to bring back the boy. The lieutenant was unlikely to take hostage the man he had just accepted as his negotiator. This is how Bascom understood the conversation. Neither he nor we know what Johnny Ward said in Spanish, although we can logically presume Ward was upset and not happy about letting the chief get away. He was convinced that Cochise had his boy and that the Chokonen was prevaricating. In a moment, in fact, he would fire his pistol at Cochise. It was unfortunate that Ward was the interpreter. Today we would not allow someone so intimately involved to serve as translator, but Morrison was under pressure to act immediately. His command had been criticized as useless against Indians, only good for mounting guard. With Ward standing in front of him, crying for action, the colonel could hardly refuse to allow him to accompany Bascom. It was an unfortunate decision.

Whatever Ward said—whether he had translated accurately, saying that Cochise would be allowed ten days to bring in the boy, or if he implied that Cochise was now a hostage against the boy's return—it enraged Cochise, who jumped up, drew his knife, and sprang to the tent flap, cutting the ties. He emerged running up Overlook Ridge. Ward was close behind and fired at the fleeing Apache. He missed. In the wagon park, Sergeant Daniel Robinson was unarmed. Suddenly, a knife-wielding Indian confronted him.

> [O]*ne of them* [Cochise] *passed close by me followed by a Sergeant, who had a musket in his hand. It seemed to be the intention of the Sergeant to capture him alive, the Indian frequently picked up stones and threw them at him defiantly. Finally, the Sergeant stopped long enough to load his piece, during this operation he lost sight of the Indian, but pushed on, the next I saw the Indian jump up from behind a rock, with his knife raised ready to strike as the Sergeant passed. The Sergeant wheeled around in time to save his own life.*[8]

Back in Bascom's tent, Coyuntura leapt toward the back flap and cut his way through the ties. Emerging, he tripped over a guy line and fell. A sentinel pinned the Indian to the ground with his bayonet, injuring him but not mortally.[9] The camp was in pandemonium. Bascom was as surprised as the Indians. His sentinels rounded up the Indians as they emerged from the tent where they'd been eating. Meanwhile, men began to load their muskets. Crucial moments passed while men grasped what was happening and began to load their weapons. A minute or maybe more passed as Cochise made good his escape. With the Indian already well up the hillside, the soldiers began to fire on him as he dodged and ran. If he received a wound, it was slight.[10] Indian accounts say Cochise still had Bascom's tin coffee cup in his hand when he reached the top of Overlook Ridge. Because the muskets were not loaded, acting with surprise, Cochise was able to escape although surrounded by dozens of soldiers who eventually fired on him.[11]

Cochise was already tense when he entered Bascom's tent. He was well aware of the treachery of Mexicans during parley. His father and elder brother had died this way. His people had been poisoned like rats with food issued by the Mexicans. They had induced his people to drink and then killed the Chokenen, who were unarmed and in a drunken stupor. They had fired cannon into crowds of peaceful Apaches. The Americans might do the same. This infantry lieutenant had come with sixty-six men arriving from two directions to confront the Chokonen.

He was alert for treachery. Before him sat an angry interpreter probably saying harsh words or employing a harsh tone. The interpreter may have said or implied that Cochise or his people would remain as hostages until the boy was returned.

Bascom had six hostages. With the exception of Cochise, none of the Chokonen in camp escaped or were killed.[12]

Before entering his tent to take dinner with Cochise, Coyuntura, and Johnny Ward, Lieutenant Bascom had set out sentries who were armed with bayonets and not loaded weapons.[13] According to Sergeant Robinson, the lieutenant instructed his men not to let the Apache leave camp. This was not an attempt to make them hostages. He would have employed loaded weapons for that. This was considered prudence at the time. Officers believed that if Indians were allowed to come and go at will from a soldier camp, they would steal everything they could carry and conceal it outside the camp. Guests were detained until their departure could be monitored. In the confusion of Cochise's flight, Bascom ended up with hostages he had not intended to take. They were too slow emerging from the tent where they had been dining and the sentries closed in on them. It wasn't perfidy or violation of hospitality on Bascom's part. In his report, he seemed genuinely confused by Cochise's flight, thinking he had an agreement and that the chief would uphold his end and seek out the boy, especially now that intentionally or not Bascom was holding his people hostage.

Once Cochise had charged off in a rage, Bascom recognized the danger and ordered his men to strike camp. They moved a half mile west to the Overland Mail station. Built of stone, the corral was eighty feet on a side,[14] with two ten by ten covered rooms at the end where supplies were stored and station personnel slept. The walls were six to eight feet high and two feet thick. The lieutenant ordered the stock watered and all kegs and canteens filled. The seven wagons parked on the southwest side of the station formed the basis for breastworks and rifle pits. Men were set to work with picks and spades digging a trench and filling empty grain sacks. The rifle pits under the wagons had overhead cover from high angle arrow fire. "By sunset everything was in pretty good shape to resist an attack or stand a siege, having on hand a fair supply of ammunition and

These are the remains of Overland Mail Station looking west toward the hill where parleys took place. Wagons were parked on the left and soldiers dug in under them. DOUG HOCKING

20 days rations."[15] On all sides were high hills that overlooked the station at a distance of five hundred or six hundred yards. On the south side, the fortified side, was a deep ravine about 120 yards off. The Overland Mail must have had at least sixteen mules on hand, and perhaps more. There can't have been enough room inside the station for sixty-six mules, sixty-seven soldiers, and four civilians. Bascom had his men pitch their tents outside the walls, and some of the men slept under the wagons in their rifle pits.

Throughout the night of Monday, February 4, 1861, the soldiers watched Apache signal fires on the highest peaks. Cochise was calling in reinforcements. Tuesday morning, February 5, the soldiers watched as a large force of Apache assembled on a hill about eight hundred yards off. Help had arrived for Cochise.

The Coyoteros came south from the White Mountains and their chief, Francisco, camped near Black Mountain. Normally it would have taken Cochise about ten days to travel to Francisco's camp, negotiate for the boy's release, and return to Apache Pass. Cochise was aware that the Coyoteros had been passing through his territory, returning from raids. Even so the presence of Coyotero chief Francisco on the very next day after the dinner meeting in Lieutenant Bascom's tent must have come as a surprise.

There was a close relationship between the Chiricahua and the Coyoteros, also known as White Mountain Apaches. The two tribes intermarried. Up to the time Cochise cut his way out of the tent, both he and Bascom seem to have been negotiating in good faith, though Bascom may have mentioned retaining some of the Apaches in camp as hostages.

Cochise's call for help went out on the evening of February 4 and Francisco's band appeared just twelve hours later, on the morning of February 5. Unfortunately for Cochise, Francisco didn't have the boy and didn't know of his presence among the Coyotero. This meant that the boy must be with Tontos, Pinals, Aravaipas, or other Western Apaches with whom Cochise was not on good terms.[16] Moreover, he had no idea which band might have had Felix Ward, or to whom to turn for assistance.

As Bascom and his men watched from their encampment, the larger force of Apache moved off and a small group approached bearing a white flag and requesting a parley. Cochise wished to speak to the soldier chief. Lieutenant Bascom agreed to the parley provided Cochise would come with not more than three others and meet under a flag of truce midway between the station and the arroyo or ravine that ran west to east 120 yards south of the station. He then ordered the breastworks manned and gave orders to fire if the Indians made any attempt at treachery. Sergeant William Smith carried the flag of truce and Johnny Ward served as interpreter while Sergeant Robinson served as guard, albeit unarmed, watching the movements of Indians in the arroyo.[17]

Cochise, Francisco, and the two accompanying them halted at a point nearer to the arroyo than to the station. The parley began with Cochise making a strong appeal at length for the release of the captive Indians.[18]

This aspect is from the mountain south of the Apache Pass Station across the arroyo/ravine to the station where Bascom's wagons are drawn up. On the left soldiers stand at the conference site. ARTWORK BY DOUG HOCKING

Bascom told him that he would not release the captives until the Apache gave up or found the boy. Cochise responded that he did not know where Felix Ward was, but would try to find him if and when Bascom set his friends at liberty. The chief's argument changed from "allow me ten days to go and get him" to "I don't know who has the boy." The talk continued for more than a half an hour. Sergeant Robinson observed Apaches entering the arroyo carrying cedar and sage bushes on their shoulders. He thought they intended to use this as camouflage when lying down to fire. "However, I supposed that the flags of truce would be respected, and this was neither the time nor place to show suspicion; but I felt it," he reported.[19] Bascom saw them as well but paid them no heed.

James Wallace, Walsh,[20] and Charles Culver,[21] Overland Mail employees, emerged from the station. At the side of the arroyo stood the two Mexican women, Juanita and the elder woman, signaling to them. Juanita especially was signaling in "a pitiful and affectionate manner with hands raised."[22] They moved toward Wallace and he moved toward them. Bascom ordered the men back to the station. He told them he would not exchange prisoners for them.

> *Juanita threw her arms around his neck and embraced him. After he had disengaged himself she caught him by the hand and led him towards the ravine to his fate. Poor fellow! Little did he think that every step was bringing him nearer it. They were now near the brink. He paused. Too late! A number of Apaches rushed out of the ravine and dragged him into it. For an instant I was spell-bound and forgot the danger we were in.*[23]

There has been speculation based on these events that Wallace had some sort of liaison with Juanita. He had a wife waiting for him in Tucson.

Cochise broke and ran as did Francisco after yelling, "Aqui! Aqui!" while pointing to Bascom's party. This was apparently indicating that his men should take the soldiers as well. Bascom and his party ran for the station at an oblique angle so as not to cross the line of fire. Bascom called on his men to fire. Robinson reported, "It was run for your life so I did not look behind; but there were others looking intently in that direction who told us a number raised up to follow but dropped down with the first volley."[24]

Meanwhile at the arroyo, Apaches accosted Culver and Walsh.[25] Culver knocked two down and received a bullet in the shoulder. The two mail employees ran into the line of fire between the soldiers at the station and the Apache. Someone, Apache or soldier, shot Walsh dead near the station.[26] Soldier fire was highly effective against the Apache, driving them back hundreds of yards. The range of the infantrymen's rifles were greater than they had previously experienced. Infantry sights, according to Robinson, were set for over five hundred yards.

It is not clear why Francisco cried out in Spanish. Perhaps this is only what Bascom thought he heard. Many Apaches were fluent in Spanish and it was the tongue that Johnny Ward, as interpreter, spoke. There is no reason that Francisco would have called out to Apache warriors in Spanish. It is clear that he cried out giving some sort of signal that ended the parley and sent everyone running in different directions. Both Bascom and Robinson thought that Cochise and Francisco had planned this treachery with the intent of taking the negotiating party captive. Perhaps Cochise felt justified, as Bascom took his people when he had come in for parley at Bascom's tent. For Bascom's part, it appears that he did not intend to take anyone captive. While Bascom had ordered his men not to let the Apache leave the camp, he had not ordered weapons loaded or that the Apaches be taken. The problem may have resulted from Ward's translation extending beyond what Bascom actually said or from the manner in which he said it.

Cochise may have been desperate. In his experience, Mexican officials often killed Chokonen they held as captives. He'd lost his father and elder brother this way and watched others lose whole families. He may have thought attack was his only recourse and that it was a fair turnabout, as the lieutenant, to his mind, may have seemed duplicitous. A great deal hinges on exactly what Johnny Ward said and how he said it. He was a poor choice for translator foisted upon Bascom by Colonel Morrison and circumstance.

During the return to the station, an Apache bullet wounded Sergeant Smith, the flag bearer. He was one of two soldiers wounded at Apache Pass; the Chokonen didn't kill any of the soldiers. Firing was general and brisk for some time. The Apache withdrew. Sergeant Robinson reports a number of Apache killed and that they were unable to retrieve their dead and wounded until darkness prevented accurate firing by the soldiers. The Chokonen were not as well armed in 1861 as they were in later times. They had just begun to use firearms and had heavy, short-ranged rifles of small caliber that took more time to load than the weapons of the soldiers. They purchased lead in bars six inches long, and then cut it into pieces and rounded the corners with their teeth to fit the bore. Their principle weapon was bow and arrow with a range of about fifty yards, giving the infantry soldiers a significant advantage in firepower and range. After the Chokonen and Coyoteros were driven back, Sergeant Robinson recalled, "Everything around us was as still as a grave-yard."[27]

Later he recalled that the night "was made hideous with the peculiar cries of the squaws on the hill sides mourning their dead, and we feared the worst fate of all had befallen the station keeper [Wallace]—that of being burned at the stake."[28]

Up until this point, both sides hoped for a peaceful solution to their mutual problem, though by now Cochise knew he could not produce the boy, Felix Ward. Bascom, in turn, had orders to bring in the boy and had the boy's stepfather there to remind him of his obligation. Cochise feared for his family. Bascom may have feared for Wallace. Sergeant Robinson did. However, Bascom had warned the man that he proceeded at his own peril and that he would not exchange hostages for him. Bascom may also have felt that Wallace was in less danger than Robinson thought. Lurid tales fueled the private soldiers' and settlers' sense of the Apache. The lieutenant knew that his hostages weren't in any danger. The Army would care for them and feed them well before eventually releasing them to their people as "goodwill ambassadors." The former hostages would have tales to tell of how well the Americans lived and ate. That was, with some terrible exceptions, the usual pattern and it is what occurred with Cochise's wife and the two boys. Wallace had bragged of his friendship with the nearby Chokonen, and Bascom may have felt that this friendship would keep him safe. Nonetheless, the lieutenant had orders and Wallace had disobeyed instructions by going off on his own hook.

On February 5 and through the night into February 6, Apache reinforcements continued to arrive. Cochise's father-in-law, Mangas Coloradas, arrived to find his daughter and grandson were hostages of the Americans. Others came in from the White Mountains, the Mogollons, the Dragoons, Chiricahuas, Peloncillos, and points east, north, and south. Accounts are not clear, but Geronimo, then still a minor player, may have arrived with the Nednhi.[29] Apache ranks swelled to what Bascom estimated to be over five hundred warriors.

In the morning of February 6, there were no Apache to be seen in the arroyo in front of the station or on the hills. Sergeant Robinson took charge of "transportation," that is, the herd of government and Overland Mail mules. He staked men in overwatch, muskets at the ready, fifty feet from Apache Spring, and left a man on the hillside of Overlook Ridge where he could see both the station and the spring and thus give warning of approaching Apache. Half of the stock were led out at a time to be watered, casks were filled, and then all returned to the station. There was no incident. Cochise may have still had hopes for a successful negotiation.

The mail stages were due in from east and west that evening. "A stage was due that night from the East and a small party was sent down the pass in hopes of meeting it," recorded Robinson. "At a narrow point they found the road obstructed with rocks placed in such a way as to upset the stage or cause a delay in removing the obstruction."[30] The soldiers cleared some of the debris and returned to the station without sighting the stage.

The westbound stage, driven by A. B. Culver, brother of the wounded station keeper, came in four hours early at 4 p.m.[31] His conductor, in charge of the mail, was Moses Lyon. Cochise was aware of the schedule and so neither he nor his men were watching the obstacle. They were busy at the other end of the pass near the Sulphur Springs Valley. The Overland Mail personnel reported that there was a pile of hay in the road which they thought might have been placed there to be burned to provide nighttime illumination. The stage drove around the hay and the rocks and came to the station without further incident.[32] Among the passengers were a lady and her husband on their way to California.

Meanwhile, at the western entrance to the pass, the eastbound Montoya wagon train with nine wagons[33] went into camp near some oak trees. As they came to a halt, Cochise and his warriors attacked. The Apache took captive a Cherokee half-breed, Frank Brunner, and two Americans, Sam Whitfield and William Sanders, killed six Mexican teamsters, and chained two others to their wagons before lighting them afire.[34] Cochise and his men now blocked the road with large stones.

After midnight that same evening, an eastbound mail wagon heading toward Apache Pass also was attacked in the same location and suffered casualties. William Buckley, a passenger and superintendent of the Overland Mail Line from Tucson to El Paso, reported:

I left Tucson on Tuesday evening by mail stage for El Paso, with six passengers, driver, and conductor. When within two miles of this sta-

tion, about one o'clock A.M., we were attacked by Indians, who fired about twelve or fourteen shots. The driver was severely wounded, one mule killed and another wounded. It being dark, it was impossible to see the Indians until they commenced firing. The passengers all left the conveyance, and as we were getting out of the stage, discovered wagon wheels and the bodies of men lying on the road. The Indians had attacked a train of immigrants, and tied eight men to the wheels and burned them. From what we could see of the remains supposed they were Mexicans. As soon as we could put the wounded driver inside the wagon, we started for the station. As the road was very heavy, it seemed impossible to reach the same, as the Indians had filled the road in several places with heavy rocks.[35]

The driver, King Lyon, suffered a broken leg from an Apache bullet.[36] Apache killed the lead mule and wounded other mules in the team. Nelson J. Davis, who had been riding on the box with Lyon, cut the dead lead mule free and drove the stage on to the Overland Mail Station two miles away, going slowly over the boulder-strewn road.[37] Among the passengers that night in addition to Mr. Buckley were Lieutenant John R. Cooke (son of the famous Philip St. George Cooke), 8th U.S. Infantry, en route from Fort Breckenridge, and Mr. W. S. Grant, of Tucson. Joining Lieutenant Bascom, although senior to him, Lieutenant Cooke willingly placed himself under Bascom's command in order to give him assistance.[38] Cooke was key in advising and assisting Bascom in negotiating with Cochise, and Bascom acknowledged his appreciation.[39] Hesperian wrote to the *Missouri Republican*, which published his letter, providing another account of the condition of the road.

A short distance this side of the station he found the remains of a wagon train and the bodies of eight men murdered by the Indians. Two of the bodies were chained to the wagons, and bore the appearance of having been burned at the stake. All the animals had been taken away. The road was barricaded with rocks for over two miles, but Mr. Culver will return in the next stage and put on a force of forty men to remove the obstructions.[40]

Still evident are the tracks of the Overland Mail Trail south of Apache Pass Station looking west. The ravine where the Apaches hid is on the left. DOUG HOCKING

Sometime during the night when the wagon train was destroyed and the two stage coaches arrived, Lieutenant Bascom received a note written by Wallace. It was found stuck on a tree branch near the station, and it stated that Cochise now had three additional prisoners, four in all, that he wished to exchange for those the soldiers were holding.[41] The note went on to state that if Bascom treated Cochise's people well, then he would treat his hostages well.

It snowed during the night and into the morning of February 7. At midmorning,[42] the Chokonen leader appeared on the bank of the arroyo south of the station, bringing James Wallace with him. In a shouted conversation with the captive, Cochise relayed the information that he would give Bascom James Wallace and sixteen government mules in exchange for the soldier's prisoners. The lieutenant enquired where he had obtained the mules and Cochise responded that he took them from a government train, of course. Bascom told him that if he brought the boy, he would make the exchange, initially assuming that the exchange would also include all four of Cochise's hostages.[43] Accepting that Cochise did not have the boy, Bascom's terms softened to an exchange to include all four of Cochise's captives. Years later, William Oury, the Tucson station keeper who would arrive at Apache Pass later in company with the dragoons, recounted the conversation as follows:[44]

[H]*aving tied Wallace's hands behind him with a long rope attached, sent him up to the level of ground to hail the people of the station for a parley, the Indians being all so thoroughly concealed in the ravine that not one was visible from the station. Lieut. Bascom held a conversation with Wallace, who told him that he would as soon be killed out-right as to longer suffer from cold and hunger as he had. He was taken, it will be remembered, in his shirt sleeves and in the month of February, the cold is very severe in Apache Pass, and the fiends had then kept him several nights without even giving him a blanket to protect him from the cold. Wallace told the Lieutenant that Cachise authorized him to say to him that if he would turn all his Indians loose, that he would liberate him (Wallace). In reply Bascom asked Wallace if Cachise still had the two other white men* [actually three]*, and being answered in the affirmative, he told Wallace to tell Cachise that if he would agree to release all three of the white men he would turn all the Indians (8 in number)* [actually 6] *loose, to which Cachise refused to consent and thus ended the parley.*[45]

This is the point at which Reuben Bernard inserts himself with the story of the "wise sergeant" who counseled Bascom to accept the trade. According to Bernard's account, he became so adamant that the lieutenant ordered him taken under guard for court martial. Bernard wasn't there. He did not counsel Bascom and was not taken under guard or court martialed. Not only did no one else have any recollection of such an incident, but military records do not reflect his presence or attachment to Bascom's unit, nor do they reflect a subsequent court martial.[46] In the 1952 movie *Battle at Apache Pass*, Cochise dragged Wallace to death behind his horse. This didn't happen, either. The exchange of words was brief. Cochise was haughty, offering to trade stolen government mules for the hostages. This did not sit well with Bascom, who related that Cochise "took them from a government train *of course*." In other words, "I stole them from you." William Oury defended Lieutenant Bascom's action:

> *The reader who had followed me through the foregoing narrative will readily understand and commend the motive which prompted Lieutenant Bascom to refuse Cachise's proposition. What fair-minded man would fail to condemn him if he had made so unfair discrimination between his own countrymen? The life of either of the other prisoners was just as sacred and as valuable as that of Wallace, and any honorable man would have done just as he did, all or none.*[47]

Bascom didn't refuse Cochise's offer simply because he was offended that the Apache haughtily offered up mules stolen from Fort Buchanan, nor was Bascom blindly following orders that he must bring back the boy, Felix Ward. Bascom was concerned with the lives of four Americans and Cochise offered him only one of them. At this point, Bascom had the advice of Lieutenant John Cooke, whose stage had been attacked the night before and who must have agreed with Bascom's decision. Bascom thanked Cooke in his report for his counsel.

Bascom must have thought as Cochise departed from his hill above the station that there would be another round of negotiations. Surely Cochise would relent and trade all four of his prisoners for Bascom's six hostages. After all, they included his brother, nephew, wife, and son. Why Cochise refused to trade all four is a mystery. His note of the previous night said that he would exchange them.

Chapter Ten

LIFE SURROUNDED BY FIVE HUNDRED APACHES

SHE SAT IN THE BACK OF THE CELERITY WAGON WITH HER HEAD REST-ing on her husband's shoulder, feeling every rock and bump in the road, and choking on dust thrown up by the wheels and mules. Crossing the San Simon River had been hard. They were thrown from side to side and almost out of the coach as they descended to the riverbed and then bounced up the other side. She didn't want to recall what Doubtful Canyon had been like: the steep descent, the stage almost upsetting as it used the canyon wall as a road. They'd been on the stage for many days, usually unable to sleep as they were jostled about. The food was terrible and tough, the rest breaks few and short.

I'm with my husband, and that's where I belong, she thought. She was a well-bred woman accustomed to better circumstances. She supposed this was a better way to travel than walking beside a Conestoga wagon or even riding on its "mule seat." Her husband had paid a small fortune for tickets on the stage.

The conductor turned as they approached the mountains and called out, "We'll be at Apache Pass Station soon. There'll be hot food for the evening meal."

As they entered the canyon the driver cursed and the stage swerved to one side then back to the other. Moses Lyon, the conductor, turned to the woman again. "Sorry, ma'am. Ole Culver ain't got no manners. There's some rocks rolled into the road. We're four hours early and we'll be there soon."

She smiled. Her husband frowned, a little offended at the conductor's overfamiliarity and the driver's foul mouth.

They bounced up the arroyo bed that was the road. The woman was glad her ample petticoats protected her a little from the hard wooden seats.

A little later Moses spoke to his partner. "Whewee, what's all the excitement? What's with all them soldier boys?"

A sergeant approached. "Glad you made it in safe. Problems with the Apache. Pull your coach up over there."

Moses Lyon called out. "What? We've got a woman on board and a schedule to keep."

The sergeant replied, "You ain't going anywhere tonight. Does that woman know anything about doctoring?"

She soon found herself in charge of a man wounded in the shoulder, apparently a relative of her driver, and of a soldier, a sergeant, who was slightly wounded. She cleaned and dressed their wounds and tried to comfort them. A lieutenant's orderly brought her dinner. It was the best she'd had in many days. She then found herself a spot in the corner of a small stone room where she curled up in her husband's arms, cold on the hard floor, and went to sleep.

Sometime after midnight she was awakened by a commotion. The eastbound stage had arrived. She emerged from her husband's arms and the small room to find snow deep on the ground. Moses Lyon and some soldiers carried in a wounded man. He'd been shot in the leg and the bone was broken.

"Please, ma'am," pleaded Moses Lyon. "Can you help my brother, King? He's hurt bad."

She cared for the man as best she could and returned to sleep. In the morning she was awakened by excitement in the station. An Apache approached the station with a white man bound by a rope.

"It's Cochise," said one of the soldiers.

The lieutenant conducted a shouted negotiation with the Apache, who wanted to exchange the bound man for the six Apache the lieutenant held as hostages. For the first time she noticed the Apache prisoners the soldiers were holding. The lieutenant at first wanted a boy plus the four prisoners the chief held. The Apache offered the bound man and fourteen mules. The lieutenant, advised by another lieutenant, softened his position, accepting that the chief didn't have the boy but demanding all four of the Apache's prisoners. The Indian departed.

She overheard the two lieutenants talking. The elder one said, "He'll be back." The bearded one said, "I hope so. He's got to let us have all four."

The woman wondered if she'd have more patients before the day was out.

During the early morning hours of Thursday, February 7, 1861, at a now very crowded Overland Mail station, men and beasts slaked their thirst on the snow that had fallen during the night. In addition to the sixty-six soldiers under Lieutenant Bascom's command, the station was occupied by one remaining station keeper, nine folks who'd come in on the eastbound stage, and at least four who had come in on the westbound. Sergeant William Smith, Charles Culver, and King Lyon lay wounded under the care of the lady who had arrived with her husband on the westbound stage. She must have been quite a lady. Sergeant Robinson said she was the least daunted of the passengers and gave her advice and attention to the wounded in the absence of a surgeon. "Her name has escaped my memory, but gratitude still lives."[1] Sergeant James Huber, first sergeant of Company C, 7th Infantry, was able to hold off watering the stock and filling water casks until noon. He then chose Sergeant Robinson, who had been in charge of transportation and who had superior knowledge of the spring and its locale, to mount the effort.

There were about fifty animals suffering from a want of water. The spring, although only half a mile away, was hidden from the station by a bend in the ravine. Huber provided Sergeant Robinson a guard of twenty men. He planned to take half of the stock at a time, water them, fill casks, and return to the station. Four men would go with him and take up overwatch positions on the steep hillside above the spring. One would go up Overlook Ridge and fire his rifle to signal if he saw Apaches approaching. The first of the animals had begun watering when Robinson saw Moses Lyon mounted in the midst of them driving the entire herd before him. The sentinel signaled and Robinson looked to the south to see a party of what he estimated to be one hundred Apaches approaching about three

Apache Spring. DOUG HOCKING

hundred yards off. They were on foot, bending low and moving rapidly to close the distance.

Robinson and the men with him opened fire with such effect that the Indians changed course to the left, climbing the steep hillside south of the spring while Robinson held the ground on the north. The Apache soon opened a plunging[2] fire on Robinson's party, firing from a position higher than his own, negating such cover as the soldiers had. Only one hundred yards separated the two forces. The sergeant ordered the guard to fall back firing, driving the herd before them and making use of the greater range of their weapons. As he turned to follow the guard, Robinson was struck by a Chokonen bullet in the right leg near the knee; the ball passed downwards and out above his ankle on the inner side. He was only able to move a few paces, and then sought concealment behind a cactus where he sat and reloaded his rifle-musket. The guard, meanwhile, had taken up positions higher on the slope and was firing over him. They kept up a steady fire, saving his life.[3]

Looking from Overland Mail Station to Apache Spring, the ravine one hundred meters south of the station where Apaches hid is to the right; Overlook Ridge where Sergeant Robinson guarded the watering party is on the left. DOUG HOCKING

At the station, Lieutenant Bascom realized that Apaches had attacked the watering party. Those at the station distinctly heard the firing of weapons by both sides. Bascom's dilemma was the arroyo to his front. The Apache had used it as a covered and concealed[4] thoroughfare since he fortified his command in the station. He now saw a very large body of Apache in this arroyo and uphill of the station to the west. Cochise's intent was clear. He wanted to lure the soldiers into the open so that he and his warriors might attack the soldiers in flank. Lieutenant John Cooke, stagecoach passenger, although senior to Bascom, placed himself under the infantryman's command and volunteered to lead a ten-man relief mission to rescue the guard. Bascom assented.

Sergeant Robinson sat in an exposed position unable to move, receiving the unkind attention of Apache marksmen. The great coat that he wore was later found to have a number of bullet holes. Lieutenant

Cooke's party appeared from the station and drove the Apache back. The Indians withdrew, killing Moses Lyon. Fire slackened. Robinson was carried to the station.[5]

The watering party lost twenty-seven government mules and all of the Overland Mail stock.[6] With four wounded men now in care of the lady from the east, Bascom decided to send to Fort Buchanan for assistance. William Buckley, the Overland Mail superintendent, imposed on A. B. Culver to undertake the dangerous mission of going to Tucson to request assistance from there and from Fort Breckenridge. Culver, driver of the westbound stage, was the brother of the wounded station keeper. He made his way to Tucson at least in part for his brother's sake and perhaps for the sake of his brother's nurse. Bascom and First Sergeant Huber selected Corporal Fraber, the oldest man in the company, and Private P. C. Daly to request reinforcements from Fort Buchanan. "A number of men volunteered for this hazardous duty out of which a few of the most experienced were selected," recorded Robinson. "They left the station singly on mules before and after midnight—using the precaution of padding the mule's hoof, so as to deaden the sound in the rocky pass."[7]

—~·~—

The snowfall may have further helped the men and mules by deadening sounds. Nonetheless, it is surprising that they made it unscathed through a cordon of so many Apache. Bascom's dispatch to Fort Buchanan said that he was surrounded by five hundred Apaches and had wounded who needed care.

The riders went first to Ewell's Station and changed for fresh mules. Miraculously, this station, although close to Apache Pass, was unscathed.[8] They then rode on to Dragoon Springs, arriving on the morning of February 8, changed mounts again, and there divided. The two soldiers rode to Fort Buchanan. A. B. Culver rode on to San Pedro Crossing, Seneca Station, and finally Tucson where he spoke first to the station keeper, William S. Oury. All riders reached their destinations on the evening of Friday, February 8. Oury sent a rider to Fort Breckenridge far to the north to request help.

At Fort Buchanan, Colonel Morrison had few men to spare. Surgeon Bernard John Dowling Irwin volunteered to lead a relief party of eleven hand-picked privates available from Company H, 7th Infantry. If more soldiers had been available to break the cordon of five hundred Apaches, it seems likely Morrison would have sent them.

Back at Apache Pass Station, the soldiers continued to water their remaining stock and fill casks. Watering parties went to the spring at night and the Apache did not interfere.[9] At the mail station, Lieutenant Bascom was probably loath to light fires for warmth. This would silhouette his soldiers in the darkness, making them easy targets for Apache in the arroyo. Food was scarce and had to be shared with the many civilians. Space was cramped. The wounded, untended by a doctor, suffered. Everyone worried that the Apache might rush the station. The occupants were outnumbered many times over. Moving out of the safety of the station would make them vulnerable. Help would come, but could not be counted on for many days yet.

As the days slowly passed, Cochise made no more attempts to lure the soldiers out. His warriors did not like to fight at night. There were spirits lurking in the dark, and they wanted no part of them. Nonetheless, Cochise had the upper hand and had strengthened his position. He had four hostages, though he was oddly unwilling to part with three of them. Perhaps Mangas Coloradas or Francisco held them and was unwilling to part with them. Cochise now held much of Bascom's livestock, crippling Bascom's ability to move. The lieutenant would have needed wagons for the woman, for the wounded, and to carry the remaining food and supplies. Cochise built his hand toward another parley with Bascom in which he could again seek freedom for his people: his wife, son, and nephew.

After the fight at the spring on February 8, the soldiers did not see any Apache. The riders sent for help did not see any either. Suddenly, Apache Pass seemed void of Indians.

Chapter Eleven

SURGEON IRWIN EARNS FIRST MEDAL OF HONOR

In 1894, Colonel Bernard John Dowling Irwin, an assistant surgeon in 1861, received the Medal of Honor for distinguished gallantry in action against hostile Indians on February 13 and 14, 1861.

Irwin's rescue mission began when Bascom sent two men to Fort Buchanan with news of his plight at Apache Pass. Irwin later wrote of Sergeant Hubert Oberly's account:

> *The statement that sixteen of them* [mules reserved from Robinson's watering party] *to mount that number of men to ride back to Fort Buchanan in quest of the medical officer is simply ridiculous, as it would have been utterly impracticable for that number of men and animals to have departed without being discovered and captured by the Indians then surrounding and watching the movements of the beleaguered party.*[1]

Success of the messengers sent to Fort Buchanan was in the hands of those few men "who during the darkness of night stealthily scaled the steep and pathless mountain side and groped [their] way out to the plain." Soon after their arrival on the evening of Friday, February 8, Surgeon Irwin volunteered to take a small number of picked men to endeavor to reach the pass. Lieutenant Colonel Pitcairn Morrison, the senior officer in Arizona, dispatched a messenger to Fort Breckenridge ninety miles to the north ordering the dragoons there under Lieutenant

Surgeon Bernard John
Dowling Irwin, ca. 1863.
COURTESY OF DR. JOHN
FAHEY COLLECTIONS

Moore to take the field and head for Apache Pass. The surgeon planned to arrive ahead of them.[2]

The commander selected eleven "reliable infantrymen,"[3] to serve as Surgeon Irwin's escort. Corporal Fraber, who had just come from Apache Pass, volunteered to return with Irwin. James "Paddy" Graydon, rancher, former dragoon, and proprietor of the best whorehouse in Arizona, joined the small party. Speed was important to relieve the wounded, and thus Irwin planned to break the cordon of Apaches ahead of the dragoons. This was indeed a bold plan. The number of riding mules available dictated the size of the party. An infantry column taking five days to march to the pass would not have delivered timely aid. Irwin made the trip in two.

The little party set out in the face of a heavy snowstorm. Snow had provided water to the men at the pass and cover for the messengers. It now concealed Irwin's move. On Saturday, February 9, he arrived at

Dragoon Springs. From here on he normally would have been not only visible to Cochise, but also of concern to the Chokonen leader as the soldiers were in Chokonen land.

The next day as the party crossed the broad plain west of the Chiricahua Mountains, the Willcox Playa and Sulphur Springs Valley, Irwin spied a group of Apaches returning from a raid. These turned out to be Coyoteros and were thus further confirmation in the shift in Apache raiding trails caused by two companies of dragoons occupying Fort Breckenridge. All of the Apache were using the Sulphur Springs Valley as a route toward home in the mountains to the north.

The Coyotero were driving a herd of cattle and horses. Irwin had every reason to avoid these raiders with his tiny force. But he was the "fighting doctor" and Paddy Graydon—who was always ready for an adventure—was at his side, so they pursued them instead. It was a long and exciting chase that resulted in the capture of three Coyotero Apache and the acquisition of two horses and thirteen steers.[4]

After crossing the Playa de los Pimos [Willcox Playa] on the 10th and while en route, I discovered a herd of cattle driven by Indians at some miles distance. My infantry escort being mounted on mules, I immediately started in pursuit and, after a hard chase of six or seven miles, succeeded in capturing the party, consisting of a Coyotero Chief and two warriors, having in their possession thirteen cattle and two horses. I bound the prisoners and with the cattle delivered them to Lieut. Bascom at Apache Pass.

I beg to speak in highest terms of the conduct of the men engaged in the capture of this party. Corpl. Adam Faber [sic], Privates W. Leiter and G. Saliot of C Company 7th Infantry are deserving of the warmest commendation for their zeal and soldierly bearing; also Private William Christy, G Company, 7th Infantry, a volunteer for this service who was ever ready to display the qualities of a good soldier. Mr. James Graydon, a citizen of this vicinity, accompanied me and was foremost in capturing and securing the prisoners. His character for daring and courage needs no commendation at my hands.[5]

Irwin had only a party of thirteen men. That wasn't enough to break a cordon of five hundred Apaches, but it was too large to go unnoticed, especially in daylight, and accompanied by thirteen head of cattle. Graydon might have been the one who proposed stampeding the cattle through the cordon, using the steers as cover. Everything the pair did was bold, if lacking in stealth and logic.

Knowing that the party to whose relief I was going was short of provisions I was determined to drive the animals before us, and for the further reason that in the event of our being attacked within the pass our escape would be facilitated through the desire of the enemy to stampede and recapture the large drive of animals in our possession.[6]

Irwin passed the site where the Chokonen had plundered and burned five wagons. In daylight he saw what the stage passengers had only glimpsed in darkness. Eight men lay dead. The Indians had lashed two of these unfortunates to their wagons and tortured them by burning them alive. This made a deep impression on Surgeon Irwin.

At the stage station Bascom's men and the stage passengers greeted Irwin's party with shouts of joy. They had feared that given the number of Apaches in the area, the enemy might have intercepted and wiped out the relief party. More than that, Irwin brought the first fresh food they had seen in many days. Surgeon Irwin immediately attended to the wounded men. Thus Irwin and his party arrived at Apache Pass undetected by the Apache force, despite the perilous threat they'd been willing to face.

In the early days of the U.S. Army, decorations for gallantry in combat came and went, existing for short periods of time. The Fidelity Medallion was authorized in 1780 and in 1782, George Washington authorized the Badge of Military Merit for soldiers of the Continental Army who performed any singular meritorious action. A Certificate of Merit was granted during the Mexican-American War (1846–1848). Officers who showed significant bravery were given brevet promotions. The number of officers in any given rank was a number fixed by Congress as a matter of budget since regular rank was tied to pay and allowances. An officer might be brevetted several ranks above his pay grade or regular rank. He was allowed to wear the uniform of his highest brevet rank and was entitled to be addressed by that rank. Provided no one with a higher regular rank was present, he was entitled to hold positions in that higher rank.

Since his October 1860 arrival in Arizona, Lieutenant Colonel Pitcairn Morrison served in his regular rank as commander of the 7th Infantry Regiment, a slot that would normally have gone to a colonel, one rank higher than he. Apparently, that colonel was not present for duty. Soon Morrison would be found unfit for duty and command of the 7th would devolve on a major. Lieutenant Colonel Isaac Van Duzer Reeve was a regular captain serving as a lieutenant colonel in command of the Arizona soldiers until Morrison arrived in Arizona, and he reverted to command of a company. Although commanding a company and getting paid as a captain, Reeve was entitled to wear a lieutenant colonel's silver oak leaf and be addressed as colonel. This has led to confusion among historians who haven't been sure whether to refer to him as colonel or captain. It led to confusion in the ranks, as well, about who was senior by date of rank and thus entitled to command. Until the late 1860s, when the commanding general of the Army decided the system was overused and being abused, this is how officers were rewarded.

The Medal of Honor is the highest and most prestigious personal military decoration and is awarded for valor only. It is awarded in the name of the U.S. Congress. The medal was first authorized during the Civil War. It was established for the Army on July 12, 1862. The Navy had its own medal established the year before. Six Union Army soldiers who hijacked a Confederate locomotive named *The General* in 1862 were the first Medal of Honor recipients, receiving the medal on March 25, 1863. Their story was told in the *Great Locomotive Chase*, a 1956 Disney movie with Fess Parker. The medal was only for enlisted personnel and not for officers. This was later changed, but for a while some stigma seems to have attached to the medal and so it was not awarded to officers. Many officers were awarded the medal during the Indian Wars, but most of these did not actually receive the medal until the 1890s and then only after application. Surgeon Irwin made his application in 1894.

Surgeon Bernard John Dowling Irwin wearing his Medal of Honor. He came to Bascom's rescue and then proposed hanging the hostages.
ARIZONA HISTORICAL SOCIETY

In 1876, after the Battle of the Little Big Horn, there were so many soldiers recommended for the medal that the criterion had to be changed. A board of officers proposed the following criterion, which was adopted:

the conduct which deserves such recognition should not be the simple discharge of duty, but such acts beyond this that if omitted or refused to be done, should not justly subject the person to censure as a shortcoming or failure.[7]

In today's words, that is, the recipient's conduct must be above and beyond the call of duty. After this, the medal began to receive much of the significance and respect that it has today. Criteria were revisited in the 1890s and in 1917.

Army Assistant Surgeon Irwin rescued the sixty-six soldiers of Lieutenant George Bascom's Company C, 7th Infantry, at Apache Pass, Arizona. Though the Medal of Honor had not yet been proposed in Congress, Irwin's relief of Bascom's command was the first heroic act for which the Medal of Honor was awarded. Irwin did not receive the medal until 1894, but his medal ranks as being awarded for the earliest action for which the medal was received. His actions in February 1861 went beyond bold.

The soldiers, now numbering eighty, and civilians, perhaps as many as twenty, settled in to wait for the cavalry, that is, dragoons, who would be delayed by another four days. They watered the stock by night and worried when the five hundred Apaches would close in to finish their slaughter. Lurid tales circulated. Irwin and his men had seen the tortured and mutilated bodies. Almost everyone was concerned with the fate of the woman trapped with them at the Apache Pass Station. Bascom was not brash and did not claim that with eighty men he could march through all of Apacheria. So far he had been prudent and none of his men had been slain.

Chapter Twelve

THE CAVALRY ARRIVES

ON THE EVENING OF FRIDAY, FEBRUARY 8, 1861, THE MESSENGER FROM Lieutenant Bascom, Corporal Fraber, arrived at Fort Buchanan. At about the same time, William Buckley's messenger arrived in Tucson. William Oury sent a messenger to Fort Breckenridge who rode all night, arriving on Saturday, February 9.[1]

> [T]he same night a courier was dispatched by Supt. Buckley to the writer of this sketch [Oury] relating what had occurred and asking him to send a messenger to Old Camp Breckenbridge (sic), (now known as Old Camp Grant) calling for military assistance and to start himself immediately for the scene of war, the same night I sent a messenger to Breckenbridge, with an account of what had occurred, at Apache Pass, and requesting Lieut. Lord and Lieut. Moore commanding respectively Co's. D. and G. first Dragoons, to meet me as speedily as possible, with their companies at Ewell's Station fifteen miles West of Apache Pass and the next morning bright and early started from Tucson with four men and a coach for the Pass, having every confidence that I would meet the Dragoons at the appointed place in which I was not disappointed; they taking the route by the head of the Arivaypa Canyon arrived at Ewells before I did, Lieut. Moore leaving a note for me at the appointed place that they would wait for me at the rock tank six miles West of the Pass where I found them and the same evening we all arrived at the station.[2]

Lieutenant Moore does not mention a messenger arriving at Apache Pass on February 9. Lieutenant Moore, in command of both Fort Breckenridge and Company G, nominally still Captain Ewell's company, waited for instructions from Lieutenant Colonel Pitcairn Morrison. It was a two-day ride from Fort Buchanan to Fort Breckenridge ninety miles to the north. The military express rider arrived about the time Surgeon Irwin reached Apache Pass.

Knowing that an infantry command was surrounded by five hundred Apache in the Pass, Moore would have awaited word from the senior officer in the area for instructions regarding a coordinated movement by all available troops. He knew that any infantry coming from Fort Buchanan would take five days to reach Apache Pass. He had time to prepare his force. Moore's livestock was in poor condition, so there were only enough mounts for seventy men. He moved relatively slowly, sparing his stock, expecting major battle when he met Cochise. The lieutenant did not want to arrive for battle on tired animals. The movement took four days. Bascom was under siege and as such was in more danger from lack of food and water than from a frontal attack by the Chokonen. Moore had been fighting Indians in the southwest for almost ten years working with Ewell. He knew the Apache were unlikely to risk a frontal attack.[3]

It is unclear if they set out on February 10 or if word came late and the dragoons set out on February 11. Lieutenants Isaiah Moore and Richard Lord arrived at Apache Pass on February 14. At that point there were four officers senior to Lieutenant Bascom at the Pass: John Cooke, Bernard Irwin, Richard Lord, and Isaiah Moore. By military protocol, and not by choice, Lieutenant Moore, the most senior, assumed command. This responsibility is not a trifling matter. It was his place to make decisions and decide for all of the soldiers present what would be done.

—•~—

Moore's seventy men were dragoons. They were a type of cavalry trained to fight either from horseback with pistol or saber, or on foot with musketoon. The musketoon was a weapon with which no one was happy. It was a shortened, smoothbore musket, with the ramrod attached by a slide. The intended purpose of the slide was so that the weapon could be loaded on horseback while on the move without fear of dropping and losing the ramrod. Shortening the musketoon decreased its range so that the weapon was rated effective at fifty yards. A pistol was accurate at twenty-five yards, a standard musket at one hundred, and the rifle-muskets issued to the infantry were rated at five hundred yards.[4] However, the rear sight had to be raised to achieve this and weapons were usually set to a shorter range like two hundred yards. At five hundred yards, with open iron sights, a human target is vanishingly small. Nonetheless, the infantry rifle-musket had a significant advantage in range. Like all muskets, the ball in the musketoon was loose in the barrel. If a soldier tilted the barrel downward while his horse was at the trot, the ball might roll out.

Dragoons were not mounted infantry who rode to the battle and dismounted to fight. They were trained to fight mounted, with pistol or saber. Dismounted, one man in four became a horse-holder. The reins of four horses were joined and one man moved a few yards to the rear, hopefully covered and concealed from direct fire, to hold the animals until needed. This substantially reduced the strength of a dragoon formation in combat. Mounted man and horse were formidable. The weight of the charging horse knocked enemies aside like ten pins. The saber once unsheathed struck again and again without reloading. Charging through a village of non-combatant women and children, they struck terror in Indian hearts as the Indian men, scrambling to protect their families, often were unable to mount a coordinated defense. Their only choice was to run and hope. Nor could an Indian defense stand up well against a cavalry charge. European infantry formed square with fixed bayonet and the stock grounded in the earth, forming an effective wall of pikes. Horses will not charge against that deadly wall of bayonets. The Apache lacked bayonets and the tactics to form square. Instead they scattered to the rocks and hillsides trying to make themselves inaccessible. Where they had rifles, still new to the Apache, they used the greater range of their weapons to hold the cavalry at bay. If only armed with bow and arrow, they employed their greater firepower: the ability to put many arrows in the air in the time it took a soldier to reload.

At the Apache Pass Overland Mail station, eighty soldiers and many civilians, including one lady from the east assisting as a nurse, waited anxiously for help to arrive. "We waited and watched day after day until the fourteenth of February, when, to our great joy,"[5] wrote Robinson, "relief arrived." They suffered from the cold and lack of firewood and from the short food rations and scarce water. At night they ventured forth under guard to gather water at the spring for the coming day not knowing when the Apache might attack. Finally, "two companies of dragoons arrived from Fort Breckenridge under command of Captain Moore and Lieutenant Lord,"[6] recorded Robinson. "Right here I must state that when Captain Moore[7] arrived at the pass he assumed command by virtue of being the senior officer and became responsible for all that happened thereafter, and not Bascom, who had been a victim of circumstances beyond his control."[8]

William Oury and four other Overland Mail employees arrived from Tucson in company with the dragoons, having met them five miles west of the pass in the Sulphur Springs Valley. After resting for a day to recruit his tired horses,[9] Lieutenant Moore mounted a reconnaissance in force using the two companies of dragoons and forty of Bascom's infantrymen,[10] leaving the remaining infantrymen and civilians in safety at the station. He might have taken more of the infantrymen, but there presumably weren't enough mounts.

Isaiah Moore wisely chose to take the infantrymen along. They would make a good base of fire[11] if he did locate the Indians. Using the longer range of their weapons, the infantry would fix the Apache in position while the cavalry maneuvered to their flank and rear to cut off retreat. There was great risk that as soon as the Army appeared the Apaches would slay their hostages and attempt to escape. Only speed, overwhelming force, and trapping them in place to force them to negotiate for the release of captives on both sides might work. Moore expected heavy combat but was disappointed.[12]

Lieutenant Bascom reported the arrival of reinforcements and the ensuing reconnaissance mission as follows, and we can sense his relief:

On the 14th Lieutenants Moore and Lord arrived with about 70 men of D & G Companies 1st Dragoons, and on the 16th we joined them with 40 men of my command in a scout against the Indians; on the 1st and 2nd days out we discovered neither Camps or fresh signs of the Indians, on the third day from 10 to 15 lodges, all of which bore evidences of having been hastily aband[on]ed several days previous. The property was all destroyed and the Camps burnt. Dr. Irwin discovered about four miles from the Station the bodies of the four prisoners; Wallace, Whitfield, Sanders and Brunner, where they had been murdered by the Indians; finding no fresh signs of Indians.[13]

As it turned out, Cochise had departed long before the cavalry arrived. On the February 8, 1861, Company B, 8th Infantry, under the command of Captain (brevet Lieutenant Colonel) Isaac Van Duzer Reeve, marched with his men north of the Dos Cabezas Mountains en route to El Paso to defend against invading Texans.[14] They had left Fort Breckenridge days before and were unaware of Bascom's plight. They were visible from Apache Pass and Cochise, Mangas Coloradas, and Francisco saw this large body of soldiers.[15] They interpreted this as the ultimate treachery, an attempt to surround their people and strike a cruel blow. The Apache slew their hostages and departed in haste before Surgeon Irwin arrived. The dragoons later found their empty camps.

In his report, Moore said:

I have the honor to report that on the 10th inst. I received information that Lt. Bascom with his company was surrounded in the Chirricaquis pass by several hundred Indians, that the Indians had burned a train and murdered the teamsters, and stopped the U.S. mail. Taking Lt. Lord and seventy men I started for the pass, but on arriving found that the Indians had left the mountains, the Coyoteros most probably for the north of the Gila, and the Chirricaquis with a band of Mimbres Indians under Mangus for the head waters of the Gila. I traversed the mountains three days to assure myself, visiting their camps, which I found to have been hastily abandoned, but did not see one fresh track in the whole march. For scouting in the mountains, I assumed the command of Lt. Bascom.[16]

Goodwin Canyon looking east. Cochise's camp was in the hollow at center. San Simon Station and Doubtful Canyon/Stein's Peak are in the distance. Sharp eyes can see semis on I-10 much as Cochise would have seen the wagons of Company B, 8th Infantry, following nearly the same route. DOUG HOCKING

William Oury recalled:

After traversing the Chiricahua in every direction and finding nothing but signs several days old, we came into a small valley on the western side of the Chiricahua range, where we came upon the carcasses of three bodies, one of which, upon examination, I knew to be that of Wallace by the gold filling of some of his teeth, and the other two could be no other than his fellow prisoners. They had been tortured to death probably two days before, most probably the very night of the day in which Wallace had held the conversation with Lieut. Bascom. All of the bodies were littered with lance holes. We commenced to gather them together and some of the Dragoons were sent to the Station to bring tools to dig a grave.[17]

Robinson also recorded this grim discovery: "[I]n the vicinity of the pass. There they found the charred remains of Wallace—who had been burned at the stake after having been led to his doom by Juanita. The charred remains of the others were also found—supposed to have been the Mexicans."[18]

Although the reconnaissance found four of Cochise's hostages tortured and slain, Oury and Robinson say three, but both were writing years after the event.[19] William Buckley reported in the *Mesilla Times* that the soldiers had found Wallace and two other Americans and a Cherokee pierced with arrows.[20] The Chokonen killed eight Mexicans at the campsite of their wagon train on February 6. Two of them had been chained to the wheels of their wagons before the wagons were burned, thus burning them alive. Burning was a torture commonly used by the Chiricahua. It is not entirely clear if the burned bodies were just those of the two Mexicans or if the Apache also burned Wallace, Whitfield, Sanders, and Brunner alive. Both Oury and Robinson make the case that they were. Wallace left behind a young wife in Tucson to mourn his untimely end. The newspaper reported that her parents resided in California, near Visalia.[21]

Surgeon Irwin later reported:

How we escaped destruction should now be related. When the Indians ran off the stock from the spring they drove the animals out on the west side of the mountains and while running them to the north-west they discovered a company of infantry on the march, changing station from Fort Breckenridge to Fort Bliss, on the Rio Grande. Suspecting that that force was marching to the east side of the pass for the purpose of attacking them in the rear the Indians followed that command and thereby left the western entrance unguarded and hence the escape of my small party which but for that fortunate incident would undoubtedly have been attacked and inevitably destroyed.[22]

It's unlikely that, when Cochise saw the large force of Company B, 8th Infantry, he would have brought his entire force out of the mountains to face this new threat in the San Simon Valley. He would have waited in ambush in the canyons. He certainly wouldn't have taken his entire force, leaving Bascom unattended in his rear. Bascom's was a formidable force—one of the largest ever sent against him—armed with weapons of much greater range and firepower than those carried by Ewell's dragoons. Cochise would have had sentinels on the peaks watching his rear, and he would have been close enough to deal with Irwin and Graydon if he had still been in the vicinity of Apache Pass. In all probability, abandoning his plan to present Bascom with his overwhelming advantage in yet another parley, he fled on February 8. Cochise was alert to deceit and treachery. The appearance of a second large force intended to encircle his people would have been enough to force Cochise to abandon his plan.

Bascom says that Irwin discovered the four bodies, suggesting that he was operating separately. What he saw thoroughly upset him. On February 18, 1861, the stagecoaches departed Apache Pass going east and west with their passengers and civilian wounded. The mail was running again. Lieutenant Bascom went on to report that after leaving a small detail to guard the station, they broke camp and headed west across the pass in company with Surgeon Irwin and the dragoons:

> *We returned to the Station and on the next day* [February 19] *started for Fort Buchanan; when near the scene of macsacre* [sic] *and about three hundred yards from the burnt train, I took the six warriors I had* [as] *prisoners to the grave of murdered men, explained through the interpreter what had taken place, and my intentions, and bound them securely hand and foot, and hung them to the nearest trees; the three remaining prisoners a woman and two boys I have turned over to the Guard at this Post.*[23]

Bascom assumes responsibility for the hanging, but Moore was in command. Moore walked around the issue in his report. He reported that he assumed command, as indeed he would have, but implies it was only of the reconnaissance. Sergeant Robinson correctly informs his readers that Lieutenant Moore was in command as the senior officer present. Bascom was the junior officer at this point.

This was not lost on Thompson Turner who wrote:

From the field where the Montoya Wagon train and the eastbound stage were attacked looking west along the Overland Trail to Apache Pass. This is where the Apaches were hanged. DOUG HOCKING

> *Lieut. Moore, who had arrived from Fort Breckenridge with 70 dragoons, had the bodies interred; and as a retaliatory measure, hanged the six Indian braves who were prisoners.*[24]

Sergeant Oberly, who was at Fort Buchanan nursing a sick child at this time, related his account of the hanging to the *New York World* in 1886:

> *After leaving the pass (going west, probably) there is a prairie known as the Round Prairie, in the center of which stand four oak trees as large as any in Carroll Park. It is a favorite camping place and the troops stopped to rest. Bascom wanted to hang the prisoners. Irwin objected and wanted to bring them to the Fort. Finally a pack of cards was borrowed from a soldier and the fate of the poor wretches hung*

on a game of Seven-up, in which the side for mercy was beaten and the death sentence pronounced. When the prisoners were made aware of their fate they asked to be shot. This was denied and then they asked for "fire-water" which was also refused. Men mounted the trees and fastened the short-noosed ropes to the branches. While this was going on the Indians sang their death-song and died gamely.[25]

Oberly's account is nothing short of fantastic. In it he includes accounts of large wagon trains being attacked by the Apache and everyone killed. No matching reference can be found anywhere. All other accounts note the place of hanging as at the spot where the Mexican wagon train was burned, two miles west of the Overland Mail station, east of Apache Pass, where there was a stand of oaks. The Oberly account enraged Surgeon Irwin with its inaccuracies, and he wrote correcting this account.

While on the march in quest of his home [Cochise's] *our presence disturbed a flock of buzzards some distance to the right of the trail leading to the chief's favorite camping-ground, and, on riding over to the place from where the birds had flown, the ghastly remains of six human bodies, upon which the vultures had been banqueting, were discovered. The evidence was indubitable that the skeletons were those of the unfortunates Wallace and his companions and three other prisoners who had fallen into the power of the savages.*

It was then and there that it was determined to execute an equal number of the Indian warriors confined at the mail-station. The silly fabrication that a game of chance decided their fate is as absurd and groundless as the ridiculous assertion that I objected to their execution and wanted to take them to the post of Fort B [Buchanan]. *So far from having remonstrated against their merited punishment, it was I who suggested their summary execution, man for man. On Bascom expressing reluctance to resort to the extreme measure proposed, I urged my right to dispose of the lives of the three prisoners captured by me, after which he then acceded to the retaliatory proposition and*

agreed that those prisoners and three of the hostages taken by him
should be brought there and executed.[26]

Bernard John Dowling Irwin was an emigrant from Ireland where
the English had often punished Irish hostages. It was a brutal environment and we should accept his statement that it was his idea to hang the
hostages man for man. It was his idea against which Lieutenant George
Bascom initially demurred, but the decision to proceed rested on Lieutenant Isaiah Moore, who was in command and whose men provided the
ropes. Bascom might have objected that the hostages were his to dispose
of and he wished to take them to Fort Buchanan. In fact, he did just that.
Irwin's insistence that he would hang the prisoners he had taken led Bascom to relent. Moore could have ended the entire proceeding at any time.

Irwin's prisoners were Coyoteros returning from a raid presumably in
Mexico. They might have been involved with Francisco and the siege at
Apache Pass, or they might not have. They might have already been prisoners when Cochise slew his hostages. For Irwin and the others, it was
enough that they were Apaches and the tribe conveniently bore collective
responsibility. Never mind that the Apache had no real political sense of
themselves as a tribe. They spoke the same language, intermarried, shared
feasts and festivals, and might on occasion, if asked, participate together
in raids. There was no overarching political system with chiefs in charge
who were elected and obeyed or who ruled by some divine right. Alliances were temporary. For the Americans, it was convenient to see them
as a tribe. Then the tribe could be punished for the crimes of the few. The
Americans could conclude treaties with the tribe and expect all to obey.
The six Apache who were hanged do not appear to have taken any part
in the killing of Wallace, Whitfield, Sanders, and Brunner. They were an
object lesson to the Apache.

The bodies hung there rotting until they fell to the ground. Surgeon
Irwin reported seeing them in late July 1861.[27] The Apache have an awful
dread of touching dead bodies. They bury their dead very quickly and
almost casually. Things that the dead loved in life go into the grave with
the body. This isn't so they'll have them in the afterlife. They fear that

things that a person loved in life may call their spirit back. For the same reason, they will not say the names of those who have passed on.

This dread may be the full explanation for why the Apache didn't take the bodies down. There was also an increased soldier presence at the pass. During the coming months until the soldiers left Arizona, Cochise was active from Doubtful Canyon on what would become the Arizona–New Mexico border in 1863 to Cooke's Canyon north of Deming, New Mexico.

Chapter Thirteen

COCHISE'S REVENGE

COCHISE SOUGHT REVENGE FOR THE HANGING OF HIS RELATIVES AT Apache Pass. He understood that he had killed many whites and they in turn had taken their revenge on him. The Apache leader was a wise man, not a psychotic out to take endless vengeance on all whites for the actions of a few. When Governor Safford interviewed Cochise in 1872, Reuben Bernard's story of the stubborn lieutenant and wise sergeant was already in circulation. Cochise knew that the whites believed Bascom had wronged him. This became something of which to remind them in negotiations. The notion that Cochise conducted a long and bloody revenge was helped along by fanciful stories like those of Sergeant Hubert Oberly and Captain James H. Tevis. In 1886, the *New York World* recorded Oberly saying:

> *I told the Captain of the Texan train, a lank individual with long hair and a big hat, of the dangers of the Pass; that the Apaches were on the warpath, and he had better return to the fort* [Fort McLane]. *He looked at me superciliously and said, or rather drawled out: "Stranger, how many men did you come through with?" I told him but reminded him they were disciplined men, and we had neither women nor children with us. "Wall, stranger, we have fifty men that fight besides the youngsters, and if I am put on the other side of Apache Pass I will get to California in spite of h—l." Further remonstrance was useless and so we parted. Clinton remained a night with them on the camping ground*

on the Round Prairie and then left for Sansamoan [San Simon] Creek to relieve my men. The Texans remained there until the next day to recruit their teams—and they never left it. That night the Apaches attacked the camp and not a soul to tell the fate of over two hundred men, women and children that composed the train. This occurred within a short distance of where the former train had been destroyed.[1]

Surgeon Irwin provided a more accurate account of the presumed death of two hundred pioneers:

The troops with which we were serving at that time remained in Arizona until August, 1861, but while the bodies of several small parties who had been captured, barbarously tortured and mutilated before having been put to death by their fiendish captors, were discovered at various times and places, we never heard of a party of two hundred emigrants having been massacred at Apache Pass or elsewhere in Arizona. When I again traversed the pass some six months after the events related (the confrontation at Apache Pass), the bodies of the Indians executed still dangled on the oak trees over the graves of our murdered people. The debris of the train burnt at the entrance to the cañon gave sad evidence of the devilish work perpetrated at that point before the execution of the Indian warriors. The remains of that time doubtless gave origin to the story that two hundred Texan emigrants had been massacred at that spot in retaliation and the perverted exaggeration forcibly illustrates that the credulity of some of those who passed through Apache Pass some months after the transactions described was grossly imposed upon at the expense of the truth and the actual and tragic occurrences that took place.[2]

Thus two hundred souls presumably sacrificed to the wrath of Cochise didn't die. Oberly also stated, "The Butterfield mail route was broken up, thousands of lives lost and millions of dollars spent to remedy the error of a hair-brained cadet of West Point."[3] On March 3, 1861, Congress ordered the Overland Mail moved from the southern Oxbow Route to a northern route along the Oregon-California Trail, the Salt Lake

Route. The Oxbow ran through Arkansas and Texas, which had entered the Confederacy. Congress was concerned that the rebels would interrupt the flow of mail. It is hardly fair to blame the Civil War on Bascom. Tevis provides another account of blood-curdling mass murder that did not occur connected with the change in the mail route. It took several months to make the change and to move stock, wagons, and personnel north. During the intervening period a competing mail service, the San Antonio and San Diego Mail, the famed Jackass Mail, ran intermittent service along with the Overland Mail and planned to purchase some of the Overland Mail's equipment and supplies.

Major McNeese [Neiss] withdrew the coaches from the Overland Mail Route, taking coaches, stock and employees. When his party, consisting of 122 men, was about two miles southeast of Stein's Peak Station the Indians attacked them and all were killed. Among them was my old partner, Anthony Elder.[4]

Events cause ripples much as a stone tossed in a pond does. The loss of 122 men out of a population of less than one thousand whites would have caused a tidal wave. We should see its echoes in military reports, in the reports of the Overland Mail Company, and in other newspapers. There is hardly a stir. The names Neiss or Niece and Elder are familiar.

According to Nelson Davis, an employee of the Overland Mail, mail service stopped around April 21, 1861, and a final move of stock and wagons began on May 17, 1861. George Giddings, of the San Antonio and San Diego Mail, was during this time attempting to purchase some of what the Overland Mail was leaving behind so that the service to California from Texas might continue on behalf of the Southern Confederacy. On April 21, or thereabouts,[5] a stage departed from Mesilla bound for Tucson carrying driver Ed Briggs, Michael Niece, conductor Anthony Elder, guard Sam Nealy, and J. J. Giddings of the San Antonio and San Diego Mail, who rode along to assess the needs of the line his brother aimed to acquire.[6] In particular, Giddings was tasked with determining the security needed to assure the safe passage of Jackass Mail stage coaches.

Cochise and his warriors lay in wait at Stein's Peak Station and the first volley claimed the lives of Briggs and Elder, who fell from the stage. The frightened mules ran wild for over a mile until finally the stage overturned into an arroyo near the base of the peak. Nealy continued to fight, slaying three Apaches before they killed him. Giddings and Niece raised their hands and surrendered to Cochise. The chief took them prisoner, suspended them upside down from trees, and lit small fires under their heads. In an interview years later, Cochise said that they "died like poor sick women."[7] Tevis's 122 was in fact only five, but was still important enough to be reported in the newspapers and in a claim by George Giddings against the government for compensation for his losses due to Indian depredation while under contract as a mail carrier.

The Overland Mail stage was running as late as April 20, 1861. On April 21, at Mesilla on the Rio Grande, Nelson J. Davis received a dispatch from Mr. Tuller, superintendent of the Eastern Division, for Mr. William Buckley at Tucson. The last mail had gone west so he picked two trusty men, Ed Conelly and A. J. Pidge, to accompany him on the ride to Tucson. Well-mounted, they set out. At Stein's Peak, Apaches caught them. Their bodies were found suspended upside down from a tree.[8] The *Mesilla Times* reported Edward Connelly and Patrick Donohue as disappearing between San Simon and the Tanks around April 23 delivering a load of flour. The newspapers reported that teamsters Paige and O'Brien disappeared in the same area about the same time.[9] The similarity of names is striking. Pidge is probably Paige. Davis' memory recorded thirty years later may be a little off the mark. It seems likely that four more men, Connelly and Donohue, Paige and O'Brien, met their fate at Doubtful Canyon by Stein's Peak in April of 1861, bringing the total who died at that location to nine.

Much has been made of the wrath of Cochise and his revenge. Some say that the revenge lasted through eleven years of bloody warfare. Cochise was a great warrior and a great leader of his people, perhaps the greatest of all. Holding out and not accepting earlier offers from the government, he won for his people the terms he'd always wanted: a reservation in his own country and an agent, Tom Jeffords, of his own choosing.[10] Apaches recognized two forms of warfare: (1) raiding for supplies and (2) raiding for revenge. When raiding for supplies they didn't usually kill people unless confronted. When raiding for revenge, killing was the whole point. To this Cochise added a third type of warfare: driving the Anglos out and keeping them out. This was alien to how Apaches had fought for centuries. They usually looked upon those they raided as a type of resource. They would raid them for food, let them live, and raid them again when in need. Cochise's revenge came in three parts: (1) murder raids for revenge immediately after the affair at Apache Pass (March–July 1861), (2) driving the Anglos out (August 1861–July 1862 or perhaps May 1864), and (3) return to resource raiding and tit-for-tat revenge raiding (1864–1872). Cochise explained how he arrived at this third phase: "Now Americans and Mexicans kill an Apache on sight. I have retaliated with all my might. My people have killed Americans and Mexicans and taken their property. Their losses have been greater than mine. I have killed ten white men for every Indian slain, but I know that the whites are many and the Indians are few."[11]

Near the end of February 1861, Apaches attacked the westbound Overland Mail twenty miles east of Tucson. They wounded the driver, Charles Clifford, while the conductor, Anthony Elder, took up the reins. They outran the Indians and escaped to Tucson.[12] In mid-March, a band of Apache herding stolen stock attacked the westbound stage twenty miles west of Apache Pass. The Overland Mail had begun sending armed guards in escort of its stages and two of them stayed behind to engage the Apache.[13] Hesperian, as Thompson Turner called himself when writing to the newspapers, noted the addition of a civilian escort to the Overland in a letter to the San Francisco *Evening Bulletin*. He also noted the heightened state of readiness at the stations, and that relations were no longer cordial between the Overland Mail and the Apache.

At present Apache Pass is in a state of quietude. On the 15th [March], nine Indians approached the station but kept at a respectful distance. One of their number advanced with a white flag but as experience had taught the employés (sic) the full value of that signal, he was warned off and it was only at the solicitation of a road agent that he was not fired upon. Upon being told to leave, he immediately hoisted a black flag, the signal of death, and disappeared—thus for the present avoiding any demonstration of a warlike nature.[14]

Toward the end of March, Apache killed a man four miles from Fort Breckenridge. This was probably the work of Pinals or Aravaipa Apache as this area is deep in their territory and they were hostile to the Chokonen. About that same time the commander of the Department of New Mexico issued orders to the military in Arizona to call in all scouting parties and refrain from action against the Indians until a general campaign was ordered.[15] Until this order was received, the commander of Fort Buchanan had kept infantry details at Stein's Peak, San Simon, Dragoon Springs, and Apache Pass. Ewell's Station may have been abandoned as too vulnerable as no guards were sent there and the newspaper does not mention the station in the attack on the stage twenty miles west of Apache Pass. It was not just Cochise who was active at this time. There was a continuation of the general uprising of Apaches. The military now pulled in its already ineffective horns and the level of mayhem increased. Thompson Turner wrote to the *Missouri Republican*:

> *The last stage from the East was several days behind time. The Texas Rangers had taken the stock at five stations near Fort Belknap [Texas], and caused the delay. It is natural to suppose that the disorderly element of Texan society will commit outrages in the existing state of political affairs there. In former years Texas was the asylum of outcasts, and for a long time desperados held full sway on the borders. . . . Such men are opposed to any government and if they now manifest their natural dispositions, justice requires that they should be blamed and not the Government of the Southern Confederacy.*[16]

Apparently Texas Rangers were part of the lawless and disorderly element of Texan society and not associated with the government. The confusion that reigned at the beginning of the Civil War was apparent to the Indians who could not help but notice that white society in Arizona was disintegrating and that its military had become ineffective. On May 4, Samuel Robinson, working for the Santa Rita Mines, wrote: "[Robert

L. Ward, who brought supplies to the mines] could not get any assistance from the Fort [Buchanan], every soldier being on duty and fearing an attack on the Fort by Apaches."[17] This was more likely the result of a Department of New Mexico order to cease patrolling until a general expedition against the Apache was mounted, but the effect was the same. In the first week of April, Apaches attacked the stage from California, eastbound, near Picacho Station, killing the driver, Parks. There were no passengers and Willis, the conductor, escaped. Another agent of the Overland Mail, Turner, disappeared between Bluewater and Picacho.[18] This was not the work of Chokonen but rather part of a more general uprising.

On May 22, the military express from Fort Fillmore, near Mesilla, was reported as overdue. It is not clear if they ever showed up. Meanwhile, Apaches allegedly killed two Americans and four Mexicans returning from Fort Fillmore.[19] These may have been mere rumors. On July 15, Apaches attacked three men at Canoa Ranch a few miles north of Tubac. Only William B. Roods escaped with his life.[20] Thompson Turner wrote to the San Francisco *Evening Bulletin*:

The Indians have been actively engaged in committing depredations upon the whites since the date of my last letter. Ranches have been despoiled, stock stolen, women and children carried into captivity, and citizens ambushed and foully murdered. It is unsafe to travel the highway and the solitary traveler, if prudent and wary, will avoid all roads and pursue his journey where less danger is to be apprehended, and bear from on landmark to another regardless of roads.[21]

The writer of the above went on to tell how on April 25, 1861, Apaches murdered three Mexicans within four miles of Tucson. Soon after, near the Santa Rita Silver Mines, eight miles from Tubac, Apaches murdered two Mexicans and Horace Grosvenor, an agent of the company. These acts may have been perpetrated by Chokonen but might as easily have been the work of Western Apache. Hesperian refers to numerous other acts, which undoubtedly include stock raids, but he does not list specifics, indicating that he is engaging in a bit of hyperbole.[22] In

July, Lieutenant Isaiah Moore oversaw the burning of Fort Breckenridge and its supplies lest they fall into rebel hands. He went on to burn and destroy Grant's flour mill at Tucson, which had been supplying flour to Arizona and the Mesilla Valley and where the Army had been storing supplies.[23] Soon he would burn and abandon Fort Buchanan as well and march with two companies of infantry and two of dragoons for the Rio Grande.

On June 22, 1861, a large party of Chiricahua Apache under Cochise attacked the herd-guard at Fort Buchanan. According to Surgeon Irwin they killed two soldiers, a citizen, and a Mexican, and captured the mule and cattle herds.[24] Sergeant Robinson wrote:

After remaining at the ranch (Paddy Graydon's) an hour or so, I mounted my horse to return to the fort. On the right side of the road were a succession of ravines that led up to the mountains. As I passed them my horse became fretful, snorted and shied to the opposite side of the road, and tried to break into a run.[25] I was in a thoughtful mood and paid little attention to all this: however, I gave him the rein and in a few moments was in the midst of the herd. I remained with the guard long enough to tell them of the fall of Fort Sumter.

After a pause, one of them innocently asked, "What was the cause?" Another paused. "Oh, D—n the cause, the flag yonder is my motto," said the old corporal, a Mexican War veteran,[26] pointing at the flag flying over the fort. "That's my sentiments," said another. "And mine too," said the first speaker. The Union flag was their guiding star, not only theirs but of every soldier in the regular army at the time.

Well, I left them and rode on to the corral, took off the saddle and turned the horse over to a stableman. Just then I heard a number of shots in the direction I had come from, and the "beat to arms" in the fort. I re-saddled my horse, picked up a rifle and some ammunition, and in a few moments was at the place where I left the guard, and herd. The herd was gone, and all that remained were the dead bodies of the soldiers, and the Mexican herder, their bodies bristling with arrows that had been shot into them by the stealthy Apaches.[27]

Lieutenant Bascom, Surgeon Irwin, and eight soldiers mounted on mules soon arrived and they immediately set off after the Apache and the herd, following a fresh trail that led across the broad Ciénega Creek to the Whetstone Mountains twenty miles east of Fort Buchanan. They heard a shot and, looking to a hilltop, saw a horseman waving his hat and pointing his rifle toward the Apache. Paddy Graydon joined the pursuit. The Apache were not moving fast because they were driving the herd and the soldiers soon came within range. When the soldiers fired, the Apache lanced slow-moving animals and sped up, leading the soldiers into rough country. The Chokonen, fifty or sixty in number, although they outnumbered the soldiers, did not make a stand, leading the sergeant to believe they were setting a trap. Lieutenant Bascom led on heedless of consequences to himself and others, and intent on recovering the herd, started to enter a deep gorge when Irwin and Robinson convinced him to go no further. Bascom ordered a halt, and the Apache rained arrows on the party, slightly wounding two soldiers. The surgeon had a narrow escape as one Chokonen paid him special attention. With a well-placed shot, Graydon silenced the Apache forever. The Apache held strong ground and Bascom's men were short of ammunition so he abandoned the pursuit. The surgeon mentioned the intense heat of the day and the lack of water. June is the hottest month in southern Arizona.[28]

The surgeon and the sergeant agree that Cochise's Apache killed four men that hot June day within sight of Fort Buchanan. Surgeon Irwin summed up the affair as follows:

The pursuit nearly led to our destruction. The officer in command seemed to have recovery of the stolen stock in view, regardless of consequences to himself or others. The trail ran through intricate gorges, and as we were about to enter one, the surgeon counseled caution before going further. A halt was ordered and no sooner made than we were assailed with a shower of arrows and defiant shouts from another band of Apaches that had been lying in wait to attack us in rear. Before we got out of that trap several soldiers were wounded slightly. The surgeon had a narrow escape; an indian [sic] had been giving him particular attention. Graydon covered the indian [sic] *with his trusty rifle and sent him to the happy hunting grounds.*[29]

Cochise and his warriors were raiding for livestock but killed four guards, a revenge measure. He set a deliberate ambush with the intent of killing as many soldiers as he could and perhaps even deliberately intended to slay Lieutenant George N. Bascom. Luring soldiers into a trap twenty miles away was a considerable tactical achievement, an act of genius, which required accurately calculating, predicting, and controlling his enemy's movements.

The final acts of his revenge came in August. Cochise and Mangas Coloradas attacked two parties at Cooke's Canyon, twenty miles north of modern Deming, New Mexico, site of Cooke's Spring and an Overland Mail station. All seven men in the first group, the Freeman Thomas party, were deliberately murdered. The second party, an Arizona wagon train, was trapped and all of its members could have been slain but Cochise and his father-in-law showed more interest in acquiring the large herd of sheep and cattle.

Cooke's Spring and the station are at the lower, eastern end of the pass. After passing through two deep arroyos, the road enters a gorge so narrow that one can almost reach out their hands and touch both walls at the same time. It extends this way for about one hundred yards and then opens out into a valley with steeply rising hills a few hundred yards' distant on each side for two miles before passing through a narrow, rocky gap and descending again toward Mimbres Crossing. Like Doubtful Canyon by Stein's Peak, it was a spot the Apache favored for ambush, as the many graves attest. During the Civil War, the California Volunteers erected Fort Cummings to help control the canyon. The soldiers situated the fort's graveyard on a hilltop next to the remains of the Overland Mail station.

On May 18, 1861, Superintendent Owen Tuller, of the Overland Mail, led a train of company property composed of one hundred men, two hundred animals, twenty-one stagecoaches, and other impedimenta from Mesilla en route to California. He left behind, stranded, seven Union men who had worked for the Overland Mail. Freeman Thomas had been a conductor. Emmett Mills at nineteen was the youngest. (He was brother to Anson Mills, later famous in Union blue and as a cavalry officer after the Civil War.) Robert Avaline was a gambler who had been employed by the Jackass Mail. Matthew Champion and John Wilson joined the group. On May 17, 1861, in Mesilla, John Portell had wounded Thomas Mastin, captain of the Arizona Guards, which became a Confederate unit, in a shootout. The town of Mesilla offered a two hundred dollar reward for his arrest. Their driver was Joseph Roescher. In late July, George Giddings, owner of the Jackass Mail, stopped in Mesilla. On July 20, the seven men of the Freeman Thomas party, armed with Sharp's rifles, stole Giddings' stage and headed west toward California.

They stopped for a day at Cooke's Spring to recruit their mules on the abundant grass. The next day as they entered the narrow gorge at the entrance to Cooke's Canyon, the Apache of Cochise's and Mangas Coloradas' bands sprung their ambush, wounding Roescher, the driver. Racing to the top of the pass, they dismounted and then chased the mules still pulling the stage downhill. They erected hasty rock shelters hoping the Apache would miss seeing them and follow the stage. The siege continued for two days and many Apache died before all seven men from the stage were slain. Cochise referred to them as the bravest men he'd ever encountered.[30]

On July 23, 1861, Captain Isaiah Moore completed the work of burning Fort Buchanan in order to destroy its stores so that they would not fall into the hands of Confederate soldiers or sympathizers. The four companies now under his command marched for the Rio Grande. Paddy Graydon went with them and soon received a commission as a captain in the New Mexico volunteers. Aware that this move was coming, settlers from Sonoita Creek had begun passing through Tubac on July 19. On July 20, Grundy Ake and General[31] William Wadsworth stayed a few days recruiting their stock, which included most of the cattle and sheep from the vicinity of Fort Buchanan. Moving on to Tucson they formed a substantial wagon train, which included more than forty adult males as well as many women and children. By July 25, mine operator Samuel Robinson reported that the country "is completely depopulated except for Tucson, Tubac, Arivaca and Patagonia."[32]

Settlers and miners would soon abandon Arivaca as well as Tubac. From Tubac, Robinson wrote:

> [On July 28, at midday, I] *had just sat down to eat it* [dinner] *when the cry of Apaches and the Apache yell came in from all directions. They were within one hundred yards of me on one side and fifty on the other. Weak as I was*[33] *I picked up my gun to defend the house if necessary. On going to shut the door I saw a dozen or two right across the street. Not caring to attract their attention to the house I did not fire but came back and finished my dinner, Charley keeping a lookout. A shot was heard every minute or two.*
>
> *It is estimated there were two hundred Indians, about seventy-five mounted and the balance on foot. They got every horse in town except mine which was in the corral, and another. Took all the stock but one old steer and four little calves. . . . There were three or four Indians killed. As soon as they got the stock they rushed on past the town out of shooting distance, and stopped a little less than a mile out and killed a couple of beeves.*[34]

The next month, the settlers abandoned Tubac, which the next day was sacked and burned by Sonorans. The midday Apache raid is interesting partly for its size and partly because it was the first attack on a large town and suggests a shift in Apache tactics to driving the whites, who were already leaving, out of the country. The departure of the soldiers must have precipitated this attack.

Meanwhile, in Tucson, Grundy Ake and William Wadsworth had formed up their wagon train and departed for the Rio Grande. On August 26, as they camped on the banks of the Mimbres River (between the modern towns of Silver City and Deming), an excited German named Eugene Zimmer entered the camp and warned them of a large party of Apaches ahead that had attacked his herd and killed his Mexican herdsmen. Ake and Wadsworth took this for some sort of ruse.

On August 27, the wagon train entered Cooke's Canyon from the pass in the west with their herds in the lead followed by mounted drovers, and Wadsworth driving the lead wagon. Cochise, Mangas Coloradas, and two hundred Apache warriors awaited them. Moving down the canyon in single file, Ake and Wadsworth discovered the naked bodies of the two Mexican herdsmen killed the day prior. Five mounted men at the rear of the wagon train took off, perhaps out of cowardice, perhaps in search of Captain Thomas Mastin's militia, the Arizona Guards. The Guards had been formed at nearby Pinos Altos (near modern Silver City) for protection from Apaches and to keep the trails open to the mining town. As the lead wagons entered the narrowest part of the canyon at the lower, eastern entrance, the Apache struck, killing John St. Claire and James May.

A horse pulling the Phillips wagon fell, blocking the road. There wasn't enough room for the wagons behind to turn. The settlers now rallied for defense. Moses Carson, elder brother of the famed scout, seemed to be everywhere directing and leading the defense. William Redding rallied the settlers and charged the Indians. Unable to turn the wagons, the settlers wedged two wagons and a buggy into a tight triangle that became their fort. Redding was driven back by the appearance of even more Apaches. A bullet broke his leg. William Wadsworth and Grundy Ake rode up the hillside to gain a vantage point. The Indians were driving the cattle herd on through the canyon. A bullet struck Wadsworth, who slid from his horse. Finally, they succeeded in turning a wagon at the rear of the column, which had not yet entered the narrowest part of the canyon. Loaded with the wounded and women and children, the crowded wagon was driven back over the pass. Abandoning their wagons, the remaining settlers withdrew to the wider part of the canyon. The Apache looted the wagons. The Arizona Guards arrived and went in pursuit of the livestock the Apache had taken.[35]

Looting and livestock took precedence over murder. Cochise's revenge was over and his war with the whites was well into a new phase, its second phase: driving the whites out. This was a new concept for the Apache who previously had conducted small-scale raids for provisions or for revenge killing. For the next year, Cochise would be conducting large-scale actions, rallying more Apache to his banner than any similar leader ever did.

On September 27, Cochise and Mangas Coloradas conducted a large-scale attack on the small town of Pinos Altos.[36] The Arizona Guards were still in the area, suggesting that the town was still occupied.[37] It fits into the scheme of Cochise's war. The *Mesilla Times* reported: "In such formidable numbers they have never assembled before on the war scout, and never before have they . . . evinced such boldness and daring as to attack a town of two or three hundred houses in open daylight. Nine-twentieths of the Territory of Arizona is under their undisputed control."[38]

More than 250 Apaches attacked at daylight from all sides at once, trapping many miners in their homes. Fighting was hand to hand. By noon the fighting centered on two stores, Bean's[39] and Roman's. The Arizona Guards were on hand, and Captain Mastin received a wound that proved mortal. A party of six women, perhaps the town prostitutes, brought a small howitzer into play, firing it down the center of the street. This rallied the miners, who drove the Apache back. The town remained under siege and a rider was sent to Mesilla for aid. The Apache shot his horse from under the rider but he tried again; returning to town for a second horse, he succeeded in getting away and returning with help.

On July 24, 1861, Lieutenant Colonel John Baylor, Confederate States Army, had occupied Mesilla with three hundred men and declared himself the governor of the Confederate Territory of Arizona. Although all he held was the Mesilla Valley along the Rio Grande, Confederate Arizona extended from Texas to the Colorado River, including roughly everything south of the Gila River. Baylor sent one hundred men to the relief of Pinos Altos, which was soon abandoned.[40]

Sent by Colonel Baylor, on February 28, 1862, Captain Sherod Hunter with a reinforced company captured Tucson for the Confederacy. In California, Colonel James Carleton was organizing the California Column, a brigade-sized element, for the Union. On May 14, Captain Hunter was forced to depart from Tucson headed back to Texas.

Hunter's livestock—horses, mules, and cattle, a commissary on the hoof—had been grazing along the San Pedro Valley thirty-five miles from Tucson. On May 5, in preparation for departure, Hunter's men, accompanied by a number of Union prisoners, were gathering in the stock. As they entered Jordan Canyon south of the abandoned Dragoon Springs Overland Mail station in search of stock at the spring there, Cochise struck, killing two. Two more soon fell. The Confederates issued arms to the Union prisoners and they fought the Apache side by side, driving them off. While the prisoners dug graves for the dead, the Confederate soldiers pursued the Apache and recovered much of their stock.[41] Cochise had again attacked a military force with the intent of both stealing their stock and driving them from the territory.

The California Column traveled the desert a few companies at a time, the most the water resources could handle. With the Confederate Texans occupying the Mesilla Valley, blocking the principal roads, Colonel Carleton lacked direct communication with the Union commander of New Mexico. A few brave couriers, such as Tom Jeffords, had come through bringing word but that word was now months old and the situation fluid. On February 20 and 21, 1862, on the Rio Grande, Colonel Edward Canby had fought a great battle against rebel commander General Henry Sibley at Valverde. Canby retained Fort Craig and its supplies while Sibley proceeded north to take Albuquerque and Santa Fe. On March 26 to 28, Colonel John Slough of the Colorado Volunteers met and halted the Texan forces at Glorieta Pass. Destitute, the rebels limped back to Texas while retaining the Mesilla Valley. Not knowing their true condition, Colonel Carleton could not risk attacking three regiments of mounted Texas troops meeting them with a single company at a time. He proceeded cautiously. On June 17, 1862, he sent Major Edward Eyre with a company to scout the way.

On June 25, Eyre's men encountered Cochise at Apache Pass. The Chokonen killed two of them before Eyre persuaded the Apache leader to come in for parley. Cochise demanded food and all Eyre had to give him was tobacco and pemmican.[42] Their resulting agreement is referred to as the Pemmican Treaty. Eyre promised friendship toward the Apache and told Cochise that a great captain, Carleton, who wished to make peace and who would give them presents, was coming. He also told the Apache that a larger group of soldiers was coming. Cochise assured Eyre that the Chokonen would not molest the men and animals of the California Column.[43]

On July 15, after marching his 126 thirsty men fifty waterless miles from Dragoon Springs, Captain Thomas Roberts of Carleton's California Column entered Apache Pass and approached the springs. Having gathered a great deal of information from Major Eyre, Cochise and Mangas Coloradas lay in wait with several hundred Chiricahua Apache in prepared positions above the spring. In one of their first assaults, Apaches captured one of Thomas' two mountain howitzers, but soldiers soon recaptured it. Apaches drove the soldiers back from the spring. The mountain howitzers were brought into play and soon drove the Apache away. The next day, soldiers approaching the spring found the Apache in position again. Colonel Carleton ordered the construction and occupation of Fort Bowie on the heights south of the spring to guard the location.[44]

The military occupied southern Arizona during the Civil War, building several new forts. The miners, ranchers, and farmers were mostly gone. Mail arrived by military express rider or not at all. In 1863, the Walker party, led by former mountain man Joseph Walker, found placer gold in the central part of the future state. In February 1863, Congress made a separate territory out of the western half of New Mexico Territory. In 1864, Prescott, where the Walker Party had camped, became the capital of the new territory. The focus of mining and settlement shifted to the north. The Chokonen made many raids, returning to old patterns of raiding for provisions and for revenge. There were few large incidents because there were few whites to attack.

Cochise made one more attempt to drive the whites out before returning completely to small-scale raiding, as reported by the May 28, 1864, San Francisco *Evening Bulletin*:

> *Tucson, May 9th, 1864—The express from the Rio Grande brings us news of a desperate fight with the Apaches in Steen's Peak Cañon* [Stein's Peak/Doubtful Canyon], *thirty miles east of Fort Bowie, or Apache Pass. It appears that on the morning of the 3rd inst., while Co. I, 5th Inf., C.V.* [California Volunteers] *fifty six strong, under the command of Lieut. H.H. Stevens, 5th Inf. C.V. were entering Steen's Peak cañon, en route to Fort Bowie from the Rio Grande, they were attacked by a large force of Indians, on both sides and in front. At the first fire one man was killed and two or three wounded, while the Lieutenant's horse was killed from under him. Deploying and placing his men as best he could, Lieut. Stevens continued the fight*

and his march through the cañon, a distance of some six miles into the
open country, when the Indians retreated. This cañon is described as
being very bad and dangerous; the sides rising several hundred feet in
a very precipitous manner, the greatest part of the way through. The
result of the fight, as stated, is one man killed and five wounded—one
mortally.[45]

In the following years, Cochise was amenable to talking peace. The American government did not authorize its War and Interior Department officials to give him the terms he demanded, which included a reservation in his own country. He was distrustful of Americans and of the U.S. military. In February 1869, Cochise met with Major Frank Perry near his central Dragoon Mountain stronghold. Cochise is reported to have said:

You mean you came to kill me or any of my tribe; that is what all your
visits means (sic) to me. I tried the Americans once and they broke
the treaty first, the officers I mean this was at the Pass. If I stop in, I
must be treated right, but I don't expect they will do all they say for
us. I won't stay Goodwin [San Carlos Reservation]; it is no place for
Indians. They die after being there a short time.[46]

In June of 1871, Cochise allowed frontiersman Tom Jeffords to enter his camp in New Mexico with a request that he come in for peace talks. The chief did not immediately acquiesce. The Camp Grant Massacre was fresh in his mind. On April 30, 1871, citizens of Tucson and Indians from San Xavier del Bac had murdered sixty-three[47] Aravaipa Apaches who were under the protection of the Army at Camp Grant and sent thirty of their children off to slavery in Mexico. In March 1872, the Chokonen leader met with Colonel Gordon Granger, military commander of New Mexico, at Cañada Alamosa. Cochise showed some interest in the Cañada Alamosa Reservation, but the Indian service was planning to close it and move the Chiricahua to the Tularosa Valley in far western New Mexico. Cochise wanted no part of Tularosa and demanded a reservation in his own country, southeast Arizona Territory between the Dragoon Mountains and the Peloncillos.

Peace was slow in coming. The nation's focus had shifted to fighting Sioux and Cheyenne along the Oregon-California Trail. The mail ran through South Pass in Wyoming, as did the telegraph. The transcontinental railroad would soon follow. In Arizona Territory, the new town of Prescott was the capital. Priorities shifted to protecting the capitol and the mining settlements in the Bradshaw Mountains from Yavapai, Mojave, and Western Apaches. Regular transcontinental mail service through Tucson did not resume until 1867. The long planned transcontinental railroad on the thirty-second degree corridor did not arrive until the 1880s.

Chapter Fourteen

AFTERMATH

My [Santiago Ward's] *mother was a Mexican, born in Santa Cruz, Mexico* [Sonora, just across the border from Arizona]. *She had been married before to a man named Tellez. He was a very light Mexican with blue eyes and brown hair and they had two children, Felix and Teodora. These children were taken into my father's family, and always went by the name of Ward.*[1]

SANTIAGO WARD, SOMETIMES CALLED BY THE ENGLISH VERSION OF HIS name, James, was an infant when nine Apaches took his half-brother, Felix Tellez Ward, from their home on Sonoita Creek. The Indians tried to break into the house, as Mr. Cole, a tradesman who lived on the property nearby, observed from his sickbed, but were deterred by the chance arrival of two of the neighbors, McCarty and Wilson, who pursued the Apache. The raiding party then divided into three groups, one taking the boy and the other taking Johnny Ward's cattle, while the third laid a decoy trail.[2] It is recorded that later in life, all Felix could recall was the long ride following his abduction[3]: "A posse of men went after the Indians but they divided in three groups. One group took my half-brother, a second took the cattle they had stolen from the ranch and . . . the other group just kept foraging. Of course they decoyed the men into taking the wrong trail."[4]

Felix was light-skinned and had gray or blue eyes with reddish-brown hair. This contributed to the rumor that Tellez had been an Irishman or that Johnny Ward was actually his father. Felix was twelve years old when taken; his sister, Teodora, was ten; their sister, Mary, was barely a year old; and brother Santiago was a newborn. Census entries for 1860, 1864, and 1867 list the family and their ages and origins. Felix's mother was Jesusa Martinez. After the Army withdrew from Fort Buchanan, Johnny Ward moved to Tucson where in 1864, he listed himself as a glassblower. Teodora did not appear in the 1864 enumeration. She may have passed away or married very young. Johnny Ward died in the fall of 1867, and Jesusa evidently passed away soon after. According to Santiago, "father and mother both died thinking that brother had been killed."[5] The family that Felix knew was gone. Only children who had been infants when he was taken away remained.

Allan Radbourne, a scholar who has studied this abduction, says the culprits who abducted Felix Ward were Aravaipa Apache and they probably would have killed him except that he looked younger than he was at age twelve.[6] The boy had little recollection that he cared to relate as he was sold from tribe to tribe until he came to reside with the Western Coyotero Apache. Tlol-dil-zil, John Rope, recounting the story in the 1920s, may have been attempting to direct blame away from his Coyotero father, Nayundiie, who adopted Felix. Rope recalled, "[Felix Ward] was raised by my father. He was given to him by the San Carlos People (Pinal) when a little boy. [Felix] and I were brought up together, so we called each other brothers."[7]

Felix established a place for himself among the Apaches, growing up as a warrior who fought alongside other warriors.[8] The Coyotero were among the first subdued by General George Crook, and he recruited Apache Scouts among them.

On December 2, 1872, Felix enlisted as an Apache Scout. His light-colored hair and one remaining eye, having lost sight in the right orb as an infant or youth, impressed the soldiers who recruited him. His Apache name was unpronounceable to them and the name Felix long forgotten. Needing something they could write on paper, they christened him Mickey Free after the servant of an Irish dragoon in the then pop-

Felix Tellez Ward, the boy who became Mickey Free, in the 1870s.

ular novel *Charles O'Malley, The Irish Dragoon*. Mickey Free of the novel was something of a scamp, no better than he had to be, "a whimsical, cunning, witty, and loveable rogue of a manservant to alternately amuse and exasperate."[9] By December 1874, Mickey had become a sergeant and a little later a first sergeant. He was next employed as an interpreter at Camp Verde where he met the famous scout Al Sieber. He became one of Sieber's favorites. Mickey Free served as a scout, tribal policeman, and interpreter until July 1893, making what by reservation standards was an excellent income. He was a member of Crook's Sierra Madre expedition against Geronimo.[10]

Mickey married four times and fathered two sons and two daughters. It's unclear how many wives he had when his brother, Santiago, came to visit him at San Carlos in 1883. He was not interested in returning to Anglo society. Multiple wives and mixed-blood children might have been an impediment. He had station in society and an income. Even if the Chiricahuas were hostile to him, thought him mean and untrustworthy, he had status within his own band. There was no family to which he might return. But he was not hostile to his mother and stepfather.

—◦—

Santiago said, "Years later a friend of the family told me that he had seen my brother at San Carlos; that he had grown up as an Indian and was an interpreter for the government. So I went up to San Carlos to see him. . . . I did not know him at first but he looked very much like his sister, fair with grayish eyes. They called him Mickey Free."[11]

—◦—

When Santiago Ward tracked him down, Mickey invited him to stay with him, which his younger half-brother did for almost two years.[12] Mickey Free passed away on the Fort Apache Reservation about 1915.

On April 20, 1861, the Army promoted Lieutenant Isaiah Moore to captain. In July 1861, Captain Moore received orders to burn Fort Breckenridge and all military stores in Arizona and proceed to Fort Fillmore, near Mesilla on the Rio Grande, to participate in the defense of New Mexico from invading Texans. He was to join with and command the two companies of infantry at Fort Buchanan currently under command of Captain Gurden Chapin (promoted to captain April 22, 1861) since the departure of Lieutenant Colonel Pitcairn Morrison in March. Captain Moore burned Fort Breckenridge on July 10, and then marched Companies D and G of the 1st Dragoons to Tucson where he destroyed the flour mill, which held large stores of flour owned by the military. That July the Army redesignated the 1st Dragoons as the 1st U.S. Cavalry. Continuing, on July 21, he burned Fort Buchanan and its stores so that they would not fall into Confederate hands.

Settlers attempted to buy the stores, but Moore would not sell them below military prices. The Arizona settlers had made overtures toward the Confederacy and were believed to be in sympathy with the rebels. The officers under Moore's command included Lieutenant Richard Lord and Surgeon Ryland from Fort Breckenridge, Captain Gurden Chapin, Lieutenant Ingraham in command of Company H, 7th Infantry, Lieutenant Bascom commanding Company C, and Surgeon Irwin. Paddy Graydon abandoned his holdings in the Sonoita Valley and may have joined the column. If not, he left for the Rio Grande soon after.[13]

Captain Moore's column began the long march to the Rio Grande. On August 6, at Cooke's Canyon, north of modern Deming, New Mexico, Moore learned of the ignominious fall of Fort Fillmore to the rebels.[14]

Major Isaac Lynde held Fort Fillmore with a combined garrison of eleven companies of infantry and cavalry, close to six hundred well-disciplined and drilled veterans. This included most of the 7th Infantry, two hundred cavalry horses, and three hundred head of cattle. On July 23, 1861, a battalion of fewer than three hundred men of the Second Texas Regiment, Mounted Rifles, led by Lieutenant Colonel John R. Baylor, entered New Mexico. Baylor planned to surprise the garrison at Fort Fillmore at daybreak but two of his pickets, U.S. Army veterans, left their post and warned Lynde. The fort was saved. That afternoon, Major Lynde approached Mesilla, then held by the Confederates, with a demand for unconditional surrender. The rebels were defiant. Lynde ordered an attack and was repulsed. Losing his nerve, he then ordered the abandonment of Fort Fillmore and a march for Fort Stanton, 150 miles to the northeast. On July 27, 1861, Colonel Baylor's forces caught up with Lynde's column and demanded its surrender. Major Lynde surrendered to a force half the size of his. On November 25, 1861, Major Isaac Lynde was dropped from the Army rolls for abandoning his post at Fort Fillmore.[15]

Captain Moore burned his wagons and excess baggage. Now unencumbered, he led his four companies over a mountain trail, avoiding a Confederate ambush. He cleverly eluded pursuit and on August 8 arrived at Fort Craig on the Rio Grande.[16]

Paddy Graydon, formerly a soldier of Moore's company, used as leverage his experience in the regular army, his tough reputation for pursuing outlaws, his intimate knowledge of the geography of southern New Mexico, and his fluency in Spanish to secure an appointment from New Mexico Governor Henry Connelly as the captain of an independent spy company, a scouting organization. He recruited eighty-four New Mexicans at Lemitar and on October 19, his command was mustered into the Union Army.[17] During the first week of January 1862, Graydon was operating out of Cañada Alamosa, south of Fort Craig, with two cavalry companies, one of them Moore's, as a cavalry screen to provide information about the enemy and deny the enemy information about Union forces. Lieutenant Colonel Baylor unexpectedly advanced with five hundred men in an attempt to capture Graydon's spy company. Graydon, suspecting a raid, had placed pickets far downriver from the village and thus was warned of the Confederate approach. The Union forces withdrew to Fort Craig.[18] On January 16, 1862, Captain Isaiah Moore was killed in action.[19]

Lieutenant John Rogers Cooke, who had been on the stagecoach that arrived at Apache Pass from Tucson, completed his journey to Virginia. Although he learned it later, he had been promoted to first lieutenant on January 28, 1861. On May 30, 1861, he resigned his commission and joined the Confederacy, eventually rising to be a brigadier general. His brother in law, J. E. B. Stuart, also resigned his commission and fought for the Confederacy, an embarrassment to John's father, Philip St. George Cooke, who remained loyal to the Union. John Cooke died at Richmond, Virginia, on April 9, 1891.[20]

Next in the chain of command under Captain Moore as the four companies marched to Fort Craig was Captain Gurden Chapin, who had achieved his rank two days after Moore. Chapin was assigned to the 7th Infantry Regiment upon graduation from West Point and promoted to first lieutenant on March 3, 1855. In 1859, while at Fort Brown in Texas, Major Samuel P. Heintzelman noted that Chapin "who had got a divorce from his wife under peculiarly atrocious circumstances & married one of the Miss Pauls, has discovered an intimacy between her [his new wife] & one of the officers of his Regiment. Everybody says he is served right." Chapin came to Arizona with the 7th Infantry in October 1860. One of his children died at Fort Buchanan. When Colonel Morrison departed in March 1861, Chapin assumed command of the post and its two companies of infantry. He was dismissed from the service in August 1861, but reinstated that November. In April 1862, he fought at the Battle of Peralta in New Mexico, earning a brevet promotion.[21]

In March 1861, Lieutenant Colonel Pitcairn Morrison returned to the East seeking a new assignment, leaving Lieutenant Gurden Chapin in command of Fort Buchanan. Morrison became colonel of the 8th Infantry. The 8th Regiment had been captured in Texas when division commander General David E. Twiggs surrendered all the federal units and supplies to the Confederacy. Morrison's task was to recruit and train a new regiment.[22]

From the summer of 1861 through the winter of 1862, Colonel Edward R. S. Canby commanded the Department of New Mexico from Fort Craig on the Rio Grande south of Socorro. These were desperate times. Most of the 7th and 8th Regiments of Infantry in the tiny Federal Army had already surrendered to the Confederacy. Henry Hopkins Sibley had been a captain of the 2nd Regiment of Dragoons assigned to Fort Union, New Mexico, fifty miles or so northeast of Santa Fe. Located on the Santa Fe Trail, it was the major supply depot for New Mexico. Sibley conceived of a plan, resigned his commission, and went to Richmond, Virginia, to present the plan to President Jefferson Davis. Sibley was commissioned a brigadier general and his plan adopted. This plan was to raise two regiments of already trained Texas mounted militia and to head west, capturing supplies at each of the forts in Texas. At El Paso he would be supplied by merchants friendly to the Confederacy. He would then invade New Mexico, whose native New Mexicans disliked the Union and would rise to join him. He would capture more supplies at Forts Craig and Union and then go on to Colorado, where there were many Southerners in sympathy with the cause who would rise to join him. Utah, which included Nevada, had just completed a war, the Mormon Rebellion, and would be happy to join the Confederacy. Sibley's army would continue on and capture southern California, where there were many Southern sympathizers. The Confederacy would then be a transcontinental power with ports on the Pacific that the Union could not blockade. The Confederacy would have mines producing specie to fight the war.

Unfortunately for General Sibley, there was no trained Texas militia and no arms. These had all found their way into other formations. He had to recruit and train his men and scrounge weapons and horses for his soldiers. Some went out armed only with lances and others with shotguns. This took time. Lieutenant Colonel Baylor's July 1861 invasion of New Mexico had put the Union on alert to the danger from Texas. Sibley's regiments crossed the desert at the driest time of the year, finding poor forage and Indians more than willing to steal their horses. The forts, surrendered by General David E. Twiggs, had been stripped of supplies. The El Paso merchants failed to come through with supplies. At El Paso part of Sibley's force became dismounted cavalry (i.e., infantry). He was forced to spend months there consolidating his force and allowing it to rest and regain strength. Finally, in February 1862, he was ready to proceed.

Forewarned, Colonel Edward Canby had consolidated his forces at Fort Craig. Fort Craig sat at the northern end of the Jornada del Muerte, the Journey of the Dead Man, a one-hundred-mile stretch of desert that was traversed coming north from Mesilla. Wagons left the Rio Grande to avoid deep canyons chancing the more level desert. A ford brought the trail back west across the river south of Fort Craig, which stood between mountains on the west with the river and Mesa de la Contedera to the east. Short of artillery, Colonel Canby armed his post with Quaker guns: logs made to look like cannon. Coming off a hard march, the Texans would face a hard fight to force their way past.

Canby consolidated various companies of cavalry, infantry, and New Mexico Volunteers,[23] as well as Captain Paddy Graydon's Independent

Spy Company, for a total of about three thousand men. Also present was Captain Theodore Dodd's seventy-one-man company of Coloradans, who would see some of the heaviest fighting, and ten companies of the 1st Regiment of New Mexico Volunteers under Colonel Kit Carson, the famous mountain man and scout.[24] Canby had very few regulars, little artillery, and few cavalry, and he didn't completely trust volunteers or New Mexico militia. Moreover, his scouts, Captain Paddy Graydon's Spies and Guides, provided information that indicated the Texans would attack up the Pecos River east of the Rio Grande, so Canby had to keep forces at Fort Stanton as well. Nonetheless, Colonel Canby had a slight (1.3:1) advantage in strength.

On February 16, 1862, General Sibley drew up the four regiments of his Texas force in battle order south of Fort Craig. Canby hoped they'd risk a frontal assault, but they did not. Impressed perhaps by Quaker guns and the numerical superiority of the Union force, after a minor skirmish, Sibley withdrew. On February 19, the Texans crossed to the east bank of the Rio Grande and proceeded north across from Fort Craig on the west bank. Formidable Mesa de la Contedera stood before them. Canby sent part of his force across the river to hold the high ground across from the fort. Concerned that the Confederates would again attempt a frontal assault, he maintained most of his force at Fort Craig. On February 20, the Texans located a steep trail over Mesa de la Contedera that descended on the northern side to the three fords of the Rio Grande at Valverde.

On February 21, the Texans began to descend on Valverde a few miles north of Fort Craig. Canby's pickets and scouts warned him in time, but he was still concerned that this was only a feint. After all, the sandy trail was steep and difficult, and only a few soldiers could pass at a time. The trail was so narrow that shepherds had used it to funnel and count their sheep, hence its name, The Counting Mesa. Committing to this move, General Sibley denied himself the capture of Fort Craig and its much-needed supplies, but placed himself in position to continue north around the Union Army to attack poorly defended Fort Union.

Both Texans and Canby's forces arrived piecemeal on the east bank of the Rio Grande. Much of the Union force was held back at Fort Craig, and then, as they came north, they had to ford the chest-deep, icy river to take positions on the east bank. The Texans trickled over the mesa into an abandoned river channel that provided a covered and concealed trench along the eastern side of the battlefield, allowing the Confederates freedom to maneuver within their lines. McRae's all-important battery was at the center, defended by the companies of the 7th Infantry. In midafternoon, Colonel Canby, arriving on the battlefield, saw an opportunity to decisively defeat the Texans. By extending to the right, Kit Carson's regiment would overlap the end of the Confederate line and be in their trench, providing the opportunity to roll up the unprotected enemy flank. In extending to the right, the New Mexicans left the center weakened and McRae's battery exposed. The Texans attacked in some of the heaviest and bloodiest fighting of the day. In his book *Bloody Valverde*, author John Taylor describes the scene:

> *The image of the onrushing Texans, combined with the shell and canister from Teel's guns, were too much for some of Mortimore's* [2nd] *New Mexico Volunteers on the left of* [McRae's] *battery. Terrified, the men fell back from the shower of lead; terror turned to panic; and the left side of Plympton's battalion, comprised mainly of men of the Tenth Infantry collapsed. Despite this problem, not all of the volunteers nor all of Plympton's battalion ran to the river; a sizable fraction of the battalion, both volunteers and regulars alike, rushed forward to defend the battery. . . . Hubbell and the men of the Fifth New Mexico rushed to the right of the battery. Rockwell and George Bascom . . . led the regulars from the Seventh and Tenth Infantry to a position on the left.*[25]

As the Texans charged to the guns, fighting was hand to hand. One of the Texans called out, "We don't want to kill you, McRae!" He yelled back, "I shall never forsake my guns!" and was shot dead, falling across his cannon. Captain Richard Lord was ordered into action to save the guns. "Draw sabres! Charge!" But soon, finding himself facing friendly fire from the 5th Infantry, ordered, "Dismount and prepare to fight on foot!"[26] The guns were lost and soon even the 7th Infantry, stubbornly defending them, recognized the lost cause. First Sergeant Daniel Robinson recalled, "Men were breaking to the rear and I thought of the low bank from which we had deployed. . . . I broke for the bank and to my surprise found it was quite steep and I was up to my waist in water . . . quite a number of men were under it, unsure whether they should cross [the river] or remain."[27]

The 7th Infantry suffered some of the heaviest losses of the battle.[28] Somewhere in this melee, Captain George N. Bascom fell. Texans drove the 7th Infantry back to the river and the mortuary detail discovered his body on a sand bar.[29] Fighting at his side was First Sergeant Daniel Robinson, who went on to fight in the battles for Albuquerque and at Peralta. On August 10, 1863, Robinson was commissioned a second lieutenant. After the war he returned to the 7th Infantry as an officer serving in Dakota, Montana, Wyoming, and Colorado. He retired in 1889 and died in 1904.[30]

Lieutenant Richard S. C. Lord had been promoted captain October 26, 1861, continuing to command Company D, 1st Dragoons, which had been redesignated the 1st U.S. Cavalry the previous summer. Sent east, he earned brevet promotions at the Battle of Gettysburg and again at the Battle of Five Forks. On October 15, 1866, in Ohio, he died of tuberculosis.[31] After the Battle of Valverde, he was accused of misconduct for delaying the charge to save the guns, but a court of inquiry cleared him. The orders were incorrectly relayed and when properly communicated were obeyed as far as they could be.[32]

On January 5, 1862, First Sergeant Reuben Bernard was promoted to second lieutenant at Fort Craig. He fought alongside Captain Lord and was instrumental in providing evidence that cleared the captain of misconduct. He served as an officer throughout the Civil War and on December 4, 1868, returned to Arizona as a captain (brevet colonel) with the 8th U.S. Cavalry. Soon after his return Colonel Thomas Devin, commanding the 8th, first made mention of the vengeance motive in Cochise's actions after October 1860,[33] a motive not previously considered. Six weeks after Bernard reached Tucson, in a district commander's report, Devin attributed Cochise's depredation to revenge for the Apache Pass episode. From this time on military correspondence began to claim that Cochise had been friendly before 1860. Bernard himself repeated this error in a letter.[34] It was after Bernard's return that a wildly distorted version of the events at Apache Pass began to circulate, becoming embedded firmly in Arizona folklore. According to one version of this account:

Cochise brought Wallace to the stage station, offering to exchange him for the Chiricahua hostages. Bascom refused unless the kidnapped boy were included. Within view of the station, Wallace was dragged to death behind Cochise's horse. Sgt. Bernard, the story continued, remonstrated with Bascom so vehemently that he was court martialed. The tale of the wise sergeant and the stupid lieutenant is totally implausible. . . . But the revenge motive was not mentioned before 1869, and events of 1861 showed Cochise's anger lasted less than a week.[35]

Another version of this implausible tale is included in Sidney DeLong's *History of Arizona*, 1903. DeLong arrived in Arizona with the California Column in 1862. He stayed after the Civil War and became sutler (the precursor to the post exchange) at Fort Bowie where Captain Bernard was assigned. This is how DeLong told Bernard's story:

[A]*t that time, an Irishman, known as Johnny Ward . . . had a Mexican woman as housekeeper. This woman had a son, at that time a small boy, whose paternal ancestor was an Apache Indian, as the mother had been a captive among them and the boy was a result of this captivity. In the absence of Mr. Ward the mountain Apaches . . . visited the ranch and packed off everything of value to them, including the boy. . . . The commanding officer of the fort sent out a new lieutenant named Bascom, accompanied by twelve men under Reuben F. Bernard, then sergeant, who afterwards became a captain in the First Cavalry . . .* [proceeded] *to Apache Pass, . . . where he would likely find Indians who could give some information regarding the lost boy and what band of Indians had committed the depredation. The lieutenant, who was not long out from West Point, upon arriving at the station with his party found there Chief Cochise and another Indian. Cochise professed entire ignorance of the depredation or what band of Apaches had committed it, but said he would find out and see that the boy was returned. This explanation and promise did not satisfy Lieutenant Bascom and he at once made prisoners of the two Indians and . . . there pitched camp giving his two captives a Sibley tent to themselves, stationing a guard in front and rear of the tent but with unloaded muskets.*

Cochise, not relishing the confinement, and not having committed any hostile act was looking for an avenue of escape, and as he had been left his sheath knife, which every Indian carries in his belt, he slashed a long cut in the tent and darted through, followed by his fellow-prisoner. The guard in the rear of the tent struck Cochise with his gun and knocked him down, but Cochise, having the agility of a cat, arose and upon his hands and feet slid off like a flash into the bushes and among the rocks, and in a moment was gone beyond hope of pursuit.[36]

Very few old-timers who had been in Arizona before 1862 remained there after the Civil War. Most of the settlers and miners departed after military protection was withdrawn. When the Confederates captured Tucson in February 1862, most of the Union sympathizers departed. When the California Column arrived in June 1862, most of the Confederate sympathizers left or were imprisoned. Tom Jeffords reported that in that June Tucson's population was below one hundred. In 1864, the focus of mining efforts shifted to the center of the territory and the capitol was established at Prescott. Mail service was not reestablished for Tucson until 1867. The southern part of the territory languished. In 1868, Bernard, a braggart at the best of times, found himself a valuable resource; he knew what had happened before 1862 and he made the most of it, making himself the hero of the tale. In 1969, historian Constance Wynn Altshuler summarized the evidence that showed that Reuben Bernard had invented the then-popular version of the story of the confrontation between Bascom and Cochise.

Up to this time [1868] the notion that Cochise raided for vengeance had not been heard. Letters of the Calif. Vols. who came to Arizona in 1862 did not mention it, nor did those of the 14th Inf. who arrived in 1866, although Cochise was a frequent topic of correspondence. Six weeks after Bernard reached Tucson came the first known written statement. A Dist. Commander's report attributed Cochise's depredations to revenge for the Apache Pass episode. From this time on, military correspondence said Cochise had been friendly before 1860 [sic], and some letters had other elements of the false version. Not only did the timing of Bernard's arrival point to him as the probable source, but he made this error—1860 instead of 1861—in dating the incident.[37]

On October 5, 1869, Cochise and his warriors ambushed the mail stagecoach, a buckboard, three miles west of the old Dragoon Springs Station, killing the driver, as well as the four-man infantry escort and Apache Pass mine owner, John Finckle Stone. The next day nearby they attacked a drove of cattle coming from Texas, killing one man and capturing 250 cows. The drovers sent word to Fort Bowie where Captain Reuben Bernard was away on patrol and Lieutenant William Winters was the senior officer. Winters mounted twenty-five troopers, all that were available, and went in pursuit. On October 8, Winters caught up with Cochise at the Pedregosa Mountains near the border with Mexico (south of the Chiricahua Mountains). Three of five Apaches in Cochise's rear guard were slain. Although outnumbered three to one, the soldiers rushed into the fight. Cochise conducted a heroic and brilliant counterattack that diverted Winters' attention. The Apaches escaped, although Winters recovered the entire herd.

On October 16, Captain Bernard set out to find Cochise, arriving at the scene of Winters' fight on October 18 and picking up the trail. Bernard followed the trail through Tex Canyon in the Chiricahuas and caught up with Cochise at Turtle Mountain. In desultory fighting, Cochise held the ground and Lieutenant Lafferty was gravely wounded. Bernard submitted recommendations for thirty-two of his men to receive the Medal of Honor.

In 1882, Reuben Bernard was promoted to major, and in 1892, to lieutenant colonel of the 9th Cavalry (Buffalo Soldiers). He retired in 1896.[38]

On September 16, 1862, Surgeon Bernard John Dowling Irwin was promoted to major. In 1882, he returned to Arizona as medical director of the department and served there until 1885. He died December 15, 1917.

All through his life, he had an interest in the sciences and investigated the flora and fauna as well as the geology of Arizona. He extended medical science as well by writing about the treatment of wounds. He inspired the hospital stewards that trained under him, and some of them went on to be scientists in their own right. He wrote of one of his assistants:

> *As he belonged to "D" troop, 1st Dragoons. . . . I had Private Charles Bendire detailed as hospital attendant, sometime in 1858. He was then comparatively young, an active efficient soldier, quiet and of modest, retiring disposition. At that time I was collecting specimens of Natural History and seeing my work he would from time to time bring me specimens of one kind or another which he supposed desirable for my collection.*
>
> *His troop having been ordered to California my impression is that he accompanied it to that State and was stationed at Fort Tejon, in the San Bernardino valley, where he commenced collecting birds' nests and birds' eggs.*[39]

Bendire is recalled as having been the first to identify Bendire's thrasher.

Captain James "Paddy" Graydon survived the fighting at Valverde. He went on to pursue Mescalero Apaches. On November 5, 1862, at Fort Stanton, Dr. John M. Whitlock accused Graydon of having acted without warrant in the Gallinas Massacre of Manuelito's band of Mescaleros. Graydon confronted the doctor, telling him, "If you come to this post again and insult an officer I will horsewhip you, I am an officer and you are a pimp that follows the army."[40] The doctor drew his pistol and fired. At the same time, Graydon returned fire. They wounded each other. Graydon's men became involved and silenced the doctor forever. Graydon lay in the hospital, his wound thought not serious; he was expected to recover. On November 8, 1862, Graydon died suddenly. Colonel Kit Carson investigated the incident and on November 20 reported to General Carleton, the commander of the Department of New Mexico. In consideration of past services, Carleton offered Graydon the opportunity to resign his commission. It was too late for that.

A militant eastern Coyotero (also known as Gila or White Mountain) Apache, Francisco was over six feet tall and is remembered as the friend and ally of Cochise. His home country was in the White Mountains north of the Gila River. Today his people reside on the White Mountain Apache Reservation. James Tevis, station keeper at Apache Pass, recalled a conversation with the chief:

The last time the Coyotero chief, Francisco, was here, he asked me if the Americans were going to buy or take Sonora? I told him I thought they would. He then wanted to know if the Americans would let the Indians steal from Sonora, and I replied that I rather thought not. He then said that as long as he lived and had a warrior to follow him, he would fight Sonora, and he did not care if the Americans did try to stop it, he would fight till he was killed. I think he would make his word true.[41]

Some sources say Francisco was a Mexican captive who rose to prominence as a major war leader. He may have participated in the Battle of Apache Pass, July 1862,[42] and was probably shot to death in 1865.[43]

Mangas Coloradas, Red Sleeves, held sway over a large number of eastern Chiricahua, the Bedonkohe, also known as Mogollon and Mimbres. He formed alliances beyond his own band partly through marriage. His daughter, Dos-teh-seh, was married to Cochise. An imposing man of fine figure, he was over six feet tall and powerfully built. Some said he was called Red Sleeves because his sleeves were soaked in the blood of his enemies. More likely, the name arose from his habit of turning the sleeves of his jacket back to expose the red lining. On October 20, 1846, he met with General Stephen Watts Kearny commanding the Army of the West at the Santa Rita Copper Mines. He promised assistance in combating their mutual enemy, the Mexicans. In February 1852, he met amicably with John Russell Bartlett's Boundary Commission. When the Stein's Peak Overland Mail station (Doubtful Canyon) opened, Mangas Coloradas appeared with his warriors demanding a gift of cornmeal. The Apache leader was generally peaceful and refrained from raiding Americans until 1860, when miners occupied his home country at Pinos Altos.

Until then, the only American presence in his land had been travelers and Overland Mail stations. In 1861, he joined Cochise in attacking the Arizona Wagon Train and Freeman Thomas party at Cooke's Canyon. Later that year he attacked Pinos Altos. On July 15, 1862, he joined Cochise and Francisco in an attack on the California Column known to history as the Battle of Apache Pass.

In September 1862, former mountain man and explorer Joseph Walker led a party of thirty-six men into New Mexico in search of gold. They would eventually find it on the Hassayampa River. This resulted in the founding of Prescott, which became the first territorial capital. At Santa Fe, the group signed loyalty oaths to the Union for General James Carleton. In January 1863, at the ruins of Fort McLane near Pinos Altos, sometime Confederate officer Jack Swilling joined the group along with a party of Union soldiers from the California Column. General Carleton's soldiers were attempting to capture Mangas Coloradas. Swilling came up with a plan to lure the chief in for a parley of friendship. The combined group executed the plan and when the old chief drew close enough, the soldiers and prospectors took him prisoner. Swilling promised the Apache leader good treatment and release after a period of time contingent on the good behavior of his people. The mixed group took him to Fort McLane, where they met General Joseph R. West and additional soldiers. The combined group mounted a two-man guard on the chief while a soldier and a civilian walked beats around the camp. The two soldiers guarding the chief goaded and tortured the old man, and then, when he protested, shot him "trying to escape."[44] Daniel Conner, a member of Walker's expedition on sentinel duty that night, reported the great chief's death as follows:

> *I could see them plainly by the firelight as they were engaged in heating their fixed bayonets in the fire and putting them to the feet and naked legs of Mangus, who was from time to time trying to shield his limbs from the hot steel. When I came up to the fire each time they would become innocent and sleepy and remain so until I departed on my beat again, when they would arouse themselves into the decided spirit of indulging this barbarous pastime. I didn't appreciate this*

conduct one particle, but said nothing to them at the time and really I had some curiosity to see to what extent they would indulge it. I was surprised at their ultimate intentions just before midnight when I was about midway of my beat and approaching the firelight. Just then Mangus raised himself upon his left elbow and began to expostulate in a vigorous way by telling the sentinels in Spanish that he was no child to be playing with. But his expostulations were cut short, for he had hardly begun his exclamation when both sentinels promptly brought down their Minnie muskets to bear on him and fired, nearly at the same time through his body.

The Chief fell back off of his elbow into the same position in which he had been lying all the forepart of the night. This was quickly followed by two shots through the head by each sentinel's six-shooter, making in all, six shots fired in rapid succession.[45]

The death of Mangas Coloradas is an outrage.[46] Nothing about the incident shines as proper military behavior. The prospectors were apparently better behaved than the soldiers of the California Column and Jack Swilling. The former Confederate captured the chief under false pretense, and then, even failing to honor the pretense, the soldiers murdered him. This should have outraged the Chiricahua Apache. Mangas Coloradas held a wider span of control than Cochise. Cochise undoubtedly thought that Lieutenant Bascom had tried to capture him under a similar pretense, though it is doubtful that the officer had this in mind. Cochise took his own captives, violating a flag of truce to do it, and then murdered his captives. He had to have suspected some form of retribution would follow from the soldiers at Apache Pass, blood for blood. In subsequent peace talks, the old chief's murder was hardly mentioned. It didn't fit into the legend of the wise sergeant and the stubborn lieutenant circulating after 1868 as an explanation for the start of the war. The legend is a white, and not an Apache, legend. The Apache learned it later.

One of the two boys at Apache Pass was likely Chie, the son of Cochise's brother, Coyuntura.[47] Taken captive by Lieutenant Bascom, he was released soon after at Fort Buchanan. His father was among those hanged, and he was raised by Cochise. Chie was one of the Apache guides who took Tom Jeffords and General Oliver O. Howard to Cochise's Stronghold in the Dragoon Mountains in 1872.

The other boy Bascom held was Cochise's own son, Naiche. He, too, was soon released. In October 1872, Naiche was with his father when Cochise negotiated a peace treaty with General Howard. Cochise died on June 8, 1874, and was succeeded by Naiche's elder brother, Taza, who died of pneumonia while on a trip to Washington, DC, on September 26, 1876, after which nineteen-year-old Naiche became chief. Troubles, including several murders, led to the closing of the reservation Cochise had negotiated and the evacuation of the Chokonen to the San Carlos Reservation. Taza and Naiche assisted in moving their father's people to the new reservation. Conditions there were unpleasant. The people were forced to wear identity tags and to report in frequently to be counted. The reservation was at a low, desert altitude, and the ten bands of Western Apache already there were not friends to the Chokonen. Discontent led to a second war. In 1880, Naiche left the reservation with Geronimo, Juh, and some of his people and headed into the Sierra Madre Mountains between the Mexican states of Chihuahua and Sonora. In 1881, he returned on a raid to San Carlos to collect more of his people and take them to Mexico. In 1882, General George Crook induced him to return to the reservation. In May 1885, he again left for Mexico. On September 4, 1886, Naiche surrendered to General Nelson Miles for the last time and was shipped off to Florida and Alabama. In 1913, when the Chokonen were finally allowed to return west, he was among those that settled at the Mescalero Reservation in southeastern New Mexico. He fathered eight sons and two daughters, and those who claim descent from Cochise do so through Naiche.[48]

Speaking with General Howard in 1872, Cochise noted the confrontation at Apache Pass as a turning point in relations with the Americans:

We were once a large people covering these mountains; we lived well; we were at peace. One day my best friend was seized by an officer of the white men and treacherously killed. . . . The worst place of all is Apache Pass. There, five Indians, one my brother, were murdered. Their bodies were hung up and kept there till they were skeletons.

Naiche, son of Cochise, and his wife, ca. 1880s. Naiche and his mother were taken hostage by Lieutenant Bascom at Apache Pass. ARIZONA HISTORICAL SOCIETY

. . . Now Americans and Mexicans kill an Apache on sight. I have retaliated with all my might. My people have killed Americans and Mexicans and taken their property. Their losses have been greater than mine. I have killed ten white men for every Indian slain, but I know that the whites are many and the Indians are few. Apaches are growing less and less every day. . . . Why shut me up on a reservation? We will make peace. We will keep it faithfully. But let us go around free as Americans do. Let us go wherever we please.[49]

By 1872, Cochise had been willing to talk peace for a number of years. He also knew by then that Americans thought that Lieutenant Bascom had done him a wrong. Bernard's story had been in circulation since 1868. Americans now thought that Cochise had always been peaceful before 1860. He capitalized on this, although he knew he had raided farms and ranches. He was Cochise who had protected the Overland Mail and he's reported in this era as offering to do so again. In Cochise's statements—whether they were about the hanging that called forth his revenge or Bascom's presumed attempt to arrest him—changed with time and audience. In the statement he made to General Howard, he paused, perhaps reflecting, after saying Apache Pass was the worst place because of the hanging. Obviously, he was hurt by the loss of his brother, Coyuntura. He resumed with a new thought. Americans and Mexicans kill Apaches on sight. And he retaliated with all his might for this wanton murder, not for the loss of his hanged brother. At Cañada Alamosa, in 1871, Cochise refused an offer of food out of fear that it was poisoned. His response to Lieutenant Bascom was conditioned by long negative experience and did not rest solely on anything George Bascom said or did.

Cochise had a longstanding distrust of councils with Mexicans. His people, including his father and elder brother, had been slain at "peaceful" meetings in Sonora and Chihuahua. Some of this distrust extended to Americans after his meeting with Lieutenant Bascom, regardless whether it was Bascom or the interpreter, Ward, who brought up detention. The lieutenant had just agreed to allow Cochise ten days to go and bring in the boy, Felix. He had no reason to detain his emissary. Ward may have said something different. A man so deeply involved in the loss should never have been allowed to serve as interpreter. Cochise expressed a fear of American councils dating from his meeting with the lieutenant, but that fear was much older, and it did not stop him from meeting with American officials later.

Two things prevented peace. One was trust, and this issue was not settled until Cochise became fast friends with a remarkable man, Tom Jeffords. Tom became his counselor, friend, and Indian agent. The second was the Apache leader's desire for a reservation in his own country. He would be an outsider at San Carlos (Camp Goodwin) or at Cañada Alamosa, which was in Chihenne Country near the Rio Grande. Worse, the Indian service wanted to close the Cañada Alamosa reservation and move the people to the Tularosa Valley in far western New Mexico, near the Arizona border. It was at higher elevation with a shorter growing season. Cochise said that the flies there ate horses' eyes and that the place was haunted. Apparently, there was a large population of owls and Apaches know that when they hear an owl hoot, someone close to them will die.

On January 20, 1869, Cochise emerged from his stronghold in the Dragoon Mountains to talk with Major Frank Perry. Cochise told him, "I won't stay at Goodwin [San Carlos], it is no place for Indians."[50] He noted that the Coyoteros would steal his stock. In December of that year, the Chokonen leader sent word to Chihenne chief Loco that he would consider joining him in his efforts to make peace once he was certain that the Americans were treating Loco's people fairly.[51] On August 13, 1870, Major John Green reported that Cochise had visited Camp Mogollon (later called Fort Apache, the Coyotero reservation): "I have the honor to report that the Indian Chief Cochise sent a message to me saying that he wanted to make peace with the whites and was tired of war."[52]

In October 1870, Cochise conferred with William Arny, special Indian agent for New Mexico at Cañada Alamosa. This was the third reservation Cochise looked into. He wanted a reservation in his own country and he wanted peace.

In 1871, the superintendent of Indian Affairs for New Mexico, Nathanial Pope, sent out a peace mission, which, somewhere west of Cañada Alamosa, passed through Cochise's camp. The chief was away on a raid into Mexico. All of the people except Cochise's immediate family were escorted peacefully to that reservation. Indian Agent Orlando Piper obeyed Pope's order to seek out Cochise by sending Jose Maria Trujillo to find him. Cochise refused to accompany him. Frontiersman, scout, and prospector Tom Jeffords next volunteered to seek out Cochise. He departed from Cañada Alamosa on June 7, 1871. These were perilous times. The Apache were in an uproar. On April 30, a mixed militia of Tucson citizens and Indians from San Xavier del Bac raided the Aravaipa Apache under the protection of the Army at Camp Grant, killing more than sixty and sending thirty children into slavery in Mexico. The Camp Grant Massacre stunned all of the Apache who had peaceful intentions. They would not be safe on the reservations. Vengeful Americans might seek them out. The newspapers clamored for the courts to hang some of them. Out of fear that he might be attacked while on an errand of peace, Cochise refused to move cross-country with his family. On June 28, Jeffords returned without them.

In September, Cochise came to Cañada Alamosa. During the ensuing months, he was nearby and Jeffords spent a great deal of time with him. At first they conversed in Spanish, but in time Jeffords picked up Apache. People noticed that a friendship had grown and that Jeffords always knew where to find the Chokonen leader. The Apache and the frontiersman became friends. Jeffords had a knack for impressing people quickly with his trustworthiness and courage. It was something developed during his time as a ship's officer on the Great Lakes. Everyone knew that the two were friends, so much so that some wondered whether Jeffords sided with the Apache or the Americans.

On March 20, 1872, a peace council between Cochise and the superintendent of Indian Affairs for New Mexico, General Gordon Granger, met. Cochise called Jeffords as his advisor. Assistant Surgeon Henry Turrill, who attended, said later that he and Colonel Willard agreed that if things went wrong at the meeting, one would "account for" Cochise and the other Jeffords. Peace was not achieved. Cochise disliked the agent and wanted no part of the Tularosa Valley. Cochise was recorded as saying:

> *I have no father and mother; I am alone in this world. No one cares for Cochise; that is why I do not care to live, and wish the rocks to fall on me and cover me up. If I had a father and a mother like you, I would be with them and they with me. When I was going around in the world, all were asking for Cochise. Now he is here—you see him and hear him—are you glad? If so, say so. Speak. American and Mexicans, I do not wish to hide anything from you nor have you hide anything from me; I will not lie to you; do not lie to me. I want to live in these mountains; I do not want to go to Tularosa. That is a long ways off. The flies on those mountains eat out the eyes of the horses. The bad spirits live there. I have drunk these waters and they have cooled me; I do not want to leave here.[53]*

In late summer 1872, General Oliver Otis Howard, the one-armed Christian general, arrived as personal emissary from President Grant authorized to grant terms he saw fit in order to achieve peace with the Chokonen Apache. At least five people told the general that the only person who could take him to Cochise was Tom Jeffords. There are two stories of how the general and the scout met. The general says he invited Tom to his tent. The other story says the general had to seek Jeffords out in a saloon where he was drinking. Both stories agree that the general asked if Tom could take him to Cochise and that the scout replied, "I can take you, but Cochise won't stand for a cavalry patrol." A tiny party, Jeffords, the general, his aide, a cook, and a packer crossed Apacheria from the Rio Grande to the western slope of the Dragoon Mountains.

At China Meadow, Cochise greeted Jeffords as a brother calling him "shdazha," or, my younger brother. Cochise asked, "Can I trust this general?" Tom relied, "I think so, but I won't let him promise too much." Eight miles farther north they talked peace at Cathedral Rock and then moved half a mile west to a circle of rocks where Cochise explained the

terms to his people and got them to agree. The next day they went farther north to the abandoned Dragoon Springs Overland Mail Station
where they met with the officers from Fort Bowie (at Apache Pass) and
explained the terms to them. Peace came in October 1872.

The terms of the treaty were oral. Cochise's reservation included
most of modern Cochise County, Arizona, its boundary running from
Dragoon Springs to Doubtful Canyon, then south through Peloncillo
Mountains to the Mexican border, then west to the western slope of the
Mule Mountains, and finally north along the Mule Mountains and Dragoons to Dragoon Springs. The modern towns of Bisbee, Willcox, and
Douglas were inside the reservation and Tombstone just outside. Cochise
insisted that Jeffords would be the agent. Tom didn't want the job but was
told there could be no peace without him.

From October 1872 until April 1876, southern Arizona had peace
and was free from Indian raids. Cochise kept the peace and his people
did as well. Jeffords administered the reservation in a manner the Apache
liked and only the Indian service could complain about.

Cochise passed away on June 8, 1874. Tom Jeffords was with him just
before his death, and Cochise asked him to remain as agent. Jeffords said,
"Your people will not listen to me." Cochise told him to gather his sub-
chiefs and this was done. It was agreed that his son, Taza, would be chief
and Taza would listen to Jeffords. On June 7, Jeffords was called away on
agency business. He recalled his last meeting with Cochise:

> In saying good-bye, Cochise said: "Chickasaw [shdazha], do you
> think you will ever see me alive again?" Jeffords replied: "I do not
> know; I don't think I will, for you have been failing very rapidly in
> the last three days, and I think that by tomorrow night you will be
> dead." Cochise said: "I think so too, about tomorrow morning, at ten
> o'clock, I will pass out, but do you think we will ever meet again?"
> Jeffords replied: "I don't know. What do you think about it?" "Well,"
> said Cochise, "I have been giving it a good deal of thought since I have
> been sick here, and I think we will." "Where?" asked Jeffords. "I don't
> know, somewhere up yonder," pointing to the skies. He never feared
> death, but rather courted it.[54]

Cochise was buried in a hidden grave near East Stronghold Canyon in the Sulphur Springs Valley. He was buried with the things he loved in life. His pistols were belted on. He was wrapped in the heavy blanket cattle baron, Colonel Henry Clay Hooker, had given him with his rifle at his side. Finally, his horse was shot and went into the grave with him. Some think the Apache do this so the departed will have these things on the other side. It isn't so. They do not wish the spirit to return for the things he loved.

Tom Jeffords never broke faith with Apache custom and his friend. He never revealed the location of the grave. The peace, based on trust and the friendship of Cochise and Tom Jeffords, lasted until 1876, two years beyond Cochise's death.[55]

Chapter Fifteen

CONCLUSIONS: WHY WAR CAME

A band of about 20 Indians stole some 80 to 90 horses and mules from the Sonora Exploring and Mining Company. Captain Isaac Van Duzer Reeve believed the Chokonen were guilty and ordered Ewell to follow them, but their trail was wiped out by a heavy rain. Ewell nevertheless concluded that the thieves were Cochise's people.[1]
—LETTER FROM ISAAC VAN DUZER REEVE TO
JOHN WILKINS, ASST. ADJUTANT GENERAL,
HEADQUARTERS DEPART OF NEW MEXICO, JULY 20, 1859

THE CHOKONEN WERE HUNTERS AND GATHERERS, MORE SETTLED THAN nomadic. When game and resources became scarce in an area, they moved, but they might stay in one spot for years or move with the seasons. They were as variable in this as the climate. One can look down the San Pedro Valley, in their old territory, on a moonlit summer evening and watch a half-dozen thunderstorms playing over different parts of the land. One side of the valley can suffer from flooding while across the way the drought is unbroken. Game animals and vegetable foods become abundant or rare in response to the disposition of moody weather patterns. Some years, food is abundant in one area but not in others. Some years food is scarce everywhere. Go-jii-ya is the most important ceremony of the Chokonen kin, the Jicarilla Apache. It is a race whose outcome determines whether plant or animal food will be more abundant in the coming year. The Chiricahua celebrate the Sunrise Ceremony, which serves to maintain the all-important balance of nature. The Chokonen ate acorns, a highly irregular crop, which they used as a thickening in stews. Game was always scarce. There were antelope, deer, and bighorn sheep, but no buffalo, the mainstay of the plains tribes that allowed them to gather in great numbers as nomads following the herds.

For the Chokonen the need to raid their neighbors for subsistence came with the climate. They might abstain for a few years, but when the weather turned on them they had to in order to survive. They did not raid for glory as the plains buffalo hunters did. They raided to survive. The purpose of the raid was to return alive to their families with food and supplies.

In the 1830s, Mexico made grants of land in Chokonen territory to *dons*[2] that were intended to finance families to populate the land. A ranch was established along Babocomari Creek, but the Chiricahua soon drove the Mexicans away. They left behind their cattle to go wild. Apaches hunted the herds, killing off the cows. In 1846, when Colonel Philip St. George Cooke passed by building a road along the San Pedro, he encountered a herd of ill-tempered bulls. Soon after, the herd without cows died out.

When natural resources failed, as during long droughts, the Apache turned to plundering their neighbors who farmed irrigated fields in the river valleys. As Spanish and then Mexicans encroached, the Apache found the meat of cattle, burro, mule, and horse enticing. The Chokonen took horses and mules as food, not as a sign of power and wealth. The newcomers brought cloth, which the Apache readily adopted for clothing, as well as corn, beans, flour, and useful metal implements. The Apache would raid in one area for plunder and trade the plundered goods in another. If their trading partners were weak, or if the Apache were short of trade goods, they'd demand presents or raid instead. If those raided killed Apaches in the process, the Apache sought revenge. When the Americans arrived, the pattern continued with one difference: The Americans brought four companies of soldiers, so it was easier and safer to continue raiding Mexicans whose government couldn't afford to send so many soldiers to defend them.

Apache fighter Captain Richard Ewell noticed the changing pattern of behavior among the Indians. As famine increased in the late 1850s, they took chances raiding Americans and risking the wrath of the dragoons. Ewell's biographer summarized what he had said in letters and reports: "The Chiricahuas routinely conducted raids into Sonora and Chihuahua, Mexico, but in recent years famine had prompted them to attack settlements in New Mexico and Arizona, too."[3]

One of Captain Richard S. Ewell's earliest campaigns against the Chiricahua began in May 1857. He rode around the Chiricahua Mountains without discerning many Indian camps. A few mutual shots were exchanged before Colonel Benjamin Bonneville, commanding the Department of New Mexico, called Ewell and the several companies of dragoons under his command away to join the Gila Expedition against the Mogollon Apache.

Raiding increased in 1859 as natural conditions worsened. By 1860, even the Chokonen became involved in raiding Americans, and Cochise's warriors raided along Sonoita Creek. Far from protecting the Overland Mail, Cochise twice raided the mail at Ewell's Station and then at Dragoon Springs Station. The Americans sent two companies of dragoon cavalry to California in response to the Mormon Rebellion and then sent another to Mesilla, replacing it with an ineffective company of infantry. In October 1860, two companies of infantry moved into Fort Buchanan while the dragoons departed from the populated region, opening the door for even more raiding, which hit a high point when Felix Ward was snatched in broad daylight as his mother and stepfather's business partner watched.

The thirty-second degree corridor runs through the heart of Chiricahua country, from the Rio Grande to Tucson. In 1846, Topographical Engineer William H. Emory, who traveled with General Stephen Watts Kearny's Army of West, noted its existence and importance. He returned to work on the survey of the border with Mexico and wrote about the corridor in 1857 in his *Report on the United States and Mexican Boundary Commission*. The corridor is a string of low passes across the Continental Divide and beyond that allow the all-weather passage of wagons and railroad. It is the only such corridor south of South Pass in Wyoming that was useful to the railroads. South Pass closes with winter weather, making the southern corridor even more important. Naturally, this became the route of an emigrant road and of the transcontinental mail service, the Overland Mail, colloquially known as the Butterfield Mail. In 1881, the Southern Pacific Railroad followed this route. Today we know it as the I-10 corridor.

It was a corridor busy with traffic. Freight wagons rolled continuously. Some fifty thousand Forty-niners are estimated to have come by the southern route. And there was mineral wealth in the area, as well. In the 1850s, Americans were working mines at Mowry in the Patagonia Mountains, at the Hacienda Santa Rita in the mountains of the same name, at Aravaipa, and along the San Pedro River at Brunckow's Mine. By 1869, John Finckle Stone was mining at Apache Pass, where the California Column established Fort Bowie in 1862. The fort remained until the 1890s. Prospectors made some of the largest strikes in 1877 at Bisbee and Tombstone, and there were many smaller ones in every range of mountains in Chiricahua country. With mining strikes came soldiers to protect the miners, farmers, hunters, and ranchers, along with cattle drives and freight lines to support them. The corridor made mining possible by providing easy access to the mines and easy transport of ores. The excess of travelers, soldiers, prospectors, and ranchers drove out and depleted game. Americans had no great record in dealing squarely with Indians. Some behaved themselves, but many did not, especially when the Indians depredated to feed themselves. Loss of property and livestock was no small matter to frontiersmen; it was often life threatening.

If they didn't invent the system, the mountain men of the 1820s and 1830s certainly perfected a manner of dealing with Indians who attacked or stole from them. They struck back harder than the Indians had struck them to teach a lesson: don't mess with us. The accounts of their bloody vengeance are hard even to read about. Other frontiersmen learned from the trappers and practiced their own versions of striking back. The Apache were not shy in seeking their own blood revenge for warriors slain while raiding.

With so many Americans traversing Chokonen territory (though they would never have recognized it as such) and stealing Apache game and resources, and with the Apache stealing from them to live, the wonder is not that war came but that it was so long in coming. It speaks to Chiricahua forbearance that war did not come sooner. War was not to the Chokonen Apache's advantage. The Apache did not think in terms of boundaries determined by land ownership. A fixed line of defense made little sense without a specific property to defend. It was better to surprise the enemy where they were weak, steal from them for the food and supplies one needed, and ambush them in the mountains and passes. For the Apache, war was an increase in raiding and an increase in revenge killing. Chokonen raiding had begun to increase in 1859. It led to Chokonen warriors being killed, and this was followed by a few random revenge killings. Immediately after Lieutenant Bascom's confrontation with Cochise there was a spate of revenge killings, but they soon ended. Cochise and Mangas Coloradas, both men of vision, took war to a new level in 1861 and 1862. They attacked towns and tried to keep the Army from coming back into their country.

The Americans practiced a two-fold system of fending off Indian war: (1) They kept the Army close at hand, when compared to the Mexicans and Spanish before them, in relatively large numbers; and (2) They fed the Indians. Of the two, the latter was probably the more successful.

Infantry was clearly unsuccessful in dealing with Indian raids, but the dragoons, the cavalry, were not much better. Writers have speculated that this was because the big cavalry horses broke down on western grasses that they could not digest as Indian ponies did. There may be some truth to this, but the real problem was in the nature of the mission. When the Indians conducted a raid, it took time for someone to ride to the fort and report. It then took time to prepare for the field, gathering equipment and stores. By that time, the Indians had a significant lead. Pursuit was traveling at the same speed as the pursued, unless the Indians were driving slow-moving stock. Catching up could only occur if the Indians stopped for some reason. The cavalry might hope to follow the trail to their village and this occasionally occurred, but not often. More often the cavalry attacked and burned at random all the villages that they discovered in a given area, since the real culprits were unknown. The tribe, defined by military leaders and not by any Indian definition, paid in blood for the attacks of a few who may or may not have been affiliated with that tribe.

In October 1860, the military moved the dragoons from Fort Buchanan to Fort Breckenridge, remote from centers of population. The Apaches noticed and raiding increased. Civilians noticed the change as well. In March 1861, the Department of New Mexico ordered the officers in Arizona to cease field operations until the department could organize a major campaign. The campaign never occurred. The Civil War intervened, and the Army sent the soldiers in Arizona to the Rio Grande to defend against invading Texans. The 7th Infantry in New Mexico and the 8th in Texas surrendered to the Confederates. The dragoons, redesignated as cavalry, had been on the frontier. Military command called many units back to the East where fighting had started. The federal army had suffered severe losses in strength by virtue of surrenders in the West and capture in the South. Weakened, the frontier languished until state and territorial governors raised volunteer regiments locally. From July of 1861 to June of 1862, Arizona was without an effective federal force. The remaining civilian population huddled in Tucson.

As early as the election of 1860, officers began to resign their commissions and head east. Unlike enlisted men who were committed to a term of service, officers served voluntarily and could resign their commissions at any time. Promotions were slow in part because there was no retirement and superannuated officers continued to serve and draw pay. Captains were often in their forties. With regiments organizing south and north, officers resigned to take up arms in new regiments at significant promotions. Captain Henry Sibley resigned at Fort Union, New Mexico, and was soon a brigadier general in Confederate service. Captain Richard S. Ewell received a similar promotion. State volunteer regiments in the north needed officers as well and also took federal officers who had resigned their commissions. With a shortage of officers, units in the field found it difficult to operate.

At the same time, American military presence in the Arizona portion of New Mexico, that is, what was then called Arizona, the part of New Mexico south of Socorro, the thirty-second degree corridor, was weakening. In the late summer and fall of 1858, Mexico began strengthening the frontier presidios in Sonora.

The second, and more effective, mode of deterrence was feeding the Indians. The American presence was disrupting game and the lives of the Indians. It only seemed fair to compensate them in some way for their loss. Many in Congress felt that the government was paying tribute and that the Indians were holding up the government unfairly. A few bad years had left the Apaches short of subsistence and they needed to raid to make up the shortfall. Raiding was part of how they survived, so the feeling that the Apache were preying upon the American government was not entirely unfair. In any event, the amount of supplies provided by Congress was small and the Apache were unhappy with semi-annual deliveries. They preferred to have supplies handed out weekly.

James L. Collins, superintendent of Indian Affairs in New Mexico, blamed Dr. Michael Steck, agent for the Chiricahua, for the uprising in the winter and spring of 1861. He claimed that if the agent had been present to issue rations, the Apaches would have been content and "the present difficulty would have been, beyond question, prevented."[4] This was unfair to Steck. The Chiricahua were upset with the infrequency and paucity of rations. Dr. Steck had no control over this. The military and civil authorities in New Mexico Territory, which included Arizona, did not point an accusing finger at Lieutenant Bascom or what had happened at Apache Pass. They understood what they were doing to control the Apache and knew their system was failing. It was not until seven years later that anyone thought to blame Bascom.

At the same time, Sonora was offering more supplies than the Americans were sending to the Chokonen. In December 1860, Cochise sent his sister-in-law, Yones, wife of Coyuntura, to Sonora to see what terms the governor there would offer. Historian Constance Altshuler speculated:

Perhaps the Bascom incident was not the cause but the occasion for an action long contemplated. Also possibly, it was merely coincidental.

The Hesperian letters show that the nature of Apache hostilities began changing the previous fall. . . . "The Apaches . . . no longer content with committing depredations, endeavor to kill all whom they encounter when not intimidated by superior numbers." . . . *To attribute Cochise's actions for the next ten years to this single incident seems both simplistic and patronizing.*[5]

Unfavorable weather for several years prior to 1861, the withdrawal of the military, insufficient and untimely rations and supplies from the Apache agent, and increased contact with Americans passing along the thirty-second degree corridor were all factors. Subsequent to 1868, informed of how American soldiers had mistreated him, Cochise would mention Bascom first in relation to the hangings and second as a reason for not trusting army officers. His statements include elements that he wouldn't have known without having been told, such as mention of the fictitious card game played to determine the fate of Bascom's and Irwin's hostages. Once Americans told Cochise that they thought Lieutenant Bascom had wronged him, naturally Cochise would not fail to mention this in bargaining. He'd committed many depredations against Americans, but this was the case where they had wronged him. He was able to assume the moral high ground. Cochise was very intelligent and a wise leader; he knew how to use a bargaining chip.

Some historians point to the Chiricahua War as having started in 1861 and extending until 1886 when Geronimo surrendered. From October 1872, when Cochise reached an agreement with General Howard, until April 1876, when Chiricahua killed three whites, there was peace in southern Arizona, a peace maintained by Cochise and Tom Jeffords. After April 1876, the Nednhi, led by Geronimo and Juh, ran to Mexico and began to raid across the border, but the Chokonen remained on the San Carlos Reservation. When they eventually did leave, it was in response to conditions and treatment at that reservation and to the fact the various Apache bands imprisoned there at close quarters were not friendly to one another. In short, the war that started in 1861 ended in 1872, and it could have ended much earlier if the American government had been willing to offer Cochise the terms he got from General Howard.

Chapter Sixteen

CONCLUSIONS: BASCOM EXONERATED

MUCH OF THE CONFUSION ABOUT THE EVENTS AT APACHE PASS IN FEBruary 1861 arises from attempts to reconcile the irreconcilable. Memory fades. Differing viewpoints record variant facts in different ways. Secondary sources record slight differences. These can be reconciled but blatant untruth cannot. Once we strip away the false accounts claiming to be primary sources, the remaining sources arising at different times and places, from different individuals, are remarkably consistent.

Former musician Oberly, who elevated himself to color sergeant in his account, is the only presumed primary source stating that George Bascom was an out-of-control, overbearing, stubborn drunk. Secondary sources pick up on this point and braid it into their tales. None of the other primary sources express anything like this. Bascom's sergeant, Daniel Robinson, and fellow lieutenants all saw him as a reasonable and responsible young officer who took his duties seriously and willingly accepted assistance and advice with appreciation. Oberly is also the origin of the tale that the assembled officers played a game of cards to decide the fate of the six adult male hostages. The presumed witnesses were all whites, assuming the hostage Apache boys and Cochise's wife were not near enough to see or understand, so Cochise would have had no way of knowing. Surgeon Irwin flatly denies that the game took place. In Oberly's tale Irwin was playing to save the hostages. Irwin goes on to state that the hanging was his idea. The hanging was an all-or-none proposition for the adult Indian males; no one suggested hanging the

woman or the two boys. They weren't playing to pick victims for deci-
mation, the killing of one in ten. A reference to the game shows up in a
statement attributed to Cochise. The statement was recorded long after
the encounter with Cochise by a third party who may have heard of this
presumed card game somewhere and inadvertently, or otherwise, added
it, so that Oberly, and not Cochise, remains the origin. On its face, the
idea of a game of 7Up seems absurd. It would have been simpler to just
cut the deck. An extended game adds drama and so with stagecoaches
leaping chasms, a drunken fool in charge, and a wise sergeant advising a
stubborn, foolish lieutenant, we want to add this to the myth. It's one of
those memorable elements.

The accounts that arise from former First Sergeant Reuben Bernard
place the abduction of Felix Ward in October 1860. These accounts
include a letter by Bernard to a fellow officer. October in southern Arizona is among the warmest months. February is cold, so cold that those
who were at Apache Pass in 1861 remember the days of snowfall. Some
secondary sources attempt to reconcile that which cannot be reconciled
by placing the abduction in October and the pursuit in February. This
makes Bascom look the fool on a cold trail selecting Cochise for per-
secution without evidence. The Bernard story makes Cochise out as the
always peaceful friend of the United States who protected the Overland
Mail, and thus the lieutenant as doubly the fool and miscreant. Lieutenant Bascom well knew that Cochise had raided along Sonoita Creek
and had raided the Overland Mail. He was following a fresh trail that
pointed toward Apache Pass and Cochise. He may have been wrong,
but he was working on valid evidence and reasonable suspicion. The
Bernard version adds to the myth, making George Bascom even more
of a villain. Many people hearing or reading the myth sympathize with
the noble savage or feel justified in accepting the sergeant as wise and
the lieutenant as a young cadet out to prove himself. We find a simple,
easily understood explanation for the start of the Cochise War that does
not point the finger at ourselves, where it belongs, but rather at one bad
lieutenant. The American public is relieved of responsibility and we don't
have to delve into the complexities of the real situation. Moreover, a
handful of raids in the spring of 1861 are then expanded into an eleven-

year war, a war that did not have to be and could have ended any time after the troops returned to Arizona.

The reason that Bernard's account cannot be reconciled is because Bernard wasn't there. His biographer places him on leave in Tennessee around the time of the election of 1860. According to the biographer, he was involved in a fistfight over Abraham Lincoln's candidacy. Political campaigns were not then as they are now. Knowing the candidate's name places the event very close to the election. The post returns for Fort Breckenridge show a man on leave—potentially Bernard—through this period. Travel times and leaves were extended affairs before the Civil War. Traveling back to Arizona was no mean feat, and winter weather would have closed the Santa Fe Trail used by military caravans. The Overland Trail ran through Texas and Arkansas. Riding the Overland stage was an expensive proposition and would have cost Bernard more than a year's pay. The evidence indicates that Bernard was in Tennessee or en route back to Arizona, and not present at Apache Pass in February 1861.

Both the civilian newspaper and the military official record, along with numerous personal accounts, all make very clear when Apaches abducted the boy and when and in what force the military responded. Lieutenant George Bascom rode out on January 29, 1861, at the head of fifty-four men of Company C, 7th Infantry. He was not leading a patrol consisting of Sergeant Bernard and twelve dragoons of the 1st Regiment of Dragoons. Such an expedition would have required a cross-attachment, which would have appeared in the records of both Fort Buchanan and Fort Breckenridge. There is no explanation as to why an infantry lieutenant would lead a patrol of dragoons. It's not impossible, but it is highly unlikely and impossible not to have appeared in the record. The story of the wise sergeant requires that the lieutenant be alone with the dragoons when he confronted Cochise. It also requires that the sergeant be court martialed, which would also appear in the record and doesn't. We know from multiple sources that Lieutenant John Cooke was present and advising Bascom when the latter met with Cochise to discuss an exchange of hostages.

The Bernard account and many secondary accounts have Lieutenant Bascom standing by his orders and refusing to make an exchange that did not include Felix Ward. Whether Bascom learned about the additional three hostages the night that Cochise took them or learned of them the next day when Cochise brought James Wallace down to trade, as William Oury wrote, may not be clear. Oury wasn't there yet, but was close to the events and he worked with Wallace and thus might have had reason to criticize the lieutenant. Instead he went on record defending Bascom's action:

[T]*he night after Wallace, the driver, was seized by the Indians; they brought him on the hill side east of the station and stuck up a stick with a paper on which Wallace, with a piece of charcoal had written ordered by Cachise, 'treat my people well and I will do the same by yours, of whom I have three.' This is the first that Lieutenant Bascom knew that the Indians had another white man than Wallace. The next morning, whilst the soldiers and employees of the overland mail co. were driving the stock to water at the spring, about six hundred yards east of the station, Cachise, who had already seen that they only went to the spring for water once a day, had placed his men in ambush in the brushy canyon which lead to the spring. . . . The next seen of Cachise was the following day, when he came down to the canyon with a large party of his warriors, concealing his men in a deep ravine which comes down from the mountain about seventy yards west of the station. . . . Wallace told the Lieutenant that Caschise authorized him to say to him that if he would turn all his Indians loose, that he would liberate him* [Wallace]. *In reply Bascom asked Wallace if Cachise still had the two other white men, and being answered in the affirmative, he told Wallace to tell Cachise that if he would agree to release all three of the white men he would turn all the Indians* [eight in number] *loose, to which Cachise refused to consent and thus ended the parley. . . . The reader who had followed me through the foregoing narrative will readily understand and commend the motive which prompted Lieutenant Bascom to refuse Cachise's proposition. What fair-minded man would fail to condemn him if he had made so unfair discrimination between his own countrymen? The life of either of the other prisoners was just as sacred and as valuable as that of Wallace, and any honorable man would have done just as he did, all or none.*[1]

The accounts arising from Bernard fault the lieutenant, saying he stood by his orders to return with the boy and thus sacrificed James Wallace's life, but Bernard was not there and those who were tell a different story. By the time the assembled officers hanged the Apache hostages in response to finding Cochise's four murdered hostages, Lieutenants Cooke, Lord, and Moore, and Surgeon Irwin were all at the pass and all senior to Bascom. Lieutenant Isaiah Moore had assumed command. The hanging was thus done under his command. Somehow Bernard overlooks the fact that his own commander, Lieutenant Richard Lord, was there. This is one more indication that Bernard was not. Daniel Robinson, who was there, mentions Bernard's arrival with the dragoons on February 14. It occurs in only one of Robinson's accounts when he says "the first sergeant of one of the two companies was Reuben F. Bernard—a soldier among soldiers."[2] That such a grand statement is left without a description of anything the first sergeant did to earn such acclaim suggests that this might include a good deal of gratuitous sarcasm aimed at Bernard as a braggart. Reuben Bernard's account cannot be reconciled because he was not there and as a result had most of his facts wrong. He set out to tell a story that made him a hero and in doing so cast Bascom as a villain. Both Bascom and Bernard fought at Valverde. Bernard knew that young Captain Bascom had died in the battle and that there was no one else in Arizona who could contradict his version.

It seems strange that Cochise, who took additional hostages from the Montoya wagon train—Frank Brunner, William Sanders, and Sam Whitfield—to strengthen his negotiating hand, would refuse to trade them. Robinson and Oury agree that Cochise offered only Wallace. Oury had reason to object to the lieutenant refusing the trade, but instead defended him. The refusal may have something to do with internal Apache politics. Those who took the hostages may have refused to give them up. The Apaches who took them captive may have killed them soon after they captured them. Cochise may have wanted something more than just return of his people for the hostages he held. He may have been playing a long game. The sources agree that the chief notified the lieutenant soon after taking them that he had Brunner, Sanders, and Whitfield. No easy answer to Cochise's motives presents itself. The fight at the spring may have taken place between the taking of the additional hostages and Cochise offering only Wallace. If this is so, soldiers may have killed Apaches, as Robinson says, and this may have necessitated revenge taken out on the unfortunate three. Cochise's coalition by then consisted of Mangas Coloradas' Bedonkohe Apaches and Francisco's Coyoteros as well as his own Chokonen. Some internal dissension seems probable. There is no reason to question the timing of when Bascom became aware of the three additional hostages taken from the burnt Montoya wagon train. He probably knew the evening the Apache captured them. If not, then he would have known by the next day when Wallace spoke for Cochise, and that was the critical juncture. Their release, and not the return of the Felix Ward, was the deciding factor in not trading his Apache hostages for James Wallace. He was not being stubborn or acting as a martinet compelled by his orders from Colonel Pitcairn Morrison. He was acting honorably in hopes of saving three more lives.

Lieutenant Bascom and his advisor, First Lieutenant John Cooke, undoubtedly believed that Cochise would return with more reasonable terms. After all, they were holding Cochise's wife, son, and brother. Espying Company B, 8th Infantry, blithely marching across the San Simon Valley, unaware of the plight of the soldiers and civilians surrounded at Apache Pass, Cochise, Managas Coloradas, and Francisco took the presence of the marching infantry as an indication that the wily Americans were trying to surround them. They slew their four hostages and departed in haste. Arriving a day later, Surgeon Irwin and his party, intending to break a cordon of encircling warriors, encountered none.

Cochise, not Bascom, violated a flag of truce. Cochise and Francisco came in under a flag of truce to parley with the lieutenant, Johnny Ward, and two sergeants. During the parley, two women from Cochise's camp lured James Wallace to the arroyo where Apache warriors captured him. At the same time they attempted to capture Charles Culver and Walsh. Francisco shouted some sort of command to the Apaches assembled in the arroyo. Sergeant Robinson and Lieutenant Bascom heard it as the Spanish "Aquí! Aquí!" meaning "Here! Here!" or perhaps "To me!" There is no reason Francisco should have called to his warriors in Spanish even though Cochise and Bascom conducted the parley in Spanish. Robinson may have misinterpreted Apache words. It's clear that Francisco was giving a signal to his and Cochise's warriors. It's important that the two women who set up Wallace were from Cochise's camp. It indicates that Cochise's Chokonen, and therefore Cochise, were responsible for seizing the stagecoach driver and thus for violating the truce and breaking trust. If this had been done without Cochise's prior knowledge, which is extremely unlikely, he could have returned Wallace as a sign of good faith. He did not.

Cochise probably thought himself justified. His people had been taken during a talk to which he had come peacefully. In his view Bascom's men had seized his people and tried to take the chief as well. Lieutenant George Bascom did not see it that way. If he had intended to take hostages, he would have had his men load their rifle-muskets. He did not. His sentries patrolled with fixed bayonets, not loaded weapons. The lieutenant gave orders that no Apache was to be allowed to leave the camp. This was not an attempt to take them hostage. At the time, soldiers and frontiersmen believed all Indians to be light-fingered. Allowing them to come and go from the camp at will was an invitation to theft. Prudence demanded that the soldiers keep the Apaches in camp until the lieutenant and sergeants could monitor their departure and recover property in an orderly fashion.

A year before, Captain Richard Ewell had taken hostages and used them to bargain for the return of Mercedes Quiroz. Although the hostage taking may have led to the abduction of the girl and Larcena Pennington Page, the action was widely applauded. Colonel Pitcairn Morrison may have included in his lost orders to Bascom instructions to take hostages if needed. Nonetheless, the lieutenant did not have his men arm their weapons and he did not deploy them in a manner consistent with taking all of the Chokonen hostage. Something happened in his tent between himself, Cochise, Coyuntura, and Johnny Ward as they shared dinner. Lieutenant Bascom does not seem to understand what happened. Some have taken it as a sign of cover up that he did not mention the attempt to take Cochise hostage. This would have been a pretty poor cover up as events spoke for themselves. Lieutenant Bascom wrote that he had agreed to allow Cochise to take ten days to go recover

Felix Ward from the people the chief thought were holding him. Bascom needed Cochise to go on this mission, which seemed to stand a good chance of success. Confronting the Pinal Apache in 1860, under similar circumstances, even though that tribe probably held Mercedes Quiroz, Captain Ewell allowed them time to bring her on the pretense that they were bringing her from Tonto Apaches. Bascom would have known this. When Cochise agreed to go look for the boy, the lieutenant had won; he had achieved his purpose. There was no reason to interfere with his emissary.[3] But something happened in the tent. Something drove Cochise to pull his knife and cut his way out.

In the tent were Cochise and Coyuntura, who spoke some Spanish but no English, Lieutenant Bascom who spoke English and French, and Johnny Ward, acting as interpreter between English and Spanish. Ward had a stake in the game. It was his stepson and his livestock that he believed Cochise had taken. Perhaps he thought the chief was prevaricating and that Bascom was being too lenient. Cochise and Coyuntura could understand his translation of the lieutenant's words, but Bascom could not. Cochise's understanding of Spanish was limited and perhaps Johnny Ward's was, as well. There may have been an innocent misunderstanding or mistranslation that enraged the chief and his brother. Or Johnny Ward may have deliberately provided the chief with his own words and not Bascom's. He may have told the chief that his people would be hostage until the boy was returned, or that Cochise himself would be hostage. It is certain that Cochise and Coyuntura believed themselves about to be taken hostage, and thus drew their knives and tried to escape.

Coyuntura tripped and a sentry captured him. Cochise escaped. He could never have escaped through a camp of sixty-six soldiers with loaded weapons who were preparing to take him hostage. The soldiers lacked prior warning and they lacked loaded weapons. Johnny Ward emerged from the tent and fired on the fleeing Apache. Soldiers remembered his shot because for a long time it was the only shot fired. The soldiers were startled and surprised, not standing ready to capture a hostage. It is apparent that Lieutenant Bascom had no prior intent to take Apache hostages that day.

The record shows him a prudent officer who behaved responsibly. During the time at Apache Pass, he took care to fortify his position, guard his livestock, and resist being lured into a trap. Bascom had sent Cochise to fetch the boy. Bascom had agreed to ten days. There is no mention in Bascom's report of an attempt to take Cochise hostage, of Johnny Ward's shot, or of Cochise drawing his knife and cutting his way out. He mentioned the hostages he held, which should have provided him assurance against Cochise's good faith effort to recover Felix Ward. The shot and the knife don't fit into what Bascom believed had occurred. Cochise had made an agreement and had reneged on it by running, but Bascom knew the Chokonen leader would act in good faith because he held some of the Apache people as hostages. Therefore, his report was complete and accurate and contained all the relevant facts with extraneous matters that he did not understand left out.

After Francisco of the Coyotero arrived unexpectedly the very next day, Cochise's situation changed. Cochise knew that Coyoteros had been passing through his country as they returned from raids. He assumed they were the culprits in Felix Ward's abduction. In ten days' time Cochise could have gone to their country and returned with the boy. But here was Francisco telling Cochise that he did not have the boy. That meant the culprits must be Western Apaches—Pinal, Araviapa, or Tontos—all of whom raided the Sonoita Creek area.[4] Cochise was not on good terms with them and thus likely realized that if they had the boy, his return would be impossible. Cochise, already feeling himself betrayed, planned to take hostages of his own. He arranged to meet with the soldier chief and lured the Overland Mail personnel out of their station to become his hostages.

To Cochise, given his experience with Mexican negotiators, it seemed that his people were already dead. He may have believed that no matter what he did they would be killed. Therefore, killing his own hostages did not create any greater risk for them. Lieutenant George Bascom, on the other hand, did not intend to harm the hostages. Surgeon Irwin makes it clear that he intended to take all of them to Fort Buchanan.

It is interesting, but not critical, that Sergeant Robinson saw the Apache seize James Wallace but didn't mention Walsh and Charles

Culver. Lieutenant Bascom noticed these latter two Overland Mail employees but not Wallace. It is not crucial because subsequently both realize that all three had been outside the station while they were talking to Cochise. Perhaps the three were not all together in one place or some intervening object blocked the view of the lieutenant and sergeant.

The false accounts that claim Lieutenant George Bascom refused to bargain for James Wallace's life without the return of Felix Ward fail to recognize that First Lieutenant[5] John Cooke was at Bascom's side advising him. This was advice that Bascom welcomed and for which he subsequently expressed thanks. George Bascom did not watch as Cochise dragged Wallace to death behind his horse. It didn't happen. Instead Bascom pled for the lives of Brunner, Whitfield, and Sanders, and Cochise refused the exchange.

The false account of former musician Oberly says George Bascom and Surgeon Bernard Irwin played 7Up, a card game to determine the fate of their hostages, and wrongly claims that Bascom had proposed the hanging. Oberly failed to note that Lieutenant Isaiah Moore had assumed command and thus the decision was Moore's. Even Thompson Turner, reporting from Tucson, was aware that Moore had taken command. Surgeon Irwin stated that, because he was appalled at the condition of the tortured captives of Cochise and the Mexican teamsters of the Montoya wagon train, he proposed hanging the hostages. He says that George Bascom objected. This tells us something about Bascom's intent concerning the hostages. He had always intended that they be exchanged unharmed. Surgeon Irwin argued that it was his right to hang the three Coyoteros he had captured and that he would whether or not Bascom agreed. Lieutenant Bascom then agreed to hang his hostages, except for the woman and boys, as well. Lieutenant Moore was in command. It was his right and duty to object to the hanging if he thought it wrong. Lieutenant Bascom could probably have interfered, claiming that Moore had no right to hang the hostages that Bascom had taken. Lieutenant Moore's report said: "For scouting in the mountains, I assumed the command of Lt. Bascom. We buried the dead bodies of four Americans who had been captured and afterwards killed by the Indians."[6]

Although Lieutenant Moore said he assumed command from Lieutenant Bascom for the purpose of conducting the reconnaissance, he doesn't mention the hanging. Nonetheless, as the senior officer present, he was in command and could have taken charge and prevented the hanging. His inaction was implied consent. Even if he did not order the hanging, it was done under his command and he, not Bascom, was responsible.

In the spring of 1861, Cochise took his revenge for the hanging: American soldiers had killed Apaches, so it was his responsibility to see their deaths avenged. The killing spree was short lived. Hostilities continued openly but had other causes that ran much deeper. Not the least of these causes was the lack of military protection for people west of the Rio Grande in southern New Mexico Territory, which the Confederates called Arizona.

Some writers have suggested that if Captain Richard Ewell had been there, matters would have gone differently. They seem to imply that Ewell had the power to read Apache minds, while poor Bascom did not, and that thus Ewell would have known that Cochise didn't have the boy. In reality Ewell wrote that he did not think Cochise dealt honestly, that the chief concealed the wrongs he and his people had done, and that the next time he had to deal with the Chokonen chief, there would be bloodshed. Lieutenant Bascom appears to have employed the same tactics Ewell did in dealing with the Pinal and had agreed to allow Cochise ten days to bring in the boy. As Ewell had accepted the intentional misdirection of the Pinals who blamed Tontos, Bascom accepted that Cochise would bring the boy in. He found himself inadvertently in possession of hostages. Ewell conducted a hostage exchange and Bascom attempted to do the same. For reasons that are unclear, after implying his intent to exchange them, Cochise offered to exchange only one, Wallace.

Unfortunately, the false story lives on. It's a great story with many exciting elements to stir the imagination. We like the idea that lieutenants are headstrong and don't take advice as well as the idea that sergeants are experienced and wise. We see the same conflict between managers, who are all stupid, and workmen who know what they are doing and don't need managers. They have experience. Our egalitarian society promotes this idea. We aren't ruled by a hereditary upper class. We like to hear that the upper class was wrong and started a war, proving their incompetence. The story also gives us a simple explanation of a bloody war, luring us away from more complex explanations that point the blame at our westward expansion and ourselves. It's the lieutenant's fault. It was management, the upper class, being wrong as usual. It wasn't our greed for land that caused the problem. It wasn't Americans in general treating Indians unfairly. It was all the fault of one lieutenant. Unfortunately, not one bit of this is true. Every element of the popular legend is false. Most of it was the invention of a self-serving, self-promoting soldier who saw the opportunity to make himself a hero at Bascom's expense.

The record shows that Lieutenant George N. Bascom was a gentleman, not a drunk, who acted prudently and earned the respect of his sergeants and men. He willingly accepted advice, acknowledging it with thanks. His brother officers liked, respected, and defended him. In confronting Cochise, he used tactics very similar to those employed by Captain Ewell. He earned his men's respect while a second lieutenant during the Mormon War before the 7th Infantry came to Arizona. It was a respect that never faltered. One of his men, Captain Daniel Robinson, who had served as a sergeant under Bascom during this period, wrote in 1896[7] in *Sports Afield* that a June 1896 article in that publication had done "great injustice to a brave and gallant officer, who was killed the following year at the battle of Valverde."[8] Things went awry at Apache Pass, probably through the actions of Johnny Ward, an individual too personally involved in the situation. Colonel Morrison should never have allowed Johnny Ward to serve as interpreter, but Bascom was stuck with him. Not knowing what Ward had said to Cochise, the lieutenant behaved as if Cochise were still serving as his emissary, especially since Bascom held hostages against performance just as Ewell had. Cochise's reaction came as a surprise to the lieutenant as did his subsequent refusal to exchange all four of the chief's hostages. The soldier tried to preserve the lives of the four men that Cochise held by refusing to trade hostages for Wallace alone. In the end, Surgeon Irwin, not Bascom, wanted to hang the hostages, but that issue was Lieutenant Moore's responsibility. He was in command.

His commander and the departmental commander commended George N. Bascom. He was promoted to captain that same year. He fought with honor and valor at Valverde against the Confederate invaders and died a hero. Fort Bascom, New Mexico Territory, was named in his honor.

Surgeon Irwin admitted to demanding the right to hang his three hostage Apaches. Lieutenant Moore was in command and could have stopped it, but instead had his dragoons provide the ropes. Nonetheless, it would be wrong to blame either of them, much less Lieutenant Bascom, for eleven years of war. At worst, their action led to a few months of retaliation. Without that action, necessity would have driven hungry Apache to steal in order to feed their families. Americans would have fired on the thieves, killing some. Apaches would have retaliated, killing Americans and Mexicans. Mexicans and Americans would have begun killing Apaches on sight and the Apache would have retaliated with all their might.

Appendix A

COMPANY C, 7TH REGIMENT OF U.S. INFANTRY, FEBRUARY 1861[1]

Captain Samuel B. Hayman—on leave from December 1860

First Lieutenant Gurden Chapin—detailed as Regimental Adjutant

Second Lieutenant George N. Bascom—commanding (killed at the Battle of Valverde)

First Sergeant James J. Huber

Sergeant Patrick Murray

Sergeant Daniel Robinson—detached service**

Sergeant William A. Smith

Corporal Adam Fraber

Corporal James Robinson—detached service

Corporal James Cavender—detached service

Corporal Anthony Canson

Musician Christian Millahn—detached service

Musician John W. Fraker—detached service

Private Leonard F. Allen

Private David Barrow

Private James W. Barry

Private Michael Bourke

Private Henry J. Buckley

Private John Burns

Private Patrick "Paddy" Carroll (wounded at Valverde)

Private Martin Collins

Private John Coonier—detached service

Private Copley Cottrell

Private Joseph Cronin

Private Thomas Cummings

Private Cornelius Daly—detached service

Private Patrick Daly—detached service**

Private George Douglas

Private Thomas Downy (wounded at Valverde)

Private Thomas Driskell

Private Charles I. East

Private Phillip Finnegan

Private John Fitzgerald (killed at Valverde)

Private Casper Frost

Private Michael Gleason

Private George Gray

Private Henry Grouse

Private Daniel Harrington (wounded at Valverde)

Private Francis E. Hayden

Private Charles C. Hein

Private Francis Hoyt

Private Cornelius Hughes—detached service

Private Robert Irvine

Private John Leibrich—detached service (killed at Valverde)

Private William Leiter—detached service**

Private James McDermott

Private James McDonald—detached service (killed at Valverde)

Private Daniel McGerry

Private Martin Miller

Private Thomas Morgan

Private Daniel Murphy—confined Albuquerque

Private Patrick Murphy

Private James Noonean

Private Bernard Norton

Private Patrick O'Brien—detached service

Private Thomas O'Leary

Private Morris Phillips

Private Thomas Reilly

Private Bernard Rooke

Private William Rooney—detached service

Private Peter Russell—enlisted February 21

Private George Salliot—detached service*,**

Private Robert Simpson (wounded at Valverde)

Private Henry Slater

Private William Smallwood

Private Charles Smith—enlisted February 21

Private Isaac M. Smith—detached service

Private John Smith

Private William Smith (wounded at Valverde)

Private John Stephens—detached service

Private John Stuart

Private Daniel Sullivan

Private Timothy Sweeny

Private Lester P. Thompson

Private Charles Tobine

Private Cornelius Toomey—detached service

Private Martin Venalstyne

Private George W. Wilson—detached service**

* Killed by Apaches in May 1861 while guarding the post herd.
** Sergeant Robinson's wagon train guard returning from Fort McLane.

Appendix B

SERGEANT DANIEL ROBINSON'S WAGON TRAIN

February 3, 1861: "At that time I was a sergeant and had been at Fort McLane in charge of a wagon train loaded with provisions for that post, and returned to the pass with an escort of twelve men on the same day as Bascom."

—"THE AFFAIR AT APACHE PASS"
BY DANIEL ROBINSON
SPORTS *AFIELD*, AUGUST 1896

SERGEANT ROBINSON SET OUT FROM FORT BUCHANAN ON JANUARY 21, 1861, taking supplies to Fort Floyd, near the Santa Rita Copper Mines and modern Silver City, New Mexico. Fort Buchanan was the regimental headquarters of the 7th Infantry and thus was tasked with supplying other 7th Infantry posts. Arizona at this time appears to have been the principal source of wheat flour from mills on the Santa Cruz River for all of southern New Mexico Territory. In January 1861, Fort Floyd was redesignated Fort McLane. Wagon trains customarily made two trips: out and back; the previous escort assignment began in mid-December with a trip to Fort Floyd. This was the second trip and on the return leg, Sergeant Robinson encountered his commander, Lieutenant Bascom, at Apache Pass.

From the 7th Infantry Regimental Returns, January 1861

Company H—"Privates Dunn, McCay, Deits, Anderson & Cooper on detached service escort to supply train to Fort Buchanan, NM, since January 21, 1861"

Company C—"Sergeant Robinson, Privates Daly, Leiter, Salliot, Wilson absent on detached service to Fort Floyd, NM, with supply train"

Company G—"Privates Christy, Burke & Sherwood on detached service to Fort Buchanan, NM, escort to supply train since January 22, 1861"

The Supply Train Escort

C Company:

Sergeant Daniel Robinson, thirty

Private Patrick Daly, twenty-four (served as a courier to Fort Buchanan)[1]

Private William Leiter, twenty-four

Private George Salliot, twenty-seven

Private George W. Wilson, twenty-seven

G Company:

Private William Burke, twenty-six

Private William Christy, twenty-five

Private Pixlee Sherwood, twenty-two

H Company:

Private Richard Anderson, twenty-seven

Private George Cooper, twenty-four

Private Albert Deits, thirty-three

Private Lewis Dunn, twenty-five

Private Joshua J. McCay, twenty

Appendix C
OTHERS AT APACHE PASS

RELIEF PARTY FROM FORT BUCHANAN
Assistant Surgeon Bernard John Dowling Irwin

Privates of Company H, 7th Infantry
Private Oliver Brown

Private Robert Burns

Private William Davison

Private Daniel Enright

Private James Graham

Private Lawrence Gillespie

Private John McGuire

Private George Power

Private Andrew Schertenlieb

Private Thomas Shea

Private William Ward

From Company C, 7th Infantry
Corporal Adam Fraber

Civilian
James "Paddy" Graydon

Relief from Fort Breckenridge
Company D, 1st Regiment of Dragoons

Second Lieutenant Richard S. C. Lord

First Sergeant Reuben F. Bernard (on leave)

Sergeant Franklin Fisher

Sergeant John Moore (left on post at Breckenridge)

Sergeant Robert J. Ward

Corporal William H. Brown

Corporal William DuBois

Corporal Jacob M. Lull

Corporal John S. Walker (left post on February 3 in charge of fourteen-man escort for Company B, 8th Infantry)

Company strength included two buglers, one farrier, and sixty-one privates. Of the non-commissioned officers and privates, thirty-six were available for duty. Thirty-five men went with the lieutenant to Apache Pass.

The company had eight men on daily detail, eight men sick, six in arrest/confinement, nine detached service to the Rio Grande, two on leave of absence, and fifty-eight serviceable horses.

Company G, 1st Regiment of Dragoons
First Lieutenant Isaiah N. Moore

First Sergeant Thomas Henderson

Sergeant John M. Hixon

Sergeant William Martin

Sergeant William T. Pennock (left on post at Breckenridge)

Corporal Sylvester Bennett

Corporal George M. Curtis

Corporal Cyrus Pennock

The company strength included two buglers, one farrier, and fifty-nine privates. Of the non-commissioned officers and privates, forty were available for duty. Thirty-five men went with the lieutenant to Apache Pass.

The company had twelve men on daily duty, six on detached service to the Rio Grande, five in arrest/confinement, five sick, one on leave, and fifty-four serviceable horses.

Appendix D

INCREASED COMMITMENT TO GUARD THE OVERLAND MAIL

GUARDS FOR OVERLAND MAIL DETAILED FROM COMPANY H, 7TH INFANTRY
To Stein's Peak Station (Doubtful Canyon) February 15
    Eight privates

GUARDS FOR OVERLAND MAIL DETAILED FROM COMPANY C, 7TH INFANTRY, AT FORT BUCHANAN
To Apache Pass Station February 19
    Sergeant Murray

    Private Carrique

    Private Cronin

    Private Driskell

    Private Harrington

    Private Hayden

    Private Hein

    Private Hoyt

Private Leibrich

Private Miller

Private O'Brien

Private Phillips

Private Sweeny

Private Tobine

Private Venalstyne

To another station either San Simon or Ewell's February 19
Four privates

GUARDS FOR OVERLAND MAIL STATION DETAILED FROM COMPANY G, 7TH INFANTRY
To Stein's Peak Station (Doubtful Canyon) February 15
Corporal Young

Four privates

GUARDS FOR OVERLAND MAIL STATIONS DETAILED FROM COMPANY H, 7TH INFANTRY, AT FORT BUCHANAN
To Dragoon Springs February 9
Private Frederick Hiller

Private John Smith

Private John A. Utchin

Private Michael Ward

Private Robert Wilson

Private Theodore Wittholz

To Dragoon Springs February 11
Private Patrick Lynch

Private Archibald Smith

To Apache Pass February 19
Private Charles Gillhauman

Private Patrick Travers

Appendix E

BIOGRAPHICAL INDEX

Ake, Felix Grundy. He was born in 1810 in Alabama. In 1855, he came to Arizona with W. C. Wordsworth (Wadsworth, Wodsworth) and settled along Sonoita Creek, selling beef and produce to the military at Fort Buchanan. His is mentioned as one of seven farms in the valley; Ward and Wordsworth owned two of the others. He was one of the leaders, with Wordsworth, of the Arizona Wagon Train ambushed by Cochise and Mangas Coloradas at Cooke's Canyon in August of 1861.

Antonio. He was a Mexican interpreter at Fort Buchanan who probably accompanied Surgeon Irwin to Apache Pass arriving on the evening of February 10, 1861. William Oury says Antonio was Bascom's interpreter when he met with Cochise on February 4, but other sources say Johnny Ward was the interpreter. Oury did not arrive at Apache Pass until February 14 and did not have direct knowledge of who served in that capacity.

Bascom, Lieutenant George Nicholas. George was born in Kentucky in 1836 and orphaned at an early age, growing up in the care of relatives. He graduated from the U.S. Military Academy (USMA) in 1858 and joined the 7th Infantry in Utah in 1859, marching with the unit from Utah to New Mexico. In December 1860, he assumed command of Company C, 7th Infantry. In January 1861, he marched his unit to Apache Pass to confront Cochise and force the return of the stolen boy, Felix Ward. Bascom died a hero at the Battle of Valverde in February 1862. Camp Bascom, New Mexico, was named in his honor.

Bernard, First Sergeant Reuben Frank. First sergeant of Company D, 1st Dragoons, he was born in Tennessee in 1834 and enlisted from there in 1855. He was commissioned during the Civil War in 1862 and rose in rank, returning to Arizona in 1868 as a captain in the 1st Cavalry. Shortly after his arrival, stories began to circulate that Lieutenant Bascom was at fault for starting the Cochise War. We find references to this in Bernard's letters and in the reports of his commander, Colonel Thomas Devin. Bernard was associated with Sidney DeLong, the sutler at Fort Bowie, who produced a history of Arizona that included the fanciful story of the wise sergeant and the stubborn lieutenant. It would appear that Bernard invented the story as an element of self-promotion. There are so many details wrong with the story that it is doubtful he was at Apache Pass. His biographer places him on leave in Tennessee about the time of the 1860 election, and unit records show a man on leave throughout the period when his unit was at Apache Pass. If he was there at all, he did not arrive before February 14 and had no knowledge of Cochise's confrontations with Bascom.

Bowman, Sarah, Great Western, Bourdette, Bourget, Bourginnis, Bourkyte. Known as the Great Western after the largest steamer of her time, she was said to be six foot, two inches, with flame-red hair. She was a military wife and laundress with the 7th Infantry in the Mexican-American War and is referred to by her several husbands' names. She organized the camp followers and officers' open mess, amassing a fortune of over ten thousand dollars. In Arizona, she operated the finest bordello in the territory at Casa Blanca on Sonoita Creek.

Brunner, Frank. He was an armed escort on the Montoya Wagon Train carrying flour to Pinos Altos that entered Apache Pass from the west on the evening of February 5, 1861. Cochise or Francisco held him as one of four hostages. The Apaches tortured and killed him. He was twenty-three in 1860, born in Baden, Germany, and had been living at Fort Buchanan.

Buckley, William. He was superintendent of the Overland Mail Tucson-El Paso division. He had been in this position when the company was building the line in 1858. He arrived at Apache Pass by stage from Tucson about 3 a.m. on February 6. He sent a dispatch to the *Alta California* newspaper (San Francisco) while still at Apache Pass.

Carroll, Private Patrick "Paddy." He was a soldier of Company C, 7th Infantry. Farrell, formerly of the 7th Infantry and working for the Overland Mail at Rough and Ready, said Paddy stood six foot, one inch, tall and was a noted wrestler and the most active man in the regiment. He also said that Paddy was selected to subdue the Indians who were taken captive and that Cochise threw the soldier over his head.

Chapin, Lieutenant Gurden. Born in the District of Columbia in 1831, he graduated from USMA in 1851. Assigned to Company C, 7th Infantry, he served with that unit during the Mormon Rebellion and he accompanied Lieutenant James Hervey Simpson of the Topographical Engineers as leader of the military escort exploring new roads west from Salt Lake City. In that capacity, he had hostile encounters with Goshutes and Mormons. In 1861, he served at Fort Buchanan as regimental adjutant of the 7th Infantry and from March as commander of the post. He and his wife lost a child while there and oversaw the burning of the fort in July.

Chie. He is thought to be the son of Cochise's brother, Coyuntura. Tradition says he was the second child accompanying Cochise to Bascom's camp, one of those taken hostage, and later released at Fort Buchanan. In 1872, he led Tom Jeffords and General O. O. Howard to Cochise's stronghold on the western side of the Dragoon Mountains.

Cochise. Chees, Cachees, and other spellings. His name means "oak." He was described as tall, erect, and of great personal dignity. Although Surgeon Irwin described him as being about thirty years old in 1860, he was probably closer to fifty. He was chief of the Chokonen Chiricahua Apache, one of four bands (Chokonen, Bedonkohe, Nednhi, and Chihenne). He was the son-in-law of Mangas Coloradas.

Cole, John. He was a blacksmith who partnered with Johnny Ward on his ranch. Cole lay in his sickbed watching the Apache take Felix Ward and twenty head of cattle on January 27, 1861.

Cooke, Lieutenant John Rogers. He was twenty-eight years old in 1861. He was the son of famed dragoon leader Philip St. George Cooke, who served with the 1st Dragoons, opened the emigrant road through southern Arizona, and later served with the Union in the Civil War. John was born at Jefferson Barracks, Missouri, in 1833. He came to Arizona in 1859 with the 8th Infantry. He fought under Captain Reeve against Pinal Apaches. In May 1860, he led Company B, 8th Infantry, from Fort Buchanan to the mouth of Arivaipa Creek on the San Pedro to build Fort Breckenridge. Promoted to first lieutenant, he left Fort Breckenridge on January 28, 1861, and boarded the eastbound stage with the intent of resigning his commission to join the Confederacy. He arrived at Apache Pass on February 6 aboard the same stage as William Buckley. Although senior, he willingly placed himself under Bascom's command and at his disposal. Bascom later expressed his gratitude for Cooke's advice and assistance. Cooke resigned his commission May 30, 1861, and fought for the Confederacy.

Coyuntura. Kin-o-tera was the brother of Cochise. His wife was Yones. He was an important and effective leader, and Cochise took him into Bascom's tent on February 4 for discussions with the lieutenant and Johnny Ward. When Cochise drew his knife to cut his way out, Coyuntura did the same, heading out the back of the tent. He tripped on a guy line and fell. A sentry pinned him to the ground with a bayonet, which didn't pierce any vital organs. He was among the six hostage Apaches hanged by the military at Apache Pass.

Crocker, Neil. He was the clerk on the eastbound stage that arrived at Apache Pass on February 6 according to Farrell, who also relates that this was the paymaster's coach, perhaps for the Overland Mail. According to another source, Neil Crocker was a daredevil and the son of Hugh Crocker of California, a director of the company. Presumed father Hugh Crocker was actually a superintendent of the company and not a director.

Culver, A. B. He was the driver on the westbound stage that arrived at Apache Pass 4 p.m. on February 5, hours ahead of schedule. His brother was Charles, the station keeper at Apache Pass. He agreed to ride to Tucson for help.

Culver, Charles. Born in New York, Charles was the station keeper at Apache Pass and brother to A. B. Culver, the driver of the westbound stage. He was wounded on February 5 while Lieutenant Bascom was negotiating with Cochise. He, Wallace, and Walsh went to the arroyo about one hundred yards south of the station beckoned by Indian women, who may have been Mexican captives. Warriors emerged and grabbed Walsh and Wallace and tried for Culver. Walsh broke away and he and Culver ran to the station. Culver was wounded. Walsh was killed—Buckley said by an Indian bullet. Culver served on the grand jury that returned indictments in the Camp Grant Massacre case in 1871.

Davis, Nelson J. He was the paymaster for the Overland Mail who was riding on the eastbound stage that arrived on February 6 with Buckley and Cooke aboard. Thomas Farrell mentions him in an account he wrote of the Bascom affair. Riding on the box, Davis took over driving after Lyon's leg was broken by an Apache bullet.

DeLong, Sidney. He was born December 28, 1828, in New York. In 1849, he sailed around Cape Horn to San Francisco. In 1862, he went to Arizona with the California Column. He was associated with the Tully-Ochoa mercantile and freighting firm. DeLong was a participant in the 1871 Camp Grant Massacre. He partnered with Tom Jeffords on a number of projects and mines. For fifteen years DeLong was the post sutler at Fort Bowie, in which capacity he was closely associated with Reuben Bernard. It was Bernard's false version of the Bascom Affair that DeLong recounted in his 1903 history of Arizona.

Driskell, Private Thomas. He served with Company C, 7th Infantry. He was left as one of the guards at the Apache Pass Station on February 19, 1861. On June 22, 1861, he was killed by Indians while on guard near Fort Buchanan minutes after speaking with Sergeant Robinson.

Elder, Anthony. He was an Overland Mail employee and conductor in charge of the mail. Apaches attacked his stage twenty miles east of Tucson in late February 1861, and when the driver was wounded, he took over the reins and drove the stage to safety. Apaches killed him at Stein's Peak Station in April 1861, in company with J. J. Giddings.

Ewell, Captain Richard Stoddert. He was born in Georgetown, District of Columbia, in 1817 and graduated from USMA in 1840, joining the

First Regiment of Dragoons under Captain Philip St. George Cooke. After fighting with distinction against Jicarilla and Mescalero Apaches in New Mexico at the head of Company G, 1st Dragoons, he came to Arizona with Major Enoch Steen, taking possession of Tucson and the Gadsden Purchase for the United States. He selected the site for Fort Buchanan and due to the illness of his superiors was often in command there until August 1860. He had many encounters with Apaches and several run-ins with Cochise. Ewell joined the Confederacy and was second in command under General Thomas "Stonewall" Jackson. He commanded a corps at Gettysburg.

Farrell, Thomas. He arrived in New Mexico with the 7th Infantry Regiment and took his discharge. He went to work for the Overland Mail Company at Rough and Ready, a station between Mesilla and Cooke's Canyon. He gave an account of the Bascom Affair that was printed in the *Prescott Courier* and reprinted in *Frontier Times* in 1923. He was not there but provides some names and also seems to be the origin of the story about the stagecoach leaping a chasm, although in his version it was only a small ditch.

Fraber, Corporal Adam. He was the oldest man in Company C, 7th Infantry. In the darkness of the snowy night of February 7, Lieutenant Bascom sent him and another man as messengers to Fort Buchanan. Sent by William Buckley, A. B. Culver accompanied them as far as Dragoon Springs where they separated, Culver continuing to Tucson and Fraber and the other soldier to Fort Buchanan. He returned to the pass with Surgeon Irwin.

Francisco. He was a chief of the Coyotero, also known as White Mountain, Apache who lived north of the Gila River and raided into Mexico through the Sulphur Springs Valley. He may have been Mexican by birth and was an ally of Cochise. He was killed at Fort Goodwin while "trying to escape" in 1865.

Free, Mickey. See Ward, Felix.

Gay, Mervin G. Born in 1827, in Louisiana, he was run out of Texas for horse stealing and came to Arizona in 1858.

Grant, W. S. He was a contractor for the regions' forts who arrived aboard the eastbound stage on February 6 with William Buckley. Grant was born in Maine in 1825. He established a flour mill in Tucson, supplying much of the wheat flour used in southern New Mexico Territory. He also owned the Canoa Hotel. In 1861, his reestablished stage line ran from Tucson to Fort Buchanan by way of Tubac. Fare was twelve dollars from either end point and six dollars from Tubac. He left for New Mexico with the troops in July 1861.

Graydon, James "Paddy." Born in Ireland in 1832, he had been a member of the 1st Dragoons at Fort Buchanan and took his discharge there, founding the United States Boundary Hotel, also known as Casa Blanca, three miles south of the post to supply soldiers' needs that the sutler could not. It was known as a rough place where there had been several shootings. Paddy accompanied Surgeon Irwin's relief party, perhaps as an interpreter. During the Civil War he was commissioned a captain of New Mexico Volunteers. On November 5, 1862, he was killed in a duel with Dr. J. M. Whitlock.

Grijalva, Merejildo. He was born about 1842 in Sonora, Mexico. He may have been an Opata Indian. Chiricahua Apache captured him when he was about ten and he was adopted by Cochise, who used him as an interpreter. Dr. Steck arranged with James Tevis to spirit him away from Cochise on an Overland stage. Thereafter he worked for Steck as an interpreter. Later he became a valued scout for the Army. The escape was a factor in the hostility between Tevis and Cochise and in Cochise's subsequent hostility toward the United States.

Hayman, Captain Samuel Brinkle. He was born in Pennsylvania about 1820 and graduated from USMA in 1842. He commanded Company C, 7th Infantry, in Utah and on the march to Fort Buchanan in 1860, arriving in October of that year. He took a leave of absence in December 1860, and Lieutenant George Bascom, the only remaining officer in the company, assumed command.

Huber, First Sergeant James J. He served with Company C, 7th Infantry. At Apache Pass he organized the watering parties that took stock to Apache Spring and brought water back to the station.

Hughes, Frederick George. Hughes was born in England in 1837 or 1838. By the winter of 1859, he was in Sierra County, California. In 1870, he was working as clerk in the Cañada Alamosa Reservation in New Mexico where he met Tom Jeffords, who hired him in 1872 as clerk for the newly formed Chiricahua Reservation in Arizona. He stayed for two years. Afterwards, he went on to be county clerk for Pima County, a member of the Arizona Legislature, and president of the Arizona Pioneers Society. He was killed by a lightning strike while sitting on his porch in Total Wreck in 1911.

Irwin, Bernard John Dowling. He was born in Ireland in 1830, and he graduated from the New York Medical College. He was appointed an assistant surgeon on August 28, 1856, and arrived at Fort Buchanan in December 1857. Irwin amputated Silas St. John's arm at Dragoon Springs and was involved in many other adventures in Arizona. He was awarded the Medal of Honor for his courage at Apache Pass. Although the award wasn't made until 1894, his was officially the first Medal of Honor, even though the award wasn't created until 1862.

Jeffords, Thomas Jefferson. Thomas Jefferson Jeffords was born on January 1, 1832, in Chautauqua, New York, and grew up in Ashtabula, Ohio. He sailed the Great Lakes as a captain and went west to the Pike's Peak Gold Rush, building the road from Fort Leavenworth, Kansas, to Denver along the way. He prospected, entering Arizona in 1860, was a civilian courier at the 1862 Battle of Valverde, returning to Arizona that year with the California Column. In 1871, he met and became friends with Cochise, then at war with the United States. He was instrumental in bringing peace to the southwest in 1872 as friend and advisor to Cochise. Thereafter he was the agent for the new reservation until 1876. (For more information see Spur Award Finalist biography *Tom Jeffords: Friend of Cochise*, TwoDot, 2017.)

Lorato. (See Antonio.) In Thomas Farrell's version of the story, he was Bascom's interpreter. He probably wasn't and may not be a real person or may be a name misremembered.

Lord, Lieutenant Richard S. C. Lord was born in 1832 and graduated from USMA in 1856. He entered Arizona that year along with Major

Steen and the First Dragoons. In 1861, he was in command of Company D. He was a part owner of the Patagonia Mine (later Mowry Mine) along with Richard Ewell and others. Reuben Bernard was his first sergeant. Initially assigned to Fort Buchanan, he was reassigned to Fort Breckenridge in 1860 along with his company. He came to Bascom's aid along with Lieutenant Moore and Company G. He commanded the 1st Cavalry detachment that served as General Sheridan's escort at New Orleans. He died in 1866.

Lyon, King. He was a twenty-four-year-old from New York working as a stage driver for the Overland Mail, driving the eastbound stage that arrived on February 6. Ambushed at the Pass two miles west of the station, an Indian ball broke his leg.

Lyon, Moses. He was the brother of King and an Overland Mail employee. On February 8, he drove the entire herd of horses and mules toward Apache Spring when the Apaches ambushed the watering party. Apaches killed him.

Mangas Coloradas. He was born around 1795 and was the father-in-law of Cochise. Mangas was the dominant chief of the Mogollon or Mimbres Apaches, that is to say, the Bedonkohe Chiricahuas. He met with General Stephen Watts Kearny, Kit Carson, and Lieutenant William Emory at the Santa Rita Copper Mines in 1846, and he promised peace and friendship to the Americans and aid against the Mexicans. He came to Cochise's aid at Apache Pass, and the two again fought side by side against the Freeman Thomas party and the Arizona Wagon Train at Cooke's Canyon and at the Battle of Apache Pass in 1862. Although legend says his name was derived from his sleeves being red with the blood of his enemies, a more likely version is that as a fashion statement he wore his sleeves turned inside out, exposing the red lining.

Marmaduke, Lieutenant John S. Graduated from USMA in 1857 and was assigned to the 1st United States Mounted Rifles, before being transferred to the 2nd U.S. Cavalry. He served under Colonel Albert Sidney Johnston in the Mormon Rebellion and was assigned to New Mexico in 1861. He participated in a court martial board at Fort Buchanan; returning to home station en route to the Rio Grande in February 1861, he encountered Sergeant Daniel Robinson at Stein's Peak and warned him that the Indians at Apache Pass were alarmed about something and to be careful. Marmaduke returned to Missouri, resigned his commission, and fought for the Confederacy. In 1885, he was elected twenty-fifth governor of Missouri.

Marshall, B. C. He was born in Kentucky in 1830. In 1858, he arrived in Arizona and began farming 160 acres between Wordsworth and Pennington. In March 1861, his house was attacked by Indians and set afire, the inhabitants escaping only because of the timely arrival of two officers from Fort Buchanan.

Mickey Free. See Ward, Felix.

Moore, Lieutenant Isaiah N. Moore was born in Pennsylvania in 1826, graduated from USMA in 1851, and served under Captain Ewell in New Mexico, fighting Apaches. He went to Arizona in 1856 with Major Steen. He served at Fort Buchanan, assuming command of Company G, 1st Dragoons, when Ewell departed, and went with the company when it was reassigned to Fort Breckenridge in October 1860. He took his company and Lord's to Apache Pass to support Bascom, arriving on February 14, 1861. Thirty-five-year-old Moore was the oldest and most senior officer at Apache Pass and one of the oldest and most experienced soldiers there; as such, he assumed command of the 136 soldiers assembled there from four companies. It was his decision to hang the six Apache hostages, although his report says that Bascom hanged them. In July 1861, he took the troops from Fort Breckenridge to Fort Buchanan and, in command of four companies, burned the fort, its supplies, and Grant's mill. He then headed east for the Rio Grande, taking his four companies successfully to Fort Craig. He died in defense of that fort on January 16, 1862.

Morrison, Lieutenant Colonel Pitcairn. He was born in New York in 1795 and was commissioned in 1820. He commanded the 7th Infantry in Utah during the Mormon Rebellion. Apparently, he was considered a bit over-the-hill as he did not command Fort Floyd even though he was the senior officer. He marched the 7th Infantry from Utah to New Mexico, arriving with two companies and the regimental headquarters at

Fort Buchanan in October 1861. His Post Order No. 4 sending Bascom to Apache Pass has been lost.

Mowry, Sylvester. He was born in Rhode Island in 1832 and graduated from USMA in 1852. Stationed at Fort Yuma from 1855 to 1857, he knew Sarah Bowman and became interested in the mineral wealth of Arizona. Resigning his commission, he headed to the area around Tubac and Sonoita Creek. In April 1860, he bought the Patagonia Mine, which had once belonged to Richard Ewell, and renamed it the Mowry Mine. It produced lead and silver.

Naiche. He was the younger son of Cochise and the boy who accompanied Cochise and his mother to Bascom's Camp. Taken hostage, he was released at Fort Buchanan. He succeeded his elder brother Taza as chief of the Chokonen Chiricahua in 1876 at San Carlos. He was chief over Geronimo and rode with him into Mexico.

Oberly, Musician Hubert (Auberly). He was the Principal Musician, a staff non-commissioned officer, for the 7th Infantry Regiment. He made inflated claims, describing himself as the color sergeant. Left behind at Fort Buchanan to nurse a sick child in January and February 1861, he claimed to the *New York World* in 1886 that he had been at Apache Pass. His account to the newspaper is full of hyperbole and a verifiable untruth. He, and he alone, accused Bascom of cowardice and drunkenness, an accusation shown groundless by Bascom's heroic behavior on multiple occasions. Oberly's motives are unclear. Perhaps he had a personal animosity toward Bascom. More likely, given his claims of being color sergeant, he was a frustrated little man who saw his chance to seem important by telling a wild story.

Oury, William S. Born in Virginia in 1817, he emigrated to Arizona from Texas. Whatever else he was, Oury was a bold frontiersman and a man who successfully held a number of positions of trust. In 1861, he was the Overland Mail agent in Tucson. He is often accused of being a liar. He was not among the defenders of the Alamo, as his family claimed. He was the leader of the 1871 Camp Grant Massacre and in 1880, as county recorder, it was he who provided the San Simon Cowboys with many more ballots than the region had eligible voters. Proof that these ballots were false led to the election being overturned. His account of the confrontation at Apache Pass has a few understandable misstatements based on his not arriving until February 14. He probably did send a messenger to alert Fort Breckenridge to Bascom's plight and ask assistance for the Overland Mail, but he did not call out the cavalry. Lieutenant Moore waited to do so until a messenger arrived from Lieutenant Colonel Morrison.

Page, Larcena Pennington. She was born in 1837 in Tennessee to Eli Pennington. In 1857, the family of four sons and eight daughters came to Arizona. In 1859, she married John Page, who was killed in the summer of 1860 by Apache. In March 1860, she was taken along with Mercedes Quiroz from a logging camp in the Santa Rita Mountains by Apaches. The Apaches speared her and threw her off a cliff. She spent the next fourteen days crawling to help.

Pennington, John (Jack). He was a settler along Sonoita Creek and brother to Larcena. The Pennington family were among the early settlers in Arizona. His father, Eli, Jack, and his four brothers died there fighting Apaches.

Poston, Charles Debrille. He was born in Kentucky in 1825. Poston first visited the Gadsden Purchase in 1854 and went east seeking funds to aid in development of Arizona silver mines. Together with other investors he founded the Sonora Exploring and Mining Company in 1856 and worked as agent for the company. He was a great booster for Arizona, which means in part that he had only passing acquaintance with the truth. He is considered the Father of Arizona as he played a part in seeing Arizona separated from New Mexico and made a territory. He was at Tubac during the confrontation at Apache Pass and his account is mostly fantasy.

Quiroz, Mercedes Sais. She was born in Tucson in 1849 and tutored by Larcena Pennington Page. In March 1860, Apache raiders took her captive along with Larcena. Captain Richard Ewell and Company G, 1st Dragoons, followed the trail and forced the Apache to return her.

Randal, Lieutenant Horace. He was born in 1834 in Tennessee and graduated from USMA in 1854. He was assigned to Fort Buchanan and his wife, Julia, accompanied him. Captain Ewell noted that his wife was blind. He resigned his commission in February 1861 and fought for the Confederacy.

Reeve, Lieutenant Colonel Isaac Van Duzer. Brevet Lieutenant Colonel Reeve was born in 1813 in New York and graduated from USMA in 1835. Transferred with part of the 8th Infantry to Fort Buchanan, he led campaigns against Western Apaches. In the spring of 1860, his unit was sent north to the mouth of Aravaipa Creek on the San Pedro, where they constructed Fort Breckenridge, which later in the year came to house two companies of dragoons. In February 1861, his unit was ordered to the Rio Grande. They began their march on February 3 and took Leach's Wagon Road north of the Dos Cabezas Mountains. Visible from Apache Pass, their presence panicked the Apache leaders into thinking the military was surrounding them. The Apache killed their hostages and departed. Colonel Reeve was unaware of Bascom's situation.

Robinson, Sergeant Daniel. He was a native of Ireland serving with Company C, 7th Infantry, which had been on detached service escorting supplies to Fort McLane. On the return journey, he arrived at Apache Pass on February 3, just hours ahead of Lieutenant Bascom and the rest of Company C. He was wounded while serving as a guard for the watering party sent to Apache Spring on February 8 and was hospitalized until April and was on limited duty for months after. His three accounts of the events at Apache Pass are the most complete and accurate in the record. During the Civil War he was commissioned and continued to serve with the Army into the 1890s.

Sanders, William. He was an armed escort on the Montoya Wagon Train carrying flour to Pinos Altos that entered Apache Pass from the west on the evening of February 5, 1861. Cochise or Francisco held him as one of four hostages. The Apaches tortured and killed him.

Tellor or Tuller, Owen. According to Farrell he was the paymaster, possibly for the Overland Mail, on the coach that arrived eastbound on February 6. Another source says that he was general superintendent of the east division of the Overland Mail, but I can find no record of him in this capacity.

Tevis, James Henry. He was born at Wheeling, then Virginia, in 1835. He traveled to Arizona in 1857 and was hired by Anthony Elder as station keeper at Apache Pass. He claimed to have assisted Meregildo Grijalva, later a famed scout for the Army, in escaping from Cochise, who held him as a slave. Tevis left Overland employ in 1859. He fought for the Confederacy.

Wallace, James F. He was born in 1828 in Massachusetts. With his wife, Mary, he owned a house in Tucson. She was seventeen in 1860. Ignoring Lieutenant Bascom's instructions to return to the station, he approached Apache women signaling to him from an arroyo one hundred yards to the south. There Apache warriors took him captive. Cochise tried to exchange him for the hostages Bascom held, but Bascom would not trade without all four hostages being released. He was later killed by Cochise or Francisco.

Walsh or Welch, first name unknown. Walsh was an assistant station keeper at Apache Pass. No one seems to recall either his first name or the correct spelling of his last name. He was slain escaping from the Apache.

Ward, Felix. Also known as Mickey Free, Felix Martinez, and Felix Tellez. He was the son of Jesusa Martinez and her first husband, Tellez, and stepson of Johnny Ward. In January 1861, Apache raiders took twelve-year-old Felix, along with Johnny Ward's herd, and headed east along Babocomari Creek toward the Chiricahua Mountains. Lieutenant Bascom was sent to get him back. Many years later, living among the Coyotero, or White Mountain, Apache, he volunteered as an interpreter and Apache scout. His grey eyes and reddish hair reminded soldiers of the character Mickey Free in the novel *Charles O'Malley, the Irish Dragoon*, and he was known by that name ever after.

Ward, John (Johnny). He was born in Ireland in 1806 and went to Arizona from California, possibly with a filibustering party, arriving too late to enter Mexico with the others. He met Jesusa Martinez, a Mexican woman, who had a child, Felix, by a scion of the Tellez family. She and John had two children of their own. He established a ranch about twelve miles south of Fort Buchanan on Sonoita Creek. Apaches took his cattle and stepson Felix on January 27, 1861. He reported this to Colonel Pitcairn Morrison at Fort Buchanan, who sent Lieutenant Bascom to retrieve them. He accompanied Bascom to Apache Pass and was in the tent with Bascom and Cochise serving as interpreter.

Whitfield, Sam. He was an armed escort on the Montoya Wagon Train carrying flour to Pinos Altos that entered Apache Pass from the west on the evening of February 5, 1861. Cochise or Francisco held him as one of four hostages. The Apaches tortured and killed him.

Wordsworth, William C., also called Woodworth and Wadsworth and the general. He was born in Mississippi in 1828. Arriving in the Sonoita Creek Valley with the Akes in 1856, he owned a farm. He had a dark secret. He and his wife had abandoned spouses and children before running away together, and they were not legally married. The Provisional Government of Arizona appointed him major general of the Territorial militia. He was killed at Cooke's Canyon.

Yones. She was the wife of Coyuntura and mother of Chie. Cochise frequently used her as a courier, possibly because she was conversant in Spanish.

Appendix F
THE ARIZONA WAGON TRAIN[1]

Forty-seven men, seven women, sixteen children

AKE FAMILY

Felix Grundy Ake

Mrs. Felix Mary Ake

Jeff Ake, age twelve

Will Ake

Emma Ake

George Davis

Mrs. George Anne Ake Davis

Thomas Thompson

Mrs. Thomas "Jinny" Virginia Ake Thompson

   Mary G., age four

   Esther, age six months

Lizzy Ake Bacon

Bob Phillips

Mrs. Robert America Phillips, niece of Mary Ake

—◦—

Sarah Bowman, Great Western

Albert Bowman (if Sarah was there, it's a good bet her husband was with her)

Moses "Ol' Mose" Carson (elder brother of Kit Carson)

Chickasaw/Cherokee Brown

Hampton Brown

Chisholm

Isaac "Jim" Cotton (wounded at Cooke's Canyon), farmed near Wadsworth

Mrs. Isaac Trinidad Cotton

    Margarita Cotton, age eight

    Joaquin Cotton, age three

Tommy Farrell, an Irishman

Irishman, name not remembered

Mr. Keith

Mrs. Keith

Luce, Mexican woman

B. C. Marshall

William May (killed in the first rush)

Old Pat, an Irishman

Pearl

Jack Pennington

William Redding (in the first rush his leg was broken; later killed)

Schaffer (tried to run but horse gave out)

Captain Nathaniel Sharpe

William W. Wadsworth (killed)

Mrs. Esther Wadsworth (eight months pregnant)

    Billy Wadsworth, age two

Those who ran away when the first shots were fired:

Sam Houston (nephew of Texas Governor Sam Houston)

John, a black man

Hatcher, a tailor

Tom Smith

Six double wagons (six yoke with trailer) plus two single wagons, a buggy and single wagon

Many cattle and sheep, one source says eight hundred cattle, twelve hundred sheep, and eight hundred goats

Appendix G

MILITARY CORRESPONDENCE[1]

MORRISON TO MAURY, ADJUTANT, DEPARTMENT OF NEW MEXICO, FEB-
ruary 11, 1861

*I have the honor to report for the information of the Commanding
Officer of the Department that the Chilicahua [sic] Indians have
become insolent, and they are now in hostile attitude toward the
United States, that they attacked a coach of the Mail Company
between Dragoon Springs and Apache Pass sometimes during last
week, killing one of the mules, and capturing the driver whom they
now hold as a prisoner of War; and they have wounded a Sergeant
of Company C 7th Infantry belonging to this Command, now on
detached service per orders No. 4 current series from these Head
Quarters of which you have been furnished with a copy. The command
under Lt. Bascom, consisting of Company C 7th Infantry and a
detachment of Company H, is now encamped at or near Apache Pass,
and by their presence will doubtless intimidate the Indians from making further depredations. Under these circumstances I am left with but
25 effective men in a country infested with hostile Indians of other
tribes, who are continually annoying the Settlers with their presence
and by their System of petty robberies. The distance to which the main
portion of the Garrison has been sent renders it inexpedient for me to
do more than protect the public property here.*

Bascom to Maury, Adjutant, Department of New Mexico, January [February] 14, 1861

I have to report that agreeable to instructions from Col. P. Morrison, to pursue the Indians and recover a boy made captive by them, I arrived here on the 3rd inst. and took six Indians as hostages until the boy should be delivered up. Co-Chis the chief denied having taken him but promised to get him if I would wait ten days; the day after he returned, accompanied by Francisco chief of the Coyoteros and a flag of truce, whist I was holding the talk with them they cut off and made prisoners of two Overland mailmen who left the station at that time. On the next day they succeeded in driving off a portion of my herd (29 mules). They also burnt a Mexican train between here and Fort Buchanan; some of the bodies they tied to the wheels and burnt, and horribly mutilated the rest. They also attacked one of the Overland Stages wounding the driver. The Coyoteros are driven from their country by the Navajos, the latter being driven down upon them by the troops; there are now in my immediate vicinity between five and six hundred warriors under the command of Mangus Colorado, although I can report with certainty but five Indians killed I think I may say twenty killed or dangerously wounded. I have two of my men slightly wounded.

Irwin to Chapin, Adjutant, Fort Buchanan, February 25, 1861

I have the honor to report that, in accordance with the instructions of the Commanding Officer of this post, I left here on the 9th instant and proceeded to the Chirricahui Mountains to render my professional services to the wounded men belonging to the command of Lieutenant G. N. Bascom, U.S. Army.

After crossing the Playa de los Pimos on the 10th and while en route, I discovered a herd of cattle driven by Indians at some miles distance. My infantry escort being mounted on mules, I immediately started in pursuit and, after a hard chase of six or seven miles, succeeded in capturing the party, consisting of a Coyotero Chief and two warriors, having in their possession thirteen cattle and two horses. I bound the prisoners and with the cattle delivered them to Lieut. Bascom at Apache Pass.

I beg to speak in highest terms of the conduct of the men engaged in the capture of this party. Corpl. Adam Faber, Privates W. Leiter and G. Saliot of C Company 7th Infantry are deserving of the warmest commendation for their zeal and soldierly bearing; also Private William Christy, G Company, 7th Infantry, a volunteer for this service who was ever ready to display the qualities of a good soldier. Mr. James Graydon, a citizen of this vicinity, accompanied me and was foremost in capturing and securing the prisoners. His character for daring and courage needs no commendation at my hands.

Being led to expect an attack from the Indians, who were reported as being assembled to the number of five hundred warriors at Apache Pass, I took every precaution to guard against surprise, and I fortunately joined Lt. Bascom on the evening of the 10th without suffering any injury from them.

Moore to Maury, Adjutant, Department of New Mexico, February 25, 1861

I have the honor to report that on the 10th inst. I received information that Lt. Bascom with his company was surrounded in the Chirricaquis pass by several hundred Indians, that the Indians had burned a train and murdered the teamsters, and stopped the U.S. mail. Taking Lt. Lord and seventy men I started for the pass, but on arriving found that the Indians had left the mountains, the Coyoteros most probably for the north of the Gila, and the Chirricaquis (sic) with a band of Mimbres Indians under Mangus for the head waters of the Gila. I traversed the mountains three days to assure myself, visiting their camps, which I found to have been hastily abandoned, but did not see one fresh track in the whole march. For scouting in the mountains, I assumed the command of Lt. Bascom. We buried the dead bodies of four Americans who had been captured and afterwards killed by the Indians. It appears that all the different tribes on this side of the Rio Grande are united in hostility, and our force is entirely inefficient as they avoid a single column, and if we divide we are too much weakened. During my absence the Pinal Indians made an attempt to drive off my herds. The vigilance of Dr. Ryland who was left in command frustrated this. Lt. Bascom's report will give more fully the details connected with this outbreak and inform you what disposition was made of the prisoners in his possession.

Bascom to Morrison, Commanding Fort Buchanan, February 25, 1861

I have the honor to report that in compliance with the foregoing Orders; I left Fort Buchanan on the 29th ult. and arrived at Apache Pass on the 3rd inst.; feeling confident that they had the boy I captured six Indians and told the Chief Ca-Ches that I would hold them as hostages until he brought in the boy; he denied having taken the boy, or having been engaged in the depredations in the vicinity of the Fort, but said it was done by the Coyoteros and that they then had the boy at the Black Mountain and if I would wait ten days at the Station he would bring him in; to this I consented.

On the 5th Ca-Ches returned, accompanied by Francisco a Coyotero Chief with about five hundred warriors, and raised a white flag. I went out to talk with them but when about one hundred and fifty yards from the house I began to suspect from their actions that all was not right and refused to go further; two of the Mail men then left the Station to go to the Indians. I ordered them back and told them that I had no prisoners to exchange for them if they were captured; they paid no attention to my orders but went into the ravine where the Indians were, and were immediately seized by them; Francisco then jerked down his white flag and crying in Spanish "Aqui! Aqui!" pointed to the [Bascom's] party with the flag. I then took down my flag and gave the command "fire" and retreated to the Station house; the fire now became general, and was carried on briskly for sometime when the Indians abandoned the ravine. Sergeant Smith of Company C 7th Infantry "bearer of the flag," was slightly wounded. Mr. Culver, one

of the captured men, in making his escape, was severely wounded &
one of the station keepers killed.

On the 6th Ca-Ches came on the hill and said he would give me
[James F.] *Wallace and sixteen Government mules for the prisoners;*
I asked him where he got the mules; his reply was [that he] *"took*
them from a government train of course." I told him if he brought
the boy also I would trade with him; that evening there was a note
written by Wallace stating that they had three other prisoners Sam
Whitfield William Sanders and Frank Brunner and that they would
come in next day and exchange; while the herd was being watered
in the morning, in charge of 1st Sergeant James Huber and fifteen
men, about two hundred Indians made a dash to get the herd; the
party headed them off in the direction they first took but were unable
to recover the herd, none of them being mounted (I had sent all the
saddle-mules with a party to escort Dr. Irwin from the Post); they
however followed the Indians keeping up a running fight for about
a mile, doing considerable execution. I can report with certainty but
five Indians killed, but think there were twelve or fifteen more killed
or badly wounded. This includes all since my arrival in the Pass.
Sergeant Daniel Robinson of Company C 7th Infty. was slightly
wounded, and one of the Mail men mortally in this last action.

The Western Stage was attacked about three miles from this place;
the drivers leg was broken by a ball; this stage was delayed here for
several days and to 1st Lieut. John R. Cooke 8th Infty. I return my
grateful thanks for his kind advice and gallant assistance; this gallant
officer though much my senior in rank and experience volu[n]*teered*
to take charge of the party at the spring on the morning of the 8th.
The Indians have burned a Mexican train between Apache Pass and
Ewell's Station killing 8 men that were with it, horribly mutilating
some of the bodies; some of them were tied to the burning wagons,
whether before or after death could not be determined; these I had
buried.

On the 10th Dr. Irwin arrived from Fort Buchanan and turned
over to me a Coyotero Chief and two warriors to-gether with a herd

of 10 cattle; the cattle I killed retaining the Indians as prisoners. On the 14th Lieutenants Moore and Lord arrived with about 70 men of D & G Companies 1st Dragoons, and on the 16th we joined them with 40 men of my command in a scout against the Indians; on the 1st and 2nd days out we discovered neither Camps or fresh signs of the Indians, on the third day from 10 to 15 lodges, all of which bore evidences of having been hastily aband[on]ed several day previous. The property was all destroyed and the Camps burnt. Dr. Irwin discovered about four miles from the Station the bodies of the four prisoners; Wallace, Whitfield, Sanders and Brunner, where they had been murdered by the Indians; finding no fresh signs of Indians, we returned to the Station and on the next day started for Fort Buchanan; when near the scene of macsacre [sic] and about three hundred yards from the burnt train, I took the six warriors I had [as] prisoners to the grave of murdered men, explained through the interpreter what had taken place, and my intentions, and bound them securely hand and foot, and hung them to the nearest trees; the three remaining prisoners a woman and two boys I have turned over to the Guard at this Post.

The men behaved excellently well, always ready for the discharge of any duty; the non-commissioned officers zealous and untiring in the discharge of their duties.

Record of Events, Post Returns, Fort Buchanan, January 1861

January - 2 Lieut. G.N. Bascom 7 Infantry with 54 enlisted men of Company G 7 Infantry left this Post, January 29, 1861, to Apache Pass & vicinity to recover a stolen boy and stock from neighboring Settlers per P.O. No. 4, dated Head Qtrs Fort Buchanan N.M. January 28, 1861

Record of Events, Post Returns, Fort Buchanan, February 1861

B.J.D. Irwin, Assistant Surgeon: on Detached service Feby. 8, 1861, Apache pass, joined from Det. service Feby. 23rd 1861. G.N. Bascom,

2nd Lt., Commanding Company C since December 15, 1861: joined from Det. service Feby. 23, 1861.

Return for Company C, 7th Infantry Regiment, February 1861

Company C 7 Infantry arrived at Apache Pass on the 3d of February 1861, took Prisoners on the 4th Inst., and a party on escort under command of Asst. Surg. Irwin U.S.A. captured 3 Indians on the 10th Instant. The Company had an engagement with the Indians on the 5th inst. Sergt. Smith slightly wounded. The Indians attacked a party on the 8th Inst. while at a spring watering animals. They ran off the herd and slightly wounded Sergt. Robinson Co C 7 Infy. The Company left apache Pass on the 19th Inst. and arrived at Fort Buchanan N.M. on the 23rd inst.

Muster Roll of Company C, Seventh Infantry, for the period from December 31, 1860, to February 28, 1861

January and February - Company left Fort Buchanan Jany. 29, 61 on scout to Apache Pass per O. No. 4 Hd. Qrs. Fort Buchanan N.M. Jany. 28th 61. Arrived at Apache pass Feby. 3d 61, captured 6 Indians on the 4th inst., and a party on escort Asst. Surgeon B.J.D. Irwin U.S.A. took 3 Indians on the 10th while en route to Apache pass. Had an engagement with Apaches on the 5th inst. Sergt. Smith wounded. A Band of about 200 Indians attacked a party of Co. C 7th [Infantry] on the 8th while they were watering the public animals. The Indians ran of [f] the Herd and wounded Sergt. Robinson. Left Apache pass on the 19th and arrived at Fort Buchanan 23d inst - distance from Fort to pass 95 miles. Left Sergt. [Patrick] Murr[a]y & 12 men at the pass guarding Mail Station. Left 2 men at Dragoon Springs with a party already there to protect Mail Station.

Muster Roll of Companies D and G, First Regiment of Dragoons, Fort Breckenridge, December 31, 1860, to February 28, 1861

The Company [D] *left this Post Feby. 10/61 in Scout against the Apache Indians and returned on the 23d marching a distance of about 300 miles. Lieut. Moore with 35 men of co.* [G] *left the post against Chiricahua Apaches Feb. 10th and returned Feb. 23, 1861.*

Maury to Chapin, commanding Fort Buchanan, March 17, 1861

The Department Commander [Canby] *directs that you will publicly express to Dr. Irwin, U.S. Army, and to Lieutenant Bascom, 7th U.S. Infantry, his approbation of the excellent conduct of those officers, and the troops under their command in the operations against the Apache Indians during the last month. He emphatically approves of Lieutenant Bascom's decided action in executing the Indian warriors, after the atrocious murders which had been committed by the tribe.*[2]

Appendix H

APACHE ACCOUNTS

THE APACHE ACCOUNTS ARE DIFFICULT TO INCORPORATE IN THE NARrative. Anglo authors put them in writing and thus they are filtered through those authors. There are strong indications that the authors of these accounts as well as the Apaches, in many cases, were aware of the post-1868 Bernard narrative that blamed Lieutenant Bascom, which had been circulated initially by Colonel Devin, in reports, and Governor Safford, in the newspaper. It was picked up by early historians DeLong, Farish, and Lockwood. It made it into popular culture through the 1947 novel *Blood Brother* and the 1950 Jimmy Stewart movie *Broken Arrow*. One of the Apache informants mentioned having seen the movie. Bits of misinformation that fit the Bernard scheme show up in the accounts.

COCHISE

Cochise said to Special Indian Agent William Arny in October of 1870, "After they took my children and I had to go to Sonora, my people got mad and went to killing."[1]

William Arny wrote to a local newspaper:

> *His history: In 1860* [1861] *he went with 6 braves and some children with a flag of truce to the camp at Apache Pass; that the commanding officer ordered them hung; that he cut his way through the tent, was fired at by the soldiers, escaped and took his people to Sonora. He has been on the warpath ever since. The six men with him were hung, and*

two officers played a game of cards to determine whether his children should be hung; that the one who opposed hanging won and one of the boys was eventually sent to the states, etc.[2]

The following account comes from General Oliver Otis Howard who met with and made peace with Cochise in October 1872. The stress of the retaliation is on Americans, Mexicans, and Apaches mutually killing each other on sight and not on the events at Apache Pass. The ellipses occur in the original text.

We were once a large people covering these mountains; we lived well; we were at peace. One day my best friend was seized by an officer of the white men and treacherously killed. . . . The worst place of all is Apache Pass. There, five Indians, one my brother, were murdered. Their bodies were hung up and kept there till they were skeletons. . . . Now Americans and Mexicans kill an Apache on sight. I have retaliated with all my might. My people have killed Americans and Mexicans and taken their property. Their losses have been greater than mine. I have killed ten white men for every Indian slain, but I know that the whites are many and the Indians are few. Apaches are growing less and less every day. . . . Why shut me up on a reservation? We will make peace. We will keep it faithfully. But let us go around free as Americans do. Let us go wherever we please.[3]

Captain Joseph Haskell recounts the 1872 Dragoon Springs Peace Treaty made by General O. O. Howard. After terms had been agreed upon, Cochise, Howard, and Jeffords went up to the old Overland Mail station at Dragoon Springs and there met with the officers from Fort Bowie to explain the terms of the treaty. Haskell attempted a verbatim account of what Cochise said. The confrontation with Bascom appears to be of much less importance in the following account than in others.

Cochise began to talk. . . . He had never lied to the white man, but the white man had lied to him. He told how he had been deceived by those in command at Bowie [Bascom], and how they had deceived him by lying at other times; how the Whites hunted Indians the way they did deer or other wild game. How they seemed pleased and laughed when they killed an Indian.[4]

The following account comes from Governor Anson Safford's interview with Cochise in November 1872, just after Cochise had accepted peace terms.

During the year 1860 [1861],[5] a boy was made captive while herding stock on the Sonoita and some believed that Cochise had taken him, hence Lieutenant Bascom with a company of soldiers marched to Apache Pass near his headquarters and camped at the overland mail station. The lieutenant told the station keepers that he was on the way to New Mexico and that he desired to see Cochise, and induced them to go and invite him in. When asked by Cochise what he wanted of him, he was informed that he desired to extend the hospitalities of his tent, as he was on his way out of the country. Cochise with four of his friends and relatives came in, and when seated in Bascom's tent, it was suddenly surrounded by soldiers. He desired to know the cause, and was informed that he and his friends were prisoners, and would be kept as such until the boy believed to be with his band was given up. Cochise protested against such treachery and declared that he could not give him up, as he knew nothing of him. Watching his opportunity, [h]e drew his knife, cut a hole through the tent, and escaped. He immediately called his warriors together, came in force near the station, and desired to have a talk. One of the station keepers [James F. Wallace] went to him to hear what he had to say, but as soon as he had reached Cochise's lines, he was seized and made a prisoner. A day or two was spent afterwards in endeavors to effect an exchange of prisoners. Cochise offering to give up his prisoner if the lieutenant would release his (Cochise's) friends. The lieutenant declined to exchange man for man unless Cochise would surrender the boy, but Cochise steadily affirmed that he knew nothing about him. Finally, he came for a last talk, leading the station keeper prisoner, with a rope around his neck tied to the horn of his saddle. He again offered to surrender him if his four friends were set free. The station keeper begged to have the exchange made as his life would be forfeited if it were not done; but the lieutenant again refused, and Cochise now "roweled" his horse and dashed off at lightning speed, dragging the poor victim at full length by the neck. The lieutenant then hung the four [six] prisoners and Cochise took the road. . . .[6]

He [Cochise] *said he was glad to see me, and the fact that I had come among them unprotected, was evidence that I had confidence in his professions of peace. He then said that prior to the ill treatment he received from Lieutenant Bascom, he had been a good friend of the Americans, and since that time he believed he had been their worst enemy; that the time was within memory when the plains were covered with herds and the mountains were filled with Apaches, but now the herds are all gone and the number of Apaches greatly reduced; that when he opened hostilities against the Americans, he and his tribe made a promise to fight until the last one was exterminated to hold the country, but now he was determined to live at peace with everyone on this side of the Mexican line. I told him that the conduct of Lieutenant Bascom was disliked by our people, and if he had not gone to war, Bascom would have been punished and many lives would have been saved. He said he was now satisfied that it was wrong to go to war on that account and that both sides were blamable and had suffered for it.*[7]

As you can see there is more Safford and Reuben Bernard here than Cochise, but Safford implies that during his interview Cochise confirmed these events. For instance, none of the primary accounts say that Bascom ever told anyone that he was en route to the Rio Grande and wanted to dine with the famous chief of the Chiricahua. In 1861, Cochise was still a rather obscure figure. Subsequent events made him famous, not the least of which was Bernard's notion of Cochise the always friendly, who guarded the Overland Mail. The deliberate violation of hospitality in the intentional taking of hostages arises from Bernard, as does the refusal of Bascom to exchange hostages without the boy, Felix. Cochise would never have admitted to dragging Wallace to death with a rope around his neck, especially since he hadn't done this. Cochise knew that he held four hostages but only offered one in exchange. Bernard, who was not there, didn't know. The governor told Cochise that the behavior of the lieutenant was disliked by the Americans. Bascom was never blamed for anything until after 1868 and then it became general knowledge. It's clear that Governor Safford was "leading the witness."

Geronimo

In the following account given by Geronimo, his timeline is highly inconsistent, jumbling events from 1860, 1861, and 1862. Fort Bowie was established after the July 1862 Battle of Apache Pass. The first time that soldiers came to Apache Pass may refer to one of Captain Richard Ewell's visits in 1860, and not to Lieutenant Bascom's visit. The taking of hostages refers to the 1861 confrontation with Lieutenant Bascom.

> *After about a year some trouble arose between them and the Indians, and I took the warpath as a warrior not as a chief. I had not been wronged, but some of my people had been, and I fought with my tribe, for the soldiers and not the Indians were at fault.*
>
> *Not long after this some of the officers of the United States troops invited our leaders to hold a conference at Apache Pass (Fort Bowie). Just before noon the Indians were shown into a tent and told that they would be given something to eat.[8] When in the tent they were attacked by the soldiers. Our chief, Mangus-Colorado, and several other warriors, by cutting through the tent, escaped; but most of the warriors were killed or captured.[9] Among the Bedonkohe Apaches killed at this time were Sanza, Kladetahe, Niyokahe, and Gopi.[10] After this treachery the Indians went back to the mountains and left the fort entirely alone. I do not think that the agent had anything to do with planning this for he had always treated us well. I believe it was entirely planned by the soldiers.*
>
> *From the very first the soldiers sent out to our western country, and the officers in charge of them, did not hesitate to wrong the Indians. They never explained to the Government when an Indian was wronged, but always reported the misdeeds of the Indians. Much that*

was done by mean white men was reported at Washington as the deeds of my people.

The Indians always tried to live peaceably with the white soldiers and settlers. One day during the time that the soldiers were stationed at Apache Pass I made a treaty with the post. This was done by shaking hands and promising to be brothers. Cochise and Mangus-Colorado did likewise. I do not know the name of the officer in command, but this was the first regiment that ever came to Apache Pass.[11] This treaty was made about a year before we were attacked in a tent, as above related. In a few days after the attack at Apache Pass we organized in the mountains and returned to fight the soldiers. There were two tribes—the Bedonkohe and the Chokonen Apache both commanded by Cochise.[12] After a few days' skirmishing we attacked a freight train that was coming in with supplies for the Fort. We killed some of the men and captured the others. These prisoners our chief offered to trade for the Indians whom the soldiers had captured at the massacre in the tent. This the officers refused, so we killed our prisoners, disbanded and went into hiding in the mountains.[13] Of those who took part in this affair I am the only one now living.[14]

BETZINEZ

Jason Betzinez fought alongside Geronimo, and had this to say about the incident at Apache Pass:

While I was still a small boy Cochise and his band were living in and around what is known as Apache Pass, a canyon just west of old Fort Bowie, which was then probably only a temporary camp.[15] An officer [Lieutenant Bascom] of the post acting, perhaps, under instruction from one of the Indian agents was attempting to secure the return of some half-breed boy captured by San Carlos Indians [Pinals]. This officer, Lieutenant Bascom, sent an invitation to Cochise to meet with him in a conference in the pass.

Not expecting any trouble and not being conscious of having committed any offense against the Government, Cochise and his subchiefs prepared to go to the meeting. They had their women give them a good scrubbing, comb their hair, paint their faces, and otherwise make them presentable for such an honored occasion.

At the meeting the officer in command of the troop detachment accused the Indians of having in captivity a small white boy named Mickey Free. Cochise replied that he had never heard of this case, which was quite true. The officer didn't believe him.

After the meeting was over, the officer told the chiefs to go into a tent where a fine dinner had been prepared for them. When they were all inside, the soldiers surrounded the tent and attacked. All the Indians except three were captured. One of those who escaped was Cochise. Evidently he reacted more quickly than the others for he sprang to the side of the tent, slashed it open with his knife, and with two others dashed out into the brush, making good his escape. This affair became known to the Apaches as "Cut Through the Tent." On account of the circumstances it aroused much indignation and interest even on the part of the Apaches of bands distant from the Chiricahua country. I have heard my parents as well as others discuss it many a time.

On their return to the rest of the tribe Cochise and his companions told the story of this act of treachery on the part of the white officer. Under Cochise's leadership the warriors established road blocks or ambushes on the wagon road leading through the pass, interrupting traffic both to the east and west. They captured a number of teamsters and other travelers. Then Cochise sent a messenger to Lieutenant Bascom offering to exchange his prisoners for the Apaches held by the military. The officer refused. A day or so afterwards Cochise and his men found these Indians hanging from trees where the soldiers had executed them. The Indians sadly took down the bodies of their friends and buried them. Then they hung all their white captives to the same trees. This affair changed a prominent, highly-thought-of chief and his band from Indians who had been friendly and cooperative with the Government to a bitterly hostile group. The warfare which was set off lasted as long as Cochise lived and cost the lives of many people.

A year after the "Cut Through the Tent" affair, soldiers attacked some Indians—not hostiles—who with their families were moving through Apache Pass. My mother told me that the soldiers fired can-non at the Apaches causing them to flee in great fright into the rocks while the shells burst over their heads. In this fight, the first in which Apaches can remember being attacked by artillery, no one was hurt by the firing.[16]

Jason Betzinez was a very young boy when these events took place. His account was not given until 1958 when he was a very old man, nearly one hundred. He conveys a sense of betrayal that the Apache felt but has a number of facts confused, particularly the relationship in time of the death of Cochise's hostages and the hanging of Bascom's. He names the boy taken as Mickey Free indicating that he, Jason, was very much aware of the Anglo accounts of the confrontation.

DAKLUGIE

Born about 1872, Daklugie was the son of Nednhi leader Juh. His account was recorded in the 1950s. The events described were already eleven years in the past when he was born. He includes the story of the wise sergeant and the dragging death of Wallace, so obviously his account is colored by Anglo intrusions.

It was when Naiche was a baby that an arrogant young officer did a stupid thing that antagonized Cochise and his Chiricahuas. That was one of our favorite stories. I've heard it about the campfire at night many, many times. A coyote [half-breed] *of Mexican and Irish parents was taken, allegedly by Cochise's men. His mother (Mexican) was living with a rancher named* [John] *Ward, not far from Fort Buchanan. This boy, later known as Mickey Free, was probably not of as much importance to Ward as were the cattle taken from him, but the man made complaint at Fort Buchanan, and Lt. George W. Bascom was sent to Apache Pass to recover the child from Cochise. He camped near the mail station where fresh horses were kept for incoming riders.*

Cochise—with his wife (daughter of Mangas Coloradas), their infant son Naiche, and three of Cochise's close male relatives—came to the station. Ward in the officer's camp, recognized Cochise and informed Bascom of his presence. Cochise denied that any of his band had done the kidnapping. Ward accused the chief of telling a lie. Cochise was very proud of making his word good, and no greater offense could have been offered to him. Apache hated liars. If a man was known to be untruthful, even though he had witnessed a murder he could not testify. He could not carry a message from one band to another because the lives of both might depend upon delivery of the sender's exact words. Ward demanded pay for both boy and cattle. Cochise offered to investigate, determine the offenders, and help restore the child.

Unknown to the Apaches, soldiers surrounded the tent in which Bascom and the Apaches were talking. The young officer informed Cochise that he and his party were prisoners and would not be released until the boy was produced. With his knife, Cochise cut a slit in the tent and escaped. The chief summoned his warriors and captured some white men to exchange for his family. Despite the protestations of an experienced old sergeant, Bascom had the men he still held captive hanged, though he released Cochise's wife and child. Cochise dragged one captive to death and had the others hanged in retaliation.

From that time on Cochise harassed the invaders, but I do not believe that he was guilty of all the atrocities attributed to him. Undoubtedly some of his young men ambushed wagon trains and stages without his even knowing of it. In general, my father knew much of his actions and they have been exaggerated by writers.[17]

JAMES KAYWAYKLA

James Kaywaykla died in 1963. His recollections were recorded in the 1950s. He includes the court martial of First Sergeant Reuben Bernard, which did not happen. Bernard wasn't present before February 14, 1861, and perhaps not even then. Kaywaykla wasn't present at Apache Pass that February, either, and has the story second hand and from Anglo sources. His observations about Mickey Free are interesting.

[B]ut we knew that Mickey Free was incapable of loyalty. . . . But because Mickey spoke our language fluently he was usually used for

interpreting. He was a half-breed—a thing abhorrent to Apaches. He had, through no fault of his own, been the cause of Cochise's outbreak. Though the trouble was precipitated by the ignorance and arrogance of a young officer, it was occasioned by the abduction of Mickey Free by other Apaches than Cochise's men, and indirectly the child was held to be responsible. Moreover, the Chiricahua considered him to be treacherous and unreliable.

It is a terrible thing for the fate of an inarticulate people to depend upon the spoken word of a renegade with no whit of integrity. My people knew well how an ambitious young lieutenant sought to arrest Cochise by inviting him to a tent for a conference. That was none other than Lt. George Nicholas Bascom. Once inside with some of his people Cochise realized that he was surrounded by troops. An experienced old sergeant went to the officer and protested against the treachery and stupidity of his commanding officer and was courtmartialed (sic) for insubordination. The chief cut his way through the tent and escaped, but his wife, his infant son, Naiche, and his two brothers were held. The wife and child were released, but the men were hanged.

For ten years Cochise exacted vengeance.

Now [1880s on the San Carlos Reservation] *the Chiricahua were at the mercy of the coyote whose kidnapping had brought war to the Chiricahua.*[18]

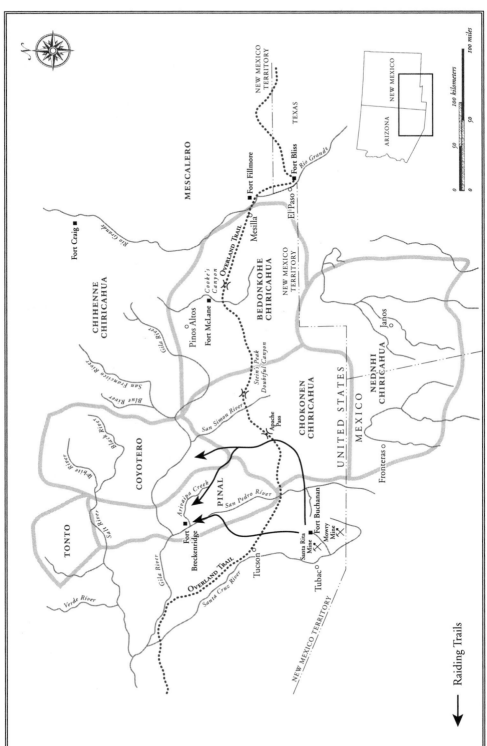

Apache Band Regions in the Gadsden Purchase (ca. 1861)

→ Raiding Trails

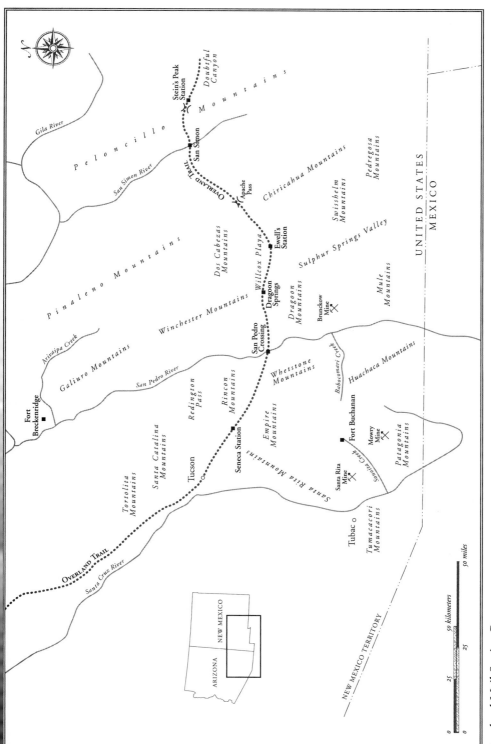

Overland Mail Station Route

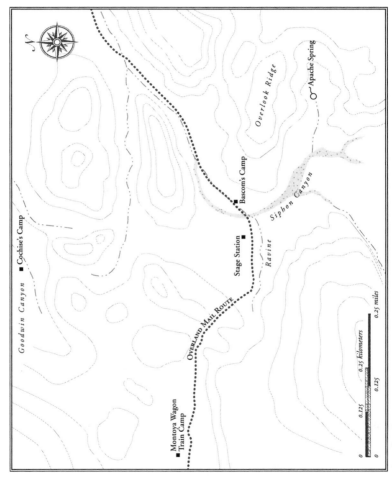

Apache Pass

ENDNOTES

CHAPTER 1: AN OVERVIEW OF THE BLACK LEGEND OF COCHISE AND LIEUTENANT BASCOM

1. Although Cochise is the accepted spelling today, it was not so in the nineteenth century when all sorts of variants were in use including: Cochise, Cachise, Coheis, Coches, Kuchies, Ka Kreese, Chies. I have not bothered to correct these in quotes from nineteenth-century texts, relying on the reader to make the adjustment. The Chokonen leader was called something like Chies by his people and the meaning was probably oak.

2. The company is commonly called the Butterfield Overland Mail, but that was never its official name. John Butterfield was instrumental in organizing the company, but its official name was always the Overland Mail.

3. In 1861, Bernard was First Sergeant of Company D, First Regiment of Dragoons, commanded by Lieutenant Richard Lord, stationed at Fort Breckenridge, ninety miles north of Fort Buchanan. Lieutenant George Bascom was commander of Company C, 7th Infantry, stationed at Fort Buchanan.

4. In the 1850s, the name Arizona was already in use for the area acquired by the 1854 Gadsden Purchase (treaty signed December 30, 1853, approved by Congress June 8, 1854). Private Roe, 7th Infantry, used the term in all that he wrote (Roe, Lewis F., edited by John P. Wilson, *From Western Deserts to Carolina Swamps: A Civil War Soldier's Journals and Letters Home*, Albuquerque, University of New Mexico Press, 2012). This was the area south of Socorro, New Mexico, from Texas in the east to the Colorado River in the west, sometimes referred to as "south of the Gila River." In August 1861, Confederate Lieutenant Colonel John Baylor declared this area to be the Territory of Arizona. Recaptured by Union forces, on February 24, 1863, Congress created the Territory of Arizona dividing it from New Mexico along the 109th line of longitude (north-south).

5. Johnny Ward was his stepfather. He had been born to an out-of-wedlock union of the Martinez and Tellez families, so he is also called Felix Tellez or Felix Martinez. In the 1870s, when he enlisted as an Apache scout, soldiers gave him a new name, one that they could pronounce, Mickey Free. Mickey Free was a character in the novel *Charles O'Malley, The Irish Dragoon*, by Charles James Lever (1841). With a blue eye and dark red hair, he seemed Irish to some and the story went around that he was Ward's natural son. Since Apache scouts had to be Apache, the story also went about that his mother

had been kidnapped, had a son by an Apache chief, and then escaped (Radbourne, Allan, *Mickey Free: Apache Captive, Interpreter, and Indian Scout,* Tucson, The Arizona Historical Society, 2005).

6. Dr. Fahey, in his fine article, says that twenty-three people lost their lives during the Bascom Affair (Fahey, John H., "Fort Buchanan and the Origins of Arizona Territory." *Journal of Arizona History* 58 [Summer 2017], p 141). We've corresponded on this topic. My count includes six Apache hostages hanged, four held hostage by Cochise murdered, one stage driver killed, one station keeper shot, and eight Mexican teamsters slain, for a total of twenty. The soldiers claimed to have killed numerous Apache in battle, but I don't have an exact number. Three is not unreasonable.

7. The earliest type of cavalry in the U.S. Army was dragoons. There were two regiments authorized in the 1830s, the 1st and 2nd, each of ten companies of about one hundred men. In 1855, Congress authorized the first regiment called cavalry. After 1861, the dragoons became cavalry. Other armies consider dragoons to be a type of cavalry. Dragoons trained to fight on foot and on horseback, as infantry and cavalry, armed with pistol, saber, and musketoon, a shortened version of the musket. Dragoons are not mounted infantry who ride to a fight and then dismount before making contact (Gorenfeld, Will, and John Gorenfeld, *Kearny's Dragoons Out West: The Birth of the U.S. Cavalry*, Norman, University of Oklahoma Press, 2016). Lieutenant Bascom's Company C, 7th Infantry Regiment, had mules, and thus was mounted infantry in all but name.

8. Twelve more men were returning from a mission and joined Bascom at Apache Pass.

9. At this time, there were five companies of soldiers in Arizona. There were two companies from the 7th Infantry stationed at Fort Buchanan, two from the 1st Dragoons (cavalry), and one from the 8th Infantry stationed at Fort Breckenridge ninety miles to the north. Three companies were at Apache Pass and a fourth marched nearby on its way to the Rio Grande to fight invading Texans, spooking Cochise into believing the army was trying to surround him. In other words, four-fifths of the entire local Army strength participated. Some readers might find an explanation of military organization useful. The smallest organization, if it can be called that, was four men who were messmates, rotating the duty of preparing food among themselves. In the dragoons, one of the four would have been the designated horse-holder, who held the horses in battle. The first formal organization was the company. Size varied from thirty to one hundred men depending on Congressional authorization. Usually a company had from thirty to fifty men available for duty. The company was supposed to be commanded by a captain assisted by a first and second lieutenant. The next largest organization was the regiment of ten companies commanded by a colonel assisted by a lieutenant colonel and a major. Above this was the department commanded by the senior colonel whose regiment was assigned to the area. The term brevet will come up. Brevet rank was an honor won in battle. An officer was paid based on his rank in the regimental structure; all the money Congress would authorize. An officer could wear the insignia of and be addressed at his brevet rank and, if no other regular officer were available, command an organization associated with that rank. Battalions/squadrons were temporary battle organizations of two or more companies. Brigades, divisions, and corps were not formed except in wartime.

10. Allan Radbourne, *Mickey Free: Apache Captive, Interpreter, and Indian Scout*, Tucson, Arizona Historical Society, 2005, p 14, says they were Aravaipa Apaches under Victor, a people closely associated with the Pinal. Over the years, the Pinal Apache have most commonly been blamed as a result of statements made by his stepbrother, John Rope. Rope who told the tale had reason to redirect blame away from his people.

11. The boy grew up among the Coyotero, also known as White Mountain Apache.

12. Richard S. Ewell was a popular and active commander of a dragoon company at Fort Buchanan from 1856 until October of 1860. He was often in command of the post and put a greater stamp on Arizona history than any other officer of the time. See Fahey, John H., "Fort Buchanan and the Origins of Arizona Territory," *Journal of Arizona History*, 58/2 (Summer 2017). In 1861, he resigned his commission and accepted appointment in the Confederate Army. He was General Thomas "Stonewall" Jackson's second in command and assumed command of Jackson's corps at Gettysburg where some blamed him for Lee's loss because he failed to take Cemetery Ridge.

13. Hutton, Paul Andrew, *The Apache Wars: The Hunt for Geronimo, the Apache Kid, and the Captive Boy who Started the Longest War in American History*, New York, Crown Publishers, 2016.

14. Sweeney, Edwin R., "Cochise and the Prelude to the Bascom Affair," *New Mexico Historical Review* 64 (Autumn 1989), p 428. Among those who according to Sweeney oversimplified the issue are Cochise and Major John Green. In August 1870, Cochise told Major John Green at Camp Mogollon that he "did not begin the war and only fought for revenge and self defense," *Alta California*, November 14, 1870. In October 1872, Cochise informed General Oliver Otis Howard that "The worst place of all is Apache Pass. There five [six] Indians, one my brother, were murdered. Their bodies hung up, and kept there till they were skeletons. . . . I have retaliated with all my might." Oliver Otis Howard, *My Life and Experience Among Our Hostile Indians*, New York, De Capo Press, 1972 (1908), p 208.

15. Howard, *My Life and Experience Among Our Hostile Indians*, p 208.

16. Utley, Robert M., "The Bascom Affair: A Reconstruction," *Arizona and the West*, 3/1 (Spring 1961), p 59.

17. Before the Civil War, there were about one thousand Anglo-Americans in Arizona, living three and four each at twenty-six Overland Mail stations, at Tubac and Tucson, the only towns, along Sonoita Creek and at Fort Buchanan, at Fort Breckenridge and environs, and at the Mowry, Santa Rita, and Cerro Colorado mines. When war came, the army was withdrawn to fight on the Rio Grande. Without protection, the miners left. Lacking customers to sell to farmers and ranchers left; they too were unprotected. The Overland Mail route was abandoned because it ran through Arkansas and Texas, now in the Confederacy. People retreated to Tubac and Tucson. Tubac was attacked by Apache and then burned by Mexican raiders. When Captain Sherrod Hunter's Confederates arrived, the Union men were forced to flee. When General Carleton's California Column arrived, the Confederates fled. Very few hardy souls returned after the war. The focus of occupation shifted for a number of years to the new capitol at Prescott far to the north of Tucson. It wasn't until the 1870s that southern Arizona came into its own again and then but slowly.

18. The Cochise War is often referred to as the Apache Wars. Jicarilla, Mescalero, and Western Apaches had been raiding the American newcomers to the southwest since the Mexican-American War that ended in 1848. The Chiricahua Apache had been at relative peace, raiding Mexicans, but seldom raiding Americans. February 1861 marks an open break with the Chokonen, Cochise's people, and Bedonkohe, Mangas Coloradas' people, of the Chiricahua. While Yavapai Apaches and Western Apaches remained at war with the United States after 1872, when Cochise accepted peace terms, the Chiricahua remained at peace until after 1876, when they were removed to the San Carlos Reservation and confined with the Western Apaches. Thereafter, Chiricahua were on and off the reservation until 1886, when Geronimo surrendered. Apache Wars refers to all of this. Cochise War refers to the Chiricahua between 1861 and 1872.

19. Governor A. P. K. Safford, "Something About Cochise," *Arizona Citizen*, December 7, 1872.

20. The sutler was an appointed, civilian position. The sutler ran the post store, the precursor to the Post Exchange, selling things the soldiers needed, clothing, sewing material, food, and alcohol.

21. DeLong, Sidney R., *History of Arizona*, San Francisco, The Whitaker & Ray Company, 1903.

22. Poston, Charles Debrille, edited by John Myers Myers, *Building a State in Apache Land*, Tempe, Aztec Press, 1963, pp 34–35.

23. Oberly, Hubert, "Why Apaches Made War: Officer Oberly, of Brooklyn, Tells What He Knows About It," *New York World*, July 1, 1886.

24. Bascom had graduated the U.S. Military Academy (West Point) in 1858 and joined the 7th Infantry Regiment in Utah at Camp Floyd in 1859. In today's Army, three years out of the U.S. Military Academy, he would have been due for promotion to captain. He was in command of Company C, holding down a captain's position. We will come back to George Nicholas Bascom's habits and personality in a future chapter; for now, note that no one else ever accused Bascom of being a drunk. With so much obvious, unsupported vituperation coming from Oberly, it is easy to suspect that he threw this in for good measure. The frontier army had few options for recreation, the most common being drinking, whoring, and gambling. Alcoholism was not uncommon.

25. *Daily Missouri Republican*, June 3, 1860. Sweeney, "Cochise and the Prelude to the Bascom Affair," pp 438–44.

26. Irwin, Brigadier General Bernard John Dowling, "The Apache Pass Fight," *Infantry Journal*, 32/4 (April 1928). In fact, though Irwin might have suggested the hanging, Lieutenant Isaiah Moore, 1st Dragoons, had assumed command and it was his decision. I suspect Irwin was being gallant by not mentioning this.

27. Post Returns, Fort Buchanan, January and February 1861, Arizona Historical Society.

28. Fontana, Bernard L., et al., "Johnny Ward's Ranch: A Study in Historic Archaeology," *The Kiva* 28 (Oct–Dec 1962).

29. Actually January 27. Other sources make it clear that the "7" in a handwritten letter was probably misread as a "1."

30. Fort Buchanan.

31. Hesperian, January 25, 1861, printed in the *Missouri Republican*, February 11, 1861. There is an error in the dates of the letter and of the report. Apaches took the boy on the January 27, 1861. Hesperian wrote the letter after January 27. Context, military reports, and his subsequent letters make his error clear.

32. Radbourne, Allan, "Salvador or Martinez? The Parentage and Origins of Mickey Free," *The Brand Book*, Taunton, Francis B., ed., London: The English Westerners Society, July 1972, p 26.

33. There were four principle bands of Chiricahua Apaches: the Chokonen, Bedonkohe, Nednhi, and Chihenne. Cochise was a leader of the Chokonen. His father-in-law, Mangas Coloradas, was Bedonkohe.

34. Fred Hughes, Tom Jeffords's clerk at the Chiricahua Agency in 1872 and 1873, reported that the women abused Geronimo who was not at all prominent at that time. He came to notice as a mouthpiece for the war leader, Juh, who stuttered. Geronimo liked to complain and since he was always loudly protesting something or other, the Army considered him a leader where the Apache did not. He was not a chief. He was not a medicine man or shaman. All Apache had "medicine" or "power." Geronimo had a war power that allowed him to detect the approach of enemies.

35. "Cochise's warriors waited here, opening a desultory fire on the approaching stage. As Cooke and the other passengers blazed away from inside the coach into the darkness, Buckley cracked his whip at the struggling team of mules. He did not see the destroyed bridge in the darkness until it was too late. It was suicide to stop and insane to cross. Buckley lashed the mules as Apache gunfire echoed across the little arroyo. The terrified animals jumped the chasm as the axles of the stage slid across the outside bridge supports. They bounced across and back onto the road and pulled into the stage station at two in the morning" (Hutton, Paul Andrew, *The Apache Wars: The Hunt for Geronimo, The Apache Kid, and the Captive Boy Who Started the Longest War in American History*, New York: Crown, 2016, pp 48–49). Lest anyone wonder, I count Dr. Hutton a friend and know him to be a brilliant historian.

36. I've seen the spot and walked the trail, but I can't tell you who built up the wash bottom or when they did it.

37. Altshuler, Constance W., ed., *Latest from Arizona! The Hesperian Letters 1859–1861*, Tucson, Arizona Pioneer's Historical Society, 1969, p 173.

38. *Daily Alta California*, February 19, 1861.

39. Farrell, Thomas, "Arizona Indian Wars," *Frontier Times* (October 1923), p 18.

40. Smith, Shannon D., *Give Me Eighty Men: Women and the Myth of the Fetterman Fight*, Lincoln, University of Nebraska Press, 2008, pp 198–99.

41. With four years drill at West Point and another year instructing recruits in New York, Bascom may have had more tactical experience than his sergeants had. Training standards were low. Units built their quarters. They conducted escort duty and spent time on sick call. In the field, there was little time for training. There was also little hostile contact with Indians.

42. The San Antonio and San Diego Mail began carrying the mail in 1857. In October 1858, the mail contract went to the Overland Mail organized by John Butterfield. The San Antonio and San Diego Mail stopped carrying the mail between El Paso and Fort

Yuma, California, on the Colorado River, but continued to run carrying passengers. The line was also known as the Jackass Mail. Across the deserts of southern California, passengers were carried, not in a stagecoach, but on mules. The Jackass Mail did not run day and night like the Overland Mail. Without stations, the mail stopped and camped out for the evening.

43. Summaries of which men went to Apache Pass at which time are found in Appendices A, B, C, and D.

44. Irwin, "The Apache Pass Fight," p 368.

45. It's interesting that Bernard mentions the unloaded condition of the rifle-muskets. The only practical way to unload one is to fire it and that wastes powder and shot, so weapons remained unloaded until trouble was expected. This is a partial explanation of how Cochise was able to escape from the midst of sixty-six infantrymen, some of them on sentry duty. This shows that leaving the weapons unloaded was common practice.

46. Hesperian, "Important from Arizona," *Missouri Republican*, February 28, 1861, describes him as a "driver on the line." The soldiers thought he was a station keeper and the key man at Apache Pass.

47. DeLong, *History of Arizona*, pp 26–29.

48. Turner, Thompson, *Latest from Arizona! The Hesperian Letters, 1859–1861*, Constance Wynn Altshuler, ed., Tucson, Arizona Pioneers' Historical Society, 1969, p 223.

49. Post returns are a long, two-sided form that folded up to letter size. It was a monthly report that recounted the names, ranks, and assignments of officers, the names of soldiers in casual status (not assigned but present), the number of enlisted men in each unit together with their status, the status of equipment and livestock, and a report of what the unit did during the month.

50. John R. Cooke was born at Jefferson Barracks, Missouri, in 1833, the son of Philip St. George Cooke. In May 1860, Cooke took Company B, 8th Infantry, to the San Pedro River at the mouth of Aravaipa Creek near the San Pedro's confluence with the Gila River in Pinal Apache country to establish Fort Breckenridge. Promotion to first lieutenant came as of January 28, 1861, but he did not receive the news in Arizona. He had started east on leave in a stagecoach that was attacked by Indians near Apache Pass. Cooke then continued east and resigned his commission as of May 30, 1861, in order to accept a commission in the Confederate Army.

51. The same stage that slid along on its axles after the driver was wounded and a lead mule slain.

52. *Bascom to Morrison*, Commanding Fort Buchanan, February 25, 1861.

53. Bernard's biographer, Don Russell (*One Hundred and Three Fights and Scrimmages: The Story of General Rueben F. Bernard*, Washington, U.S. Cavalry Association, 1936, pp 14–27), corrects some of these oversights by referring to the published accounts of William Oury and Surgeon Irwin, among others.

54. Russell (*One Hundred and Three Fights and Scrimmages*, pp 14–27), has Bernard on leave in Tennessee about the time of the 1860 election. Post returns confirm a man on leave November 1860 through March 1861. A soldier in Tennessee in November would have reported to Fort Leavenworth, Kansas, for transportation back to his post and likely found the trail closed for the winter.

55. Sacks, Benjamin H., "New Evidence on the Bascom Affair," *Arizona and the West* 4/3 (1962), p 267. He was quoting directly from Bascom to Morrison, February 25, 1861, Letters Received, Department of New Mexico.

56. Kessel, John L., "So What's Truth Got to Do with It? Reflections on Oñate and the Black Legend," New Mexico Historical Review 86 (Summer 2011). Quote from Jacques Barzun and Henry F. Graff, *The Modern Researcher*, fifth edition, New York, Harcourt Brace Javonovich, 1992.

57. Hocking, Doug, *Tom Jeffords: Friend of Cochise*, Guilford, CT, TwoDot, 2017.

58. Robinson, Daniel, "Another Apache Affair," undated manuscript, Daniel Robinson Collection, Fort Laramie National Historic Site. Irwin, Bernard John Dowling, April 18, 1893, Letter from Irwin's Medal of Honor packet by courtesy of Dr. John Fahey. Post Returns, Fort Buchanan, June 1861, Arizona Historical Society.

59. Tevis, James H., *Arizona in the '50s*, edited by Betty Barr and William J. Kelly, Tucson, Brocking J. Books, 2007, p 115. Originally published by the University of New Mexico Press, 1953.

60. Sweeney, Edwin R., *Cochise: Chiricahua Apache Chief*, Norman, University of Oklahoma Press, 1991, p 171.

61. Irwin, "The Apache Pass Fight," p 375.

62. DeLong, Sidney R., *History of Arizona*, San Francisco, The Whitaker & Ray Company, 1903, p 44.

63. *Indian* has long been the accepted term even though we've long known that these people do not come from the Indian subcontinent.

64. Letter Bascom to Lieutenant Colonel Pitcairn Morrison, January 14, 1861 (actually February), National Archive and Records Administration RG 353, Letters Received, Department of New Mexico, Arizona Historical Society.

65. Colonel Irwin, Bernard John Dowling, "Additional Explanatory Memoranda," April 18, 1893, quoting Captain Daniel Robinson, from Irwin's support packet for the Medal of Honor by the kindness of Dr. John Fahey who is researching Irwin. It is interesting to speculate that this may have been an attempt by Cochise to lure Lieutenant Bascom out of the fort for the purpose of revenge. The ambush seems to have been prepared ahead of time.

66. Irwin, "The Apache Pass Fight," p 374.

Chapter 2: George Nicholas Bascom

1. Schoenberger, Dale T., "Lieutenant George N. Bascom At Apache Pass, 1861," *Chronicles of Oklahoma* 51 (Spring 1973), p 84.

2. Robinson, Daniel, "The Affair at Apache Pass," *Sports Afield* XVII/2 (August 1896), p 79.

3. Irwin, Bernard John Dowling, "The Chiricahua Apache Indians: A Thrilling Incident in the Early History of Arizona Territory," *Infantry Journal* 32/4 (April 1928), p 368.

4. Szynalski, Susie, personal correspondence, June 22, 2017.

5. Waugh, John C., *The Class of 1846*, New York, Ballantine Books, 1994, p 13.

6. Morrison, James L., *The Best School in the World: West Point, the Pre-Civil War Years, 1833–1866*, Kent, Kent State University Press, 1986, p 70.

7. Maximum effective range is drawn from a combination of factors. Some weapons, with a light charge, pistols, for instance, lose penetrating power over twenty-five yards and become unlikely to kill or wound an opponent. Other weapons, muskets and rifles, might penetrate a man at one thousand yards but be limited by the inaccuracy of the weapon so that a hit at anything over one hundred yards was unlikely. This had to do with the uneven weight of the ball, defects in barrel construction, and limitations of the sights. European armies, for the most part, didn't bother much with marksmanship. At one hundred yards the soldier pointed his weapon at the massed troops approaching. American soldiers didn't get much practice either, though many came with skills learned at home.

8. The rifle had a maximum effective range of about two hundred yards. However, because the ball had to be patched and forced down the barrel, it was much slower to load. A soldier might manage one round per minute, whereas a soldier with a musket could manage three. Muskets with a higher rate of fire provided more firepower and were preferred by the military until the Civil War when breach-loading weapons removed the need to drive the ball down the barrel and expanding Minié balls reduced loading time and made the rifle a viable military weapon for purposes other than sniping.

9. Gorenfeld, Will, and John Gorenfeld, *Kearny's Dragoons Out West: The Birth of the U.S. Cavalry*, Norman, University of Oklahoma Press, 2016.

10. Alright, Sir Arthur Conan Doyle who wrote the Sherlock tales.

11. The conclusions rendered here are my own drawn from a career in the military as a sergeant in military intelligence and then as an officer in armored cavalry conducting the same missions that dragoons performed. Background information comes from many sources. Hardee, W. J., *Hardee's Rifle and Light Infantry Tactics*, Union City, Pioneer Press, 1997 (originally published 1862). Ball, Durwood, *Army Regulars on the Western Frontier, 1848–1861*, Norman, University of Oklahoma Press, 2001. Cooke, Philip St. George, *Cavalry Tactics or Regulations*, Union City, Pioneer Press, 1997 (originally published 1862). Utley, Robert M., *Frontier Regulars: The United States Army and the Indian: 1866–1891*, New York, Macmillan, 1973. Utley, Robert M., *Frontiersmen in Blue: The United States Army and the Indian, 1848–1865*, New York, Macmillan, 1967. Michno, Gregory, and Susan Michno, *Forgotten Fights: Little-known Raids and Skirmishes on the Frontier, 1823 to 1890*. Missoula, Mountain Press Publishing, 2008. Michno, Gregory, *Encyclopedia of the Indian Wars: Western Battles and Skirmishes 1850–1890*, Missoula, Mountain Press Publishing, 2003. Gorenfeld, Will, and John Gorenfeld, *Kearney's Dragoons Out West: The Birth of the U.S. Cavalry*, Norman, University of Oklahoma Press, 2016. Coffman, Edward M., *The Old Army: A Portrait of the American Army in Peacetime, 1784–1898*, New York, Oxford University Press, 1986.

12. *The Missouri Republican*, St. Louis, December 27, 1861, letter from New Mexico dated November 25, 1861.

13. The Apache lanced her and threw her off a cliff. They and everyone else thought her dead. She spent fifteen days crawling through the mountains to safety.

14. Or very likely, Aravaipa Apaches. Ewell met with Apaches at Aravaipa Creek on the San Pedro River in Aravaipa Apache country. He described them as Pinals who

lived nearby. Ewell may not have been precise in his language. He was holding Pinal hostages who had been taken in the same area. Were they Pinals or Aravaipas? He reported that he met with Pinal Apaches who said they were assisting him in getting her from Tonto Apaches. It is unlikely they'd have risked war with their neighbors in order to take the girl away from other Apaches. They demanded a large ransom on a pretense of helping.

15. Callum, George W., *List of Officers of the Army of the United States from 1779 to 1900*, Boston, Houghton-Mifflin, 1903.

16. Among them are George A. Custer, the boy general, who achieved great things during the Civil War, and George Pickett, the Confederate General who led the charge at Gettysburg.

17. Post returns, Fort Columbus, October 1858.

18. Johnson, A. B., "The 7th Regiment of U.S. Infantry," Center of Military History, www.history.army.mil/books/R&H/R&H=7IN.htm.

19. Johnson, "The 7th Regiment of U.S. Infantry."

20. She married several times and thus bore many names. The name Great Western came from the name of the largest steamship of the time.

21. This summary is drawn from Bigler, David L., and Will Bagley, *The Mormon Rebellion: America's First Civil War 1857–1858*, Norman: University of Oklahoma Press, 2011; and Bagley, Will, *Blood of the Prophets*, Norman, University of Oklahoma Press, 2002.

22. Wilson, John P., ed., *From Western Deserts to Carolina Swamps: A Civil War Soldier's Journals and Letters Home*, Albuquerque, University of New Mexico Press, 2012.

23. Post returns, Fort Buchanan, October 1860.

24. Irwin, Bernard J. D., "The Chiricahua Apache Indians, A Thrilling Incident in the Early History of Arizona Territory," *Infantry Journal* 32/4 (April 1928), p 368.

CHAPTER 3: RICHARD S. EWELL, THE OCCUPATION OF ARIZONA, AND THE FOUNDING OF FORT BUCHANAN

1. Edward Dunbar letter of June 19, 1858, in *Daily Alta California*, July 18, 1858.

2. Fahey, John H., "Fort Buchanan and the Origins of Arizona Territory," *Journal of Arizona History* 58 (Summer 2017), p 124.

3. National Archive and Records Administration, RG 393., LR, DNM, E22, 1860, Ewell to Maury, July 24, 1860. Sweeney, Edwin R., *Cochise: Chiricahua Apache Chief*, Norman, University of Oklahoma Press, 1991, p 146.

4. Bascom lost his father at about the same age.

5. Pfanz, Donald, *The Letters of General Richard S. Ewell: Stonewall's Successor*, Knoxville, University of Tennessee Press, pp 15–16.

6. The musketoon was a shortened musket. Its ramrod was attached to the stock with a slide and pivot so that soldiers could reload while mounted without danger of losing the ramrod. The ball fit loosely in the barrel and if the barrel was tilted downward, as it was intended to be carried, the ball could roll out. Its range was little greater than that of a pistol.

7. Pfanz, *The Letters of General Richard S. Ewell*, p 29.

8. Pfanz, *The Letters of General Richard S. Ewell*, p 34.

9. Pfanz, *The Letters of General Richard S. Ewell*, p 35.

10. Pfanz, *The Letters of General Richard S. Ewell*, p 44.

11. Thrapp, Dan L., *Encyclopedia of Frontier Biography*, Lincoln, University of Nebraska Press, 1988, p 475.

12. Pfanz, *The Letters of General Richard S. Ewell*, p 67.

13. Pfanz, *The Letters of General Richard S. Ewell*, pp 90–91.

14. Today known as Cottonwood Spring.

15. Pfanz, *The Letters of General Richard S. Ewell*, p 92.

16. Pfanz, *The Letters of General Richard S. Ewell*, p 92.

17. This is the same Benjamin Bonneville that Washington Irving wrote about in 1837 in *The Adventures of Captain Bonneville.*

18. Pfanz, *The Letters of General Richard S. Ewell*, p 93.

19. Hamlin, Percy Gatling, *The Making of a Soldier: Letters of General R. S. Ewell*, Richmond, Whittet & Shepperson, 1935, pp. 85–86.

20. Pfanz, *The Letters of General Richard S. Ewell*, pp 95–96.

21. Pfanz, *The Letters of General Richard S. Ewell*, p 98.

22. Pfanz, *The Letters of General Richard S. Ewell*, p 103.

23. Pfanz, *The Letters of General Richard S. Ewell*, pp 112–13.

24. Fahey, "Fort Buchanan," pp 123–33.

25. Pfanz, *The Letters of General Richard S. Ewell*, p 105.

26. Pfanz, *The Letters of General Richard S. Ewell*, p 108.

27. Pfanz, *The Letters of General Richard S. Ewell*, pp 108–09.

28. Altshuler, Constance W., ed., *Latest from Arizona! The Hesperian Letters 1859–1861*, Tucson, Arizona Pioneer's Historical Society, 1969, pp 47–48. April 3, 1860, St. Louis *Missouri Republican*. Ewell also said of this incident that the Pinals took captives in response to Ewell taking their people captive in December 1859.

29. Altshuler, *Latest from Arizona!*, pp 50–53. Hesperian, Tubac, March 23, 1860, April 10, 1860, St. Louis *Missouri Republican*.

30. Altshuler, *Latest from Arizona!*, pp 64–67. Tubac, April 9, 1860, May 8, 1860, St. Louis *Missouri Republican*.

31. Altshuler, *Latest from Arizona!*, pp 50–53. Tubac, March 19, 1860, April 10, 1860, St. Louis *Missouri Republican*.

32. Fahey, "Fort Buchanan," pp 133–34.

33. There is some confusion about exactly which Apaches Ewell was dealing with. He was in the Aravaipa homeland, which is next to Pinal country with whom they were closely allied. The names are drawn from their locations: Pinal Mountains, Aravaipa Creek. Tribal designations have more to do with locale than with political affiliation. Whichever of the two Ewell was dealing with, and he may not have made a clear distinction himself, the Apache claimed that Tonto Apaches were the culprits. Tonto is Spanish for mute or dummy, and it's unclear if they are named for the Tonto Basin or if the basin draws its name from the people.

34. The author has found nothing in primary sources that would support this contention.

35. The story also appears in Roberts, Virginia Culin, *With Their Own Blood: A Saga of Southwestern Pioneers*, Fort Worth, Texas Christian University Press, 1992.

36. Hamlin, Percy Gatling, *The Making of a Soldier: Letters of General R.S. Ewell*, Richmond, Whittet & Shepperson, 1935, pp 94–95.

37. DeVault, Tracy, "Finding Ewell's Station," *Desert Tracks* (January 2016), p 25.

38. Altshuler, *Latest from Arizona!*, p 26. January 30, 1860, St. Louis *Missouri Republican*.

39. Fahey, "Fort Buchanan," p 136.

40. Altshuler, *Latest from Arizona!*, p 102. July 18, 1860, St. Louis *Missouri Republican*.

41. Altshuler, *Latest from Arizona!*, p 105. August 6, 1860, St. Louis *Missouri Republican*.

42. Sweeney, Edwin R., *Cochise: Chiricahua Apache Chief*, Norman, University of Oklahoma Press, 1991, p 146. July 24, 1860, Ewell to Maury, LR DNM, RG393.

CHAPTER 4: THE SETTLEMENTS OF ARIZONA

1. Colonel B. L. E. Bonneville to Adjutant General, July 15, 1859, Adjutant General's Office, Letters Received, RG 94, National Archive and Records Administration. Radbourne, Allan, "Salvador or Martinez? The Parentage and Origins of Mickey Free," *The Brand Book*, Taunton, Francis B., ed., London, The English Westerners' Society, 1972, p 28.

2. *The Weekly Arizonian*, May 12, 1859.

3. Fahey, John H., "Fort Buchanan and the Origins of Arizona Territory," *Journal of Arizona History* 58 (Summer 2017), p 130, quoting *Cincinnati Times*, March 17, 1859.

4. Mexico and many of the Latin American states were deeply in debt often to France and England who threatened to foreclose by occupying the land. Bankrupt governments despaired of maintaining law and order as outlying provinces fended for themselves often run by strongmen of one stripe or another. This made these outlying areas tempting targets for small, armed parties of American soldiers of fortune to take over and run as separate countries, often in hope of later attaching their prize to the United States.

5. Who soon became the husband of Larcena Pennington. He was slain by Apache in 1860.

6. This might be John Ward, stepfather of Felix Ward.

7. O'Neal, James B., ed., *They Die But Once: The Story of a Tejano*, New York, Knight Publications, 1935, p 28.

8. San Francisco *Evening Bulletin*, November 15, 1860. Murphy's Bar is undoubtedly a place name drawn from a placer mining term for the sort of spot placers were found. It's not a reference to a saloon.

9. "Shooting Scrape Graydon," *Weekly Arizonian*, April 21, 1859.

10. "Mowry-Cross Duel," *Weekly Arizonian*, July 14, 1859.

11. Farrell, Thomas, "Arizona Indian Wars," *Frontier Times* (October 1923), p 18.

12. The San Antonio–San Diego Mail continued to run during the years that the Overland Mail held the mail contract carrying passengers and express matter and apparently taking advantage of Overland Mail stations at least as watering points.

Having no stations of its own, the Jackass Mail did not run day and night, but rather stopped and camped. From the vicinity of Fort Yuma across the southern deserts of California to San Diego, passengers and the mail traveled on mule-back, hence the name, Jackass Mail.

13. Writing many years later, St. John gave Burr's name as "James Hughes" of Watertown. The *Daily Alta California*, October 11, 1858, quoting a letter from Sylvester Mowry (who was in Arizona in 1858), gives the name as "Burr." Mr. Archibald, who discovered St. John's plight, also gave the name as "Burr" in the *Memphis Appeal*, October 19, 1858. Preston Cunningham has his name recorded as "Preston" (Warner and Henry), unknown (*Memphis Appeal*), James (Ormsby), and Peyton (Mowry, *Daily Alta California*). In Farish's *History of Arizona*, Silas St. John gives Cunningham's name as "William." However, he gave it as Preston in a letter dated November 15, 1915, to Professor Forbes (Conkling, Roscoe P., and Margaret B. Conkling, *The Butterfield Overland Mail, 1857–1869*, Volume 2, Glendale, The Arthur H. Clark Co., 1947, p 375.) James Laing has his name recorded as "Long" (Archibald, *Memphis Appeal*) and Loring (Mowry, *Daily Alta California*).

14. Farish, Thomas F., *History of Arizona*, Volume II, San Francisco, Filmer Brothers Electrotype Co., 1915, pp 5–6. Farish quotes directly out of a letter from St. John.

15. Farish, *History of Arizona*, p 5.

16. "The shot struck Pablo, and his bones were found some days after picked by the wolves" (Barber, John Warner, and Henry Howe, *Our Whole Country – Or, The Past and Present of the United States, Historical and Descriptive*, Volume II, Cincinnati, Charles Tuttle, 1863, p 1448). This is the only account that mentions St. John's shot taking effect. St. John doesn't mention it. The source is H. C. Grosvenor, manager of the Santa Rita Mines, who was in Tubac at the time.

17. In a talk at Dragoon Springs, Dr. John Fahey noted that these unlikely survivals were entirely possible. The pressure of swelling and bleeding inside the skull usually kills men wounded in the head. Since their skulls were split open, the pressure was released.

18. St. John referred to Archibald's newspaper as the Memphis *Avalanche*, but the *Appeal* was not known by that name until the 1890s (Farish, Thomas F. *History of Arizona, Vol. II.*).

19. Farish, *History of Arizona*.

20. Barber and Howe, *Our Whole Country*.

21. Horace Grosvenor was killed by Apaches on April 25, 1861. Altshuler, Constance Wynn, "Arizona in 1861: A Contemporary Account by Samuel Robinson," *Journal of Arizona History* (Spring 1984).

22. Farish, *History of Arizona*.

23. Irwin, Bernard John Dowling. "Amputation at the Shoulder-Joint," *American Journal of Medical Science* 37 (1859).

24. Ibid. Irwin, "Amputation . . ."

25. An event that occurred two years later serves to show what life was like for the men who worked at the Butterfield stations in Apache country. The Overland Mail Company completed the station at Dragoon Springs and constructed a new station, called "Ewell's," to the east between Dragoon Springs and Apache Pass. On May 20,

1860, Apaches attacked the Dragoon Springs Station. "An express just in from the Rio Mimbres, reports that a pack train of 24 mules, heavily loaded with 'panocha' or Mexican sugar from Sonora, was attacked by the Apaches near the Hanover Copper Mines, worked by Messrs. Hinkle and Thibault, on the morning of the 20th—five persons killed and the whole train captured. The same Indians have also succeeded in stealing all the mules from Ewell's Station Overland Mail Company as well as from Dragoon Springs Station" (*Daily Missouri Republican*, June 3, 1860. Quoted in DeVault). Overland Mail employees were heroes in their own right!

26. Altshuler, Constance W., ed., *Latest from Arizona! The Hesperian Letters 1859–1861*, Tucson, Arizona Pioneer's Historical Society, 1969, p 107.

27. O'Neal, *They Die But Once*, p 29.

28. "Sonoita Valley Murders," *Weekly Arizonian*, May 19, 1859.

29. A nephew of settler Felix Grundy Ake and a very bad outlaw.

30. "Sonoita Valley Murders," *Weekly Arizonian*, May 19, 1859.

31. "United States Boundary Hotel," *Weekly Arizonian*, August 4, 1859.

32. O'Neal, *They Die But Once*, p 30.

33. Tevis, James H., *Arizona in the '50s*, edited by Betty Barr and William J. Kelly, Tucson, Brocking J. Books, 2007, p 115. Originally published by the University of New Mexico Press, 1953, p 41. Originally published by the University of New Mexico Press, 1953.

34. O'Neal, *They Die But Once*, p 35.

35. Pinpointing the Casa Blanca today has proved all but impossible. There is a canyon in the correct locale that bears that name but there are no remains, no foundations or datable trash in the mouth of the canyon. They may lie elsewhere nearby. Old-timers and local historians point to a building that cannot possibly have been the Casa Blanca. Graydon's establishment was described as being three miles from Fort Buchanan and as being called the United States Boundary Hotel, as has been quoted. In a column titled "Indian Depredations," *Weekly Arizonian*, March 3, 1859, the writer refers to stock being taken from Graydon at Casa Blanca on February 12. Other references call his establishment Casa Blanca as well. Solomon Warner refers to Sarah Bowman's place of business as the Casa Blanca but places it in Patagonia, eleven miles south of Fort Buchanan. The Patagonia Mine was the name of what became the Mowry Mine. However, elsewhere the entire area of Sonoita Creek and the Patagonia Mountains is referred to as Patagonia. Solomon Warner, "Memoir," p 22 manuscript in Folder 59, Box 6, Warner Collection, Arizona Historical Society. Although Graydon and Bowman are never referred to as being at the Casa Blanca at the same time, there appears to have been only one Casa Blanca.

36. Coffman, Edward M., *The Old Army: A Portrait of the American Army in Peacetime, 1784–1898*, New York, Oxford University Press, 1986, p 112.

37. Soldiers were organized into messes and shared cooking duties. Officers didn't cook for themselves. Sometimes they might arrange to dine with the family of a married officer or they might hire a servant, often an enlisted man, although this was expensive. More commonly, bachelor officers and officers in the field organized an open mess and hired a servant to do the cooking.

38. Pumpelly, Raphael, *My Reminiscences*, two volumes, New York, Holt and Company, 1948, volume 1, pp 258–59. Great Western is variously reported at this time as being in Yuma and being with the Arizona Wagon Train. Perhaps she only accompanied the wagon train as far as Tucson, or Jeff Ake's memory may have been faulty.

39. O'Neal, *They Die But Once*, p 29.

40. O'Neal, *They Die But Once*, p 40.

41. Spring of 1861.

42. Robinson, Daniel, "Another Apache Affair," Fort Laramie National Historic Site, undated. Daniel Robinson Collection, Fort Laramie National Historic Site.

43. A contraction of the Spanish for one hundred waters, it refers to a marsh.

44. O'Neal, *They Die But Once*, p 24.

45. *Arizonian*, May 12, 1859.

46. No record of a marriage has been found, and there was great difficulty in locating in Arizona an official of either church or state to conduct a ceremony.

47. Federal Decennial Census of 1860.

48. Radbourne, Allan, "Salvador or Martinez? The Parentage and Origins of Mickey Free," *The Brand Book*, Taunton, Francis B., ed., London, The English Westerners' Society, 1972, pp 28–29. Radbourne uses the census and the recollections of Santiago Ward to find that John Ward's wife and Felix's mother was Jesusa Martinez and her former spouse, whether Mexican or Irish, was Tellez. It is pronounced Tay-ehz. Ez is the equivalent of -son in English. So the Irish name might have been Tay or Tayes. Felix had gray eyes and light brown to reddish hair. Radbourne gives no other explanation of why he thinks Tellez was Irish. The name is known in New Mexico and common in Sonora.

49. Fontana, Bernard L., and J. Cameron Greenleaf, et al., "Johnny Ward's Ranch: A Study in Historic Archaeology," *The Kiva* 28/1&2 (October–December 1962).

50. Cady, John Henry, and Basil Dillon Woon, eds., *Arizona's Yesterday: Being the Narrative of John H. Cady Pioneer*, Tucson, Adobe Corral, 1995 (original publication 1915), p 76.

51. This points to Cochise and his people.

52. Estevan Ochoa partnered with Pinkney Tully as freighters. Ochoa ran sheep in the San Pedro Valley. In the 1870s, they partnered with Tom Jeffords on several mining ventures.

53. In the days before refrigeration, the "commissary" was maintained alive and on the hoof. On many larger military expeditions, a herd of cattle was driven along behind to feed the troops.

54. "Indian Depredations," *Weekly Arizonian*, March 3, 1859.

55. Tubac *Arizonian*, March 3, 1859.

56. The superintendent, not an outlaw.

57. *Missouri Republican*, May 25, 1860.

58. Ahnert, Gerald T., *The Butterfield Trail and Overland Mail Company in Arizona: 1858–1861*, Canastota, Canastota Publishing Co., 2011.

59. Tevis, *Arizona in the '50s*, p 102.

60. Hesperian, "From Arizona and Sonora," *Missouri Republican*, February 11, 1861.

61. Altshuler, *Latest from Arizona!*, p 163.

62. Mesilla *Times*, February, 23, 1861, quoted in Altshuler, *Latest from Arizona!*, p 234.
63. San Francisco *Evening Bulletin*, December 4, 1860, in Altshuler, *Latest from Arizona!*, p 153.

Chapter 5: Life at Fort Buchanan

1. St. Louis *Missouri Republican*, December 7, 1860, in Altshuler, Constance W., ed., *Latest from Arizona! The Hesperian Letters 1859–1861*, Tucson, Arizona Pioneer's Historical Society, 1969, p 149.
2. Barrera, William, "The Fort Buchanan Project, Archeological Salvage Operations of State Highway 82," S-900-298, C.O. No. 2, Arizona State Highway Department, July 1965.
3. Spanish-English dictionary gives the meaning as prison. Cobos, Ruben, *A Dictionary of New Mexico and Southern Colorado Spanish*, Santa Fe, Museum of New Mexico Press, 1983, says: "a group of citizens armed for defense." In Spanish colonial times, the Crown sent soldiers and their families to the borders to protect citizens and the missions. It was intended that by sending families with the soldiers that they would stay on and farm and thus become the core of new colonies as well as providing defense. The forts that they built are referred to as presidios.
4. Frazer, Robert W., *Forts and Supplies: The Role of the Army in the Economy of the Southwest, 1846–1861*, Albuquerque, University of New Mexico Press, 1983, p 125.
5. Fahey, John H., "Fort Buchanan and the Origins of Arizona Territory," *Journal of Arizona History* 58/2 (Summer 2017).
6. "Our Arizona Correspondence," September 7, 1857, in San Francisco *Daily Alta California*, December 25, 1857.
7. Pfanz, Donald, *The Letters of General Richard S. Ewell: Stonewall's Successor*, Knoxville, University of Tennessee Press, pp 107–08.
8. Mort, Terry, *The Wrath of Cochise: The Bascom Affair and the Origins of the Apache Wars*, New York, Pegasus, 2013, p 225.
9. Pfanz, *The Letters of General Richard S. Ewell*, pp 100–07.
10. Thompson, Jerry D., ed., *Texas & New Mexico On the Eve of the Civil War: The Mansfield and Johnston Inspections, 1859–1861*, Albuquerque, University of New Mexico Press, 2001, p 63.
11. Fahey, "Fort Buchanan," p 122.
12. Fahey, "Fort Buchanan," p 122.
13. Fahey, "Fort Buchanan," p 123.
14. Pfanz, *The Letters of General Richard S. Ewell*, p 103.
15. Tevis, James H. *Arizona in the '50s*, edited by Betty Barr and William J. Kelly, Tucson, Brocking J. Books, 2007, p 42.
16. Pfanz, *The Letters of General Richard S. Ewell*, p 90. This originates in Frazer, Robert W., *Forts and Supplies: The Role of the Army in the Economy of the Southwest, 1846–1861*, Albuquerque, University of New Mexico Press, 1983, p 94; and is also reported in Sacks, Benjamin, "The Origins of Fort Buchanan: Myth and Fact," *Arizona and the West* 7 (1965): 207–26. Originally recorded from Benjamin S. Roberts to Nich-

ols, September 28, 1856, and February 12, 1857, RG 393, DNM, LR. Pfanz, Donald C., *Richard S. Ewell: A Soldier's Life (Civil War America)*, The University of North Carolina Press. Kindle Edition, p 636.

17. Pfanz, *The Letters of General Richard S. Ewell*, p 105.

18. Hamlin, Percy Gatling, *The Making of a Soldier: Letters of General R.S. Ewell*, Richmond, Whittet & Shepperson, 1935, pp 93–94.

19. Hamlin, *The Making of a Soldier*, p 82.

20. Hamlin, *The Making of a Soldier*, p 85.

21. Hamlin, *The Making of a Soldier*, pp 87–88.

22. Rold, Robert L., "Six Apaches and the Medal of Honor," *Journal of the West*, July 1995.

23. Fahey, "Fort Buchanan," pp 127–28.

24. Fahey, John H., "More than 'The Fighting Doctor': Brigadier General Bernard J.D. Irwin," *Military Medicine*, 180 (November 2015).

25. Pfanz, *Richard S. Ewell*, p 108.

26. Pfanz, *Richard S. Ewell*, p 110.

27. Thompson, *Texas & New Mexico*, p 64.

28. Thompson, *Texas & New Mexico*, p 64.

29. When the two new cavalry regiments were formed in 1855, the secretary of war offered appointment as a major to William H. Emory. Others received promotion the same way.

30. St. Louis *Missouri Republican*, December 7, 1860, in Altshuler, *Latest from Arizona!*, p 149.

31. Lieutenant Colonel Custer rightfully wore major general's stars and was addressed as general.

32. Pfanz, *Richard S. Ewell*, p 74.

33. Thrapp, Dan L., *Encyclopedia of Frontier Biography*, Lincoln, University of Nebraska Press, 1988, Volumes 1 to 3, p 1010. Altshuler, Constance W., *Cavalry Yellow & Infantry Blue: Army Officers in Arizona Between 1851 and 1886*, Tucson, The Arizona Historical Society, 1991, p 236.

34. Thrapp, *Encyclopedia of Frontier Biography*, p 877. Altshuler, *Cavalry Yellow*, p 206.

35. Altshuler, *Cavalry Yellow*, pp 271–72.

36. On government contract, Colonel Leach built his road in 1858, much of it coinciding with or parallel to the Overland Mail road. However, his road went north of the Dos Cabezas Mountains where the Overland route was south of these mountains through Apache Pass. His road struck the San Pedro River many miles north of the San Pedro Crossing Overland Mail Station and then continued north along the river completely bypassing Tucson, the only town for six hundred miles. The route was unpopular.

37. Altshuler, *Latest from Arizona!*, p 84.

38. Faulk, Odie B., *Destiny Road: The Gila Trail and the Opening of the Southwest*, New York, Oxford University Press, 1973, pp 109–13.

39. Thrapp, *Encyclopedia of Frontier Biography*, pp 1202–03.

40. *Arizonian*, 15 December 1860. Altshuler. *Latest*, p 135.

41. Altshuler, *Cavalry Yellow*, pp 123 and 177.

42. Post returns, January 1861, Fort Buchanan, Arizona Historical Society.
43. National Archive and Records Administration, RG 393. LR, DNM, E22, 1860, Ewell to Maury, July 24, 1860. Sweeney, Edwin R., *Cochise: Chiricahua Apache Chief*, Norman, University of Oklahoma Press, 1991, p 146.
44. Pfanz, *Richard S. Ewell*, p 75.

Chapter 6: Cochise and the Overland Mail

1. Bernard to Lt. W. H. Winters, March 23, 1869, 357 P 1869, LR AGO, RG 94. Altshuler, Constance Wynn, *Chains of Command: Arizona and the Army, 1856–1875*, Tucson, The Arizona Historical Society, 1981, p 18.
2. Devin to Major J.P. Sherbourne, January 25, 1869, District Arizona Letters Sent. Schmitt, Martin F., ed., *General George Crook, His Autobiography*, Norman, University of Oklahoma Press, 1960, p 78. Altshuler, *Chains of Command*, p 18.
3. Ahnert, Gerald T., *The Butterfield Trail and Overland Mail Company in Arizona, 1858–1861*, Canastota, Canastota Publishing Co., Inc., 2011, pp 3–16.
4. The distances are those between the scheduled stations. Conkling, Roscoe P., and Margaret B. Conkling, *The Butterfield Overland Mail, 1857–1869, Vol. 2*, Glendale, The Arthur H. Clark Company, 1947, plate 18.
5. Faulk, Obie B., *Destiny Road: The Gila Trail and the Opening of the Southwest*, New York, Oxford University Press, 1973, p 88.
6. Ahnert, *The Butterfield Trail*, p 14.
7. Ahnert, *The Butterfield Trail*, p 13.
8. Worcester, Donald Emmet, *The Apaches: Eagles of the Southwest*, Norman, University of Oklahoma Press, 1992, p 72.
9. Conkling and Conkling, *The Butterfield Overland Mail*, p 127.
10. "Indian News," *Weekly Arizonian*, March 10, 1859.
11. *Missouri Republican*, May 2 and June 3, 1860.
12. Francisco was a friend and ally of Cochise. He would be at Cochise's side during negotiations with Lieutenant Bascom.
13. Tevis, James H., "Indian News," *Weekly Arizonian*, July 14, 1859.
14. Thrapp, Dan L., *Encyclopedia of Frontier Biography*, Lincoln, University of Nebraska Press, 1988, Volumes 1 to 3, pp 589–90.
15. *Chief* was a term used for: family head, war leader, leader. All have connotations that go beyond the actual scope and range of the Indian leader's role. Tevis should not be taken at face value because his book, *Arizona in the '50s*, was written to sell to a wide audience with many tall tales, untruths, and exaggerations.
16. He did not enter the post himself, but sent in two warriors. Cochise was wary of being trapped or taken prisoner. Sweeney, Edwin R., "Cochise and the Prelude to the Bascom Affair," *New Mexico Historical Review* 64 (Autumn 1989), p 435.
17. Reeve to Wilkins, July 21, 1859. R31-1859, LR, RG 393. Sweeney, "Cochise and the Prelude," p 436.
18. Gustafson, A. M., ed., *John Spring's Arizona*, Tucson, University of Arizona Press, 1966. Sweeney, "Cochise and the Prelude," pp 435–36.

19. The author grew up on the Jicarilla Apache reservation and observed firsthand their respect to claims to traditional campsites and sites for the collection of plant foods.

20. Sweeney, "Cochise and the Prelude," pp 428–30.

21. After the assimilation of the Bedonkohe into the Chokonen only the Chokonen, Chihenne, and Nednhi remained.

22. Sweeney, "Cochise and the Prelude," p 5.

23. Irwin, Bernard John Dowling, "The Apache Pass Fight," *Infantry Journal*, 32/4 (April 1928), p 369.

24. Sweeney, "Cochise and the Prelude," p 6.

25. *Arizona Daily Star*, Tucson, January 31, 1886.

26. Sweeney, "Cochise and the Prelude," p 430.

27. *Missouri Republican*, June 3, 1860.

28. Cozzens, Samuel W., *Explorations & Adventures in Arizona and New Mexico*, Secaucus, Castle, 1988, pp 222–24. This was the title given the new release of *The Marvelous Country*. Early Arizona historian Sidney DeLong panned this book saying: "One of the associate justices in this provisional government scheme, Samuel W. Cozzens, published a book on Arizona, which came out in 1874, called '*The Marvelous Country*.' From its careful perusal one can hardly avoid the conclusion that the author was never in what now is Arizona, but only in that portion along the Rio Grande at Mesilla, and Donna Ana, which finally fell to New Mexico; so his 'book' is largely made up of fancied adventures and descriptions of scenery that are fictitious or taken at second-hand from descriptions of others." DeLong, Sidney R., *History of Arizona*, San Francisco, The Whitaker & Ray Company, 1905, p 44.

29. Captive or not, Jose was probably considered a member of the tribe.

30. Sweeney, "Cochise and the Prelude," p 438.

31. Pfanz, Donald C., *Richard S. Ewell: A Soldier's Life (Civil War America)*, The University of North Carolina Press. Kindle Edition, p 109.

CHAPTER 7: APACHE FIGHT FOR SURVIVAL

1. Some tribes, notably the Cheyenne, ate dogs. The Apache did not.

2. Pfanz, Donald C., *Richard S. Ewell: A Soldier's Life* (Civil War America), The University of North Carolina Press. Kindle Edition, p 91.

3. Sweeney, Edwin R., "Cochise and the Prelude to the Bascom Affair," *New Mexico Historical Review* 64 (Autumn 1989), p 442.

4. My knowledge of the Apache comes from having grown up on the Jicarilla Apache Reservation in New Mexico and from graduate studies in social anthropology. I recommend the following sources: Basso, Keith H., *Cibecue Apache*, New York, Holt, Rinehart and Winston, 1970. Basso, Keith, *Wisdom Sits in Places: Landscape and Language Among the Western Apache*, Albuquerque, University of New Mexico Press, 1996. Cremony, John Carey, *Life Among the Apache*, Lincoln, Nebraska, University of Nebraska Press, 1983. Delgadillo, Alicia, and Miriam A. Perrett, eds., *From Fort Marion to Fort Sill: a Documentary History of the Chiricahua Apache Prisoners of War 1886 to 1913*, Lincoln, University of Nebraska Press, 2013. Goodwin, Grenville, *The Social Organization of the Western Apache*, Chicago, University of Chicago Press, 1942. Goodwin, Grenville,

Western Apache Raiding & Warfare, Keith H. Basso, ed., Tucson, University of Arizona Press, 1971. Gunnerson, Dolores A., *The Jicarilla Apaches: A Study in Survival*, Dekalb, Northern Illinois University Press, 1974. Lockwood, Frank C., *The Apache Indians*, Lincoln, University of Nebraska Press, 1938. Mails, Thomas E., *The People Called Apache*, Englewood Cliffs, NJ, Rutledge/Prentice-Hall, 1974. Markstrom, Carol A., *Empowerment of North American Indian Girls*, Lincoln, University of Nebraska Press, 2008. Opler, Morris Edward, *An Apache Life-way: The Economic, Social and Religious Institutions of the Chiricahua Indians*, Lincoln, University of Nebraska Press, 1941.

5. Sweeney, "Cochise and the Prelude," p 7.

6. Pfanz, *Richard S. Ewell*, p 108.

7. Sweeney, "Cochise and the Prelude," p 445.

8. Sweeney, "Cochise and the Prelude," p 438.

9. Much is made of the Cochise who never lied. War is deception. Lying in this context is very different from lying to those with whom you have a bond of trust. In *Tom Jeffords: Friend of Cochise*, we see a Cochise who never broke his bound of trust with Tom Jeffords or General O. O. Howard. He gave his word and that was his bond.

10. Fahey, John H. "Fort Buchanan and the Origins of Arizona Territory," *Journal of Arizona History* 58/2 (Summer 2017), p 136. Sweeney, "Cochise and the Prelude," p 435.

11. Altshuler, Constance W., ed., *Latest from Arizona! The Hesperian Letters 1859–1861*, Tucson, Arizona Pioneer's Historical Society, 1969, p 130.

12. Altshuler, *Latest from Arizona!*, p 135.

13. Altshuler, *Latest from Arizona!*, p 141.

14. Altshuler, *Latest from Arizona!*, p 141.

Chapter 8: The Raid on Johnny Ward's Ranch

1. Fontana, Bernard L., et al., "Johnny Ward's Ranch: A Study in Historic Archaeology," *The Kiva* 28, (October–December 1962), pp 13–15.

2. Fontana, "Johnny Ward's Ranch," p 17.

3. "Nickerson & Cole," *Weekly Arizonian*, 31 March 1859.

4. *Los Angeles Star*, February 16, 1861.

5. A smithy or a wheelwright's shop both leave distinctive signs for the archaeologist. Charcoal does not easily disintegrate. The forge leaves hardened brick and red soil. Bits of iron remain behind as well. Perhaps the road destroyed the shops or perhaps they are still somewhere near the stream waiting to be found. None of these signs were seen by archaeologists in 1962.

6. Additionally, the post returns show an enlisted man on leave all through this period. Bernard's biographer has him on leave in Tennessee about the time of the 1860 election. Russell, Don, *One Hundred and Three Fights and Scrimmages: The Story of General Rueben F. Bernard*, Washington, U.S. Cavalry Association, 1936.

7. In common parlance this is known as the Article 15, which allows the soldier to accept punishment without the need for court martial. It's much like a civilian *nolo contendere* plea except that it does not result in a lasting criminal record.

8. In a passage quoted in the previous chapter, James Tevis spoke of an interview with Francisco, a Coyotero chief, at Apache Pass in 1860. It was clear that Francisco was

returning from a raid into Mexico and even this early was returning to the White Mountains by way of Apache Pass. Felix Ward eventually resurfaced among the Western Coyotero. They and not the Pinal Apache may always have been the culprits in his abduction.

9. Unfortunately, Order No. 4 has been lost and we don't know exactly what instructions it contained.

10. *Bascom to Morrison*, Commanding Fort Buchanan, February 25, 1861.

11. *Record of Events, Post Returns, Fort Buchanan*, January 1861.

12. Robinson, Daniel, "The Affair at Apache Pass," *Sports Afield* XVII/2 (August 1896), p 80.

13. Surgeon Irwin included this information in his report. Captain Daniel Robinson, formerly sergeant in Company C, 7th Infantry, reported that Lieutenant Marmaduke had warned him that there had been trouble with the Chiricahua before he departed from Fort Buchanan. He warned Robinson to be on the alert.

14. Michno, Gregory, *Encyclopedia of the Indian Wars: Western Battles and Skirmishes 1850–1890*, Missoula, Mountain Press Publishing, 2003, pp 55–56.

15. Michno, *Encyclopedia of the Indian Wars*, p 71.

16. Robinson, Daniel, "Apache Affairs in 1861," Fort Laramie National Historic Site, p 5.

17. Self-striking or farmer's matches use the same fulminate of mercury. We used to throw them at the pavement causing them to burst into flame with a loud crack.

18. Purists will insist that one can use a worm attached to the ramrod. This destroys the ball and one then disposes of the powder. The cartridge is destroyed, and this wastes ammunition.

19. Robinson's unedited manuscript says they had Sibley tents. Scott, H. L., *Scott's Military Dictionary*, USA, 1861, p 142.

20. Daniel Robinson was born in Ireland in 1830 and enlisted in the 7th Infantry in 1849 when he was nineteen. Robinson was commissioned during the Civil War and rose to the rank of major before retiring in the 1890s.

21. Robinson, "Apache Affairs," p 3.

22. Today it is misspelled Stein's. There is a railroad town by the name of Stein's on I-10 nine miles south of Stein's Peak and Doubtful Canyon.

23. In April 1861, he would resign his commission and join the Confederacy. The ambulance was the most comfortable wagon the Army had at the time. Units often used the ambulance to carry senior officers and officers traveling with their families.

24. If Marmaduke and Morrison had suspected Western Apaches as perpetrators of the raid on Johnny Ward's ranch, there would have been no need for a warning. The route the Army believed they used led north from Fort Buchanan and Robinson would not have encountered them. There was no need to inform Robinson of an Apache raid. Raids were a constant hazard. The need to issue a warning arose because Robinson was headed to the same spot as the returning raiding party.

25. Robinson, Daniel, "A Narrative of Events Pertaining to C, F and H Companies of the Seventh Infantry while Serving in New Mexico and Arizona from October 1860, to April 1862," Fort Laramie National Historic Site, p 3. The steep road levels out for a while near the Overland Mail station, but the summit is still two miles to the west.

Overlook Ridge separates Siphon Canyon from the spring with the mail station at the peak or western end of a rough triangle.

26. Robinson, Daniel, "The Affair at Apache Pass," *Sports Afield* 37/2 (August 1896); "Apache Affairs in 1861," Unpublished, Fort Laramie National Historic Site; and "A Narrative of Events Pertaining to C, F and H Companies of the Seventh Infantry while Serving in New Mexico and Arizona from October 1860, to April 1862," Fort Laramie National Historic Site. Of these, the last is the most complete.

27. Today the remains of Tom Jeffords' Apache Agency building are close to where Robinson camped.

28. Robinson, "A Narrative," p 6.

29. In McChristian, Douglas C., and Larry L. Ludwig, "Eyewitness to the Bascom Affair: An Account by Sergeant Daniel Robinson, Seventh Infantry," *Journal of Arizona History* 42 (Autumn 2001), p 293, Robinson is noted as saying that Bascom's camp was two hundred yards west of the stage station. References to the location of the spring and subsequent material as well as archaeological analysis make it clear that the campsite was at the foot of Overlook Ridge two hundred yards east of the station.

30. Robinson says the column approached from the south but given the topography that is most unlikely. They'd have had to scale cliffs. He also says that Bascom camped west of the station. This would have put him a mile from the spring. Moreover, archaeology has recovered bullets presumably fired at Cochise from the side of Overlook Ridge. Ludwig, Larry L., "An Archeological Survey of Possible Bascom Affair Sites," MS, 1993, Fort Bowie National Historic Site, 1993.

31. Robinson, "A Narrative," p 4. This account is so detailed and so in line with other accounts available to us now, but not available to Robinson, that I think he must have kept a journal or diary. Post Order No. 4 has been lost. "Assistant Surgeon Irwin, who was at Fort Buchanan, stated however, that Bascom was under orders to use force against Cochise to recover the Ward boy." Schoenberger, Dale T., "Lieutenant George N. Bascom At Apache Pass, 1861," *Chronicles of Oklahoma* 51 (Spring 1973), p 87.

32. Report of February 25, 1861, Lieutenant George N. Bascom, Seventh Infantry, to Lieutenant Colonel Pitcairn Morrison, commanding at Fort Buchanan, New Mexico Territory. Letters Received, Department of New Mexico. National Archive and Records Administration RG 353, Letters Received, Department of New Mexico.

CHAPTER 9: NEGOTIATING WITH COCHISE

1. One source, Oury, William S., "True History of the Outbreak of the Noted Apache Chieftain Cochise in the Year 1861," *Arizona Star* June 28, July 5, and July 12, 1877, says the interpreter was Antonio, a Mexican who worked at Fort Buchanan. Oury was not at Apache Pass until many days later. Robinson in all writings says that Johnny Ward was the interpreter.

2. Robinson, Daniel, "The Affair at Apache Pass," *Sports Afield* 37/2 (August 1896), p 80. It is clear that word was sent twice to Cochise. Robinson only mentions the women in the *Sports Afield* article. Since Wallace was imposed upon later in the day, someone has to have been sent with the message and these women are as likely as any other messenger.

3. "That day passed and so did the next [with no word from Cochise]" according to Robinson in *Sports Afield*. However, in "A Narrative" he makes it clear that it was the same day. If it had been several days, problems would arise in the timeline, so it seems likely that "A Narrative" is the more correct version. There are signs in the *Sports Afield* article that some things were added and amended to appeal to a popular audience. Later on in the article there are soldiers, civilians, and Indians wounded and slain that do not appear in other sources or in the documentary accounts. *The Chronological List of Actions from January 15, 1837 to January 1891* lists two enlisted men wounded and nine Indians captured. Also the post returns list two enlisted men wounded and none killed.

4. Robinson, "The Affair," p 79.

5. *The Chronological List*, post returns, and Bascom's account say that nine hostages were taken. Cochise escaped. Some accounts say there was only one boy. This may relate to perception of the boy's age with some thinking him an adult. Cochise's son, Nai-che, would have been the right age. He was about nineteen in 1876 when he assumed leadership of the tribe and so would have been about four years old. However, Irwin brought in three captives and six were eventually hung. That means that Bascom provided three adult male hostages including Coyuntura. Since there were nine hostages altogether and six were hung, that leaves three unaccounted for: a woman and two boys eventually released at Fort Buchanan. Ed Sweeney thinks the second boy may have been Cochise's favorite nephew the son of Coyuntura, Chie. Sweeney, Edwin R., ed., *Making Peace with Cochise: The 1872 Journal of Captain Joseph Alton Sladen*, Norman, University of Oklahoma Press, 1997, p 6.

6. Robinson, Daniel, "A Narrative of Events Pertaining to C, F and H Companies of the Seventh Infantry while Serving in New Mexico and Arizona from October 1860, to April 1862," Fort Laramie National Historic Site, p 4.

7. Report of February 25, 1861, Lieutenant George N. Bascom, Seventh Infantry, to Lieutenant Colonel Pitcairn Morrison, commanding at Fort Buchanan, New Mexico Territory. Letters Received, Department of New Mexico. National Archive and Records Administration RG 353, Letters Received, Department of New Mexico.

8. Robinson, "A Narrative," p 4. Robinson goes on to say that the sergeant saved his own life by shooting the Indian dead. There is no corroboration for any Indians having been killed at this time. The Indian who ran up the hill was Cochise, and he seems to have been the only one to escape. Moreover, this event was added in later versions of the story and does not appear in the earliest account.

9. Apparently inflicting only a flesh wound as Coyuntura was able to walk a few days later.

10. Ludwig, Larry L., "An Archeological Survey of Possible Bascom Affair Sites," MS, 1993, Fort Bowie National Historic Site, 1993.

11. Surgeon Irwin, who would arrive several days later and so did not directly observe the event, described it as follows:

> [W]*hen demand was made upon him for the restoration of the stolen property he scoffed at the idea of force having been brought there to compel obedience on his part. Argument having failed to produce any effect upon the disposition of the*

Chief, Lieutenant Bascom then determined to detain him and some others of his party as hostages until the tribe should deliver up a captive boy carried off with the herd and surrender the stolen animals. That determination was only reached as a dernier resort after every effort at peaceful persuasion had proved futile. When Cochise was informed that he would not be allowed to depart until after the demand made by the representative of the government had been complied with he arose from where the party was seated and yelling to his companions to follow him boldly dashed through the bystanders and with some of the warriors escaped into the adjacent ravines. . . . Next day an Indian woman was dispatched with a message informing the Chief that the hostages detained would be taken to Fort Buchanan and confined there until the captive and the cattle were restored. The Overland mail-coach from California was attacked from a well prepared ambuscade on entering the pass that night, but, after a wounded horse had been cut adrift, miraculously, escaped. Irwin, Bernard John Dowling, "The Chiricahua Apache Indians: A Thrilling Incident in the Early History of Arizona Territory," Infantry Journal 32/4 (April 1928), p 371.

12. Both Irwin and Robinson make vague references to slain Apache. These do not appear in Bascom's reports. The numbers are vague and vary between accounts. Probably none were slain at this time. Only four .58 caliber minie balls have been found by archaeologists working the site along with four .44 caliber pistol balls. Firing was very light. Ludwig, "An Archeological Survey."

13. Everyone remembered the one shot from Johnny Ward. If everyone had been firing, no one would have recalled this shot, nor would Cochise have escaped. Archaeologists have recovered from the site "line of four .58-caliber minie balls and four .44 caliber revolver bullets extending from mid-slope to the top of the hill, a pattern that suggests Cochise's possible escape route." Personal communication Larry Ludwig, park archaeologist, Fort Bowie National Historic Site. Johnny Ward had a revolver. Not many shots were fired at Cochise. He was far up the hillside before the soldiers got their weapons loaded.

14. Estimates vary. Eighty by sixty feet seems likely judging from the foundations.

15. Robinson, "Unedited Account of the Bascom Affair," p 6.

16. In 1872, the boy Felix Ward enlisted as an Apache scout from the Western Coyoteros with whom he had been living. It had long been believed that he had been abducted by Pinals or even Tontos who sold him to the Coyotero (or White Mountain) Apache. Recent research has shown that the abductors were in fact Aravaipa Apaches. See Radbourne, Allan, *Mickey Free*, for a full discussion.

17. Ibid, "Unedited Account of the Bascom Affair."

18. Robinson, "A Narrative." Robinson refers to two hostages, but everything else points to Bascom holding six hostages at this point, the wounded Coyuntura, two adult males, a woman, and two children. Perhaps Cochise referred only to the two adult males not being concerned for the immediate safety of the others. Or Robinson's memory may be faulty.

19. Robinson, "The Affair at Apache Pass," p 81.

20. "Mr. Chas. W. Culver, the Station keeper, and his assistant, Mr. Walch, with Mr. Jas. F. Wallace, driver on the line" from Hesperian, "Important from Arizona," *Missouri Republican*, February 28, 1861.

21. Robinson does not mention Culver and Walsh. In the excitement and seeing what was happening to Wallace, he may not have noticed them. Later both were back at the station, although Walsh was dead. Bascom, on the other hand, mentions two "mail men." He has to have known Wallace was a captive and that Walsh had been shot dead. He may not have realized that Culver had been with him. It seems likely that Culver and Walsh went to one spot along the arroyo and that Wallace went to another. Hence, Robinson saw one man and Bascom saw two.

22. Robinson, "A Narrative," p 7.

23. Robinson, "The Affair at Apache Pass," pp 81–82.

24. Robinson, "The Affair at Apache Pass," p 82.

25. "Southern Overland Troubles," *Sacramento Union*, March 4, 1861. This and other sources make it clear that Wallace, Walsh, and Culver all went out to the arroyo against Bascom's instructions.

26. Friendly fire isn't. Friendly fire incidents have been common as long as there have been soldiers. Running toward men firing at the enemy is very dangerous, and it would not have taken carelessness or intent on the part of a soldier to have shot Walsh. With confusion and smoke of more than sixty soldiers firing, the soldier may not even have known that his bullet dropped the man. On the other hand, it may as easily have been an Apache who shot him. The statement that a soldier shot and killed Walsh first shows up in Russell, Don, *One Hundred and Three Fights and Scrimmages: The Story of General Reuben F. Bernard*, Mechanicsburg, Stackpole Books, 2003, p 21.

27. Russell, *One Hundred and Three Fights and Scrimmages*, p 82.

28. Robinson, "A Narrative," p 7.

29. Geronimo's own account confuses several events from this period, making it unclear what his role, if any, was and whether he was there at all. Among other things he said that the initial confrontation was between Mangas Coloradas and Bascom.

30. Robinson, "The Affair at Apache Pass," p 82.

31. Hesperian, "Overland Stage Attacked!" Tucson, February 9, 1861. St. Louis *Missouri Republican*, February 28, 1861.

32. Hesperian, "Overland Stage Attacked!" This account mentions that there was hay stacked in the road and does not mention the stones, which the soldiers may have already moved before the stage arrived. The Apache may have intended the hay to be ignited so as to illuminate the stage and its passengers when the stones stopped them.

33. Oury, "True History of the Outbreak."

34. *Sacramento Union*. Buckley, William, "The Apaches' Attacks on the Overland Mail," *Daily Alta California*, February 19, 1861. *Bascom to Morrison*.

35. Buckley, "The Apaches' Attacks on the Overland Mail."

36. His brother, Moses Lyon, was the conductor in the charge of the mail on the westbound stage that had arrived the previous (it now being after midnight) afternoon unscathed.

37. Letter Nelson J. Davis, dated August 20, 1894. Transcript in author's personal collection.

38. Thrapp, *Encyclopedia of Frontier Biography*, p 314.

39. Hesperian, "Overland Stage Attacked!"

40. Altshuler, *Latest from Arizona!*, p 173. There was no chasm to leap, nor any burned out bridge. The road was obstructed, and the going was slow.

41. *Bascom to Morrison*. Other sources give a slightly different count. Some apparently didn't consider the half-breed, Frank Brunner, an American and count a total of three hostages in Cochise's possession.

42. The timeline here is an educated guess. Accounts of the attack on the watering party and the negotiation for Wallace seem to make it appear that they occurred on different days. We know the stage came in on the night of February 6 and that this is when the additional three captives were taken and Lieutenant Cooke arrived. We know that First Sergeant Huber waited until midday on February 7 to send out the watering party. It seems unlikely that Cochise would have come to negotiate after the shooting affray, so the negotiation must have taken place before the watering party went out.

43. *Bascom to Morrison*, Commanding Fort Buchanan, February 25, 1861. Robinson's timeline is a little confused at this point. He does not recall this meeting and recounts his wounding on this date. Lieutenant Cooke had not yet arrived on the morning of February 6 and he was involved in the rescue of Sergeant Robinson. So the last negotiation with Cochise must have taken place on the morning of February 7 and the attack at the spring at noon that day. The mules had been stolen from John Doyle's fifteen-wagon government train which left Fort Buchanan on December 26, 1860, and arrived at Albuquerque on February 4, 1861. The train was attacked by Apaches near Burro Canyon on January 11 and lost fourteen mules. Mills, Charles K. III, "Incident at Apache Pass," *Journal of America's Military Past* (Spring/Summer 2000), p 85.

44. Oury heard about it from those present at the station including many employees of the Overland Mail of which he was an agent. Oury is not a primary source on this interaction, but he did hear about it soon after the events. He had every reason to be upset at the loss of Wallace's life as Wallace was a fellow employee of the Overland Mail. Nonetheless, he defends Bascom's action lending credence to his account. This is not the only account of the exchange between Cochise and Bascom. Robinson talks about it as well. Oury's account is more complete and comes from a source that might have been expected to be hostile to Bascom.

45. Oury, William S., "A True History of the Outbreak of the Noted Apache Chieftain, Cachise, in the Year 1861," Tucson *Arizona Star*, June 28, 1877, and following.

46. Robinson, Daniel, "Apache Affairs in 1861," Fort Laramie National Historic Site, p 17. Robinson says: "The following day [February 14] two companies of dragoons arrived from Fort Breckenridge, under command of Captain Moore and Lieutenant Lord. The first sergeant of one of the companies was Reuben F. Bernard—a soldier among soldiers—afterward Lieutenant Colonel, 9th Cavalry, and in charge of the National Soldiers Home at Washington, D.C." Robinson implies that Bernard may have arrived on this date. He could not have been there any earlier. This is the only account in which Robinson mentions Bernard who thus is not otherwise important to the story. This

writer believes that "soldier among soldiers" drips with heavy sarcasm at Bernard's many boastful claims including the damage that he did to Bascom's reputation.

47. Oury, William Sanders, "A True History of the Outbreak of the Noted Apache Chieftain Cachise in the Year 1861," Tucson *Arizona Weekly Star*, June 28, 1877.

CHAPTER 10: LIFE SURROUNDED BY FIVE HUNDRED APACHES

1. Ibid. Robinson, Daniel. "The Affair at Apache Pass," *Sports Afield* 37/2 (August 1896) p 83.

2. Plunging fire: firing so that the natural arching fall of the round causes it to strike targets behind cover.

3. Robinson, Daniel, "A Narrative of Events Pertaining to C, F and H Companies of the Seventh Infantry while Serving in New Mexico and Arizona from October 1860, to April 1862," Fort Laramie National Historic Site, pp 7–8. A very disjointed version of this fight in Geronimo's autobiography possibly places him among this group of attackers.

4. Cover protects soldiers from direct, straight-line fire. Concealment keeps them from being seen. A bush might provide concealment while a tree would provide cover.

5. Robinson, "A Narrative," p 8, and "The Affair at Apache Pass," *Sports Afield* 37/2 (August 1896), p 83.

6. Robinson, "A Narrative," p 8, and "The Affair at Apache Pass," *Sports Afield* 37/2 (August 1896), p 83.

7. Robinson, "The Affair at Apache Pass," p 83.

8. Ewell's Station was about five miles south of Ewell's Spring in the Dos Cabezas Mountains. The station may have had adobe walls and stood in the open on the prairie.

9. The Apache believe that spirits roam the dark and thus they do not like to move about at night or to fight in the hours of darkness. Nonetheless, they were known to fire at parties around campfires.

CHAPTER 11: SURGEON IRWIN EARNS FIRST MEDAL OF HONOR

1. Irwin, Bernard John Dowling, "The Apache Pass Fight," *Infantry Journal*, 32/4 (April 1928), p 372.

2. Irwin, "The Apache Pass Fight," p 372. Several accounts conflict on the exact number of men that went with Surgeon Irwin. Unit records say eleven to which we might add Irwin and civilian Paddy Graydon.

3. Irwin recalled fourteen infantrymen in his article, but post returns and other sources place the number at eleven and the entire party at thirteen.

4. Irwin, "The Apache Pass Fight," p 373. *Irwin to Chapin*, Adjutant, Fort Buchanan, February 25, 1861, the official report says thirteen cattle and two horses. Cattle move slowly and attempting to drive and retain them would have slowed the Indians. Irwin's "The Apache Pass Fight" says forty head. The herd seems to have grown between 1861 and 1886.

5. *Irwin to Chapin*, Adjutant, Fort Buchanan, February 25, 1861.

6. Irwin, "The Apache Pass Fight," p 373.

7. The Congressional Medal of Honor Society, http://www.cmohs.org/medal-history
.php.

CHAPTER 12: THE CAVALRY ARRIVES

1. Depending if he rode all night or waited for daybreak, he would have arrived on the evening of February 9 or morning of February 10.

2. Oury, William, "A True History of the Outbreak of the Noted Apache Chieftain Cachise in 1861," Tucson *Arizona Star*, June 28, 1877.

3. Alternatively, Lieutenant Moore may have planned to arrive on February 14, St. Valentine's Day. Dragoons are cavalry after all.

4. And lethal at over one thousand.

5. Robinson, Daniel, "Apache Affairs in 1861," Fort Laramie National Historic Site, p 17.

6. Robinson, Daniel, "The Affair at Apache Pass," *Sports Afield* 37/2 (August 1896), p 83.

7. Moore was promoted to captain soon after these events.

8. Robinson, "The Affair," p 84.

9. Oury, William, "A True History of the Outbreak of the Noted Apache Chieftain Cachise in 1861," Tucson *Arizona Star*, June 28, 1877.

10. Oury and Moore say all hands were mounted. Ibid. Moore, *Moore to Maury*, Adjutant, Department of New Mexico, February 25, 1861. Oury, "A True History." Robinson refers to a detachment of "foot soldiers," which might just mean infantry or mounted infantry. Robinson, "The Affair," p 83.

11. The firepower of the infantrymen would amount to a point almost like a fortification around which the cavalry could maneuver to advantage.

12. Accounts suggest the doctor explored the pass on his own.

13. *Bascom to Morrison*, Commanding Fort Buchanan, February 25, 1861.

14. Hesperian, Tucson, February 8, 1861. St. Louis *Missouri Republican*, February 28, 1861.

15. The distance is about fifteen miles. The Apache may have had sentinels closer to the trail. The dust of so many soldiers, wagons, and livestock, their commissary on the hoof, would have made the force look very large.

16. *Moore to Maury*, Adjutant, Department of New Mexico, February 25, 1861.

17. Oury, "A True History."

18. Robinson, "The Affair," p 83.

19. Wallace's body may have been found separately or they may not have counted Frank Brunner, the half-breed Cherokee.

20. Buckley, William, *Mesilla Times*, February 23, 1861.

21. Tucson, February 24, 1861. San Francisco *Evening Bulletin*, March 6, 1861.

22. Tucson, February 24, 1861. San Francisco *Evening Bulletin*, March 6, 1861.

23. *Bascom to Morrison*, Commanding Fort Buchanan, February 25, 1861.

24. Hesperian, "Letter from Arizona," Tucson, February 24, 1861. *Evening Bulletin*, March 6, 1861. Altshuler, *Latest from Arizona!* pp 177–78.

25. Oberly, Hubert, "Why Apaches Made War: Officer Oberly, of Brooklyn, Tells What He Knows About It," *New York World*, July 1, 1886.

26. Irwin, Bernard John Dowling, "The Apache Pass Fight," *Infantry Journal*, 32/4 (April 1928), pp 373–74.

27. Irwin, "The Apache Pass Fight," p 375.

CHAPTER 13: COCHISE'S REVENGE

1. "Why the Apaches Made War. Officer Oberly, of Brooklyn, Tells What He Knows About It," *New York World*, Sunday, July 1, 1886.

2. Irwin, Bernard John Dowling, "The Apache Pass Fight," *Infantry Journal*, 32/4 (April 1928), pp 374–75. Irwin's statement points to Oberly not having been at Apache Pass with Bascom but only much later since he has the location of the hanging wrong and mistakes the remains of the Mexican wagon train for that of an emigrant train.

3. Oberly, Hubert, "Why Apaches Made War: Officer Oberly, of Brooklyn, Tells What He Knows About It," *New York World*, July 1, 1886. Bascom was no cadet and would be a captain within the year.

4. Tevis, James H., *Arizona in the '50s*, edited by Betty Barr and William J. Kelly, Tucson: Brocking J. Books, 2007. In this book, Tevis emerges time and again as a much larger-than-life hero. We're told he composed his memoirs for his children. The book is full of exaggeration and tall tales.

5. Michno, Gregory, *Encyclopedia of the Indian Wars: Western Battles and Skirmishes 1850-1890*, Missoula, Mountain Press Publishing, 2003, p 85. Michno records the date as around March 28, 1861. Hackler, George, *The Butterfield Trail in New Mexico*, Rock Hill, Yucca Enterprises, 2003, p 184. Hackler gives the date as April 12. *Mesilla Times*, May 11, 1861. The *Times* says late April.

6. Letter, Nelson J. Davis to Charles B. Howry, Asst. Atty. General, Department of Justice, Washington, DC, dated August 20, 1894. Transcript in author's personal collection.

7. Michno, *Encyclopedia of the Indian Wars*, places the date as early as March 28.

8. Letter, Nelson J. Davis to Charles B. Howry, Asst. Atty. General, Department of Justice, Washington, DC, dated August 20, 1894. Transcript in author's personal collection.

9. *Mesilla Times*, May 11, 1861. Ibid. Sweeney, *Cochise, Chiricahua Apache Chief*, p 171. Altshuler, Constance Wynn, "Arizona in 1861: A Contemporary Account by Samuel Robinson," *Journal of Arizona History* (Spring 1984), pp 40–41. Robinson reports the murders on May 14 and 19, but they were slain earlier. The same names appear and the same body count as the author has summarized: nine total in three parties at Doubtful Canyon/Stein's Peak.

10. See Hocking, Doug, *Tom Jeffords: Friend of Cochise*, Helena, TwoDot, 2017.

11. Howard, Oliver Otis, *My Life and Experience Among Our Hostile Indians*, New York, De Capo Press, 1907, taken from the Kindle edition.

12. Hesperian, Tucson, March 5, 1861. San Francisco *Evening Bulletin*, March 18, 1861. Altshuler, Constance W., ed., *Latest from Arizona! The Hesperian Letters 1859–1861*, Tucson, Arizona Pioneer's Historical Society, 1969, p 179.

13. Hesperian, Tucson, March 20, 1861. San Francisco *Evening Bulletin*, April 3, 1861. Altshuler, *Latest from Arizona!*, p 182.

14. Hesperian, Tucson, March 20, 1861. San Francisco *Evening Bulletin*, April 3, 1861. Altshuler, *Latest from Arizona!*, p 182.

15. Hesperian, Tucson, April 1, 1861. St. Louis *Missouri Republican*, April 25, 1861. Altshuler, *Latest from Arizona!*, p 189.

16. Altshuler, *Latest from Arizona!*, pp 189–90.

17. Altshuler, Constance Wynn, "Arizona in 1861: A Contemporary Account by Samuel Robinson," *Journal of Arizona History* (Spring 1984), p 37.

18. Hesperian, Tucson, April 8, 1861. San Francisco *Evening Bulletin*, April 24, 1861. Altshuler, *Latest from Arizona!*, p 195.

19. Altshuler, "Arizona in 1861," p 42.

20. Altshuler, "Arizona in 1861," p 57.

21. Hesperian, Tucson, May 1861. San Francisco *Evening Bulletin*, June 25, 1861. Altshuler, *Latest from Arizona!*, pp 197–98.

22. How unlike a nineteenth-century newspaper writer!

23. Altshuler, "Arizona in 1861," p 57.

24. Letter Irwin, Bernard John Dowling, dated April 18, 1893. Xerox copy in author's personal collection. Post returns for June 1861 show only one soldier slain. It is probable that four men were slain but that only one was a soldier.

25. He was still suffering from the wound received at Apache Pass in February and had to ride to go about on light duty.

26. This would seem to refer to Corporal Fraber.

27. Robinson, Daniel, "Apache Affairs in 1861," Fort Laramie National Historic Site.

28. Robinson, "Apache Affairs." Letter Irwin, Bernard John Dowling, dated April 18, 1893. Altshuler, "Arizona in 1861," p 51. Samuel Robinson wrote: "The Indians turned on them and gave fight. It is said Lieut. [George N.] Bascom would not allow the soldiers to get off their mules or fire. [James T.] Paddy Graydon, Antonio the interpreter and a soldier who would not obey orders, did all the fighting a few feet in front of the soldiers. Antonio killed one, the soldier one, and Graydon two. It is almost impossible to believe that the Lieut. would act as he did. He was afraid if they dismounted to fire, the Indians would get their mules, but the fight occurred on an open plain and there was no danger of the Indians charging on them." Samuel Robinson was not there, and this is at considerable variance to what Sergeant Daniel Robinson and Surgeon Irwin wrote.

29. Letter Irwin, Bernard John Dowling, dated April 18, 1893.

30. Kuhn, Berndt, "Siege in Cooke's Canyon: The Freeman Thomas Fight in 1861," *Journal of Arizona History* (Summer 1997).

31. As noted elsewhere, Wadsworth had been elected general of the non-existent militia of the yet to be formed Territory of Arizona.

32. Altshuler, "Arizona in 1861," p 60.

33. He had been ill.

34. Altshuler, "Arizona in 1861," pp 62–63.

35. Roberts, Virginia Culin, *With Their Own Blood: A Saga of Southwestern Pioneers*, Fort Worth, Texas Christian University Press, 1992, pp 105–16. Michno, Gregory, and

Susan Michno, *Forgotten Fights: Little-known Raids and Skirmishes on the Frontier, 1823 to 1890*. Missoula, Mountain Press Publishing, 2008, pp 171–72. O'Neil, James B., *They Die But Once: The Story of a Tejano*, New York, Knight Publications, 1935, Kessinger Legacy Reprints, pp 38–46.

36. Michno, Roberts, and Sweeney all believe there was such a raid. Thrapp believed the town had already been abandoned by then and could find little supporting evidence.

37. Thrapp, Dan L., *Victorio and the Mimbres Apaches*, Norman, University of Oklahoma Press, 1974, p 338. Michno, *Forgotten Fights*, pp 175–76. Roberts, *With Their Own Blood*, pp 118–20. Sweeney, Edwin R., *Mangas Coloradas*, Norman, University of Oklahoma Press, 1998, p 424.

38. New Orleans *Daily Picayune*, November 1, 1861, from the *Mesilla Times*, October 3, 1861. Roberts, *With Their Own Blood*, p. 118.

39. Owned by Roy Bean, later Judge Roy Bean, and his brother.

40. Michno, *Forgotten Fights*, pp 175–76.

41. Hocking, Doug, "The Graves at Dragoon Springs," *Desert Tracks* (June 2017), pp 13–19.

42. Pemmican is a mixture of pounded jerked meat mixed with berries and nuts with animal fat as a preservative.

43. Michno, *Forgotten Fights*, pp 184–85.

44. Michno, Gregory, *Encyclopedia of the Indian Wars: Western Battles and Skirmishes 1850–1890*, Missoula, Mountain Press Publishing, 2003, p 93.

45. "Stein's Peak Cañon Fight," San Francisco *Evening Bulletin*, May 28, 1864.

46. Occasional, "Letter from Camp Goodwin," *The Weekly Arizona Miner*, March 20, 1869.

47. The number is disputed some saying as many as 130. This was the highest number I could find in primary sources.

CHAPTER 14: AFTERMATH

1. Ward, Santiago, *Reminiscences*, Arizona Historical Society. Radbourne, Allan, "Salvador or Martinez? The Parentage and Origins of Mickey Free," *The Brand Book*, Taunton, Francis B., ed., London, The English Westerner's Society, July 1972, p 28.

2. Radbourne, "Salvador or Martinez?," p 31.

3. Radbourne, "Salvador or Martinez?," p 23.

4. Ward, *Reminiscences*.

5. Radbourne, "Salvador or Martinez?," pp 26, 33–34.

6. Radbourne, Allan, *Mickey Free: Apache Captive, Interpreter, and Indian Scout*, Tucson, Arizona Historical Society, 2005, p 14.

7. Radbourne, *Mickey Free*, p 34. The San Carlos People include the Aravaipa as well as the Pinal, Tonto, and other Western Apache and Yavapai. San Carlos is a reservation home to many tribes and not a tribal designation.

8. Thrapp, Dan L., *Encyclopedia of Frontier Biography*, Lincoln, University of Nebraska Press, 1988, Volumes 1 to 3, p 518. Radbourne, *Mickey Free*, p 34.

9. Radbourne, Allan, "The Naming of Mickey Free," *The Journal of Arizona History* XII (Autumn 1976), p 343.

10. Thrapp, *Encyclopedia of Frontier Biography*, p 518.
11. Radbourne, "The Naming of Mickey Free." Ward, *Reminiscences*, pp 85–86.
12. Radbourne, "Salvador or Martinez?," p 36.
13. Thrapp, *Encyclopedia of Frontier Biography*, p 1010.
14. Colton, Ray C., *The Civil War in the Western Territories: Arizona, Colorado, New Mexico, and Utah*, Norman, University of Oklahoma Press, 1959, p 18.
15. Colton, *The Civil War*, pp 14–16.
16. Altshuler, Constance W., *Cavalry Yellow & Infantry Blue: Army Officers in Arizona Between 1851 and 1886*, Tucson, The Arizona Historical Society, 1991, p 236.
17. Thompson, Jerry D., *Desert Tiger, Captain Paddy Graydon and the Civil War in the Far Southwest*, El Paso, Texas Western Press, 1992, p 27.
18. Thompson, *Desert Tiger*, p 32.
19. Altshuler, *Cavalry Yellow*, p 236. Colton, *The Civil War*, p 18.
20. Thrapp, *Encyclopedia of Frontier Biography*, p 314.
21. Altshuler, *Cavalry Yellow*, p 65.
22. Altshuler, *Cavalry Yellow*, p 238.
23. These included five companies of the 5th, three of the 10th and three of the 7th U.S. Infantry (all that remained of the 7th), two companies of the 1st Cavalry (formerly 1st Dragoons, the rest of the regiment having been sent east, only D and G, Moore and Lord, remained), four companies of the 3rd Cavalry, six artillery pieces under Captain Alexander McRae attached to 10th Infantry, along with ten companies of Colonel Miguel Pino's 2nd New Mexico Volunteers, eight companies of Colonel Jose Gallegos's 3rd New Mexico Volunteers, one company of Colonel Paul's 4th New Mexico Volunteers, and two of Colonel Robert's 5th New Mexico Volunteers.
24. Whitlock, Flint, *Distant Bugles, Distant Drums: The Union Response to the Confederate Invasion of New Mexico*, Denver, University of Colorado Press, 2006, p 100.
25. Taylor, John, *Bloody Valverde: A Civil War Battle on the Rio Grande, February 21, 1862*, Albuquerque, University of New Mexico Press, 1995, pp 87–88.
26. Taylor, *Bloody Valverde*, p 91–94.
27. Taylor, *Bloody Valverde*, p 92. Daniel Robinson Collection, Fort Laramie National Historical Site, U.S. National Park Service.
28. *War of the Rebellion*, Series 1, Volume IX, Chapter XXI, No. 1, Headquarters Department of New Mexico, February 22, 1862, report of Col. Edward R.S. Canby.
29. Taylor, *Bloody Valverde*, p 102.
30. Thrapp, *Encyclopedia of Frontier Biography*, p 1230.
31. Thrapp, *Encyclopedia of Frontier Biography*, p 877.
32. *War of the Rebellion*, Series 1, Volume IX, Chapter XXI, General Orders #92, Headquarters Department of New Mexico, October 13, 1862.
33. Stories originating with Bernard use October 1860 for the date when Felix Ward was taken.
34. Altshuler, *Cavalry Yellow*, pp 31–32.
35. Altshuler, *Cavalry Yellow*, p 24.
36. DeLong, Sidney R., *History of Arizona*, San Francisco, The Whitaker & Ray Company, 1905, pp 26–29. It's interesting that even DeLong notes that the muskets were

not loaded. DeLong was the sutler (post trader precursor to the post exchange) at Fort Bowie in Apache Pass when Reuben Bernard was assigned there as company and post commander.

37. Altshuler, *Cavalry Yellow*, p 32. Reuben Bernard to William Winters, March 23, 1869, Letter Received, AGO, 357 P 1869.

38. Thrapp, *Encyclopedia of Frontier Biography*, p 101–02.

39. Irwin, BG Bernard, Letter of September 21, 1901.

40. Thompson, *Desert Tiger*, p 58.

41. Tevis, James, *Weekly Arizonian*, July 14, 1859.

42. Sweeney, *Cochise, Chiricahua Apache Chief*, p 199.

43. Sweeney, *Cochise, Chiricahua Apache Chief*, p 424 n 21.

44. Thrapp, *Encyclopedia of Frontier Biography*, p 935. Bates, Albert R., *Jack Swilling: Arizona's Most Lied About Pioneer*, Tucson, Wheatmark, 2008, pp 35–39.

45. Conner, Daniel Ellis, *Joseph Reddeford Walker and the Arizona Adventure*, Berthrong, Donald J., ed., Norman, University of Oklahoma Press, 1956, pp 38–39.

46. Conner, *Joseph Reddeford Walker*. The version given here comes from Conner. There are problems in his overall account. Army sources do not mention the Walker party or the part played by Jack Swilling. There is no doubt that Mangas Coloradas died in custody of the California Column under highly suspicious circumstances.

47. Sweeney, *Cochise, Chiricahua Apache Chief*, p 166.

48. Thrapp, *Encyclopedia of Frontier Biography*, pp 1037–38.

49. Howard, Oliver Otis, *My Life and Experience Among Our Hostile Indians*, New York, De Capo Press, 1907, taken from the Kindle edition. Ed Sweeney misquotes this passage going directly from the word "skeletons" to "I have retaliated with all my might," leaving out "Now Americans and Mexicans kill an Apache on sight." This makes it appear that Cochise is retaliating for the hangings at Apache Pass, which he is in part, but ignoring that he's primarily retaliating for the general slaying of Apaches. In so doing Sweeney lays undo blame on the Bascom incident.

50. Sweeney, Edwin, *Cochise, Firsthand Accounts of the Chiricahua Apache Chief*, Norman, University of Oklahoma Press, 2014, p 125.

51. Sweeney, *Cochise, Firsthand Accounts*, p 127.

52. Sweeney, *Cochise, Firsthand Accounts*, p 131.

53. Hocking, Doug, *Tom Jeffords: Friend of Cochise*, Helena, TwoDot, 2017, p 101.

54. Hocking, *Tom Jeffords*, p 121.

55. Hocking, *Tom Jeffords*, p 121.

CHAPTER 15: CONCLUSIONS: WHY WAR CAME

1. Sweeney, Edwin R., "Cochise and the Prelude to the Bascom Affair," *New Mexico Historical Review* 64 (Autumn 1989), p 435. Drawing on Isaac Van Duzer Reeve to John Wilkins, July 20, 1859, Letter Received, Department of New Mexico, R30-1859, RG 393.

2. *Don* in Spanish is a title of courtesy roughly equivalent to sir in English.

3. Pfanz, Donald C., *Richard S. Ewell: A Soldier's Life (Civil War America)*, The University of North Carolina Press. Kindle Edition, p 92.

4. Collins to Greenwood, February 24, March 3, 1861. Sweeney, *Cochise, Chiricahua Apache Chief*, p 168.
5. Altshuler, Constance W., ed., *Latest from Arizona! The Hesperian Letters 1859–1861*, Tucson, Arizona Pioneer's Historical Society, 1969, p 226.

Chapter 16: Conclusions: Bascom Exonerated

1. Oury, William, "A True History of the Outbreak of the Noted Apache Chieftain Cachise in 1861," Tucson *Arizona Star*, June 28, 1877.
2. Robinson, Daniel, "Apache Affairs in 1861," Fort Laramie National Historic Site, p 17.
3. Rick Collins pointed this out to me many times before it sunk in. I hope I've taken it a bit further than Rick did, and I owe him thanks. Having read many of the secondary accounts, I had formed opinions based on them before I ventured into the realm of primary sources. It was a process of relearning what I thought I knew. I had to check each fact to see if it could be supported from a primary source.
4. It seems that Felix Ward was either taken by Pinals who traded him to Western Coyoteros or was always with the Western Coyotero and Francisco had no knowledge of him. Either happenstance put the boy beyond Cochise's reach.
5. Cooke was promoted in January but didn't know it yet. He was senior to Bascom by many years.
6. *Moore to Maury*, Adjutant, Department of New Mexico, February 25, 1861.
7. Formerly Sergeant Robinson who served in Company C, 7th Infantry, under Lieutenant Bascom.
8. Robinson, Daniel, "The Affair at Apache Pass," *Sports Afield* XVII/2 (August 1896), p 79.

Appendix A

1. From the regimental returns and Fort Buchanan post returns.

Appendix B

1. Robinson, Daniel, "The Affair at Apache Pass," *Sports Afield* XVII/2 (August 1896), p 84.

Appendix F

1. List consolidated from Felix Ake Hayden File, Arizona Historical Society; O'Neil, James B., *They Die But Once: The Story of a Tejano*, New York, Knight Publications, 1935, Kessinger Legacy Reprints, pp 42–43. Roberts, Virginia Culin, *With Their Own Blood: A Saga of Southwestern Pioneers*, Fort Worth, Texas Christian University Press, 1992, pp 105–07. Altshuler, Constance W., ed., *Latest from Arizona! The Hesperian Letters 1859–1861*, Tucson, Arizona Pioneer's Historical Society, 1969.

Appendix G

1. Quoted from Sacks, Benjamin H., "New Evidence on the Bascom Affair," *Arizona and the West* 4/3 (1962), pp 263–68.

2. Irwin, Bernard John Dowling, "The Apache Pass Fight," *Infantry Journal*, 32/4 (April 1928), p 374. RG 98 Vol. 10 Letter Sent, Department of New Mexico, p 565. Maury to Chapin, March 17, 1861.

APPENDIX H

1. Sweeney, Edwin, *Cochise, Firsthand Accounts of the Chiricahua Apache Chief*, Norman, University of Oklahoma Press, 2014, p 138.

2. Santa Fe *New Mexican*, November 1, 1870. Sweeney, *Cochise, Firsthand*, p 143. This is a little different version of the card game. It's very unlikely that Cochise would have had actual knowledge of any such game of cards. His wife and two boys were somewhere nearby but unlikely to have been close enough to observe or understand what was happening. It seems likely that Arny got this information somewhere other than from Cochise.

3. Howard, Oliver Otis, *My Life and Experience Among Our Hostile Indians*, New York, De Capo Press, 1907, taken from the Kindle edition. Ed Sweeney misquotes this passage going directly from the word "skeletons" to "I have retaliated with all my might," leaving out "Now Americans and Mexicans kill an Apache on sight." This makes it appear that Cochise is retaliating for the hangings at Apache Pass, which he is in part, but ignoring that he's primarily retaliating for the general slaying of Apaches. In so doing Sweeney lays undo blame on the Bascom incident.

4. Sweeney, *Cochise*, Firsthand, p 213.

5. The events took place in 1861. The error as to the year first appears in a letter from Colonel Thomas Devin, Captain Reuben Bernard's commanding officer, in 1869, and thus may be attributed to Bernard who makes the same error in his account. The error is an indication that Devin had made Safford aware of Bernard's account. Thus, we don't know if Safford is relaying something Cochise said or something Bernard said.

6. *Arizona Citizen*, December 7, 1872. Sweeney, *Cochise, Firsthand*, p 242. Sweeney notes that Wallace was not dragged to death behind Cochise's horse, as indeed he was not. It is doubtful Cochise would have admitted to any such action.

7. *Arizona Citizen*, December 7, 1872. Sweeney, *Cochise*, Firsthand, p 242.

8. This seems to refer to Bascom's conference with Cochise.

9. Mangas Coloradas was not present for Cochise's conference with Bascom. He arrived a few days later. No Apaches were killed at that time.

10. These Bedonkohe (Mogollon/Mimbres) Apaches, who were not people of Cochise's Chokonen, may have died in the fighting at the spring. Bascom and Robinson mention killing a number of Apaches.

11. This may refer to Captain Richard Ewell's visit in 1860, or to the Pemmican Treaty of June 1862, when Major Eyre came through with the lead scout company of the California Column. In July 1862, Cochise and Mangas Coloradas lay in wait for the lead companies of the California Column and ambushed them at the spring. Cannon fire drove the Apache away.

12. This seems to refer to the July 1862 battle, not the 1861 meeting with Bascom.

13. This references the prisoners taken and killed during the confrontation with Lieutenant Bascom.

14. Geronimo, as told to S. M. Barrett, *Geronimo: His Own Story, the Autobiography of a Great Patriot Warrior,* New York, Meridian, 1906, edition of 1996, pp 114–15.

15. The events described occurred in February 1861. Fort Bowie was established July 28, 1862, eighteen months later.

16. Betzinez, Jason, with Wilbur Sturtevant Nye, *I Fought with Geronimo*, Lincoln, University of Nebraska Press, 1959, pp 40–42.

17. Ball, Eve, with Nora Henn and Lynda A. Sanchez, *Indeh: An Apache Odyssey*, Norman, University of Oklahoma Press, 1980, p 25.

18. Ball, Eve, *In the Days of Victorio: Recollections of a Warm Springs Apache*, Tucson, University of Arizona Press, 1970, p 155.

BIBLIOGRAPHY

1. On November 7, 1864, the Arizona Historical Society was established in Prescott, then the capitol of the Territory of Arizona, by the territorial legislature. On March 3, 1884, the Arizona Pioneers Historical Society was established in Tucson and membership was open to those who had arrived in Arizona prior to January 1, 1870. It was a private institution. In the 1960s, the Arizona Historical Society absorbed the Pioneers Society becoming a hybrid organization, part public and part private. Publications appear under both names.

BIBLIOGRAPHY

Newspapers

The Arizona Citizen (Tucson)
Citizen (Tucson)
Daily Alta California (San Francisco)
Daily Missouri Republican (St. Louis)
Evening Bulletin (San Francisco)
Los Angeles Star (Los Angeles)
Marysville Daily Appeal (Marysville)
Memphis Appeal (Memphis)
Mesilla Times (Mesilla)
New York Times (New York City)
New York World (New York City)
Sacramento Union (Sacramento)
The Weekly Arizonian (Tubac)

Archival Material

Abbreviations:
AHS (Arizona Historical Society)[1]
NARA (National Archive and Records Administration)
8th Census 1860 Arizona County, New Mexico Territory. Washington: U.S. Government Printing Office, 1860.
Ake, Grundy. Hayden File. AHS, Tucson.
Bascom Biofile, AHS, Tucson.
Centennial of the US Military Academy at West Point, NY, 1802 to 1902. Washington: Government Printing Office, 1904.
Company Returns, February 1861, Company C, Seventh Infantry, Fort Buchanan. NARA.
Irwin, Bernard John Dowling, April 18, 1893, Letter from Irwin's Medal of Honor packet by courtesy of Dr. John Fahey.
Moore, I. N., September 1, 1861. William S. Grant v. the United States. RG 123. NARA.
Muster Rolls, December 31, 1860, to February 28, 1861, Company C, Seventh Infantry, Fort Buchanan. NARA.

Muster Rolls, December 31, 1860, to February 28, 1861, Company D and Company G, First Dragoons, Fort Breckenridge. NARA.

Report of February 11, 1861—Lieutenant Colonel Pitcairn Morrison, seventh Infantry, commanding at Fort Buchanan, New Mexico Territory, to First Lieutenant Dabney H. Maury, Assistant Adjutant General for the Department of New Mexico, Santa Fe. NARA RG 353, Letters Received, Department of New Mexico.

Report of February 14, 1861—Second Lieutenant George N. Bascom, Seventh Infantry to Lieutenant Colonel Pitcairn Morrison, commanding Fort Buchanan, New Mexico Territory, NARA RG 353, Letters Received, Department of New Mexico. Report is misdated January.

Report of February 25, 1861—Assistant Surgeon Bernard J. D. Irwin, Fort Buchanan to First Lieutenant Gurden Chapin, Adjutant, Seventh Infantry. Letters Received, Department of New Mexico. NARA RG 353, Letters Received, Department of New Mexico.

Report of February 25, 1861—First Lieutenant Isaiah N. Moore, First Dragoons, commanding at Fort Breckenridge, New Mexico Territory to First Lieutenant Dabney H. Maury, Assistant Adjutant General for the Department of New Mexico, Santa Fe. Letters Received, Department of New Mexico. NARA RG 353, Letters Received, Department of New Mexico.

Report of February 25, 1861—Lieutenant George N. Bascom, Seventh Infantry, to Lieutenant Colonel Pitcairn Morrison, commanding at Fort Buchanan, New Mexico Territory. Letters Received, Department of New Mexico. NARA RG 353, Letters Received, Department of New Mexico.

Post Returns, Fort Breckinridge, 1860 and 1861, AHS.

Post Returns, Fort Buchanan, 1860 and 1861, AHS.

Post Returns, Fort Jay, New York, October 1858. Ancestory.com.

Regimental Returns, 1861, 1st U.S. Dragoons, NARA.

Regimental Returns, 1861, 7th U.S. Infantry, NARA.

Robinson, Daniel. "Another Apache Affair." Undated manuscript, Daniel Robinson Collection, Fort Laramie National Historic Site.

Silas St. John Biofile, AHS.

Benjamin H. Sacks Collection. Arizona Historical Foundation, Hayden Library, Tempe, Arizona.

U.S. Census, 1850, Kentucky, Division 2, Bath. Ancestory.com.

Ward, Santiago. "Reminiscences of Santiago Ward as told to Mrs. Geo F. Kitt." Oral history. Tucson, March 12, 1934. AHS, Tucson.

Journal Articles

Altshuler, Constance Wynn. "Arizona in 1861: A Contemporary Account by Samuel Robinson," *Journal of Arizona History*, Spring 1984.

Anonymous. "Some Unpublished History of the Southwest." *Arizona Historical Review* (January 1935).

Biertu, F., and Frank C. Lockwood. "A Diary: An Account of a Trip via Overland Mail from Los Angeles to Fort Yuma and Tucson." Diary. San Marino, 1861. AHS, Tucson.

Crimmins, Martin L., Colonel, retired. "The Apache Pass Fight," *Infantry Journal* 32/4 (April 1928).

———. "Recollections of the Old Medical Officers. Brigadier General B.J.D. Irwin, U.S. Army, Retired: The Fighting Doctor." *Military Engineer* (March–April 1931).

"Crabb Massacre." *Wikipedia,* https://en.wikipedia.org/wiki/Crabb_massacre.

DeVault, Tracy. "Finding Ewell's Station." *Desert Tracks* (January 2016): 24–27.

Fahey, John H. "Fort Buchanan and the Origins of Arizona Territory." *Journal of Arizona History* 58/2 (Summer 2017).

———. "More Than 'The Fighting Doctor': Brigadier General Bernard J. D. Irwin." *Military Medicine* 180 (2015): 1116–17.

Farrell, Thomas. "Arizona Indian Wars." *Frontier Times* quoting *Prescott Courier* (October 1923), pp. 18–19.

Fontana, Bernard L., and J. Cameron Greenleaf, et al. "Johnny Ward's Ranch: A Study in Historic Archaeology." *The Kiva* 28/1&2 (October–December 1962).

Hocking, Doug. "The Graves at Dragoon Springs." *Desert Tracks* (June 2017).

Irwin, Colonel Bernard John Dowling, "Additional Explanatory Memoranda." April 18, 1893, quoting Captain Daniel Robinson, from Irwin's support packet for the Medal of Honor by the kindness of Dr. John Fahey.

———. "Amputation at the Shoulder-Joint." *American Journal of Medical Science* 37 (1859).

———. "The Chiricahua Apache Indians: A Thrilling Incident in the Early History of Arizona Territory." *Infantry Journal* 32/4 (April 1928).

———. "Why the Apaches Made War: Irwin Articles, 1876–1934." For publication. Tucson, Arizona.

Johnson, A. B. "The 7th Regiment of U.S. Infantry." Center of Military History. www.history.army.mil/books/R&H/R&H=7IN.htm.

Kessel, John L. "So What's Truth Got to Do with It? Reflections on Oñate and the Black Legend." *New Mexico Historical Review* 86 (Summer 2011).

Kuhn, Berndt. "Siege in Cooke's Canyon: The Freeman Thomas Fight in 1861." *Journal of Arizona History* (Summer 1997).

Leckenby. "Indian Affairs." *Sports Afield* XVI/12 (June 1896).

Ludwig, Larry L. "An Archeological Survey of Possible Bascom Affair Sites." MS, 1993. Fort Bowie National Historic Site, 1993.

McChristian, Douglas C., and Larry L. Ludwig. "Eyewitness to the Bascom Affair: An Account by Sergeant Daniel Robinson, Seventh Infantry." *Journal of Arizona History* 42 (Autumn 2001), pp 277–300.

Mills, Charles K., III. "The Bascom Affair." *Cochise Quarterly* (Summer 1993), pp 3–22.

———. "Incident at Apache Pass." *Journal of America's Military Past* (Spring/Summer 2000), pp 76–88.

Mulligan, Raymond A. "Sixteen Days in Apache Pass." *The Kiva* 24/2 (1958).

Oberly, Hubert, and Colonel Martin L. Crimmins. "Why Apaches Made War: Officer Oberly, of Brooklyn, Tells What He Knows About It." *New York World*, July 1, 1886.

Opler, Morris Edward. "The Jicarilla Apache Ceremonial Relay Race." *American Anthropologist* 46 (1944), pp 75–97.

———. "Jicarilla Apache Territory, Economy, and Society in 1850." *Southwestern Journal of Anthropology* 27 (1971), pp 309–29.

Ormsby, Waterman L. *The Butterfield Overland Mail*, eds. Lyle H. Wright and J. M. Bynum. San Marino: Huntington Library, 1954.

Oury, William S. "True History of the Outbreak of the Noted Apache Chieftain Cochise in the Year 1861." *Arizona Star* June 28, July 5, and July 12, 1877.

Radbourne, Allan. "The Naming of Mickey Free." *Journal of Arizona History* 17 (Autumn 1976), pp 341–46.

———. "Salvador or Martinez? The Parentage and Origins of Mickey Free." *The Brand Book*, ed. Francis B. Taunton. London: The English Westerners' Society, 1972, pp 20–45.

Robinson, Daniel. "The Affair at Apache Pass." *Sports Afield* 37/2 (August 1896).

———. "Another Apache Affair." Fort Laramie National Historic Site, undated. Daniel Robinson Collection, Fort Laramie National Historic Site.

———. "Apache Affairs in 1861." Unpublished. Fort Laramie National Historic Site.

———. "A Narrative of Events Pertaining to C, F and H Companies of the Seventh Infantry while Serving in New Mexico and Arizona from October 1860, to April 1862." Fort Laramie National Historic Site.

———. "Unedited Account of the Bascom Affair." Fort Laramie National Historic Site.

Rold, Robert L. "Six Apaches and the Medal of Honor." *Journal of the West* (July 1995).

Russell, Don. "Chief Cochise vs. Lieutenant Bascom: A Review of the Evidence." *Winners of the West* (December 1936), pp 1–3, 7.

Sacks, Benjamin H. "Creation of Arizona Territory, Part 1 and 2." *Arizona and the West* 5 (Spring and Summer 1963).

———. "New Evidence on the Bascom Affair." *Arizona and the West* 4/3 (1962).

———. "The Origins of Fort Buchanan: Myth and Fact." *Arizona and the West* 7 (1965).

Safford, Gov. A. P. K. "Something About Cachise." *Arizona Citizen* (December 7, 1872).

———. "Something About Cochise." Chapter in *The Struggle for Apacheria*. Mechanicsburg, PA: Stackpole, 2001.

Schoenberger, Dale T. "Lieutenant George N. Bascom at Apache Pass, 1861." *The Chronicles of Oklahoma* LI/1 (Spring 1973).

———. "Lieutenant George N. Bascom At Apache Pass, 1861." *Chronicles of Oklahoma* 51 (1973), pp 84–91.

Seymour, Deni J. "1762 On the San Pedro: Reevaluating Sobaipuri-O'odham Abandonment and New Apache Raiding Corridors." *Journal of Arizona History* 52 (Summer 2011), pp 169–88.

Sweeney, Edwin R. "Cochise and the Prelude to the Bascom Affair." *New Mexico Historical Review* 64 (Autumn 1989).

Tyler, Barbara Ann. "Cochise: Apache War Leader, 1858–1861." *Journal of Arizona History* VI (1965), pp 1.

Utley, Robert M. "The Bascom Affair: A Reconstruction." *Arizona and the West* 3/1 (Spring 1961).

Ward, Santiago, and Mrs. George F. Kitt. "As Told by the Pioneers: Santiago Ward (Reminiscences as told to Mrs. Geo. F. Kitt)." *Arizona Historical Review* 6 (March 1934), pp 85–86.

Books

Ahnert, Gerald T. *The Butterfield Trail and Overland Mail Company in Arizona 1858–1861*. Canastota: Canastota Publishing Co., 2011.

Aleshire, Peter. *Cochise: The Life and Times of the Great Apache Chief*. New York: John Wiley & Sons, Inc., 2001.

Altshuler, Constance W., editor. *Latest from Arizona! The Hesperian Letters 1859–1861*. Tucson: Arizona Pioneer's Historical Society, 1969.

———. *Cavalry Yellow & Infantry Blue: Army Officers in Arizona Between 1851 and 1886*. Tucson: AHS, 1991.

———. *Chains of Command Arizona and the Army 1856–1875*. Tucson: AHS, 1981.

Bagley, Will. *Blood of the Prophets*. Norman: University of Oklahoma Press, 2002.

Ball, Durwood. *Army Regulars on the Western Frontier, 1848–1861*. Norman: University of Oklahoma Press, 2001.

Ball, Eve. *Indeh, An Apache Odyssey*. Provo: Brigham Young Press, 1980.

———. *In the Days of Victorio: Recollections of a Warm Springs Apache*. Tucson: University of Arizona Press, 1970.

Barber, John Warner, and Henry Howe. *Our Whole Country—Or, The Past and Present of the United States, Historical and Descriptive, Volume II*. Cincinnati: Charles Tuttle, 1863.

Barrett, S. M., editor. *Geronimo's Story of His Life*. New York: Duffiel and Company, 1906.

Basso, Keith H. *Cibecue Apache*. New York: Holt, Rinehart and Winston, 1970.

———. *Wisdom Sits in Places: Landscape and Language Among the Western Apache*. Albuquerque: University of New Mexico Press, 1996.

Bates, Albert R. *Jack Swilling: Arizona's Most Lied About Pioneer*. Tucson: Wheatmark, 2008.

Betzinez, Jason, with W. S. Nye. *I Fought With Geronimo*. New York: Bonanza Books, 1959.

Bigler, David L., and Will Bagley. *The Mormon Rebellion: America's First Civil War 1857–1858*. Norman: University of Oklahoma Press, 2011.

Cady, John Henry, and Basil Dillon Woon. *Arizona's Yesterday: Being the Narrative of John H. Cady Pioneer*. John H. Cady, 1916.

Cobos, Ruben. *A Dictionary of New Mexico and Southern Colorado Spanish*. Santa Fe: Museum of New Mexico Press, 1983.

Coffman, Edward M. *The Old Army: A Portrait of the American Army in Peacetime, 1784–1898*. New York: Oxford University Press, 1986.

Colton, Ray C. *The Civil War in the Western Territories: Arizona, Colorado, New Mexico, and Utah*. Norman: University of Oklahoma Press, 1959.

Conkling, Roscoe P., and Margaret B. Conkling. *The Butterfield Overland Mail, 1857–1869, Vol. 2*. Glendale: The Arthur H. Clark Co., 1947.

Conner, Daniel Ellis, edited by Donald J. Berthrong. *Joseph Reddeford Walker and the Arizona Adventure*. Norman: University of Oklahoma Press, 1956.

Cooke, Philip St. George. *Cavalry Tactics or Regulations*. Union City: Pioneer Press, 1997 (originally published 1862).

Cozzens, Samuel Woodworth. *Explorations & Adventures in Arizona and New Mexico*. Secaucus: Castle, 1988.

Cullum, George W. *Biographical Register of the Officers and Graduates of the U.S. Military Academy*. Boston: Houghton Mifflin, 1891.

———. *List of Officers of the Army of the United States from 1779 to 1900*. Boston: Houghton-Mifflin, 1903.

Davis, Goode P., Jr. *Man and Wildlife in Arizona: The American Exploration Period 1824–1865*, ed. Neil B. Carmony and David E. Brown. Scottsdale: Somers Graphics, Inc., 1982.

Delgadillo, Alicia, and Miriam A. Perrett, eds. *From Fort Marion to Fort Sill: A Documentary History of the Chiricahua Apache Prisoners of War 1886 to 1913*. Lincoln: University of Nebraska Press, 2013.

DeLong, Sidney R., *History of Arizona*. San Francisco: The Whitaker & Ray Company, 1903.

Farish, Thomas F. *History of Arizona, Vol. II*. San Francisco: Filmer Brothers Electrotype Co., 1915.

Faulk, Obie B. *Destiny Road: The Gila Trail and the Opening of the Southwest*. New York: Oxford University Press, 1973.

Floyd, Dale E. *Chronological List of Actions from January 15, 1837 to January 1891*. Old Army Press, 1979, reprinted from 1891.

Frazer, Robert W. *Forts and Supplies: The Role of the Army in the Economy of the Southwest, 1846–1861*. Albuquerque: University of New Mexico Press, 1983.

Geronimo, as told to S. M. Barrett. *Geronimo: His Own Story, the Autobiography of a Great Patriot Warrior*. New York: Meridian, 1906, edition of 1996.

Goodwin, Grenville. *The Social Organization of the Western Apache*. Chicago: University of Chicago Press, 1942.

———. *Western Apache Raiding & Warfare*, ed. Keith H. Basso. Tucson: University of Arizona Press, 1971.

Gorenfeld, Will, and John Gorenfeld. *Kearny's Dragoons Out West: The Birth of the U.S. Cavalry*. Norman: University of Oklahoma Press, 2016.

Gunnerson, Dolores A. *The Jicarilla Apaches: A Study in Survival*. Dekalb: Northern Illinois University Press, 1974.

Gustafson, A. M. *John Spring's Arizona*. Tucson: University of Arizona Press, 1966.

Hamlin, Percy Gatling. *The Making of a Soldier: Letters of General R. S. Ewell.* Richmond: Whittet & Shepperson, 1935.

Hardee, W. J. *Rifle and Light Infantry Tactics: For the Instruction, Exercises and Manoeuvres of Riflemen and Light Infantry, including School of the Soldier and School of the Company.* New York: J. O. Kane, Publisher, 1862. Union City: Pioneer Press, 1997.

Hedren, Paul L. *Powder River: Disastrous Opening of the Great Sioux War.* Norman: University of Oklahoma Press, 2016.

Hocking, Doug. *Tom Jeffords: Friend of Cochise.* Helena, MT: TwoDot, 2017.

Howard, Oliver Otis. *My Life and Experience Among Our Hostile Indians.* New York: De Capo Press, 1970.

Hunt, Aurora. *Major General James Henry Carleton, 1814–1873, Western Frontier Dragoon.* Glendale: Arthur H. Clark and Company, 1958.

Hutton, Paul Andrew. *The Apache Wars: The Hunt for Geronimo, the Apache Kid, and the Captive Boy Who Started the Longest War in American History.* New York: Crown Publishers, 2016.

Kaywaykla, James, with Eve Ball. *In the Days of Victorio.* Tucson: University of Arizona Press, 1981.

Lever, Charles James. *Charles O'Malley, The Irish Dragoon, 1841.* BibioLife, 2008.

List of Cadets Admitted into the United States Military Academy, West Point, NY, from its Origin till 1901. Washington, DC: Government Printing Office, 1902.

Lockwood, Frank C. *The Apache Indians.* Lincoln: University of Nebraska Press, 1938.

Mails, Thomas E. *The People Called Apache.* Englewood Cliffs, NJ: Rutledge/Prentice-Hall, 1974.

Markstrom, Carol A. *Empowerment of North American Indian Girls.* Lincoln: University of Nebraska Press, 2008.

Michno, Gregory. *Encyclopedia of the Indian Wars: Western Battles and Skirmishes 1850–1890.* Missoula, MT: Mountain Press Publishing, 2003.

Michno, Gregory and Susan Michno. *Forgotten Fights: Little-known Raids and Skirmishes on the Frontier, 1823 to 1890.* Missoula, MT: Mountain Press Publishing, 2008.

Morrison, James L. *The Best School in the World: West Point, the Pre-Civil War Years, 1833–1866.* Kent: Kent State University Press, 1986.

Mort, Terry. *The Wrath of Cochise: The Bascom Affair and the Origins of the Apache Wars.* New York: Pegasus, 2013.

Mulligan, Raymond A. *Apache Pass and Old Fort Bowie.* Tucson: Tucson Corral of the Westerners Press, 1965.

North, Diane M. T. *Samuel Peter Heintzelman and the Sonora Exploring & Mining Company.* Tucson: University of Arizona Press, 1980.

O'Neil, James B. *They Die But Once: The Story of a Tejano.* New York: Knight Publications, 1935. Kessinger Legacy Reprints.

Opler, Morris Edward. *An Apache Life-way: The Economic, Social and Religious Institutions of the Chiricahua Indians.* Lincoln: University of Nebraska Press, 1941.

———. *Childhood and Youth in Jicarilla Apache Society*. Los Angeles: Southwest Museum, 1946.

———. *Myths and Tales of the Jicarilla Apache Indians*. New York: Dover Publications, 1995.

Pfanz, Donald. *The Letters of General Richard S. Ewell: Stonewall's Successor*. Knoxville, University of Tennessee Press, 2012.

———. *Richard S. Ewell: A Soldier's Life*. The University of North Carolina Press, 2000.

Pumpelly, Raphael. *My Reminiscences*, two volumes. New York: Holt and Company, 1948.

Radbourne, Allan, *Mickey Free: Apache Captive, Interpreter, and Indian Scout*. Tucson: AHS, 2005.

Register of Officers and Cadets of the United States Military Academy. West Point, NY: Military Academy Press, 1875.

Roberts, Virginia Culin. *With Their Own Blood: A Saga of Southwestern Pioneers*. Fort Worth: Texas Christian University Press, 1992.

Robinson, Sherry. *Apache Voices: Their Stories of Survival as Told to Eve Ball*. Albuquerque: University of New Mexico Press, 2000.

Robinson, Will H. *The Story of Arizona*. Phoenix, 1919.

Roe, Lewis F., edited by John P. Wilson. *From Western Deserts to Carolina Swamps: A Civil War Soldier's Journals and Letters Home*. Albuquerque: University of New Mexico Press, 2012.

Russell, Don. *One Hundred and Three Fights and Scrimmages: The Story of General Rueben F. Bernard*. Washington: U.S. Cavalry Association, 1936.

Sacks, Benjamin H. *Be It Enacted: The Creation of the Territory of Arizona*. AHS, 1964.

Schmitt, Martin F. ed. *General George Crook, His Autobiography*. Norman: University of Oklahoma Press, 1960.

Scott, H. L., Col., Inspector General. *Scott's Military Dictionary*. USA, 1861.

Smith, Shannon D. *Give Me Eighty Men: Women and the Myth of the Fetterman Fight*. Lincoln: University of Nebraska Press, 2004.

Sweeney, Edwin R. *Cochise: Chiricahua Apache Chief*. Norman: University of Oklahoma Press, 1991.

———. *Cochise: Firsthand Accounts of the Chiricahua Apache Chief*. Norman: University of Oklahoma Press, 2014.

———. *Making Peace with Cochise: The 1872 Journal of Captain Joseph Alton Sladen*. Norman: University of Oklahoma Press, 1997.

———. *Mangas Coloradas*. Norman: University of Oklahoma Press, 1998.

Taylor, John. *Bloody Valverde: A Civil War Battle on the Rio Grande, Feb 21, 1862*. Albuquerque: University of New Mexico Press, 1995.

Tevis, James H. *Arizona in the '50s*, ed. Betty Barr and William J. Kelly. Tucson: Brocking J. Books, 2007. Originally published by the University of New Mexico Press, 1953.

Thompson, Jerry D. *Desert Tiger, Captain Paddy Graydon and the Civil War in the Far Southwest*. El Paso: Texas Western Press, 1992.

———. *Texas & New Mexico on the Eve of the Civil War: The Mansfield & Johnston Inspections, 1859–1861*. Albuquerque: University of New Mexico Press, 2001.

Thrapp, Dan L. *The Conquest of Apacheria*. Norman: University of Oklahoma Press, 1988.

———. *Encyclopedia of Frontier Biography*. Lincoln: University of Nebraska Press, 1988. Volumes 1 to 3.

———. *Victorio and the Mimbres Apaches*. Norman: University of Oklahoma Press, 1974.

Tiller, Veronica E. Velarde. *The Jicarilla Apache Tribe*. Lincoln, NE: University of Nebraska Press, 1992.

Turner, Thompson, edited by Constance Wynn Altshuler. *Latest from Arizona! The Hesperian Letters, 1859–1861*. Tucson: Arizona Pioneers' Historical Society, 1969.

Utley, Robert M. *Frontier Regulars: The United States Army and the Indian: 1866–1891*. New York, Macmillan, 1973.

———. *Frontiersmen in Blue: The United States Army and the Indian, 1848–1865*. New York: Macmillan, 1967.

Waldman, Carl. *Atlas of the North American Indian*. Revised Edition. New York: Checkmark Books, 2000.

Washburn, Wilcomb E., and Robert M. Utley. *Indian Wars*. New York: Mariner Books, 2002.

Waugh, John C. *The Class of 1846*. New York: Ballantine Books, 1994.

Whitlock, Flint. *Distant Bugles, Distant Drums: The Union Response to the Confederate Invasion of New Mexico*. Boulder: University Press of Colorado, 2006.

Wilson, John P., ed. *From Western Deserts to Carolina Swamps: A Civil War Soldier's Journals and Letters Home*. Albuquerque: University of New Mexico Press, 2012.

Worcester, Donald Emmet. *The Apaches: Eagles of the Southwest*. Norman: University of Oklahoma Press, 1992.

INDEX

ABOUT THE AUTHOR

Doug Hocking grew up on the Jicarilla Apache Reservation in New Mexico where he formed close friendships with Native Americans and Mexican Americans learning the peoples, cultures, and terrain of the Southwest.

As a young man, he joined Army Intelligence. He later earned a degree in business administration and then attended graduate school in social anthropology (ethnography), honing his ability to understand and express differences in culture. Returning to the Army as an Armored Cavalry (scout) officer, Doug completed his career teaching military tactics and tactical intelligence to military intelligence officers.

Since retiring he has earned a master's degree with honors in American history and a field work certification in historical archaeology. Doug lives in southeast Arizona, where he has frequently visited the site of Forts Buchanan and Breckenridge, Cochise's stronghold, Johnny Ward's ranch, and Apache Pass, seeing them through the eyes of historian, ethnographer, and archaeologist.

His biography of Tom Jeffords, *Tom Jeffords: Friend of Cochise*, was recognized by his peers in the Western Writers of America as a Spur Award Finalist (like winning Silver in the Olympics) and won 2nd Place for the Co-Founders Award for Best Western History from Westerners International. He has twice been recognized by Westerners International with the Danielson Award for excellent historical presentations.